FO

ANNUAL 1984-85

Edited by Peter Dunk and Lionel Francis

Queen Anne Press

A *Queen Anne Press* BOOK

Photograph courtesy of Colorsport

First published in Great Britain in 1984 by
Queen Anne Press
Macdonald & Co (Publishers) Ltd
London and Sydney
A BPCC plc Company

ISBN 0 356 10444 3

Typeset in Times by SIOS Limited, London NW6
Printed and bound in Great Britain by
Hazell, Watson and Viney Limited,
a BPCC Company, Aylesbury, Bucks.

Macdonald & Co (Publishers) Ltd
Maxwell House
74 Worship Street
London
EC2A 2EN

CONTENTS

Addresses 256

Cups

European tournaments report 1983-84 138
European tournaments results 1983-84 139
European tournaments past finals 142
FA Cup report 1983-84 98
FA Cup results 1983-84 98
FA Cup past finals 102
FA Challenge Trophy 1983-84 220
FA Challenge Vase 1983-84 222
FA Youth Challenge Cup 1983-84 224
FA Sunday Cup 1983-84 225
Football League Cup report 1983-84 107
Football League Cup results 1983-84 108
Football League Cup past finals 109
Charity Shield 210
World Club Championship 211
Welsh FA Cup past winners 135
Scottish Cup 1983-84 129
Scottish Cup past finals 130
Scottish League Cup 1983-84 132
Scottish League Cup past finals 132
Northern Irish Cup finals 136

Fixtures

International and Cup dates 1984-85 250
Football League 1984-85 236
Alliance Premier League 1984-85 244

Football Awards

European Footballer of the Year 255
Footballer of the Year 254
Manager of the Year 255
PFA Player of the Year 255
Scottish PFA Player of the Year 255

Football League

Football League results 1983-84 64
Final League tables 1983-84 72
Attendances 133
Honours List 86
League club directory 9
League position charts 74
League goalscorers 84
League tables 1983-84 72
Transfers 103

Final Honours 1983-84 8

Internationals

British International Championship 1983-84 report 156
British International Championship 1982-83 results 157
Other British international matches 1983-84 159
International goalscorers since 1946 161
European Championship past finals 144
European Championship Qualifying 1982-84 146
European Championship 1982-84 Finals 153
Post-war international appearances 164
UEFA under-21 competition 1983-84 206
World Cup past finals 203

Other League Tables 212

Scottish League

League results 1983-84 121
Honours List 125
League club directory 113
League tables 1983-84 124

EDITORIAL

As England set out on another World Cup campaign this autumn, manager Bobby Robson has to face the fact that the League remains unprepared to rearrange fixtures on more than one Saturday during 1984-85 in order to give the England squad more time to prepare for the important qualifying fixtures. Robson had asked for four free weekends, but League Chairman Jack Dunnett said after the League Annual General Meeting in June: 'If we ask the clubs for too much we will have a lot of trouble. Bobby Robson is frustrated because he's not winning matches and one of the ways to do this is to have his players together longer. But we must remember that it's the clubs who pay the players' wages.'

It is easy to feel sympathy for both Dunnett and Robson, and there is certainly no easy solution to this clash of interests. It really all comes back to the old problem of fixture congestion. The problems that faced Bobby Robson during 1983-84, when he was unable to field his first choice team for a single England game, will stay with us until the League as a whole, and the First Division in particular, is reduced in size. It is clearly preferable for an international squad to spend some time together before a game, and this was highlighted during the past year when a makeshift England XI lost miserably in Wales. Later, after spending a week or more together, the squad went to Rio de Janiero and beat the Brazilians for the first time in 28 years, and the first time ever in Brazil.

On the other hand the clubs, who do indeed pay the players' wages, and in some cases make huge investments in acquiring the services of these players in the first place, are looking for that elusive profit at the end of each season. Given that they are reluctant even to rearrange present fixtures – which would result in more mid-week games and therefore lower attendances – it is hard to see how they would agree to reduce the number of fixtures per club. At present, First Division clubs play 42 League games per season. If the Division was reduced from 22 to, say, 18 clubs, it would mean a reduction of eight games, and although it is difficult to predict what effect this would have on a club's finances, it is almost certain to be detrimental.

However, it should be recognised that success at international level does rub off on attendance figures at League games. Immediately after England's World Cup truimph in 1966, First Division attendances jumped by more than 1.7 million in 1966-67 compared with 1965-66, and a further million was added to the total in 1967-68. The benefit was felt for no fewer than seven seasons, and it wasn't until after England's disappointing departure from the European Championship quarter-finals in 1972 at the hands of West Germany that attendances fell back below their 1965-66 level.

In 1966, of course, the England squad didn't face the problem of having to qualify for the World Cup finals, as host status ensures automatic qualification, and in 1970 there was another free pass, this time because England were the holders. But since then England have managed to qualify only once in three attempts, and although it would be unrealistic to suggest that these failures were due entirely to fixture congestion, it would seem reasonable to suppose that the national squad would have a better chance if they had more time to prepare before an important game.

There seems little likelihood of the League chairmen either changing their minds about rearranging fixtures or agreeing to reduce the size of the League, and their arguments for not doing so are powerful indeed. However, a reduction in the size of the League may well be forced upon them in the years ahead. Already, several near-bankrupt clubs have seen the writing on the wall in vivid close-up, but somehow they've all managed to survive. The League have said that any club falling by the wayside due to lack of funds will probably not be replaced and so a League which has contained 92 teams for the past 65 years may be forced to shrink in the near future.

If and when the England squad reach Mexico for the 1986 World Cup finals, it will be 20 years since Alf Ramsey fielded a team without wingers and took the greatest prize in soccer. Many club managers followed the trend, and wingers in the style of Matthews, Finney et al virtually disappeared from the game. We were into the era of 'total football', 4-3-3 formations (4-4-2 in away games!) and overlapping full-backs. Bobby Robson, however, is setting his sights on Mexico with different ideas.

Following the debacle against Wales at the beginning of May, he started using wingers – initially Barnes and Chamberlain – and a 4-2-4 formation which relied on the wingers dropping back to help in midfield more than on full-backs coming forward. Victory proved elusive at the first two attempts – especially against the Soviet Union at Wembley – but the policy paid dividends in Rio de Janeiro, and at the time of writing it seems likely that the new strategy will be persevered with. When Ramsey's England tactics proved so influential with the clubs in the late sixties, it was a case of the tail wagging the dog, but this time the dog (the League clubs) is wagging the tail (the national squad), and the time is probably right. Wingers have been reappearing in club sides recently, with marked success, and our most successful club, Liverpool, has virtually always used wingers.

A manager with less nerve might have abandoned the idea after the 2-0 defeat by the Soviets, but as Robson pointed out to the Press contingent on Galvea Beach just outside Rio prior to the Brazilian game, the defeat at Wembley had not been caused by weakening the midfield in order to play two wingers, but by defensive errors which had led to two goals being conceded in a match in which England were hardly outclassed. One of the by-products of using wingers is that they tend to tie down the opposing full-backs, and the dangerous Brazilian pair, Junior and Leandro, were certainly tied down on the day. When England lose possession of the ball in this new formation, the obvious danger is that they will be out-numbered between the penalty areas, but with alert wingers who move back in that situation and then have the pace to attack quickly when possession is regained, that should not be a great problem.

If the new tactics continue to work well in the forthcoming World Cup Qualifying matches, we may yet see an England squad in Mexico. The last time that happened, England were desperately unlucky to go out at the quarter-final stage, and were certainly the only team in the tournament to worry the brilliant Brazilians. This time the Brazilians have not only been worried, but stunned. It could be an interesting two years ahead.

FINAL HONOURS 1983-84

European Championship:
France

British Championship:
Northern Ireland

European Cup:
Liverpool

European Cup Winners' Cup:
Juventus

U.E.F.A. Cup:
Tottenham Hotspur

Football League:
Division One: Liverpool
Division Two: Chelsea
Division Three: Oxford United
Division Four: York City

F.A. Cup:
Everton

League Cup:
Liverpool

Scottish League:
Premier Division: Aberdeen
Division One: Morton
Division Two: Forfar Athletic

Scottish Cup:
Aberdeen

Scottish League Cup:
Rangers

F.A. Charity Shield:
Manchester United

Welsh Cup:
Shrewsbury Town

Northern Irish Cup:
Ballymena

League Associate Members' Cup:
AFC Bournemouth

F.A. Challenge Vase:
Stansted

F.A. Challenge Trophy:
Northwich Victoria

Alliance Premier League:
Maidstone United

Northern Premier League:
Barrow

Southern League Premier Division:
Dartford

Southern League Midland Division:
Willenhall Town

Southern League Southern Division:
R.S. Southampton

F.A. Youth Cup:
Everton

F.A. Sunday Cup:
Lee Chapel North

FOOTBALL LEAGUE CLUBS AND THEIR PLAYERS

ALDERSHOT DIV. 4

Banton, Dale C.
Briley, Leslie
Burvill, Glen
Coles, David A.
Day, Clive A.
Gillard, Ian T.
Lawrence, Leslie O.
McDonald, Ian C.
Mazzon, Georgio
Shrubb, Paul
Souter, Don D.

League Appearances: Ampofo, C.J.K. 4; Banton, D.C. 46; Berry, S.A. 5(2); Briley, L. 36; Burvill, G. 33(5); Coles, D.A. 45; Compton, P.D. 13; Day, C.A. 28(3);Fielder, C.M.R. 2; Gillard, I.T. 26; Hatcher, D.T. 1; Jopling, J. 24(2); Lawrence, L.O. 39; Lucas, B.A. 20(3);Mazzon, G. 45; McDonald, I.C. 46; O'Sullivan, P.A. 13(1); Shrubb, P. 29(4); Souter, D.D. 39; Wooler, A.T. 12.
Goals – League (66): Lawrence 23, Banton 19, Burvill 12, McDonald 11 (7 pens), Lucas 5, Mazzon 3, Briley 1, own goals 2.
Milk Cup (9): Banton 2, Lawrence 2, McDonald 2 (1 pen), Burvill 1, Day 1, Lucas 1.
FA Cup (2): Banton 1, Burvill 1.
Ground: Recreation Ground, High St., Aldershot GU11 1TW (0252 20211)
Nearest station: Aldershot
Manager: Len Walker **Secretary:** T. H. C. Green
Colours: Red and blue striped shirts with blue trim; blue shorts
Record home gate: 19,138 v Carlisle, January 1970 (FA Cup)
Honours: Nil

ARSENAL DIV. 1

Adams, Tony A.
Allinson, Ian J.R.
Caesar, Gus C.
Campbell, Gary
Caton, Thomas
Cork, David
Davis, Paul V.
Hayes, Martin
Hill, Colin F.
Isaacs, Anthony L.
Jennings, Patrick A.
Kay, John
Keown, Martin R.
Lee, Terence D.
Lukic, Jovan
McDermott, Brian J.
Mariner, Paul
Meade, Raphael J.
Nicholas, Charles
Nicholas, Peter
O'Leary, David A.
Quinn, Niall J.
Rix, Graham
Robson, Stewart I.
Sansom, Kenneth G.
Talbot, Brian E.
Whyte, Christopher A.
Wilmot, Rhys J.
Woodcock, Anthony S.

League Appearances: Adams, T.A. 3; Allinson, I.J.R. 7(2); Caton, T. 26; Chapman, L.R. 3(1); Cork, D. 5(2); Davis, P.V. 31(4); Gorman P.A. 1(1); Hill, C.F. 37; Jennings, P.A. 38; Kay, J. 6(1);Lukic J. 4; Madden, D.J. 2; Mariner P. 15; Meade, R.J. 9(4);McDermott, B.J. 6(7); Nicholas, C. 41; O'Leary, D.A. 36; Rix, G. 34; Robson, S.I. 28; Sansom, K.G. 40; Sparrow, B.E. 2; Sunderland, A. 11(1); Talbot, B.E. 26(1); Whyte, C.A. 14(1); Woodcock, A.S. 37.

Goals – League (74): Woodcock 21, Nicholas 11 (5 pens), Mariner 7, Robson 6, Talbot 6, Meade 5, Rix 4, Sunderland 4, McDermott 2, Whyte 2, Chapman 1, Cork 1, Davis 1, Hill 1, Sansom 1, own goals 1.
Milk Cup (5): Nicholas 1, Rix 1, Robson 1, Sunderland 1, Woodcock 1.
FA Cup (2): Nicholas 1, Woodcock 1.
Ground: Arsenal Stadium, Avenell Road, N5 1BU (01-226 0304)
Nearest stations: Arsenal (Piccadilly Line), Drayton Park (British Rail) or Finsbury Park (BR, Piccadilly Line or Victoria Line)
Manager: Don Howe **Secretary:** Ken Friar
Colours: Red shirts, with white sleeves; white shorts
Record home gate: 73,295 v Sunderland, March 1935 (League)
Honours – Champions: Division 1: 1930-31, 1932-33, 1933-34, 1934-35, 1937-38, 1947-48, 1952-53, 1970-71
FA Cup winners: 1929-30, 1935-36, 1949-50, 1970-71, 1978-79
Fairs Cup winners: 1969-70

ASTON VILLA — DIV. 1

Birch, Paul
Blair, Andrew
Bremner, Desmond G.
Bradley, Darren M.
Cowans, Gordon S.
Curbishley, Llewellyn C.
Day, Mervyn R.
Deacy, Eamonn S.
Dorigo, Anthony R.
Evans, Allan
Foster, Stephen R.
Gibson, Colin J.
Glover, Dean V.
Greenhalgh, Andrew R.
Kerr, Paul A.
McMahon, Stephen
Mortimer, Dennis G.
Norton, David W.
Obi, Anthony I.
Ormsby, Brendan T.
Palin, Leigh G.
Poole, Kevin
Rideout, Paul D.
Shaw, Gary R.
Spink, Nigel P.
Walker, Raymond
Walters, Mark
Williams, Gary
Withe, Peter

League Appearances: Birch, P. 22; Blair, A. 9; Bremner, D.G. 14(3); Curbishley, L.C. 25(1);Day, M.R. 14; Deacy, E. 12(1); Dorigo, A.R. (1); Evans, A. 36; Foster, S.B. 7; Gibson, C.J. 28; Jones, M.A.W. 5; Kerr, P.A. 1(1); Morley, W.A. 6(1); Mortimer, D.G. 37; McMahon, S. 37; Ormsby, B.T.C. 34; Rideout, P.D. 22(3); Shaw, G.R. 11(1); Spink, N.P. 28; Walker, R. 5(3); Walters, M. 33(4); Williams, G. 40; Withe, P. 36
Goals – League (59): Withe 16, Walters 8, Evans 7 (6 pens), McMahon 5, Mortimer 5, Rideout 5, Shaw 5, Birch 2, Ormsby 2, Curbishley 1, Foster 1, Gibson 1, Morley 1.
Milk Cup (13): Evans 3 (1 pen), Gibson 2, Mortimer 2, Rideout 2, Walters 2, Shaw 1, Withe 1.
FA Cup (1): Withe 1.
Ground: Villa Park, Birmingham B6 6HE (021-327 6604)
Nearest station: Birmingham, New Street
Manager: Graham Turner **Secretary:** Steven Stride
Colours: Claret shirts; Claret shorts.
Record home gate: 76,588 v Derby, March 1946 (FA Cup)
Honours – Champions: Division 1: 1893-94, 1895-96, 1896-97, 1898-99, 1899-1900, 1909-10, 1980-81; Division 2: 1937-38, 1959-60; Division 3: 1971-72

FA Cup winners: 1886-87, 1894-95, 1896-97, 1904-05, 1912-13, 1919-20, 1956-57. (Seven wins stands as the record)
League Cup winners: 1960-61, 1974-75, 1976-77
European Champions Cup: 1981-82

BARNSLEY DIV. 2

Agnew, Stephen M.
Airey, Carl
Campbell, Winston R.
Cross, Paul
Futcher, Paul
Geddis, David
Glavin, Ronald M.
Goodison, Christopher W.
Gray, Stuart
Ironside, Ian
Jeffels, Simon
Joyce, Joseph P.
Law, Nicholas
Lowe, Simon J.
McGuire, Michael J.
Marshall, Craig
Martin-Chambers, Philip
May, Lawrence C.
Plummer, Calvin A.
Rhodes, Andrew C.
Ronson, William
Semley, Alan
Thomas, David G.
Wilkes, David A.

League Appearances: Agnew, S.M. (1); Airey, C. 20(7); Campbell, W.R. 31; Cunningham, A.E. 13; Findlay, J.W. 6; Fletcher, M.R.J. 1; Futcher, P. 10; Geddis, D. 31; Glavin, R.M. 34(1); Gray, S. 16(1); Horn, R.I. 5; Jeffels, S. 3; Johnson, D.E. 4; Joyce, J.P. 39(1); Law, N. 30(1); Lowe, S.J. 2; Martin-Chambers, P. 37; May L.C. 41; McCarthy, M. 12; McGuire, M.J. 36; Pickering, M.J. 3; Plummer, C.A. 1(1); Rhodes, A.C. 31; Ronson, W. 31(1); Semley, A. 1(3); Thomas, D.G. 13; Whitehouse, D. 1(1); Wilkes, D.A. 10(1).
Goals – League (57): Geddis 14, Glavin 11, Gray 8 (2 pens), McGuire 5 (1 pen), Cunningham 4, Airey 3, Campbell 2, Ronson 2, Wilkes 2, Chambers 1, Johnson 1, Joyce 1, Law 1, May 1, Plummer 1.
Milk Cup (0)
FA Cup (0)
Ground: Oakwell, Grove Street, Barnsley S71 1ET (0226-295353)
Nearest station: Barnsley
Manager: Bobby Collins **Secretary:** Michael Spinks
Colours: Red shirts; white shorts
Record home gate: 40,255 v Stoke 1936 (FA Cup)
Honours – Champions: Division 3 North: 1933-34, 1938-39, 1954-55
FA Cup winners: 1911-12

BIRMINGHAM CITY DIV. 2

Blake, Noel L.G.
Blyth, James A.
Broadhurst, Kevan
Coton, Anthony P.
Ferguson, Michael J.
Gayle, Howard
Hagan, James
Halsall, Michael
Harford, Michael G.
Hopkins, Robert
Kuhl, Martin
Rees, Anthony A.
Roberts, Brian L.F.
Stevenson, William B.
Van den Hauwe, Patrick W.R.
Wright, William

League Appearances: Blake, N.L.G. 39; Broadhurst, K. 22(1); Coton, A.P. 41; Gayle, H. 32(1); Hagan, J. 30(3); Halsall, M. 21; Handysides, I.R. 4(1); Harford, M.G. 39; Hopkins, R. 32; Kendall, M.I. 1; Kuhl, M. 20(2); Linton, I. 3(1); Muir, I.J.

1; Mumford, W.E. 3(1); McCarrick, M.B. 12(3); Phillips, L.M. 18(2); Rees, A.A. 22(3); Roberts, B.L.F. 11; Rogers, K.P. 8(1); Stevenson, W.B. 21(4); Van den Hauwe, P.W.R. 42; Wright, W. 40.
Goals – League (39): Gayle 8, Harford 8, Hopkins 5, Wright 5 (5 pens), Blake 2 (1 pen), Halsall 2, Rees 2, Stevenson 2, Broadhurst 1, Kuhl 1, Rogers 1, own goals 2.
Milk Cup (13): Harford 5, Gayle 2, Hopkins 2, Handysides 1, Phillips 1, Rees 1, own goals 1.
FA Cup (9): Wright 3 (3 pens), Harford 2, Hopkins 1, Kuhl 1, Rees 1, own goals 1.
Ground: St Andrews, Birmingham B9 4NH ((021-772 0101 and 2689)
Nearest station: Birmingham, New Street
Manager: Ron Saunders **Secretary:** A. R. Waterhouse
Colours: Royal blue shirts with 3 white vertical stripes on sleeves; white shorts with two royal blue bands down right leg.
Record home gate: 66,844 v Everton, February 1939 (FA Cup)
Honours – Champions: Division 2: 1892-93, 1920-21, 1947-48, 1954-55; League South: 1945-46
League Cup winners: 1962-63

BLACKBURN ROVERS — DIV. 2

Barker, Simon
Branagan, James P.
Brotherston, Noel
Byrom, David J.
Fazackerley, Derek W.
Garner, Simon
Gennoe, Terence W.
Glenn, David A.
Hamilton, David
Keeley, Glenn M.
Lowey, John A.
Mail, David
Miller, Ian
O'Keefe, James V.
Patterson, Mark A.
Randell, Colin W.
Rathbone, Michael J.
Thompson, Christopher D.

League Appearances: Barker, S. 28; Bell, N. 1; Branagan J.P. 41; Brotherston N. 18(3); Devine, P. 7; Fazackerley, D.W. 39; Garner, S. 42; Gennoe, T.W. 30; Glenn, D.A. 21(1); Hamilton, D. 24(2); Keeley, G.M. 35; Lowey, J.A. 42; Mail, D. 8(3); Miller, I. 35(1); O'Keefe, J.V. 12; Patterson, M.A. 27(2); Randell, C.W. 10(1); Rathbone, M.J. 11, Thompson, C.D. 31(2).
Goals – League (57): Garner 19 (2 pens), Thompson 8, Patterson 7, Fazackerley 4 (2 pens), Keeley 4, Barker 3, Miller 3, Devine 2, Hamilton 2, Randell 2, Brotherston 1, Mail 1, own goal 1.
Milk Cup (4): Garner 3, Miller 1.
FA Cup (): Brotherston 1, Garner 1, Keeley 1.
Ground: Ewood Park, Blackburn BB2 4JF (0254 55432/3)
Nearest station: Blackburn
Manager: Bobby Saxton **Secretary:** John W. Howarth F.A.A.I.
Colours: Shirts: blue and white halves; white shorts
Record home gate: 61,783 v Bolton Wanderers, March 1929 (FA Cup)
Honours – Champions: Division 1: 1911-12, 1913-14; Division 2: 1938-39; Division 3: 1974-75
FA Cup winners: 1883-84, 1884-85, 1885-86, 1889-90, 1890-91, 1927-28

BLACKPOOL DIV. 4

Britton, Ian
Davies, Michael J.
Deary, John S.
Dyer, Alexander C.
Ferns, Philip D.
Greenall, Colin A.
Hetzke, Stephen E.R.
Mercer, Keith
Moore, David
Stewart, Paul A.
Stonehouse, Kevin
Walsh, Michael T.
Windridge, David H.

League Appearances: Bardsley, D.J. 16; Brand, A.S. 3; Britton, I. 29(1); Davies, M.J. 3; Deary, J.S. 27(4); Downes, R.D. 1; Dyer, A.C. 4(5); Ferns, P.D. 37(1); Greenall, C.A. 39; Hetzke, S.E.R. 45; Mercer, K. 31; Moore, D. 28; McNiven, D.S. 28(4); O'Rourke, W.J. 6; Pierce, G. 27; Pritchett, K.B. 10(1); Rodaway, W.V. 41; Serella, D.E. 8; Siddall, B. 7; Steele, S.P. 3; Stewart, P.A. 40(4); Stonehouse, K. 13; Walker, N.S. 8(2); Walsh, M.T. 20; Windridge, D.H. 32(2).
Goals – League (70): Stewart 10, Britton 9, Mercer 9, Hetzke 7 (4 pens), Deary 6 (2 pens), McNiven 6, Windridge 6, Stonehouse 5, Greenall 4, Walker 3, Serella 2 Moore 1, Walsh 1, Wright 1.
Milk Cup (3): Bardsley 1, McNiven 1, Stewart 1.
FA Cup (8): Mercer 3, McNiven 2, Deary 1, Stewart 1, own goal 1.
Ground: Bloomfield Road, Blackpool FY1 6JJ (0253 404331)
Nearest station: Blackpool North
Manager: Sam Ellis **Secretary:** D. Johnson
Colours: Tangerine shirts with white stripe on sleeves, white collar and cuffs; white shorts.
Record home gate: 39,118 v Manchester United, April 1952 (League)
Honours – Champions: Division 2: 1929-30
FA Cup winners: 1952-53
Anglo-Italian Cup winners: 1971

BOLTON WANDERERS DIV. 3

Bell, Graham T.
Berry, Neil
Booth, Paul
Borrows, Brian
Caldwell, Anthony
Came, Mark R.
Chandler, Jeffrey G.
Deakin, Raymond J.
Farnworth, Simon
Foster, Wayne P.
Joyce, Warren G.
McElhinney, Gerard
Oghani, George W.
Phillips, James N.
Platt, John R.
Redfearn, Neil D.
Rudge, Simon J.
Saunders, Steven J.P.
Thompson, Stephen J.
Valentine, Peter

League Appearances: Bell, G.T. 20; Berry, N. 9(5); Borrows, B. 44; Caldwell, A. 32(1); Chandler, J.G. 46; Deakin, R.J. 41; Farnworth, S. 36; Foster, W.P. 27(3); Joyce, W.G. 45; McElhinney, G. 43; McGovern, J.P. 2; Oghani, G.W. 1(2); Phillips, J.N. (1); Platt, J.R. 10; Redfearn, N.D. 25; Rudge, S.J. 27(5); Saunders, S.J.P. 3; Snookes, E. 6; Thompson, S.J. 40; Valentine, P. 42; Whatmore, N. 7.
Goals – League (56): Caldwell 19, Chandler 14 (2 pens), Rudge 7, Foster 3, Joyce 3, Thompson 3, Whatmore 2, Bell 1, Deakin 1, McElhinney 1, Redfearn 1, Valentine 1.
Milk Cup (3): Caldwell 2, Joyce 1.
FA Cup (8): Chandler 3 (2 pens), Rudge 2, Caldwell 1, Foster 1, Joyce 1.
Ground: Burnden Park, Manchester Rd., Bolton BL3 2QR (0204-389200)

Nearest station: Bolton
Player/Manager: John McGovern **Secretary:** Des McBain F.A.A.I.
Colours: Shirts: white, shorts: navy blue
Record home gate: 69,912 v Manchester City, February 1933 (FA Cup)
Honours – Champions: Division 2: 1908-09, 1977-78; Division 3: 1972-3
FA Cup winners: 1922-23, 1925-26, 1928-29, 1957-58

AFC BOURNEMOUTH — DIV. 3

Beck, John A.
Brignull, Philip A.
Brown, Roger W.
Graham, Milton M.
La Ronde, Everald
Leigh, Ian R.
Morrell, Paul D.
Nightingale, Mark B.D.
Rafferty, William H.
Savage, Robert J.
Shaw, Christopher J.
Smeulders, John
Sulley, Christopher S.
Thompson, Ian P.

League Appearances: Beck, J.A. 44(1); Brignull, P.A. 44; Brown, R.W. 23; Carter S.C. 4(3); Dawtry, K.A. (1); Duffield, M.J. 6; Graham, M.M. 24(6); La Ronde, E. 18; Lee, T.C. 4(3); Leigh, I.R. 41; Lewis, M.R. 1; Morgan, T.J. 29; Morrell, P.D. 19(3); Nightingale, M.B.D. 46; O'Driscoll, S.M. 19; Rafferty, W.H. 17; Ramsbottom, N. 4; Savage, R.J. 22(1); Schiavi, M.A. 10; Shaw, C.J. 1(2); Smeulders, J. 1; Sulley, C.S. 46; Thompson, I.P. 42(2); Thompson, M.S. 9; Train, R. 7; Williams, K.D. 25(1).
Goals – League (63): Morgan 13 (1 pen), I. Thompson 12, Brignull 6, Rafferty 5, Savage 5 (3 pens), Graham 4, Beck 3, Brown 2, Lee 2, Morrell 2, Nightingale 2, Sulley 2, Duffield 1, O'Driscoll 1, own goals 3.
Milk Cup (5): Brignull 1, Graham 1, Morgan 1 (1 pen).
FA Cup (8): Thompson 3, Beck 2, Graham 1, Lee 1, Morgan 1.
Ground: Dean Court, Bournemouth, Dorset BH7 7AF (0202-35381)
Nearest station: Bournemouth
Manager: Harry Redknapp **Secretary:** Mrs. C. B. Dowsett.
Colours: Shirts: red with single white stripe under arm and down side, red shorts with white stripe
Record home gate: 28,799 v Manchester United, March 1957 (FA Cup)
Honours: Nil

BRADFORD CITY — DIV. 3

Abbott, Gregory S.
Campbell, Robert M.
Cherry, Trevor J.
Clegg, Tony
Ellis, Mark E.
Fee, Gregory P.
Gray, Terence I.
Haire, Garry
Hawley, John E.
Jackson, Peter A.
McCall, Stuart M.
McManus, Charles E.
Withe, Christopher
Yorath, Terence C.

League Appearances: Abbott, G.S. 30(5); Airey, C. 4(1); Campbell, R.M. 32; Cherry, T.J. 44; Clegg, T. 2; Cooke, J. 5(1); Ellis, M.E. 37; Fee, G.P. 3(1); Goodman, D. (2); Gray, T.I. 29(2); Griffiths, P.J. 2; Haire, G. 39(4); Hawley, J.E. 42; Hill, D. (1); Jackson, P.A. 42; Lampkin, S.C.A. (1); Mellor, I. 2(4); McCall, S.M. 46; McManus, C.E. 46; Pickering, M.J. 4; Podd, C.C.M. 30; Watson, G. 4;

Withe, C. 45; Yorath, T.C. 18(3).
Goals – League (73): Hawley 22 (6 pens), Haire 13, Campbell 9, Ellis 8, Gray 7, McCall 5, Abbott 3 (1 pen), Jackson 3, Withe 1.
Milk Cup (1): Podd 1.
FA Cup (2): Haire 1, Hawley 1.
Ground: Valley Parade, Bradford BD8 7DY (0274-306062)
Nearest station: Bradford Exchange
Manager: Trevor Cherry **Secretary:** T. F. Newman
Colours: Claret shirts with amber panelled front, claret shorts
Record home gate: 39,146 v Burnley, March 1911 (FA Cup)
Honours – Champions: Division 2: 1907-08; Division 3 North: 1928-29
FA Cup winners: 1910-11 (first holders of present trophy)

BRENTFORD DIV. 3

Bolton, Ian R.
Booker, Robert
Bullivant, Terence P.
Cassells, Keith B.
Finney, Tom
Fisher, Robert P.
Hurlock, Terence A.
Joseph, Francis
Kamara, Christopher
Lynch, Anthony J.
Mahoney, Anthony J.
Roberts, Gary P.M.
Roberts, Paul
Rowe, Norman T.S.
Salman, Danis M.M.
Spencer, Anthony R.
Swinburne, Trevor

League Appearances: Bolton, I.R. 14; Booker, R. 26(3); Bowles, S. 7(1); Bullivant, T.P. 24; Cassells, K.B. 26(4); Davies, I.C. 2; Finney, T. 14(1); Fisher, R.P. 17; Garner, W.D. 2(1); Gray, N.R. 16; Harris, R.E. 3; Hurlock, T.A. 32; Joseph, F. 42(1); Kamara, C. 37(1); Lynch, A.J. 2; Mahoney, A.J. 15(8); McNichol, J.A. 19(1); Roberts, G.P.M. 40(1); Roberts, P. 34; Roche, P.J. 25; Roffey, W.R. 13; Rollings, A.N. 1; Rowe, N.T.S. 18(3); Salman, D.M.M. 21; Spencer, A.R. 5(1); Swinburne, T. 21; Whitehead, A. 18; Wilkins, G.G. 12(1).
Goals – League (69): Joseph 18, G. Roberts 10, Cassells 9(1 pen), Kamara 6, Booker 4, Hurlock 4, McNichol 4, Mahoney 3 (1 pen), Finney 2, Bolton 1, Bullivant 1, Garner 1, Gray 1, Roffey 1, Rowe 1, own goals 3.
Milk Cup (5): Joseph 2, P. Roberts 2, own goal 1.
FA Cup (10): G. Roberts 3, Joseph 2, Cassells 1, Hurlock 1, Kamara 1, Mahoney 1, P. Roberts 1.
Ground: Griffin Park, Braemar Road, Brentford TW8 0NT (01-560 2021)
Nearest stations: Brentford (BR) or South Ealing (Piccadilly line).
Manager: Frank McLintock **Chief Development Executive:** Miss C. Mathews
Colours: Shirts: Red and white stripe, shorts: white with red stripe down side.
Record home gate: 39,626 v Preston North End, March 1968 (FA Cup)
Honours – Champions: Division 2: 1934-35; Division 3 South: 1932-33; Division 4: 1962-63.

BRIGHTON & HOVE ALBION DIV. 2

Case, James R.
Connor, Terence F.
Corrigan, Thomas J.
Digweed, Perry M.
Fleet, Mark R.
Gatting, Stephen P.
Howlett, Gary P.
Hutchings, Christopher
Jones, Mark A.W.
Kraay, Hans
Lambert, Martin C.
Moseley, Graham

Muir, Ian J.	Ramsey, Christopher I.	Wilson Daniel
O'Reagan, Kieran	Ryan, Gerard J.	Young, Alexander F.
Pearce, Graham	Smillie, Neil	Young, Eric
Penney, Steven A.	Stille, Giles K.	

League Appearances: Case, J.R. 35; Connor, T.F. 40; Corrigan, T.J. 36; Digweed, P.M. 4; Foster, S.B. 16; Gatting, S.P. 35; Grealish, A.P. 23(2); Howlett, G.P. 15(2); Hutchings, C. 26; Jones, M.A.W. 6; Kraay, H. 2(3); Lambert, M.C. 2(1); Moseley, G. 1; Muir, I.J. 2; O' Reagan, K. 30(1); Pearce, G. 18; Penney, S.A. 22(3); Ramsey, C.L. 4; Ring, M.P. (3); Ryan, G.J. 20(4); Smillie, N. 25(1); Smith, G.D. 11(4); Steele, S.P. 1; Stille, G.K. 1(1); Wilkins, D.M. 2; Wilson, D. 26; Young, A.F. 25(1); Young, E. 30; Young, W.D. 4.
Goals – League (69): Connor 13, A. Young 12, Wilson 10 (3 pens), Ryan 5, Case 4, Gatting 4 (1 pen), Smith 4 (2 pens), E. Young 4, Grealish 3, Smillie 2, Foster 1, Hutchings 1, O'Reagan 1, Penney 1, Price 1, own goals 2.
Milk Cup (5): Connor 2, Smith 2, Ryan 1.
FA Cup (5): Connor 2, Ryan 1, Wilson 1 (pen), own goal 1.
Ground: Goldstone Ground, Old Shoreham Road, Hove, Sussex BN3 7DE (0273-739535)
Nearest station: Hove
Manager: Chris Cattlin **Secretary:** Kenneth J. Calver
Colours: Blue shirts with red and white trim, white shorts
Record home gate: 36,747 v Fulham, December 1958 (League)
Honours – Champions: Division 3 South: 1957-58; Division 3: 1971-72; Division 4: 1964-65
FA Cup winners: Nil

BRISTOL CITY — DIV. 3

Cooper, Terence	Llewellyn, Andrew D.	Riley, Glyn
Crawford, Alan P.	Morgan, Trevor J.	Ritchie, Thomas G.
Curle, Keith	Newman, Robert N.	Shaw, John
Halliday, Bruce	Nicholls, Alan	Smith, Nigel K.
Hirst, Martyn P.	Phillipson-Masters, Forbes	Stevens, Paul D.
Hooper, Michael D.	Pritchard, Howard K.	Stroud, Kenneth A.

League Appearances: Cooper, T. 1(20); Crawford, A.P. 31; Curle, K. 5(1); Economou, J. 11(1); Halliday, B. 41; Hirst, M.P. 22(2); Kerr, J. 13(1); Marshall, G. (1); Morgan, T.J. 15; Musker, R. 2(1); Newman, R.N. 29(1); Phillipson-Masters, F.E. 44; Pritchard, H.K. 46; Riley, G. 42; Ritchie, T.G. 45; Shaw, J. 46; Stevens, P.D. 45(1); Stroud, K.A. 34; Williams, G.A. 29(1); Williams, P.S. 5(3).
Goals – League (70): Riley 16, Crawford 15, Ritchie 12 (8 pens), Pritchard 10, Morgan 5, Kerr 4, Stroud 3, Stevens 2, Hirst 1, Newman 1, Phillipson-Masters 1.
Milk Cup (1): Riley 1.
FA Cup (8): Pritchard 3, Ritchie 2, Crawford 1, Hirst 1.
Ground: Ashton Gate, Bristol BS3 2EJ (0272-632812)
Nearest station: Bristol Temple Mead
Manager: Terry Cooper **Secretary:** Robert C. Twyford
Colours: Shirts: red, shorts: white.

Record home gate: 43,335 v Preston, February 1935 (FA Cup)
Honours – Champions: Division 2: 1905-06; Division 3 South: 1922-23, 1926-27, 1954-55

BRISTOL ROVERS DIV. 3

Bannon, Paul A.
Barrett, Michael J.
Bater, Philip T.
Cashley, Alec R.
Holloway, Ian S.
Hughes, Mark
Kite, Philip D.
McCaffery, Aidan
Parkin, Timothy J.
Pulis, Anthony R.
Randall, Paul
Slatter, Neil J.
Stephens, Arthur
Vassall, Paul R.
White, Stephen J.
Williams, Brian
Williams, David G.
Williams, David M.

League Appearances: Bannon, P.A. 11; Barrett, M.J. 33(3); Bater, P.T. 30(2); Cashley, A.R. 27; Holloway, I.S. 36; Hughes, M. 9; Kite, P.D. 19; McCaffery, A. 45; Parkin, T.J. 39; Pulis, A.R. 28; Randall, P. 24(8); Slatter, N.J. 43; Stephens, A. 24(10); White, S.J. 38(5); Williams, B. 46; Williams, D.G. 33(1); Williams, D.M. 21(3).
Goals – League (68): Stephens 13, B. Williams 11 (4 pens), Barrett 9, White 9, Randall 6, Bannon 3, D.M. Williams 3, D.G. Williams 3, Parkin 2, Pulis 2, Bater 1, Holloway 1, Slatter 1, own goals 4.
Milk Cup (8): Barrett 2, Holloway 1, Randall 1, Slatter 1, Stephens 1, White 1, B. Williams 1.
FA Cup (4): Barrett 1. Holloway 1, Slatter 1, Stephens 1.
Ground: Bristol Stadium, Eastville, Bristol BS5 6NN (0272-573687)
Nearest stations: Bristol Temple Mead, Stapleton Road or Parkway
Manager: David Williams **Secretary:** G. J. Bennett
Colours: Shirts: blue and white quarters, shorts: white with blue trim.
Record home gate: 38,472 v Preston, January 1960 (FA Cup)
Honours – Champions: Division 3 South: 1952-53

BURNLEY DIV. 3

Biggins, Wayne
Daley, Stephen
Flynn, Brian
Gallagher, Joseph A.
Hamilton, William R.
Hansbury, Roger
Hutchison, Thomas
Kennedy, Stephen
Malley, Philip
Miller, David B.
Overson, Vincent D.
Phelan, Michael C.
Ray, Philip
Reeves, Kevin P.
Scott, Derek E.

League Appearances: Baker, S. 10; Biggins, W. 20; Daley, S. 20(3); Dixon, L.M. 1; Dobson, J.M. 28; Donachie, W. 37; Donovan, T.C. (1); Flynn, B. 42; Gallagher, J.A. 1; Glendon, K.W. 4; Gow, G. 8(1); Hamilton, W.R. 46; Hansbury, R. 46; Hutchison, T. 46; Kennedy, S. 7; Malley, P. 1(1); Miller, D.B. 15(2); Overson, V.D. 38; Phelan, Marcus C. 1; Phelan, Michael C. 44; Reeves, K.P. 20(1); Scott, D.E. 38(2); Tueart, D. 8(7); Waldron, M. 16; Wharton, A. 7; Young, K. 2.
Goals – League (76): Hamilton 18, Reeves 12 (3 pens), Flynn 9, Biggins 8, Tueart 5 (1 pen), Daley 4, Dobson 4, Hutchison 4, Scott 4, Donachie 3, Miller 2, Michael Phelan 2, own goal 1.
Milk Cup (3): Flynn 2 (1 pen), Wharton 1.

FA Cup (8): Hamilton 3, Reeves 3 (1 pen), Dobson 1, Waldron 1.
Ground: Turf Moor, Brunshaw Road, Burnley BB10 4BX (0282 27777 and 38021)
Nearest station: Burnley Central
Manager: John Bond **Secretary:** R. Bradshaw
Colours: Shirts: claret and blue; shorts: white
Record home gate: 54,775 v Huddersfield, February 1924 (FA Cup)
Honours – Champions: Division 1: 1920-21, 1959-60; Division 2: 1897-98, 1972-73; Division 3: 1981-82
FA Cup winners: 1913-14

BURY — DIV. 4

Bramhall, John
Brown, David J.
Carrodus, Frank
Cutler, Christopher P.
Dobson, John M.
Entwhistle, Wayne P.
Gardner, Paul A.
Jakub, Yanek
Madden, Craig
Pashley, Terence
White, Eric W.

League Appearances: Bramhall, J. 45; Brown, D.J. 28; Buckley, G. 8(1); Butcher, J.M. 11; Carrodus, F. 31(3); Coleman, G.M. 24(5); Cutler, C.P. 7(5); Deacy, N.S. 30(1); Dobson, J.M. 10; Entwhistle, W.P. 35(3); Gardner, P.A. 44; Hilton, G. 1; Hilton, P. 19; Jakub, Y. 46; Madden, C. 46; Mountford, R. 4; O'Keefe, J.V. 2; Park, T. 18(3); Pashley, T. 40; Potts, E.T. 19(1); Spence, D.W. 9(4); White, E.W. 29.
Goals – League (61): Madden 17, Entwhistle 11 (1 pen), Jakub 11 (1 pen), Bramhall 6 (1 pen), Hilton 6, Cutler 2, Potts 2, Carrodus 1, Park 1, Spence 1, White 1, own goals 2.
Milk Cup (5): Madden 2, Bramhall 1, Entwhistle 1, Jakub 1.
FA Cup (3): Entwhistle 2, Madden 1.
Ground: Gigg Lane, Bury BL9 9HR (061-764 4881/2)
Nearest station: Bury
Manager: Martin Dobson **Secretary:** John Heap
Colours: Shirts: white; shorts: royal blue
Record home gate: 35,000 v Bolton, January 1960 (FA Cup)
Honours – Champions: Division 2: 1894-95; Division 3: 1960-61
FA Cup winners: 1899-1900, 1902-03

CAMBRIDGE UNITED — DIV. 3

Beattie, Andrew H.
Branagan, Keith G.
Cartwright, Leslie
Christie, Derrick H.M.
Clark, Steven
Cooke, Robert L.
Daniels, David G.
Fallon, Stephen P.
Greygoose, Dean
Lockhart, Keith S.
Massey, Kevin J.
Moyes, David W.
Murray, James G.
Pyle, Stephen
Sinton, Andrew
Smith, Kevin J.
Spriggs, Stephen

League Appearances: Beattie, A.H. 21; Bennett, M. 11; Branagan, K.G. 1; Cartwright, L. 11(1); Christie, D.H.M. 20(3); Clark, S. 16; Cooke, R.L. 34(3); Cooper, M.D. 1(1); Daniels, D.G. 20; Davis, I.C. 5; Donaldson, D.J. 13(1); Evans, I.P. 1; Fallon, S.P. 33; Finney, T. 22; Fisher, R. P. 17; Goldsmith, M.S. 13(2); Greygoose,

D. 16; Heward, G.K. 1; Mardenborough, S. A. 6; Massey, K.J. 1; Measures, G. A. 4; Moyes, D.W. 30; Murray, J.G. 24; Nicholls, R.I. 2(1); Pyle, S. 11(8); Sinton, A. 32(2); Smith, K.J. 20(5); Spriggs, S. 27(1); Turner, C.J. 9; Webster, M.W. 17.
Goals – League (28): Cooke 6, Sinton 6 (4 pens), Christie 3, Lockhart 3, Daniels 2, Pyle 2, Smith 2 (1 pen), Spriggs 2, Fallon 1, Goldsmith 1.
Milk Cup (5): Cooke 2, Fallon 1, Goldsmith 1, Smith 1.
FA Cup (0).
Ground: Abbey Stadium, Newmarket Road, Cambridge CB5 8LL (0223-241237)
Nearest station: Cambridge
Manager: John Ryan **Secretary:** Paul Daw
Colours: Amber shirts with black trim; amber shorts with black trim.
Record home gate: 14,000 v Chelsea (friendly), May 1970
Honours – Champions: Division 4: 1976-77

CARDIFF CITY — DIV. 2

Bennett, Gary
Bodin, Paul J.
Dibble, Andrew
Dwyer, Philip J.
Elsey, Karl W.
Gibbins, Roger G.
Grant, David
Mullen, James
Owen, Gordon
Plumley, Gary E.
Smith, Colin R.
Tong, David J.
Vaughan, Nigel M.

League Appearances: Baird, I.J. 12; Bennett, G. 32; Bodin, P.J. 26; Burke, M. 3; Crawford, A. 6; Dibble, A. 41; Dwyer, P.J. 42; Elsey, K.W. 29; Evans, P.A. (2); Gibbins, R.G. 42; Goldsmith, M.S. 3(6); Grant, D. 12; Hemmerman, J.L. 10(1); Jones, L. 6; Lee, T.C. 21; Lewis, J. 6; Matthews, W.J. 4(10); Mullen, J. 8(4); Owen, G. 38(1); Plumley, G.E. 1; Rodon, C.P. 4; Smith, C.R. 34; Tong, D.J. 42; Townsend, C.G. 2(3); Vaughan, N.M. 36; Walker, P.A. 2.
Goals – League (53): Owen 14 (3 pens), Vaughan 8, Baird 6, Lee 5, Gibbins 4, Bodin 3, Bennett 2, Dwyer 2, Goldsmith 2, Smith 2, Crawford 1, Elsey 1, own goals 3.
Milk Cup (5): Crawford 2, Bennett 1, Dwyer 1, Owen 1.
FA Cup (0).
Ground: Ninian Park, Sloper Road, Cardiff CF1 8SX (0222-398636/8)
Nearest station: Cardiff Central
Manager: J. Goodfellow **Secretary:** R. Jones
Colours: Blue shirts, white shorts
Record home gate: 61,655 Wales v England, October 1961 (Club record); 57,800 v Arsenal, Division 1: 22 April, 1953
Honours – Champions: Divison 3 South: 1946-47
FA Cup winners: 1926-27

CARLISLE UNITED — DIV. 2

Ashurst, Jack
Coughlin, Russell
Craig, Thomas B.
Dixon, Kevin L.
Haigh, Paul
Hill, Andrew R.
McCartney, Michael
McKellar, David
O'Riordan, Donald J.
Poskett, Malcolm
Rushbury, David
Shoulder, Alan

League Appearances: Ashurst, J. 41; Bannon, P.A. 3(1); Bell, G.T. 11(3); Buckley, M.J. 24(1); Coughlin, R. 22(8); Craig, T.B. 34; Dixon, K.L. 5(4); Haigh, P. 32(2); Hill, A.R. 26; Hornsby, B.G. 1; Horswill, M.F. 1; Moore, D. 13; McCartney, M. 21; McKellar, D. 42; Nicholson, P. 1(1); O'Riordan, D.J. 42; Parker, R. 35(1); Poskett, M. 41; Rushbury, D. 27(1); Shoulder, A. 40.
Goals – League (48): Poskett 17, O'Riordan 8, Shoulder 8, Coughlin 3, Hill 3, Buckley 2, Craig 2, Ashurst 1, Bannon 1, Moore 1, Parker 1, Rushbury 1.
Milk Cup (2): Poskett 2.
FA Cup (2):Ashurst 1, Shoulder 1 (pen).
Ground: Brunton Park, Warwick Road, Carlisle CA1 1LL (0228-26237)
Nearest station: Carlisle
Manager: Bob Stokoe **Secretary:** N. Irving
Colours: Blue shirts with red and white trim; blue shorts
Record home gate: 27,500 v Birmingham, January 1957 (FA Cup) and v Middlesbrough, February 1970 (FA Cup)
Honours – Champions: Division 3: 1964-65

CHARLTON ATHLETIC DIV. 2

Aizlewood, Mark
Anderson, Darren I.
Berry, Leslie D.
Curtis, Paul A.E.
Dickenson, Kevin J.
Dowman, Stephen J.
Flanagan, Michael A.
Gritt, Stephen J.
Hales, Derek D.
Harris, Carl S.
Johns, Nicholas P.
Lange, Anthony S.
Lee, Robert M.
Moore, Ronald.
Mountford, Peter
Robinson, Martin J.
Scott, Geoffrey
Smith, Kevin P.
Westley, Shane L.M.

League Appearances: Aizlewood, M. 31; Anderson, D.I. 1; Berry, L.D. 42; Curtis, P.A.E. 23(1); Dickenson, K.J. 42; Dowman, S.J. 35; Flanagan, M.A. 18; Gritt, S.J. 33; Hales, D.D. 27(2); Harris, C.S. 24; Johns, N.P. 36; Jones, C.H. 17(6); Lange, A.S. 6; Lee, R.M. 10(1); Moore, R.D. 27(1); Mountford, P. 10(1); Naylor, T.M.P. 6; O'Shea, D.E. 9; Paye, M.C. 2; Robinson, M.J. 25(2); Smith, K.P. 30(6); Westley, S.L.M. 8.
Goals – League (53): Hales 10 (3 pens), Moore 8, Robinson 8, K. Smith 6 (2 pens), Lee 4, Curtis 3, Dowman 3, Flanagan 2, Harris 2, Jones 2, Aizlewood 1, Dickenson 1, Gritt 1, Mountford 1, own goal 1.
Milk Cup (2): Aizlewood 1, Jones 1.
FA Cup (1): own goal 1.
Ground: The Valley, Floyd Road, Charlton, SE7 8AW (01-853 0444)
Nearest station: Charlton (SR)
Manager: Lennie Lawrence **Secretary:** G.I.S. Hortop
Colours: Red shirts with red and white trim; shorts: white
Record home gate: 75,031 v Aston Villa, February 1938 (FA Cup)
Honours – Champions: Division 3 South: 1928-29, 1934-35
FA Cup winners: 1946-47

CHELSEA DIV. 1

Beste, Robin A.
Bumstead, John
Canoville, Paul K.
Dixon, Kerry M.
Donnellan, Leo J.
Droy, Michael R.
Dublin, Keith B.L.
Francis, Stephen S.
Hollins, John W.
Howard, Terence
Isaac, Robert C.
Jasper, Dale W.
Johnstone, Derek J.
Jones, Joseph P.
Jones, Keith A.
Lee, Colin
McAndrew, Anthony
McLaughlin, Joseph
Nevin, Patrick K.F.
Niedzwiecki, Andrew E.
Nolan, Martin J.
Pates, Colin G.
Priest, Philip
Shearer, Duncan N.
Spackman, Nigel J.
Speedie, David R.
Thomas, Reginald M.
Walker, Clive

League Appearances: Bumstead, J. 30(1); Canoville, P.K.17(3); Dixon, K.M. 42; Dublin, K.B.L 1; Hollins, J.W. 29; Hutchings, C. 4; Jasper, D.W. 3; Johnstone, D.J. (2); Jones, J.P. 34; Lee, C. 25(8); McAndrew, A. 13; McLaughlin, J. 41; Nevin, P.K.F. 38; Niedzwiecki, A.E. 42; Pates, C.G. 42; Rhoades-Brown, P. 6; Spackman, N.J. 40; Speedie, D.R. 32(5); Thomas, R.M. 17; Walker, C. 6.
Goals – League (90): Dixon 28 (2 pens), Nevin 14 (1 pen), Speedie 13, Bumstead 7, Canoville 6, McAndrew 4 (2 pens), Thomas 4, Lee 3, Spackman 3 (1 pen), Walker 3, Hollins 1, Hutchings 1, Jones 1, Rhoades-Brown 1, own goal 1.
Milk Cup (8): Dixon 6, Canoville 1, Walker 1.
FA Cup (0).
Ground: Stamford Bridge, Fulham Road, London SW6 1HS (01-385 5545/6), also information service 381 0111.
Nearest station: Fulham Broadway (District Line)
Manager: John Neal **Secretary:** Miss S. F. Marson
Colours: Shirts: royal blue with vertical pinstripes and red and white trim; shorts: royal blue.
Record home gate: 82,905 v Arsenal, October 1935 (League)
Honours – Champions: Division 1: 1954-55; Division 2: 1983-4
FA Cup winners: 1969-70
League Cup winners: 1964-65
European Cup-Winners' Cup winners: 1970-71

CHESTER CITY DIV. 4

Blackwell, Paul
Bulmer, Peter
Cooke, Terence A.
Dixon, Lee M.
Evans, David
Harrington, Phillip
Holden, Andrew I.
Lane, Martin J.
O'Rourke, William J.
Sanderson, Paul D.
Wharton, Andrew
Zelem, Peter R.

League Appearances: Allen, J. 40(2); Blackwell, P. 36(3); Brett, D.S. 24(5); Bulmer, P. 10(9); Burke, J. 3; Camden, C.E. 9; Coy, R.A. 14; Dixon, L.M. 16; Donnelly, P.J. 1; Elliott, A. 24(8); Evans, D. 10; Harrington, P. 41; Hildersley, R. 9; Holden, A.I. 44; Lane, M.J. 38; Manns, P.H. 16; O'Rourke, W.J. 5; Parker, S.J. 9; Phillips, T. 9(1); Raynor, P.E. 3; Ryan, J.G. 4; Sanderson, P.D. 24; Storton, T.G. 18; Sutcliffe, P.D. 11; Wann, J.D. 2(1); Wharton, A. 15; Williams, M. 18(2); Williams, P.J. 6(1); Wintersgill, D. 5; Zelem, P.R. 42.

Goals – League (45): Holden 7, Zelem 7 (3 pens), Parker 5, Allen 3, Blackwell 3, Elliott 3, Sanderson 3, Brett 2, Camden 2, Phillips 2, Wharton 2, M. Williams 2, Dixon 1, Storton 1, own goals 2.
Milk Cup (5): Zelem 2 (1 pen), Elliott 1, Holden 1, Phillips 1.
FA Cup (1): Holden 1.
Ground: The Stadium, Sealand Road, Chester CH1 4LW (0244 371376)
Nearest station: Chester
Manager: John McGrath **Secretary:** J. A. Eckersley
Colours: Royal blue shirts with white stripes; royal blue shorts with red and white trim
Record home gate: 20,500 v Chelsea, January 1952 (FA Cup)
Honours: Nil

CHESTERFIELD DIV. 4

Baines, Stephen J.
Bellamy, Gary
Brown, James G.
Brown, Neil R.
Brown, Philip J.
Hunter, Leslie
Kendal, Stephen J.
Klug, Bryan P.
Newton, Robert
Scrimgeour, Brian
Spooner, Stephen A.
Stimpson, Barrie G.

League Appearances: Baines, S.J. 45; Bell, D.M. 15(2); Bellamy, G. 38; Birch, A. 30(2); Boxall, A.R. 4(1); Brown, J.G. 40; Brown, N. R. 5; Brown, P.J. 16; Clayton, J. 25(8); Grant, D. 7; Gregory, P.G. 6; Henderson, W.M. 3; Higginbottom, M. 4(1); Hornsby, B.G. 1; Hoskin, M.A. (1); Hunter, L. 21; Kendal, S.J. 43; King, J. 1; Klug, B.P. 27(7); Newton, R. 33; O'Neill, J.J. 34; Scrimgeour, B. 41; Spooner, S.A. 20; Stimpson, B.G. 27; Waddington, S. 14(4); Walker, G.G. 6; White, E.W. (1).
Goals – League (59): Newton 14 (2 pens), Kendal 9, P. Brown 6, Birch 5 (1 pen), Clayton 4, Baines 3, Bell 3 (1 pen), Scrimgeour 3, Spooner 3, Hunter 2, Klug 2, O'Neill 2, Bellamy 1, J. Brown 1, Waddington 1.
Milk Cup (3): Baines 1, Birch 1 (pen), Scrimgeour 1.
FA Cup (6): Newton 3, Birch 2 (2 pens), Bellamy 1.
Ground: Recreation Ground, Chesterfield S40 4SX (0246 209765)
Nearest station: Chesterfield
Manager: John Duncan **Secretary:** R. F. Pepper
Colours: Royal blue shirts; white shorts
Record home gate: 30,968 v Newcastle United, April 1939 (League)
Honours – Champions: Division 3 North: 1930-31, 1935-36; Division 4: 1969-70

COLCHESTER UNITED DIV. 4

Adcock, Anthony C.
Bowen, Keith B.
Burman, Simon J.
Chamberlain, Alec F.R.
Cook, Michael
Farrell, Andrew
Groves, Perry
Hadley, Antony P.F.
Houston, Stewart
Hull, Jeff
Leslie, Steven R.W.
Mutrie, Leslie A.
Osborne, Roger C.
Phillips, Ian A.
Walker, Michael S.G.
Wignall, Steve L.

League Appearances: Adcock, A.C.41(2); Bowen, K.B. 46; Chamberlain, A.F.R. 46; Coleman, P. 7(1); Cook, M. 36; Farrell, A.J. 15; Groves, P. 38(4); Hadley, A.P.F. 44(1); Hedman, R. 3(1); Houston, S. 42; Hubbick, D. 3(7); Hull, J. 33; Leslie, S.R.W. 25; Mutrie, L.A. 10(4); Nichols, A.A. 4(2); Oldfield, C. (3); Osborne, R.C. 34(2); Phillips, I.A. 43; Wignall, S.L. 36.
Goals – League (69): Adcock 26 (8 pens), Bowen 12, Wignall 8, Phillips 5 (1 pen), Houston 4, Cook 2, Groves 2, Mutrie 2, Hull 1, Leslie 1, Nichols 1, Osborne 1, own goals 4.
Milk Cup (8): Adcock 5, Wignall 2, Bowen 1.
FA Cup (6): Bowen 5, Houston 1.
Ground: Layer Road, Colchester CO2 7JJ (0206-574042)
Nearest station: Colchester
Manager: Cyril Lea **Secretary:** M. R. Bennet
Colours: Blue and white vertical striped shirts; blue shorts
Record home gate: 19,072 v Reading, November 1948 (FA Cup)
Honours: Nil

COVENTRY CITY — DIV. 1

Adams, Michael R.
Bennett, David A.
Butterworth, Ian S.
Daly, Gerard A.
Gibson, Terence B.
Grimes, Augustine A.
Gynn, Michael
Hormantschuk, Peter A.
Kelly, Errington E.
Langley, Thomas W.
McDonald, James R.S.
McGrath, Lloyd A.
Peake, Trevor
Pearce, Stuart
Platnauer, Nicholas R.
Singleton, Martin D.
Spring, Andrew J.
Suckling, Perry J.
Thompson, Keith A.
Withey, Graham A.

League Appearances: Adams, M.R. 16(1); Allardyce, S. 28; Avramovic, R. 18; Bamber, J. D. 18(1); Bennett, D.A. 32(2); Butterworth, I.S. 22(2); Daly, G.A. 27(1); Ferguson, M.J. 7; Gibson, T.B. 35(1); Grimes, A.A. 29(3); Gynn, M. 20(3); Hendrie, J.G. 1(2); Hormantschuk, P.A. 8; Hunt, S.K. 13(2); Jacobs, S.D. 18; Langley, T.W. 2; McGrath, L.A. 1; Peake, T. 33; Pearce, S. 23; Platnauer, N.R. 29(5); Roberts, B.L.F. 30; Singleton, M.D. 12(1); Spring, A.J. (1); Suckling, P.J. 24; Thompson, K.A. 6; Withey, G.A. 10(10).
Goals – League (57): Gibson 17 (1 pen), Daly 7 (2 pens), Bennett 6, Platnauer 6, Withey 4, Bamber 3, Ferguson 3, Peake 3, Gynn 2, Adams 1, Allardyce 1, Grimes 1, Hunt 1, own goals 2.
Milk Cup (3): Bamber 1, Bennett 1, Grimes 1.
FA Cup (7): Withey 3, Gibson 2, Hunt 1, Peake 1.
Ground: Highfield Road Stadium, King Richard Street, Coventry CV2 4AW (0203-57171)
Nearest station: Coventry
Manager: Bobby Gould **Secretary:** G. P. Hover
Colours: Sky blue shirts with navy and white trim; shorts: sky blue with navy trim.
Record home gate: 51,455 v Wolverhampton, April 1967 (League)
Honours – Champions: Division 2: 1966-67; Division 3: 1963-64; Division 3 South: 1935-36

CREWE ALEXANDRA DIV. 4

Blissett, Gary P.
Brady, Paul J.
Cliss, Tony
Crabbe, Steven A.J.
Davis, Steven A.J.
Grimshaw, Christopher A.
Hart, Nigel
King, Peter
Leonard, Mark A.
Longley, Nicholas
Pullar, David R.
Scott, Robert W.
Thomas, Geoffrey R.
Waller, David H.
Williams, Philip J.

League Appearances: Bishop, I.W. 4; Blissett, G.P. 20(2); Bowers, I. 19(2); Brady, P.J. 24(1); Cliss, T. 36(1); Crabbe, S.A.J. 37; Davis, S.P. 23(1); Edwards, S.G. 38(1); Grimshaw, C.A. 1(2); Hart, N. 36(1); King, P. 38(4); Leonard, M.A. 36(2); Naylor, S.W. 38; Newell, M.C. 3; Puller, D.H. 33(1); Scott, R.W. 46; Sheldon, K.J. 2; Smith, S.J. 8; Spittle, P.D. 4(2); Thomas, G.R. 5(3); Thornhill, K.E. 1; Waller, D.H. 40(2); Williams, P.J. 14(6).
Goals – League (56): Leonard 10, Waller 10, Pullar 6, Scott 6, Crabbe 4 (2 pens), King 4 (2 pens), Blissett 3, Cliss 3, Hart 3, Williams 3, Brady 1, Spittle 1, Thomas 1, own goal 1.
Milk Cup (9): Waller 4 (1 pen), Blissett 1, Bowers 1, Crabbe 1, Leonard 1, King 1.
FA Cup (0).
Ground: Gresty Road, Crewe CW2 6EB (0270 213014)
Nearest station: Crewe
Manager: Dario Grady **Secretary:** Mrs G. C. Palin
Colours: Red shirts; shorts: white
Record home gate: 20,000 v Tottenham, January 1960 (FA Cup)
Honours: Nil

CRYSTAL PALACE DIV. 2

Barber, Phillip A.
Cannon, James A.
Cummins, Stanley
Gilbert, William A.
Hilaire, Vincent M.
Hughton, Henry T.
Lacy, John
Lindsay, David J.
Locke, Gary R.
McCulloch, Andrew
Mabbutt, Kevin R.
Murphy, Jeremiah M.
Nebbeling, Gavin M.
Stebbing, Gary S.
Wood, George

League Appearances: Barber, P.A. 8(1); Brooks, S. 3(1); Cannon, J.A. 30; Cummins, S. 17(1); Evans, A. 19(2); Fashanu, J. 1; Gilbert, W.A. 33(1); Giles, D.C. 26(3); Hilaire, V.M. 40; Hughton, H.T. 35; Lacy, J. 24(3); Lindsay, D.J. 1; Locke, G.R. 36; Mabbutt, K.R. 9(2); Martin, W.L. 1; Murphy, J.M. 30(2); McCulloch, A. 25; Nebbeling, G.M. 13(3); Nicholas, P. 25; Stebbing, G.S. 30(1); Strong, L. 7; Wilkins, P. 7; Wood, G. 42.
Goals – League (42): Evans 7, Giles 5, Cummins 4, Mabbutt 3, McCulloch 3, Murphy 3, Nicholas 3, Barber 2, Cannon 2, Hilaire 2, Stebbing 2, Gilbert 1, Locke 1, Wilkins 1, own goals 3.
Milk Cup (3): Hilaire 2, Brooks 1.
FA Cup (2): Gilbert 1, McCulloch 1.
Ground: Selhurst Park, SE25 6PU (01-653 4462)
Nearest stations: Selhurst, Norwood Junction or Thornton Heath
Manager: Steve Coppell **Secretary:** Alan J. Leather

Colours: Shirts:royal blue and red vertical stripes; shorts, royal blue with three red stripes down sides.
Record home gate: 51,801 v Burnley, May 1979 (League)
Honours – Champions: Division 2: 1978-79; Division 3 South: 1920-21

DARLINGTON DIV. 4

Barber, Frederick	Johnson, Peter E.	Smith, Kevan
Cartwright, Peter	McLean, David J.	Todd, Kevin
Craggs, John E.	Ross, Colin	Walsh, Alan

League Appearances: Angus, M.A. 13; Bannon, P.A. 2; Barber, F. 46; Barton, D. 30; Cartwright, P. 39(2); Craggs, J.E. 44; Davies, R. 10; Forster, M.E. 10(2); Gilbert, T.H. 25(2); Hannah, J. 9(4); Honour, B. 32(9); Hulse, R.J. 3(1); Johnson, P.E. 44; Lee, R.G. 5; Lloyd, P.R. 14; McLean, D.J. 43; Pugh, K.J. (2); Ross, C. 7; Smith, K. 44; Todd, K. 36(1); Wakefield, D. 4(12); Walsh, A. 36(2); Wilson, J.H. 9(1); Young, D.A. 1(2).
Goals – League (49): Walsh 10 (1 pen), Todd 9, Angus 7, Forster 4, Cartwright 3, Hannah 3, McLean 3, Gilbert 2, Smith 2, Barton 1, Davies 1, Honour 1, Johnson 1, own goals 2.
Milk Cup (6): Walsh 3, Cartwright 1, Honour 1, Pugh 1.
FA Cup (12): Walsh 5, McLean 2, Todd 2, Barton 1, Cartwright 1, Davies 1.
Ground: Feethams Ground, Darlington DL1 5JB (03254-65097)
Nearest station: Darlington
Manager: Cyril Knowles **Secretary:** D. A. Thorne
Colours: White shirts; black shorts
Record home gate: 21,023 v Bolton, November 1960 (League Cup)
Honours – Champions: Division 3 North: 1924-25

DERBY COUNTY DIV. 3

Blades, Paul A.	Davison, Robert	Powell, Stephen
Buckley, Steven	Devine, Stephen B.	Pratley, Richard G.
Burns, Kenneth	Garner, Andrew	Robertson, John N.
Cherry, Steven R.	Harbey, Graham K.	Wilson, Kevin J.
Clifford, Mark	Hooks, Paul	

League Appearances: Attley, B.R. 13(1); Banovic, V. 3; Barton, J.S. 19; Blades, P.A. 4; Buckley, S. 31; Burns, K. 11; Campbell, R.M. 11; Cherry, S.R. 38; Davison, R. 40; Deacy, E. 5; Devine, S.B. 9(1); Findlay, J.W. 1; Futcher, P. 18; Garner, A. 13; Gemmill, A. 38; Harbey, G.K. 19; Hill, A.R. 1; Hooks, P. 17; Lane, S.B. 1; McAlle, J.E. 14(2); McFarland, R.L. 3(5); O'Brien, R.C. 4; Plummer, C.A. 23(4); Powell, S. 36; Pratley, R.G. 1(1); Robertson, J.N. 31; Watson, D.V. 34; Wilson, K.J. 24(8).
Goals – League (36): Davison 14, Garner 5, Campbell 4, Plummer 3, Gemmill 2 (2 pens), Robertson 2 (1 pen), Wilson 2, Hooks 1, McAlle 1, Powell 1, Watson 1.
Milk Cup (0):
FA Cup (8): Davison 4, Gemmill 1 (pen), McAlle 1, Plummer 1, Wilson 1.

Ground: The Baseball Ground, Shaftesbury Crescent, Derby DE3 8NB (0332-40105)
Nearest station: Derby
Manager: Arthur Cox **Secretary:** M. J. Dunford
Colours: White shirts; blue shorts
Record home gate: 41,826 v Tottenham, September 1969 (League)
Honours – Champions: Division 1: 1971-72, 1974-75; Division 2: 1911-12, 1914-15, 1968-69; Division 3 North: 1956-57
FA Cup winners: 1945-46.

DONCASTER ROVERS — DIV. 3

Brown, Allan
Dobbin, James
Douglas, Colin F.
Green, William
Gregory, Paul G.
Harle, David
Humphries, Glenn
Kowalski, Andrew M.
Lister, Stephen H.
Peacock, Dennis
Philliben, John,
Russell, William M.
Snodin, Glynn
Snodin, Ian
Woods, Neil S.
Yates, Stephen

League Appearances: Allanson, G.E. 1(1); Boyd, W. 8; Breckin, J. 17(1); Brown, A. 9; Bukovina, J.F. 1; Dobbin, J. 11; Douglas, C.F. 44; Green, W. 10(1); Harle, D. 28(1); Humphries, G. 44; Kowalski, A.M. 32; Lister, S.H. 30(1); Miller, M.J. 21(9); Moss, E. 41(3); Mutrie, L.A. 6; Peacock, D. 38; Philliben, J. 12; Russell, W.M. 41; Snodin, G. 41(2); Snodin, I. 39; Tomlinson, A.D. 2(2); Woods, N.S. 3(4); Yates, S. 27.
Goals – League (82): Douglas 15, Moss 15, G. Snodin 13 (1 pen), I. Snodin 9 (4 pens), Harle 6, Russell 6, Miller 4, Brown 2, Dobbin 2 (1 pen), Humphries 2, Lister 2, Green 1, Kowalski 1, Mutrie 1, Woods 1, Yates 1, own goal 1.
Milk Cup (6): Douglas 2, Moss 2, Humphries 1, I. Snodin 1 (pen).
FA Cup (0):
Ground: Belle Vue Ground, Doncaster DN4 5HT (0302 535281)
Nearest station: Doncaster
Manager: Billy Bremner **Secretary:** Mrs C.I. Heeley
Colours: Shirts: red and white hoops, shorts: white
Record home gate: 37,149 v Hull City, October 1948 (League)
Honours – Champions: Division 3 North: 1934-35, 1946-47, 1949-50; Division 4: 1965-66, 1968-69

EVERTON — DIV. 1

Arnold, James A.
Bailey, John A.
Bishop, Ian W.
Curran, Edward
Gray, Andrew M.
Harper, Alan
Heath, Adrian P.
Higgins, Mark N.
Hughes, Darren J.
Irvine, James A.
Macowat, Ian S.
Marshall, Ian P.
Morrisey, John
Mountfield, Derek N.
Ratcliffe, Kevin
Reid, Peter
Richardson, Kevin
Rimmer, Stuart A.
Sharp, Graeme M.
Sheedy, Kevin M.
Southall, Neville
Steven, Trevor M.
Stevens, Michael G.
Wakenshaw, Robert A.

League Appearances: Arnold, J.A. 7; Bailey, J.A. 33; Bishop, I.W. (1); Curran, E. 8; Gray, A.M. 23; Harper, A. 26(3); Heath, A.P. 36; Higgins, M.N. 14; Hughes, D.J. 1; Irvine, J.A. 19(2); Johnson, D.E. 7(2); King, A.E. 19(1); Mountfield, D.N. 31; Ratcliffe, K. 38; Reid, P. 34(1); Richardson, K. 25(3); Rimmer, S.A. 1; Sharp, G.M. 27(1); Sheedy, K.M. 28; Southall, N. 35; Steven, T.M. 23(4); Stevens, M.G. 26(1); Wakenshaw, R.A. 1.
Goals – League (44): Heath 12 (1 pen), Sharp 7 (1 pen), Gray 5, Richardson 4, Sheedy 4 (1 pen), Mountfield 3, King 2 (1 pen), Reid 2, Harper 1, Johnson 1, Steven 1, Stevens 1, Wakenshaw 1.
Milk Cup (16): Heath 4, Sheedy 4, Sharp 3, Richardson 2, King 1, Reid 1, Steven 1.
FA Cup (13): Gray 3, Heath 2, Irvine 2, Sheedy 2, Reid 1, Richardson 1, Sharp 1, own goal 1.
Ground: Goodison Park, Liverpool L4 4EL (051-521 2020)
Nearest station: Liverpool Lime Street
Manager: Howard Kendall **Secretary:** Jim Greenwood
Colours: Royal blue shirts with white trim; white shorts
Record home gate: 78,299 v Liverpool, September 1948 (League)
Honours – Champions: Division 1: 1890-91, 1914-15, 1927-28, 1931-32, 1938-39, 1962-63, 1969-70; Division 2: 1930-31
FA Cup winners: 1905-06, 1932-33, 1965-66, 1983-84

EXETER CITY — DIV. 4

Bond, Leonard A.
Francis, Gerald C.J.
Harrower, Steven G.
Howarth, Frank
Kirkup, Graeme S.
Ling, Martin
McDonough, Roy
Marker, Nicholas R.T.
Neville, Steven F.
Pratt, Raymond E.
Rogers, Martyn
Sims, John
Viney, Keith R.

League Appearances: Atkinson, H.A. 28; Auguste, J. 7(3); Bond, L.A. 45; Crabtree, R.E. 1; Dennis, J.A. 3(1); Evans, I.P. 4; Francis, G.C.J. 28; Harle, D. 6; Harrower, S.G. 10(3); Hicks, J.M. 3; Howarth, F. 6(5); Kellow, T. 7(1); Kirkup, G.S. 36; Lane, M.E. 1; Ling, M. 23(6); Marker, N.R.T. 28(3); Musker, R. 6; McDonough, R. 15(1); McEwan, S. 28; Neville, S.F. 40(3); O'Connor, M.A. 38; Pratt, R.E. 30(6); Rogers, P.P. 25; Sims, J. 12(2); Taylor, P.J. 8; Viney, K.B. 42; Webster, S.P. 26.
Goals – League (50): Pratt 16 (1 pen), McEwan 9 (4 pens), Neville 9, Rogers 5, Francis 3, Sims 3, Atkinson 1, Harrower 1, Kirkup 1, O'Connor 1, own goal 1.
Milk Cup (3): Kellow 1, McEwan 1, Rogers 1.
FA Cup (2): Neville 1, O'Connor 1.
Ground: St James' Park, Exeter, Devon EX4 6PX Exeter (0392 54073/59466)
Nearest stations: Exeter Central or St David's
Manager: Jim Iley **Secretary:** C. Davey
Colours: Red and white vertical striped shirts; black shorts with white trim
Record home gate: 20,984 v Sunderland, March 1931 (FA Cup)
Honours: Nil

FULHAM DIV. 2

Carr, Clifford P.
Coney, Dean H.
Cottington, Brian A.
Davies, Gordon J.
De Graft Rosenior, Leroy
Elkins, Gary
Gale, Anthony P.
Hopkins, Jeffrey
Houghton, Raymond J.
Kerrins, Wayne M.
Lewington, Raymond
Lock, Kevin J.
Marshall, John P.
O'Driscoll, Sean M.
Parker, Paul A.
Peyton, Gerald J.
Reeves, John C.
Scott, Peter R.
Stannard, James
Tapley, Steven
Tempest, Dale M.
Wilson, Robert J.

League Appearances: Brown, R.W. 13; Carr, C.P. 38(3); Coney, D.H. 26(1); Cottington, B.A. (1); Davies, G.J. 35(1); De Graft Rosenior, L. 22(1); Foley, S. 2(1); Gale, A.P. 35; Hopkins, J. 31(2); Houghton, R.J. 40; Lewington, R. 32(1); Lock, K.J. 15; Marshall, J.P. 21(4); O'Driscoll, S.M. 10(2); Parker, P.A. 34; Peyton, G.J. 27; Reeves, J.C. 2(1); Scott, P.R. 31(1); Sealy, A.J. 5; Stannard, J. 15; Tapley, S. 1; Tempest, D.M. 13(2); Wilson, R.J. 14(2).
Goals – League (60): Davies 21, Rosenior 8, Coney 7, Carr 4 (3 pens), Scott 4, Tempest 4, Houghton 3, Wilson 3, Lock 2 (1 pen), Gale 1, Sealey 1, own goals 2.
Milk Cup (8): Davies 3, Lock 2 (2 pens), Lewington 1, Scott 1, Tempest 1.
FA Cup (0)
Ground: Craven Cottage, Stevenage Road, Fulham SW6 6HH (01-736 6561)
Nearest stations: Putney Bridge (District) or Hammersmith (Metropolitan, District and Piccadilly)
Manager: Ray Harford **Secretary:** Mrs. Y. Haines
Colours: White shirts with black trim; black shorts with white trim
Record home gate: 49,335 v Millwall, October 1938 (League)
Honours – Champions: Division 2: 1948-49; Division 3, South: 1931-32.
FA Cup winners: Nil

GILLINGHAM DIV. 3

Bruce, Stephen R.
Cascarino, Anthony G.
Cochrane, George T.
Fry, David P.
Handford, Philip M.
Hillyard, Ronald W.
Johnson, Jeffrey D.
Leslie, John A.
Mehmet, David
Musker, Russell
Sage, Melvyn
Sharpe, John W.H.
Shaw, Peter K.
Sitton, John E.
Weatherly, Colin M.

League Appearances: Armstrong, G.S. 7(1); Bruce, S.R. 39(1); Cascarino, A.G. 33(4); Cavener, P. 4(6); Clarke, C.J. 8; Cochrane, G.T. 34; Daniel, R.C. 5; Duncan, C.J. 1; Fry, D.P. 38; Garner, P. 5; Handford, P.M. 17(3); Hillyard, R.W. 8; Johnson, J.D. 31(1); Leslie, J.A. 44(1); Mehmet, D. 42(1); Musker, R. 23(4); Sage, M. 40; Scotting, A. 2; Sharpe, J.W.H. 16; Shaw, P.K. 32(1); Sitton, J.E. 40(2); Sparrow, B.E. 5; Stokes, W.D. (1); Tydeman, R. 2; Weatherly, C.M. 29(3); Woodhead, A. 1(1).
Goals – League (74): Mehmet 16 (1 pen), Cascarino 12, Leslie 9, Weatherly 9, Bruce 6 (1 pen), Cochrane 6, Musker 5, Johnson 2, Sage 2, Sitton 2, Cavener 1, Clarke 1, Shaw 1, Sparrow 1, Sutton 1.

Milk Cup (1): Shaw 1.
FA Cup (12): Weatherly 3, Leslie 2, Cascarino 1, Cochrane 1, Handford 1, Mehmet 1, Musker 1, Sage 1, Shaw 1.
Ground: Priestfield Stadium, Gillingham, Kent ME7 4DD (0634-51854)
Nearest station: Gillingham
Manager: Keith Peacock **Secretary:** R. J. Dennison
Colours: Blue shirts: white shorts
Record home gate: 23,002 v Queen's Park Rangers, January 1948 (FA Cup)
Honours – Champions: Division 4: 1963-64

GRIMSBY TOWN — DIV. 2

Agnew, Paul
Batch, Nigel A.
Bonnyman, Philip
Crombie, Dean M.
Cumming, Robert
Drinkell, Kevin S.
Emson, Paul
Ford, Tony
Grotier, Peter D.
Hannay, David M.
Henshaw, Gary
Hine, Mark
Lund, Gary J.
Moore, Andrew R.
Moore, Kevin T.
Nicholl, Christopher J.
Speight, Michael
Wilkinson, Paul

League Appearances: Agnew, P. 1; Batch, N.A. 42; Bonnyman, P. 27(2); Cooper, N. 7; Crombie, D.M. 40; Cumming, R. 27(3); Drinkell, K.S. 35(1); Emson, P. 39; Ford, T. 42; Henshaw, G. 3(1); Lund, G.J. 4(3); Moore, A.R. 8(1); Moore, K.T. 41; Nicholl, C.J. 39; Shearer, D.J. 1(3); Speight, M. 23(2); Waters, J.J.W. 37; Whymark, T.J. 9(2); Wilkinson, P. 37.
Goals – League (60): Drinkell 15, Wilkinson 12, Ford 8, Waters 7 (3 pens), Emson 5, Lund 4, Bonnyman 3 (1 pen), Speight 2, Whymark 2, Cumming 1, Moore 1.
Milk Cup (4): Drinkell 2, Wilkinson 2.
FA Cup (1): Drinkell 1.
Ground: Blundell Park, Cleethorpes, DN35 7PY (0472-697111)
Nearest stations: Cleethorpes or Grimsby Town
Manager: Dave Booth **Secretary:** B. J. Fleming
Colours: Black and white striped shirts with red line on collar and cuffs; black shorts with red and white stripes
Record home gate: 31,657 v Wolverhampton, February 1937 (FA Cup)
Honours – Champions: Division 2: 1900-01, 1933-34; Division 3 North: 1925-26, 1955-56; Division 3: 1979-80; Division 4: 1971-72

HALIFAX TOWN — DIV. 4

Cook, Jeffrey, W.
Gallagher, Barry P.
Greenway, Mark
Hendrie, Paul
Kendall, Paul S.
Little, Alan
Nobbs, Alan K.
Wards, Stephen C.

League Appearances: Cook, J.W. 25(5); Cooper, S.B. 7; Evans, D.G. 46; Gallagher, B.P. 32(3); Gallagher, J.A. 4; Greenway, Mark 10(1); Hanson, N. 1(1); Hendrie, P. 40; Kendall, P.S. 36 (3); Little, A. 27; Mell, S.A. 22(8); Nobbs, A.K. 41;

Nuttall, M. 13(8); Smelt, L.A. 44; Smith, A. 37(2); Staniforth, D.A. 28(2); Thornber, S.J. 3(1); Vesey, K.G. 2; Ward, S.C. 46; Wood, M. J. 42(1).
Goals – League (55): B. Gallagher 14 (2 pens), Mell 8, Cook 6 (2 pens), Staniforth 6, Little 3 (1 pen), Nuttall 3, Ward 3, Evans 2, Hendrie 2, Kendall 2, Cooper 1, Greenway 1, Smith 1, Thornber 1, own goals 2.
Milk Cup (2): Kendall 1, Staniforth 1.
FA Çup (2): Evans 1, Ward 1.
Ground: The Shay, Halifax HX1 2YS (0422-53423)
Nearest station: Halifax
Manager: Micky Bullock **Secretary:** Mrs. C Bell
Colours: Royal blue shirts with white trim; white shorts with blue trim
Record home gate: 36,885 v Tottenham, February 1953 (FA Cup)
Honours: Nil

HARTLEPOOL UNITED — DIV. 4

Barker, Allan
Blackburn, Edwin H.
Brown, Phillip
Dobson, Paul
Harrington, Paul
Hogan, Roy D.
Kennedy, Raymond
Linighan, David
Robinson, David A.
Smithies, Michael H.
Wilson, Harry

League Appearances: Bainbridge, T. 11(1); Barker, A. 27; Bassett, G.R. 4(3); Bird, J.C. 15; Blackburn, E.H. 41; Borthwick, J.R. 8(1); Brown, P. 29(2); Buckley, M.J. 6; Campbell, P. 1(2); Dixon, C. 1; Dixon, K.L. 6; Dobson, P. 27; Finch, M. 1; Harrington, P. (2); Hogan, R.D. 27; Johnson, K.P. 15(2); Kennedy, R. 18(5); Lawrence, M. 7; Linacre, J. 15; Linacre, P. 19; Linighan, A. 42; Linighan, D. 19(4); Lowe, K. 27(1); Malley, P. (1); Prudhoe, M. 3; Ray, P. 5; Roberts, J. 1; Robinson, D.A. 6(1); Robinson, M.W. 18; Smithies, M.H. 15(1); Staff, P. 32(1); Stimpson, B.G. 2(1); Taylor, M. 5; Taylor, P.M.R. 1; Waddle, A.R. 12; Weir, A. 9(1); Whitfield, M. 15(1); Wilson, H. 16.
Goals – League (47): Dobson 12, Linacre 7 (2 pens), Staff 5 (1 pen), Bird 3, Dixon 3, Kennedy 3, Hogan 2, A. Linighan 2, Lowe 2, Robinson 2, Waddle 2, Barker 1, Ray 1, own goals 2.
Milk Cup (0)
FA Cup (0)
Ground: Victoria Ground, Clarence Road, Hartlepool (0429-222077)
Office: 60, Avenue Road, Hartlepool (0429-222077)
Nearest station: Hartlepool
Manager: Billy Horner **Secretary:** Mrs L. Holmes
Colours: Shirts: blue and white; shorts: white
Record home gate: 17,426 v Manchester United, January 1957 (FA Cup)
Honours: Nil

HEREFORD UNITED — DIV. 4

Beacock, Gary C.
Bray, Ian M.
Carter, Michael
Dalziel, Ian
Delve, John F.
Emery, Stephen R.

Harvey, James
Hicks, Keith
Kearns, Oliver A.
Larkin, Anthony G.
Leonard, Carleton C.
Maddy, Paul M.
Pejic, Melvyn
Phillips, Stewart G.
Price, Christopher J.
Rose, Kevin P.

League Appearances: Beacock, G.C. 13(1); Black, J. 8(1); Bray, I.M 21(2); Butler, P.J. 16; Dalziel, I. 30; Delve, J.F. 35(1); Emery, S.R. 32(2); Francis, C.E. 5; Harvey, J. 43(1); Hendrie, J.G. 6; Hicks, K. 43; Kearns, O.A. 39(2); Larkin, A.G. 10(1); Leonard, C.C. 24(1); Maddy, P.M. 10; Pejic, M. 44; Phillips, S.G. 46; Price, C.J. 35(2); Rose, K.P. 46.
Goals – League (54): Phillips 17, Kearns 10, Harvey 9 (3 pens), Dalziel 4, Beacock 3, Delve 3, Butler 2, Bray 1, Emery 1, Larkin 1, Maddy 1, Price 1, own goal 1.
Milk Cup (4): Phillips 2, Beacock 1, Pejic 1.
FA Cup (0)
Ground: Edgar Street, Hereford HR4 9JU (0432 276666)
Nearest station: Hereford
Manager: John Newman **Secretary:** J. Finney
Colours: Shirts: white with navy trim; shorts: navy blue with white side stripe.
Record home gate: 18,114 v Sheffield Wednesday, 1958 (FA Cup)
Honours – Champions: Division 3: 1975-76

HUDDERSFIELD TOWN DIV. 2

Burke, David I.
Cowling, David R.
Cox, Brian R.
Doyle, Stephen C.
Jones, Paul B.
Laws, Brian
Lillis, Mark A.
Mason, Keith M.
Measham, Ian
Pugh, Daral J.
Russell, Colin
Stanton, Brian
Sutton, David
Wilson, Philip
Winter, Julian

League Appearances: Bird, K. 1; Burke, D.I. 42; Cooper, G. 3; Cowling, D.R. 40(1); Cox, B.R. 23; Doyle, S.C. 34(2); Eastoe, P.R. 8(2); Eves, M.J. 7; Greenwood, R.T. 1(3); Hanvey, K. 9; Jones, P.B. 36; Laws, B. 31; Lillis, M.A. 36(1); Mason, K.M. 19; Pugh, D.J. 19(10); Robinson, S.L. 4(1); Russell, C. 23(2); Stanton, B. 33; Stonehouse, K. 15(2); Stoutt, S. 3; Sutton, D. 34; Wilson, P. 41.
Goals – League (56): Lillis 11, Jones 7 (5 pens), Russell 7 (3 pens), Stanton 6, Eves 4, Pugh 4, Stonehouse 4 (1 pen), Cowling 3, Wilson 3, Doyle 2, Cooper 1, Hanvey 1, Robinson 1, Sutton 1, own goal 1.
Milk Cup (11): Sutton 3, Jones 2, Lillis 2, Cowling 1, Russell 1, Stanton 1, own goal 1.
FA Cup (3): Stonehouse 2, Lillis 1.
Ground: Kirklees Stadium, Leeds Road, Huddersfield HD1 6PE (0484-20335/6)
Nearest station: Huddersfield
Manager: Mick Buxton **Secretary:** G. S. Binns
Colours: Blue/white striped shirts; white shorts
Record home gate: 67,037 v Arsenal, February 1932 (FA Cup)
Honours–Champions: Division 1: 1923-24, 1924-25, 1925-26; Division 2: 1969-70; Division 3: 1979-80
FA Cup winners: 1921-22

HULL CITY — DIV. 3

Askew, William
Davies, John G.
Davis, Ian
Flounders, Andrew J.
Hollifield, Michael
McClaren, Stephen
McEwan, Stanley
McNeil, Robert M.
Marwood, Brian
Massey, Stephen
Norman, Anthony J.
Olsson, Paul
Roberts, Garreth W.
Roberts, James D.
Skipper, Peter D.
Swann, Gary
Whitehurst, William

League Appearances: Askew, W. 29(4); Booth, D. 14; Flounders, A.J. 22(8); Gill, G. (1); Hollifield, M. 33; Marwood, B. 39; Massey, S. 11(2); Mutrie, L.A. 11(1); McClaren, S. 36(4); McEwan, S. 16; McNeil, R.M. 46; Norman, A.J. 46; Roberts, G.W. 37(1); Roberts, J.D. 28(1); Saville, A.V. 1; Skipper, P.D. 46; Swann, G. 41; Taylor, A.D. 13(1); Wassell, K. 1; Whitehurst, W. 36(1).
Goals – League (71): Marwood 16, Whitehurst 10, Flounders 9, G. Roberts 9, Mutrie 5, Massey 4 (1 pen), McClaren 3, McNeil 3, Taylor 3, D. Roberts 2, Swann 2, Askew 1, Hollifield 1, Johnson 1, McEwan 1 (pen), Skipper 1.
Milk Cup (1): Skipper 1.
FA Cup (3): Flounders 1, G. Roberts 1, Whitehurst 1.
Ground: Boothferry Park, Hull HU4 6EU (0482-51119)
Nearest stations: Hull or Boothferry Park Halt
Manager: Brian Horton **Secretary:** I.E White
Colours: Shirts: amber with black and red trim; shorts: black with amber and red stripe.
Record home gate: 55,019 v Manchester United, February 1949 (FA Cup)
Honours – Champions: Division 3 North: 1932-33, 1948-49; Division 3: 1965-66

IPSWICH TOWN — DIV. 1

Barnes, David
Brennan, Mark R.
Burley, George E.
Butcher, Terence I.
Cole, Michael W.
Cooper, Paul D.
Crane, Andrew D.
Cranson, Ian
D'Avray, Jean M.
Gates, Eric L.
Gernon, Frederick A.J.
Gorman, Keith
Grew, Mark
Hallworth, Jonathan G.
Humes, Anthony
Linford, John R.
McCall, Stephen H.
O' Callaghan, Kevin
Osman, Russell C.
Parkin, Thomas A.
Putney, Trevor A.
Steggles, Kevin P.
Stockwell, Michael T.
Turner, Robin D.
Yallop, Frank W.
Zondervan, Romeo

League Appearances: Barnes, D. 10(1); Brennan, M.R. 19; Burley, G.E. 28; Butcher, T.I. 34; Cooper, P.D. 36; Cranson, I. 8; D'Avray, J.M. 17(6); Dozzell, J.A.W. (5); Gates, E.L. 37; Gernon, F.A.J. 19; Kinsella, A.S. 4(1); Mariner, P. 23; McCall, S.H. 42; O'Callaghan, K. 23(2); Osman, R.C. 37; Parkin, T.A. 18(3); Putney, T.A. 32(3); Sivell, L. 6; Steggles, K.P. 5; Sunderland, A. 15; Turner, R.D. 3(7); Wark, J. 32; Yallop, F.W. 6; Zondervan, R. 8.
Goals – League (55): Gates 13, Mariner 12, D'Avray 6, Wark 5 (2 pens), Osman 3, Sunderland 3, O'Callaghan 2, Putney 2, Zondervan 2, Brennan 1, Burley 1, Butcher 1, Dozzell 1, McCall 1, Turner 1, own goal 1.
Milk Cup (9): Wark 6 (1 pen), Mariner 2, own goal 1.

FA Cup (3): Gates 3.
Ground: Portman Road, Ipswich IP1 2DA (0473 219211)
Nearest station: Ipswich
Manager: Bobby Ferguson **Secretary:** D. C. Rose
Colours: Blue shirts with three white stripes down sleeves; white shorts with three blue stripes
Record home gate: 38,010 v Leeds United, March 1975 (FA Cup)
Honours – Champions: Division 1: 1961-62; Division 2: 1960-61, 1967-68; Division 3 South: 1953-54, 1956-57
FA Cup winners: 1977-78

LEEDS UNITED DIV. 2

Aspin, Neil
Barnes, Peter S.
Brown, Anthony J.
Butterworth, Aidan J.
Dickinson, Martin J.
Donnelly, John
Eli, Roger
Gavin, Mark W.
Gray, Francis T.
Hamson, Gary
Harvey, David
Hughes, Philip
Irwin, Denis J.
Linighan, Andrew
Lorimer, Peter P.
McCluskey, George M.C.
Ritchie, Andrew T.
Sellars, Scott
Sheridan, John J.
Stiles, John
Watson, Andrew
Wright, Thomas

League Appearances: Aspin, N. 21; Barnes, P.S. 25(2); Brown, A.J. 22; Burns, K. 13; Butterworth, A.J. 4(7); Dickinson, M.J. 34; Donnelly, J. 23(2); Gavin, M.W. 10(2); Gray, E. 4; Gray, F.T. 24; Hamson, G. 23(2); Harvey, D. 40; Hird, K. 16(2); Hughes, P. 2; Irwin, D.J. 12; Lorimer, P.P. 20(2); McCluskey, G.M.C. 24(8); McGoldrick, J. 7; Ritchie, A.T. 38; Sellars, S. 19; Sheridan, J.J. 11; Thomas, D.G. 16(1); Thompson, N.D. 1; Watson, A. 30(1); Wright, T. 23(2).
Goals – League (55): McCluskey 8, Wright 8, Ritchie 7, Watson 7, Barnes 4, F. Gray 4 (2 pens), Lorimer 4 (1 pen), Donnelly 3, Sellars 3, Aspin 1, A. Brown 1, Butterworth 1, Gavin 1, Hird 1, Sheridan 1, own goal 1.
Milk Cup (6): Burns 2, Ritchie 2, Barnes 1, McCluskey 1.
FA Cup (4): Wright 3, Ritchie 1.
Ground: Elland Road, Leeds LS11 0ES (0532-716037/9)
Nearest station: Leeds
Manager: Eddie Gray M.B.E **Secretary:** D. J. Dowse
Colours: white shirts, blue and yellow trim; white shorts with blue and yellow trim
Record home gate: 57,892 v Sunderland, March 1967 (FA Cup)
Honours – Champions: Division 1: 1968-69, 1973-74; Division 2: 1923-24, 1963-64
FA Cup Winners: 1971-72
League Cup winners: 1967-68
European Fairs Cup winners: 1967-68, 1970-71

LEICESTER CITY DIV. 1

Andrews, Ian E.
Banks, Ian F.
Burnside, Scott H.
Feeley, Andrew J.
Ford, Michael P.
Hazell, Robert J.

Hutchinson, Colin M.	MacDonald, Kevin D.	Smith, Alan M.
Jones, Robert	O'Neill, John P.	Smith, Robert N.
Kelly, Robert A.	Peake, Andrew M.	Wallington, Francis M.
Lineker, Gary W.	Ramsey, Paul	Williams, Thomas E.
Lynex, Steven C.	Rennie, David	Wilson, Ian W.

League Appearances: Andrews, I.E. 2; Banks, I.F. 22(4); Eastoe, P.R. 5; English, T.S. 4(12); Feeley, A.J. 2(1); Grew, M. 5; Hazell, R.J. 27; Jones, R. 6(2); Kelly, R.A. 1; Lineker, G.W. 38(1); Lynex, S.C. 40; MacDonald, K.D. 38; O'Neill, J.P. 31; Peake, A.M. 22(2); Ramsey, P. 33; Rennie, D. 15; Smith, A.M. 39(1); Smith, R.N. 35(1); Wallington, F.M. 35; Williams, T.E. 21(1); Wilson, I.W. 41.
Goals – League (65): Lineker 22, A. Smith 15, Lynex 12 (5 pens), Peake 4, Banks 3, Hazell 2, Jones 2, O'Neill 2, Eastoe 1, MacDonald 1, Ramsey 1.
Milk Cup (2): English 1, A. Smith 1.
FA Cup (0)
Ground: City Stadium, Filbert Street, Leicester LE2 7FL (0533-555000/2; match information 551155)
Nearest station: Leicester
Manager: Gordon Milne **General secretary:** . K Bennett
Colours: Blue shirts with white collar and cuffs; white shorts
Record home gate: 47,298 v Tottenham Hotspur, February 1928 (FA Cup)
Honours–Champions: Division 2: 1924-25, 1936-37, 1953-54, 1956-57, 1970-71, 1979-80
League Cup winners: 1963-64

LINCOLN CITY — DIV. 3

Fashanu, John	Naylor, Stuart W.	Thomas, John W.
Felgate, David W.	Neale, Philip A.	Thompson, Steven P.
Hobson, Gordon	Shipley, George M.	Turner, Philip
Houghton, Keith	Simmonite, Gordon	Walker, Alan
Jack, James R.	Strodder, Gary	

League Appearances: Burke, M. 14(1); Cockerill, G. 33; Fashanu, J. 22(4); Felgate, D.W. 46; Hobson, G. 35(1); Houghton, K. 26; Jack, J.R. 34(2); Johnson, R.S. 4; Moyses, C.R. 2(2); Neale, P.A. 36; Redfearn, N.D. 10; Saxby, M.W. 10; Shipley, G.M. 42; Simmonite, G. 35; Strodder, G. 21(1); Thomas, J.W. 31(6); Thompson, S.P. 16; Turner, P. 41(1); Walker, A. 32(1); Webb, A.R. 11; Williamson, C.H. 5.
Goals – League (59): Thomas 13 (1 pen), Jack 9 (2 pens), Fashanu 7, Cockerill 6, (1 pen), Hobson 6, Shipley 4, Turner 3, Burke 2 (1 pen), Walker 2, Neale 1, Redfearn 1, Saxby 1, Strodder 1, Thompson 1, own goals 2.
Milk Cup (6): Shipley 2, Thomas 2, Houghton 1, Jack 1 (pen).
FA Cup (2): Jack 1, Shipley 1.
Ground: Sincil Bank, Lincoln LN5 8LD (0522-2224)
Nearest stations: Lincoln Central and St Mark's
Manager: Colin Murphy **Secretary:** P. M. Hough
Colours: Red and white striped shirts; white shorts
Record home gate: 23,196 v Derby, November 1967 (League Cup)
Honours–Champions: Division 3 North: 1931-32, 1947-48, 1951-52; Division 4: 1975-76

LIVERPOOL DIV. 1

Ablett, Gary I.	Johnston, Craig P.	Robinson, Michael J.
Beglin, James M.	Kennedy, Alan P.	Rush, Ian J.
Bolder, Robert	Lawrenson, Mark T.	Seagraves, Mark
Dalglish, Kenneth M.	Lee, Samuel	Souness, Graeme J.
Gillespie, Gary	McGregor, John R.	Thompson, Philip B.
Grobbelaar, Bruce D.	de Mange, Kenneth J.P.P.	Wardle, Robert I.
Hansen, Alan D.	Mooney, Brian J.	Wark, John
Hodgson, David J.	Neal, Philip G.	West, David C.
Jewell, Paul	Nicol, Stephen	Whelan, Ronald A.

League Appearances: Dalglish, K.M. 33; Grobbelaar, B.D. 42; Hansen, A.D. 42; Hodgson, D.J. 1(4); Johnston, C.P. 28(1); Kennedy, A.P. 41; Kenney, R. 1; Lawrenson, M.T. 42; Lee, S. 42; Neal, P.G. 41; Nicol, S. 19(4); Robinson, M.J. 23(1); Rush, I.J. 41; Souness, G.J 37; Wark, J.H. 9; Whelan, R.A. 20(3).
Goals – League (73): Rush 32 (1 pen), Dalglish 7, Souness 7 (1 pen), Robinson 6, Nicol 5, Whelan 4, Johnston 2, Kennedy 2, Lee 2, Wark 2, Hansen 1, Neal 1, own goals 2.
Milk Cup (25): Rush 8 (1 pen), Souness 5 (1 pen), Robinson 3, Whelan 3, Dalglish 2, Nicol 2, Hodgson 1, Neal 1 (pen).
FA Cup (4): Rush 2, Johnston 1, Robinson 1.
Ground: Anfield Road, Liverpool L4 0TH(051-263 2361/2)
Nearest stations: All stations, Liverpool
Manager: Joe Fagan **Secretary:** P. Robinson
Colours: Red shirts with thin white pinstripe; red shorts
Record home gate: 61,905 v Wolverhampton, February 1952 (FA Cup)
Honous– Champions: Division 1: 1900-1, 1905-06, 1921-22, 1922-23, 1946-47, 1963-64, 1965-66, 1972-73, 1975-76, 1976-77, 1978-79, 1979-80, 1980-81, 1982-83; Division 2: 1893-94, 1895-96, 1904-05, 1961-62
FA Cup winners: 1964-65, 1973-74
League Cup winners;1980-81, 1981-82
Milk Cup winners: 1981-82, 1982-83, 1983-84
European Champions Cup: 1976-77, 1977-78, 1980-81
UEFA Cup winners: 1972-73, 1975-76
Super Cup winners: 1977

LUTON TOWN DIV. 1

Aylott, Trevor K.C.	Hill, Ricky A.	Sealey, Leslie J.
Breacker, Timothy S.	Horton, Brian	Stein, Brian
Bunn, Frankie S.	Johnson, Robert S.	Stein, Earl M.S.
Daniel, Raymond C.	Moss, David J.	Stephens, Kirk W.
Donaghy, Malachy	North, Mark V.	Thomas, Mitchell A.
Elliot, Paul M.	North, Stacey S.	Turner, Wayne L.
Findlay, John W.	Nwajiobi, Chukwuemeka	Walsh, Paul A.
Goodyear, Clive	Parker, Garry S.	

League Appearances: Antic, R. 8(14); Aylott, T.K.C. 20; Breacker, T.S. 2; Bunn, F.S. 29(1); Daniel, R.C. 7; Donaghy, M. 40; Elliot, P.M. 38; Goodyear, C. 13(4);

Hill, R.A. 26; Horton, B. 37; Johnson, R.S. 2; Moss, D.J. 16; North, S.S. 1; Nwajiobi, C. 2(2); Parker, G.S. 13; Sealey L.J. 42; Stein, B. 42; Stein, E.M.S. 1; Stephens, K.W. 40: Thomas, M.A. 26; Turner, W.L. 18(1); Walsh. P.A. 39.
Goals – League (53): Walsh 11, Stein 9, Aylott 8 (1 pen), Moss 4 (1 pen), Bunn 3, Horton 3 (2 pens), Daniel 2, Elliot 2, Hill 2, Parker 2, Antic 1, Donaghy 1, Nwajiobi 1, own goals 4.
Milk Cup (3): Aylott 1, Bunn 1, Walsh 1.
FA Cup (5): Walsh 2, Donaghy 1, Nwajiobi 1, Stein 1.
Ground: 70-72 Kenilworth Road, Luton LU1 1DH (0582 411622)
Nearest station: Luton
Manager: David Pleat **Secretary:** John Wilkinson
Colours: White shirts with orange collars and cuffs, white shorts with two orange and three navy blue vertical stripes
Record home gate: 30,069 v Blackpool, March 1959 (FA Cup)
Honours – Champions: Division 2: 1981-82; Division 3 South: 1936-37; Division 4: 1967-68

MANCHESTER CITY DIV. 2

Adams, Richard M.
Baker, Graham E.
Beresford, John
Bond, Kevin J.
Dalziel, Gordon
Hoyland, Jamie W.
Jackson, Gary
Johnson, David E.
Kinsey, Stephen
Lomax, Geoffrey W.
McCarthy, Michael
McNab, Neil
May, Andrew M.
Nixon, Eric W.
Parlane, Derek J.
Power, Paul C.
Ranson, Raymond
Reid, Nicholas S.
Simpson, Paul D.
Smith, Gordon D.
Tolmie, James
Williams, Alexander
Wilson, Clive

League Appearances: Baker, G.E. 36; Bond, K.J. 33(1); Caton, T. 16; Dalziel, J. 4(1); Davidson, G. 2(4); Davies, I.C. 5; Hartford, R.A. 7; Hoyland, J. W. 1; Johnson, D.E. 4(2); Kinsey, S. 16(7); Lomax, G.W. 16(1); May, A.M. 42; McCarthy, M. 24; McNab, N. 33; Parlane, D.J. 40(1); Power, P.C. 37; Ranson, R. 25(1); Reid, N.S. 18(1); Smith, G.D. 9; Tolmie, J. 38(3); Walsh, M.T. 3(1); Williams, A. 42; Wilson, E.A. 11.
Goals – League (66): Parlane 16, Tolmie 13 (4 pens), Baker 8, Kinsey 7, May 5, Bond 4 (3 pens), Caton 2, Power 2, Reid 2, Davidson 1, Hartford 1, Johnson 1, Lomax 1, McCarthy 1, McNab 1, Smith 1.
Milk Cup (6): Parlane 3, Tolmie 2 (1 pen), Hoyland 1.
FA Cup (1): own goal 1.
Ground: Maine Road, Moss Side, Manchester M14 7WN (061-226 1191/2)
Nearest station: Manchester Piccadilly
Manager: Billy McNeill M.B.E. **Secretary:** J. B. Halford
Colours: Sky blue shirts with white trim; sky blue shorts
Record home gate: 84,569 v Stoke City, March 1934 (FA Cup)
Honours–Champions: Division 1: 1936-37, 1967-68; Division 2: 1898-99, 1902-03, 1909-10, 1927-28, 1946-47, 1965-66
FA Cup winners: 1903-04, 1933-34, 1955-56, 1968-69
League Cup winners: 1969-70, 1975-76
European Cup-Winner's Cup winners: 1969-70

MANCHESTER UNITED DIV. 1

Albiston, Arthur R.
Bailey, Gary R.
Blackmore, Clayton G.
Davies, Alan
Dempsey, Mark J.
Duxbury, Michael
Garton, William F.
Gidman, John
Graham, Arthur
Hogg, Graeme J.
Hughes, Leslie M.
Kelch, Patrick J.
McGarvey, Scott T.
McGrath, Paul
McQueen, Gordon
Moran, Kevin B.
Moses, Remi M.
Muhren, Arnoldus J.H.
Olsen, Jesper
Pears, Stephen
Robinson, Andrew
Robson, Bryan
Russell, Martin
Scott, Kenneth
Stapleton, Francis A.
Wealands, Jeffrey
Whiteside, Norman
Wood, Nicholas A.
Wynn, David

League Appearances: Albiston, A.R. 40; Bailey, G.R. 40; Blackmore, C.G. 1; Crooks, G.A. 6(1); Davies, A. 3; Duxbury, M. 39; Gidman, J. 4; Graham, A. 33(4); Hogg, G. J. 16; Hughes, L.M. 7(4); Macari, L. (5); Moran, K.B. 38; Moses, R.M. 31(4); Muhren, A.J. 26; McGrath, P. 9; McQueen, G. 20; Robson, B. 33; Stapleton, F.A. 42; Wealands, J. 2; Whiteside, N. 30(7); Wilkins, R.C. 42.
Goals – League (71): Stapleton 13, Robson, 12, Whiteside 10, Muhren 8 (4 pens), Moran 7, Graham 5, Hughes 4, Wilkins 3 (1 pen), Albiston 2, Crooks 2, Moses 2, Hogg 1, McGrath 1, McQueen 1.
Milk Cup (8): Stapleton 2, Graham 1, Hughes 1, McQueen 1, Moses 1, Whiteside 1, Wilkins 1 (pen).
FA Cup (0).
Ground: Old Trafford, Manchester M16 0RA (061-872 1661/2)
Nearest stations: All stations Manchester
Manager: Ron Atkinson **Secretary:** R. L. Olive
Colours: Red shirts with red and white trim; white shorts
Record home gate: 76,962 FA Cup semi-final (Wolverhampton v Grimsby Town) March 1939; **Club:** 70,504 v Aston Villa, December 1920 (League)
Honours – Champions: Division 1: 1907-08, 1910-11, 1951-52, 1955-56, 1956-57, 1964-65, 1966-67; Division 2: 1935-36, 1974-75
FA Cup winners: 1908-09, 1947-48, 1962-63, 1976-77, 1982-83
European Champions Cup: 1967-68

MANSFIELD TOWN DIV. 4

Barrowclough, Stewart J.
Calderwood, Colin
Caldwell, David W.
Foster, George W.
Galloway, Michael
Keegan, Gerard A.
Kearney, Mark J.
Lowery, Anthony W.
Whitworth, Stephen
Woodhead, Simon C.

League Appearances: Arnold, R.J. 11; Ayre, W. 25; Barrowclough, S.J. 36(2); Calderwood, C. 27(3); Caldwell, D.W. 37(1); Daines, B.R. 21; Dungworth, J.H. 14(3); Foster, G.W. 42; Frain, P.A. 1(1); Galloway, M. 12(5); Hitchcock, K. 14; Hutchinson, R. 10; Juryeff, I.M. 12; Kearney, M.J. 17; Kee, P.J. (1); Keegan, G.A. 18; Lowery, A.W. 45; Matthews, J.M. 31(1); Nicholson, G.A. 38(3); Partridge, J.T. 1; Sindall, M. 9(1); Storer, S.J. (1); Taylor, P. 3; Whitworth, S. 41; Woodhead, S.C. 41(2).
Goals – League (66): Caldwell 21, Barrowclough 10 (1 pen), Nicholson 8, Lowery 6,

Juryeff 5, Ayre 4, Matthews 3, Dungworth 2, Kearney 2, Calderwood 1, Keegan 1, Woodhead 1, own goals 2.
Milk Cup (2): Barrowclough 1 (pen), Caldwell 1.
FA Cup (3): Barrowclough 1, Calderwood 1, Caldwell 1.
Ground: Field Mill, Quarry Lane, Mansfield (0623- 23567)
Nearest stations. Alfreton and Mansfield Parkway
Manager: Ian Greaves **Secretary:** J. D. Eaton
Colours: Yellow shirts; blue shorts
Record home gate: 24,567 v Nottingham Forest, January 1953 (FA Cup)
Honours – Champions: Division 3: 1976-77; Division 4: 1974-75

MIDDLESBROUGH DIV. 2

Baxter, Michael J.
Beagrie, Peter S.
Bell, Stephen
Currie, David N.
Gill, Gary
Hamilton, Gary J.
Kennedy, Michael F.
Mowbray, Anthony M.
Nattrass, Irving
O'Hanlon, Kelham G.
Otto, Hendrikus M.
Roberts, Alan
Sugrue, Paul A.
Ward, Paul T.
Wood, Darren T.

League Appearances: Baxter, M.J. 41; Bell, S. 21(4); Crawford, A. 8(1); Currie, D.N. 35(4); Gill, G. 4(2); Hamilton, G.J. 26(5); Kennedy, M.F. 30; Mowbray, A.M. 33(2); MacDonald, G. 24(5); Nattrass, I. 42; O'Hanlon, K.G. 30; Otto, H.M. 42; Pears, S. 12; Roberts, A. 7; Sugrue, P.A. 39(1); Ward, P.T. 26(2); Wood, D.T. 42.
Goals – League (41): Currie 15 (3 pens), Otto 7, Hamilton 3, MacDonald 3, Sugrue 3, Baxter 2, Bell 2, Wood 2, Crawford 1, Mowbray 1, Roberts 1, Ward 1.
Milk Cup (1): Otto 1.
FA Cup (5): Sugrue 3, Baxter 1, MacDonald 1.
Ground: Ayresome Park, Middlesbrough TS1 4PB (0642-819659 and 815996)
Nearest station: Middlesbrough
Manager: Willie Maddren **Secretary:** C. Edon
Colours: Red shirts with white shoulders and sleeves with red/white collar and cuffs; white shorts
Record home gate: 53,596 v Newcastle United, December 1949 (League)
Honours – Champions: Division 2: 1926-27, 1928-29, 1973-74

MILLWALL DIV. 3

Bremner, Kevin J.
Chatterton, Nicholas J.
Coleman, Nicholas
Cusack, David S.
Lovell, Stephen J.
Lowndes, Stephen R.J.
McCleary, Alan T.
Martin, David
Neal, Dean J.
Neal, John J.
Nutton, Michael W.
Otulakowski, Antoni
Robinson, Paul
Sansome, Paul E.
Sheringham, Edward P.
Stevens, Keith
Wells, Peter A.

League Appearances: Bremner, K.J. 41(1); Burke, S.J. 7; Chatterton, N.J. 26(1); Cowley, C. 2(1); Cusack, D.S. 39; Lovell, S.J. 46; Lowndes, S.R. 20; Martin, D. 26(5); Massey, A.T. 8(5); McLeary, A.T. 24(6); Neal, D.J. 29(5); Neal, J.J. 3(3);

Nutton, M.W. 43; Otulakowski, A. 33; Robinson, P. 32(1); Sansome, P.E. 31; Sheringham, E.P. 4(3); Sparrow, B.E. 5; Stevens, K.H. 17; Stride, D.R. 28; Wells, P.A. 15; White, D. 27
Goals – League (71): Bremner 16, D. Neal 13, Lovell 7 (3 pens), Otulakowski 7, Chatterton 6 (2 pens), Lowndes 3, Martin 3, Nutton 2, Robinson 2, Sparrow 2, Stride 2, Bruce 1, Burke 1, Massey 1, J. Neal 1, Sheringham 1, own goals 2.
Milk Cup (9): Neal 3, Chatterton 2 (1 pen), Martin 2, Lowndes 1, Otulakowski 1.
FA Cup (4): Cusack 1, Lovell 1 (pen), Martin 1, Massey 1.
Ground: The Den, Cold Blow Lane, London SE14 5RH (01-639 3143/4)
Nearest stations: New Cross or New Cross Gate (SR and Metropolitan line)
Manager: George Graham **Secretary:** Mrs. S. Shaw
Colours: Blue shirts with white trim; white shorts with blue trim
Record home gate: 48,672 v Derby County, February 1937 (FA Cup)
Honours – Champions: Division 3 South: 1927-28, 1937-38; Division 4: 1961-62

NEWCASTLE UNITED DIV. 1

Anderson, John
Beardsley, Peter A.
Brown, Malcolm
Carney, Stephen
Carr, Kevin
Carver, John W.
Clarke, Jeffrey D.
Dawes, Ian M.
Ferris, Paul J.
Haddock, Peter M.
Hedworth, Christopher
McCreery, David
McDermott, Terence
cDonald, Neil R.
Roeder, Glenn V.
Ryan, John B.
Saunders, Wesley
Thomas, Martin R.
Trewick, John
Waddle, Christopher R.
Wharton, Kenneth

League Appearances: Anderson, J. 41; Beardsley, P.A. 34(1); Carney, S. 32(1); Carr, K. 19; Clarke, J.D. 14; Haddock, P.M. 1(2); Keegan, J.K. 41; Mills, D.J. 10(6); McCreery, D. 40; McDermott, T. 42; McDonald, N.R. 10(2); Roeder, G.V. 23; Ryan, J.B. 22; Saunders, W. 16; Thomas, M.R. 23; Trewick, J. 14(2); Waddle, C.R. 42; Wharton, K. 38(3).
Goals – League (85): Keegan 27 (4 pens), Beardsley 20, Waddle 18, McDermott 6, Mills 5, Wharton 4, Anderson 1, Ryan 1, Trewick 1, own goals 2.
Milk Cup (2): Keegan 1, McDermott 1.
FA Cup (0)
Ground: St James' Park, Newcastle-upon-Tyne NE1 4ST (0632 328361 answer service 611571)
Nearest station: Newcastle
Manager: Jack Charlton **Secretary:** R. Cushing
Colours: Black and white vertical striped shirts; black shorts
Record home gate: 68,386 v Chelsea, September 1930 (League)
Honours – Champions: Division 1: 1904-5, 1906-07, 1908-09, 1926-27; Division 2: 1964-65
FA Cup winners: 1909-10, 1923-24, 1931-32, 1950-51, 1951-52, 1954-55
European Fairs' Cup winners: 1968-69
Anglo-Italian Cup winners: 1973

NEWPORT COUNTY — DIV. 3

Boyle, Terence D.J.
Carter, Roy W.
Jones, Linden
Kendall, Mark
Lewis, John
Matthewson, Trevor
Oakes, Keith B.
Pratt, Michael W.
Reid, Anthony J.
Relish, John D.
Williams, Ceri

League Appearances: Aldridge, J.W. 28; Bailey, N. 5; Boyle, T.D.J. 45; Carter, R.W. 37(2); Chamberlain, N.P. 6; Elsey, K.W. 7; Green, P. 8(1); Jones, G.A. 3; Jones, L. 32; Jones, V. 24(1); Kendall, M. 43; Layton, J.H. 1; Lewis, J. 25; Lilygreen, C.L. 15(6); Martinez, E. 18(2); Mather, S.L. (1); Matthewson, T. 30(2); Micallef, C. 22(2); Morse, R.A. (1); Oakes, K.B. 37; Pratt, M.W. 3(3); Randell, C.W. 15; Reid, A.J. 37; Relish, J.D. 30(4); Stroud, K.A. 4(1); Vaughan, N.M. 7; Williams, C. 15(7); Woodruff, R.J. 9(1).
Goals – League (58): Aldridge 20 (2 pens), Reid 6 (1 pen), Vaughan 5 (2 pens), Carter 4, Jones 4 (1 pen), Lilygreen 4, Chamberlain 2, Green 2, Micallef 2, Pratt 2, Boyle 1, Elsey 1, Lewis 1, Martinez 1, Oakes 1, Williams 1, own goal 1.
Milk Cup (2): Aldridge 1, Boyle 1.
FA Cup (8): Aldridge 5, Chamberlain 1, Lewis 1, Oakes 1.
Ground: Somerton Park, Newport, Gwent NPT OHZ (0633 277543)
Nearest station: Newport
Manager: Colin Addison **Secretary:** P. Dauncey
Colours: Amber shirts; black shorts
Record home gate: 24,268 v Cardiff, October 1937 (League)
Honours – Champions: Division 3 South: 1938-39

NORTHAMPTON TOWN — DIV. 4

Belfon, Frank
Burrows, Adrian M.
Gage, Wakeley A.J.
Gleasure, Peter
Hayes, Austin W.P.
Lewis, Russell
Mundee, Brian G.

League Appearances: Austin, T.W. 42(1); Belfon, F. 35(5); Brough, N.K. 3(2); Brown, S.F. (1); Burrows, A.M. 45; Forster, M.G. 41(1); Gage, W.A.J. 40; Gleasure, P. 46; Hayes, A.W.P. 40(3); Jeffrey, W.G. 44(1); Lewis, R. 45; Mann, A.G. 2; Martinez, E. 12; Muir, M.M. 5(10); Mundee, B.G. 33(3); O'Neill, T. 43; Syrett, D.K. 5(1); Tucker, W.B. 25(1).
Goals – League (53): Austin 10, Belfon 9, Hayes 9, Gage 6, O'Neill 6 (1 pen), Jeffrey 4, Lewis 4, Martinez 2, Mundee 1, Syrett 1, Tucker 1.
Milk Cup (1): Gage 1.
FA Cup (7): Austin 2, Gage 1, Jeffrey 1, Muir 1, Mundee 1, O'Neill 1.
Ground: County Ground, Abington Avenue, Northampton NN1 4PS (0604 31553)
Nearest station: Northampton
Manager: Tony Barton **Secretary:** Dave Bowen
Colours: Shirts maroon with white trim; shorts maroon
Record home gate: 24,523 v Fulham, April 1966 (League)
Honours – Champions: Division 3: 1962-63

NORWICH CITY — DIV. 1

Barham, Mark F.
Bennett, David P.
Bertschin, Keith E.
Channon, Michael R.
Clayton, Paul S.
Crowe, Mark A.
Deehan, John M.
Devine, John A.
Donowa, Brian L.
Downs, Gregory
Farrington, Mark A.
Gordon, Dale A.
Goss, Jeremy
Haylock, Paul
McIntyre, Brendan A.
Mendham, Peter S.
Metcalf, Mark P.
Rigby, Jonathan K.
Riley, Neil P.
Rosario, Robert M.
Spearing, Anthony
Van Wijk, Dennis J.
Waddell, John R.
Watson, David
Williams, Gregory
Woods, Christopher
Young, William D.

League Appearances: Barham, M.F. 10(1); Bennett, D.P. 12(1); Bertschin, K.E. 33; Channon, M.R. 37; Clayton, P.S. 3(4); Deehan, J.M. 34; Devine, J.A. 31(1); Donowa, B.L. 23(2); Downs, G. 42; Farrington, M.A. 1(1); Godbold, D.M. (2); Goss, J. (1); Hareide, A.F. 26(2); Haylock, P. 38(1); Mendham, P.S. 41; Pickering, M.J. (1); Rigby, J.K. 3(2); Rosario, R.M. 6(2); Spearing, A. 4; Van Wijk, D.J. 31(2); Watson, D. 40, Woods, C.C.E. 42; Young, W.D. 5(1).
Goals – League (48): Deehan 15 (4 pens), Bertschin 7, Channon 5 (1 pen), Donowa 4, Downs 4, Devine 3, Barham 2, Hareide 2, Bennett 1, Mendham 1, Rosario 1, Watson 1, own goals 2.
Milk Cup (6): Channon 4, Bertschin 2.
FA Cup (7): Channon 2, Deehan 2, Bertschin 1, Mendham 1, Van Wijk 1.
Ground: Carrow Road Stadium, Norwich NR1 1JE (0603 612131)
Nearest station: Norwich
Manager: Ken Brown **Secretary:** Nigel Pleasants
Colours: Yellow shirts, green collar and cuffs; green shorts with yellow trim
Record home gate: 43,984 v Leicester, March 1963 (FA Cup)
Honours – Champions: Division 2: 1971-72; Division 3 South: 1933-34
FA Cup winners: Nil
League Cup winners: 1961-62

NOTTINGHAM FOREST — DIV. 1

Anderson, Vivian A.
Birtles, Garry
Bowyer, Ian
Campbell, David A.
Davenport, Peter
Fairclough, Courtney H.
Gunn, Brynley C.
Hart, Paul A.
Heyes, Darren L.
Hitchcock, Kevin
Hodge, Stephen B.
Longhurst, David J.
Mills, Gary R.
Raynor, Paul J.
Riley, David S.
Shaw, Adrian
Sinclair, Ronald M.
Smalley, Mark A.
Sutton, Stephen J.
Swain, Kenneth
Van Breukelen, Hans
Walker, Desmond S.
Wallace, Ian A.
Walsh, Colin D.
Wigley, Steven

League Appearances: Anderson, V.A. 40; Birtles, G. 33(1); Bowyer, I. 42; Davenport, P. 32(1); Fairclough, C.H. 31; Gunn, B.C. 4; Hart, P.A. 36; Hodge, S.B. 39; Mills, G.R. 5(2); Riley, D.S. (1); Smalley, M.A. (1); Sutton, S.J. 6; Swain, K. 41; Thijssen, F.J. 17; Todd, C. 13; Van Breukelen, H. 36; Walker, D.S. 3(1); Wallace, I.A. 22(5); Walsh, C.D. 35(3); Wigley, S. 27(8).

Goals – League (76): Birtles 15, Davenport 15 (2 pens), Walsh 13 (5 pens), Hodge 10, Anderson 6, Bowyer 6, Thijssen 3, Wallace 3, Swain 1, Wigley 1, own goals 3.
Milk Cup (1): Wallace 1.
FA Cup (1): Hart 1.
Ground: City Ground, Pavilion Road, Nottingham NG2 5FJ (0602 822202)
Nearest station: Nottingham
Manager: Brian Clough **Secretary:** K. Smales
Colours: Red shirts; white shorts
Record home gate: 49,945 v Manchester United, October, 1967 (League)
Honours – Champions: Division 1: 1977-78; Division 2: 1906-07, 1921-22; Division 3 South: 1950-51
FA Cup winners: 1897-98, 1958-59
League Cup winners: 1977-78, 1978-79
European Champions Cup: 1978-79, 1979-80

NOTTS COUNTY — DIV. 2

Beaver, David
Benjamin, Tristam
Chiedozie, John O.
Christie, Trevor
Clarke, David A.
Downing, Keith G.
Fashanu, Justinus S.
Goodwin, Mark A.
Harkouk, Rachid P.
Hodson, Simeon
Hunt, David
Jones, Mark R.
Kilcline, Brian
Lahtinen, Aki A.
Leonard, Michael C.
McCulloch, John
McDonagh, James M.
McParland, Ian J.
Mair, Gordon
O'Neill, Martin H.M.
Richards, Peter

League Appearances: Armstrong, K.C. 10; Benjamin, T. 15; Chiedozie, J.O. 39(1); Christie, T. 36(3); Clarke, D.A. 18(2); Davis, D.J. 1; Fashanu, J.S. 17; Goodwin, M.A. 27(2); Harkouk, R.P. 27(5); Hodson, S. 13; Hunt, D. 39; Jones, M.R. (2); Kilcline, B. 24; Lahtinen, A.A. 6; Leonard, M.C. 18; Mair, G. 15(2); McCulloch, J. 20(2); McDonagh, J.M. 24; McParland, I.J. 15(6); O'Neill, M.H.M. 37(1); Richards, P. 33(1); Roeder, G.V. 4; Worthington, N. 24.
Goals – League (50): Christie 19 (6 pens), Chiedozie 9, Harkouk 6, Fashanu 5, O'Neill 4, Hunt 2, McParland 2 (1 pen), Kilcline 1, Richards 1, Worthington 1.
Milk Cup (11): Christie 4, Hunt 2, Chiedozie 1, Fashanu 1, Harkouk 1, Kilcline 1, O'Neill 1.
FA Cup (8): Chiedozie 2, Christie 2 (1 pen), Kilcline 2, Harkouk 1, McCulloch 1.
Ground: Meadow Lane, Nottingham NG2 3HJ (0602 861155)
Nearest station: Nottingham
Manager: Larry Lloyd **Secretary:** K. H. Mott
Colours: Black and white striped shirts; black shorts
Record home gate: 47,310 v York, March 1955 (FA Cup)
Honours – Champions: Division 2: 1896-97, 1913-14, 1922-23; Division 3 South: 1930-31, 1949-50; Division 4: 1970-71
FA Cup winners: 1893-94

OLDHAM ATHLETIC DIV. 2

Bowden, John
Buchan, Martin M.
Clements, Kenneth H.
Colville, Robert J.
Goram, Andrew L.
Henry, Anthony
Hodkinson, Andrew J.
Hoolickin, Garry J.
Hudson, Christopher J.
Jones, Alexander
McBride, Joseph
McDonough, Darron K.
Palmer, Roger N.
Parker, Derrick
Parkin, Brian
Quinn, Michael
Sinclair, Nicholas J.T.
Ward, Mark W.

League Appearances: Anderson, D.E. (2); Bowden, J. 31; Bromage, R. 2; Buchan, M.M. 24; Bullock, S. (1); Clements, K.H. 41; Collins, J.P. (1); Colville, R.J. 4; Cross, D. 18(4); Goram, A.L. 22; Grew, M. 5; Heaton, P.J. 10; Henry, A. 39(3); Hodkinson, A.J. 3(1); Hoolickin, G.J. 34; Hudson, C.J. 12(1); Humphreys, J.S. 5(5); Jones, A. 2; McBride, J. 19(6); McDonough, D.K. 38; Palmer, R.N. 42; Parker, D. 22(3); Parkin, B. 5; Quinn, M. 14; Sinclair, N.J.T. 18; Ward, M.W. 42; Wealands, J. 10.

Goals – League (47): Palmer 13, Cross 6, Ward 6, Quinn 5, Henry 4, McBride 4, Heaton 2 (2 pens), Parker 2, Bowden 1, Colville 1, Hodkinson 1, Hoolickin 1, own goal 1.

Milk Cup (5): McDonough 2, Cross 1, Palmer 1, Parker 1.

FA Cup (0).

Ground: Boundary Park, Oldham OL1 2PA (061-624 8110 information service 4972)

Nearest station: Oldham, Werneth

Manager: Joe Royle **Secretary:** T. M. Finn

Colours: Blue shirts, with white trim; white shorts

Record home gate: 47,671 v Sheffield Wednesday, January 1930 (FA Cup)

Honours – Champions: Division 3 North: 1952-53; Division 3: 1973-74

ORIENT DIV. 3

Brooks, Shaun
Castle, Stephen C.
Corbett, Patrick A.
Cornwell, John A.
Foster, Colin J.
Godfrey, Kevin
Hales, Kevin
McNeil, Mark
Silkman, Barry
Sussex, Andrew R.

League Appearances: Banfield, N. 6; Brooks, S. 33(3); Corbett, P.A. 43; Cornwell, J.A. 42; Cunningham, T.E. 36; Foster, C.J. 10(1); Godfrey, K.A. 9(2); Hales, K.P. 43; Harvey, L.D. (4); Houchen, K.M. 28(2); Key, R.M. 42; Kitchen, M.P. 26(3); Mancini, M.L. 2; McNeil, M. 37(2); Osgood, K. 12; Roffey, W.R. 28(1); Shoemake, K.P. 4; Silkman, B. 41; Sussex, A.R. 24(5); Wilkins, D.M. 10.

Goals – League (71): Kitchen 12 (1 pen), Godfrey 10, Brooks 9 (2 pens), Houchen 9 (4 pens), Cornwell 7, Cunningham 6, Sussex 6, McNeil 4, Silkman 4, Hales 2, Corbett 1, Foster 1.

Milk Cup (4): Cornwell 1, Godfrey 1, Houchen 1, Kitchen 1.

FA Cup (1): own goal 1.

Grounds: Leyton Stadium, Brisbane Road, Leyton, E10 5NE (01-539 2223/4)

Nearest station: Leyton (Central line)

Manager: Frank Clark **Secretary:** Miss C. Stokes
Colours: Red shirts; red shorts
Record home gate: 34,345 v West Ham United, January 1964 (FA Cup)
Honours – Champions: Division 3: 1969-70; Division 3 South: 1955-56

OXFORD UNITED DIV. 2

Aldridge, John W.
Aries, Steven J.
Barnett, Gary L.
Biggins, Stephen J.
Briggs, Gary
Brock, Kevin S.
Butcher, John M.
Fogg, David
Hardwick, Steven
Hebberd, Trevor N.
Hinshelwood, Paul A.
Jones, Mark
Lawrence, George R.
McDonald, Robert W.
Phillips, Leslie M.
Rhoades-Brown, Peter
Shotton, Malcolm
Thomas, Andrew M.
Vinter, Michael
Whatmore, Neil

League Appearances: Aldridge, J.W. 5(3); Barnett, G.L. 18(1); Biggins, S.J. 35(7); Briggs, G. 36(2); Brock, K.S. 45; Fogg, D. 3; Grant, D. 4; Hardwick, S. 46; Hebberd, T.N. 46; Hinshelwood, P.A. 43; Jones, M. 13(7); Lawrence, G.R. 34; McDonald, R.W. 39; Phillips, L.M. 2(4); Rhoades-Brown, P. 19(1); Shotton, M. 43; Thomas, A.M. 23; Todd, C. 12; Train, R. 1; Trewick, J. 3; Vinter, M. 25(1); Whatmore, N. 11(2).
Goals – League (91): Biggins 19, Hebberd 11 (4 pens), Vinter 11, Lawrence 9, Barnett 7, Thomas 7, Aldridge 4, McDonald 4 (4 pens), Rhoades-Brown 4, Briggs 3, Brock 3, Whatmore 3, Jones 2, Shotton 1, own goals 3.
Milk Cup (16): Biggins 3, Brock 3, McDonald 3, Thomas 2, Vinter 2, Hinshelwood 1, Lawrence1, Whatmore 1.
FA Cup (10): McDonald 4 (2 pens), Biggins 2, Brock 1, Lawrence 1, Vinter 1, own goal 1.
Ground: Manor Ground, Beech Road, Headington, Oxford OX3 7RS (0865 61503)
Nearest station: Oxford
Manager: Jim Smith **Secretary:** Jim A. Hunt
Colours: Yellow shirts with blue pinstripe; blue shorts
Record home gate: 22,730 v Preston, February 1964 (FA Cup)
Honours – Champions: Division 3: 1967-68, 1983-84

PETERBOROUGH UNITED DIV. 4

Beech, Kenneth
Chard, Phillip J.
Firm, Neil J.
Hankin, Raymond
Holmes, James
Pike, Martin R.
Quow, Trevor
Rayment, Patrick J.
Seaman, David A.
Slack, Trevor C.
Tydeman, Richard
Waddle, Alan R.
Worrall, Gary G.

League Appearances: Beech, K. 38; Benjamin, I.T. 31(3); Buchanan, D. 13(3); Chard, P.J. 38; Clarke, C.J. 17(1); Firm, N.J. 24(1); Hankin, R. 25(2); Holmes, J. 20(1); Imlach, M.T. 29(3); Kelly, E.E. 11; Linton, I. 3; Pike, M.R. 28(7); Quow, T.

24(4); Rayment, P.J. 8(5); Seaman, D.A. 45; Slack, T.C. 39; Tydeman, R. 29; Waddle, A.R. 33; Wile, J.D. 32; Worrall, G.G. 7(1); Zenchuk, S.J. 1.
Goals – League (72): Waddle 12, Benjamin 8, Chard 7 (4 pens), Hankin 7, Kelly 7, Clarke 5, Buchanan 4, Quow 4, Beech 3, Slack 3, Holmes 2 (2 pens), Pike 2, Wile 2, Worrall 2, Imlach 1, Rayment 1, own goals 2.
Milk Cup (4): Chard 1 (pen), Clarke 1, Hankin 1, Quow 1.
FA Cup (0).
Ground: London Road Ground, Peterborough PE2 8AL (0733 63947)
Nearest station: Peterborough
Manager: John Wile **Secretary:** A. V. Blades
Colours: Blue shirts with white trim; white shorts with blue trim
Record home gate: 30,096 v Swansea, February 1965 (FA Cup)
Honours – Champions: Division 4: 1960, 1973-74

PLYMOUTH ARGYLE — DIV. 3

Cooper, Leigh V.
Crudgington, Geoffrey
Ham, Michael T.
Harrison, Christopher C.
Hodges, Kevin
Nisbet, Gordon J.M.
Phillips, David O.
Rogers, Andrew
Rowe, Mark T.
Smith, Lindsay
Staniforth, Gordon
Tynan, Thomas E.
Uzzell, John E.

League Appearances: Cassidy, F.J.A. 1; Chamberlain, N.P. 7(4); Cooper, L.V. 43; Crudgington, G. 46; Forbes, R.J. 3; Ham, M.T. 5(1); Harrison, C.C. 44; Hodges, K. 41(2); Kellow, T. 8(2); Nisbet, G.J.M. 44; Pearson, I.T. 5(3); Phillips, D.O. 39(3); Price, N. 1; Rogers, A. 36(1); Rowe, M.T. 24(4); Smith, L. 42; Smith, M. 3; Staniforth, G. 36(3); Swiggs, B. 1(1); Tynan, T.E. 35; Uzzell, J. E. 42.
Goals – League (56): Tynan 12 (4 pens), Staniforth 11 (1 pen), Phillips 6, Hodges 4, Nisbet 4, Rogers 4, Smith 4, Cooper 3, Chamberlain 2, Kellow 2, Pearson 1, Rowe 1, own goals 2.
Milk Cup (5): Nisbet 2, Smith 1, Staniforth 1, Tynan 1.
FA Cup (11): Tynan 3 (1 pen), Rogers 2, Hodges 1, Rowe 1, Smith 1, Staniforth 1, Uzzell 1, own goal 1.
Ground: Home Park, Plymouth, Devon PL2 1BQ (0752 52561)
Nearest station: Plymouth
Manager: John Hore **Secretary:** Graham Little
Colours: Green shirts; black shorts
Record home gate: 43,596 v Aston Villa, October 1936 (League)
Honours – Champions: Division 3 South: 1929-30, 1951-52; Division 3: 1958-59

PORTSMOUTH — DIV. 2

Ball, Kevin A.
Biley, Alan P.
Dillon, Kevin P.
Doyle, Robert
Gosney, Andrew R.
Hardyman, Paul G.
Knight, Alan E.
Money, Richard
Morgan, Nicholas
Stanley, Gary E.
Sullivan, Colin J.
Tait, Michael P.
Thomas, David
Waldron, Malcolm
Walsh, Mario M.
Webb, Neil J.
Wimbleton, Paul P.
Wood, Paul A.

League Appearances: Aizlewood, S. 22; Ball, K.A. 1; Biley, A.P. 37; Dillon, K.P. 36; Doyle, R. 37; Ellis, P.J. 10(2); Hardyman, P.G. 2(1); Hateley, M.W. 38; Hindmarch, R. 2; Howe, E.J. 8; Knight, A.E. 42; Money, R. 16; Morgan, N. 16(9); McLaughlin, J. 33; Rogers, A.J. 13(1); Stanley, G.E. 11(1); Sullivan, C.J. 30; Tait, M.P. 36; Thomas, D. 12(2); Waldron, M. 12; Webb, N.J. 40; Wimbleton, P.P. 1(1); Wood, P.A. 7(1).
Goals – League (73): Hateley 21 (1 pen), Biley 17, Webb 10, Dillon 9 (4 pens), Morgan 9, Tait 3, Howe 2, Doyle 1, Wood 1.
Milk Cup (9): Dillon 3 (2 pens), Biley 2, Hateley 2, Webb 1, own goal 1.
FA Cup (2): Hateley 1, Morgan 1.
Ground: Fratton Park, Frogmore Road, Portsmouth, PO4 8RA (0705-734129)
Nearest stations: Fratton or Portsmouth and Southsea
Manager: Alan Ball **Secretary:** W. J. B. Davis
Colours: Blue shirts; white shorts
Record home gate: 51,385 v Derby County, February 1949 (FA Cup)
Honours – Champions: Division 1: 1948-49, 1949-50; Division 3 South: 1923-24; Division 3: 1961-62
FA Cup winners: 1938-39

PORT VALE — DIV. 4

Armstrong, Terry
Banks, Christopher
Bright, Mark A.
Bromage, Russel
Cegielski, Wayne
Earle, Robert
Gore, Thomas J.
Henderson, William M.M.
Hunter, Geoffrey
O'Keefe, Eamon G.
Pearce, Christopher L.
Pollard, Gary
Ridley, John
Shankland, Andrew J.
Siddall, Barry
Sproson, Philip J.
Tartt, Colin

League Appearances: Armstrong, T. 18(1); Bright, M.A. 17(9); Bromage, R. 38; Cegielski, W. 38(1); Earle, R. 8(4); Fox, S.D. 37(2); Gore, T.J. 33(3); Henderson, W.M. 27; Hunter, G. 42; Massey, A.T. 4; Newton, R. 7; O'Keefe, E.G. 34(3); Oakes, A.A. 1; Pearce, C.L. 7; Pollard, G. 17(1); Ridley, J. 30; Shankland, A.J. 6(1); Siddall, B. 39; Sproson, P.J. 38; Steel, W.J. 14(1); Tartt, C. 21(1); Thompson, M.S. 2; White, E.W. (1); Young, K. 28.
Goals – League (51): O'Keefe 10 (1 pen), Bright 9, Henderson 7, Young 4, Fox 3, Steele 3, Armstrong 2, Gore 2 (2 pens), Newton 2, Ridley 2, Sproson 2, Tartt 2, Bromage 1, Hunter 1, Massey 1 (pen).
Milk Cup (8): Newton 2, Sproson 2, Gore 1, Hunter 1, O'Keefe 1 (pen), Steele 1.
FA Cup (1): Bright 1.
Ground: Vale Park, Hamil Road, Burslem, Stoke-on-Trent ST6 1AW (0782 814134)
Nearest station: Stoke-on-Trent
Manager: John Rudge **Secretary:** P. A. Shaw
Colours: White shirts with black trim; black shorts with white stripes down seams
Record home gate: 50,000 v Aston Villa, February 1960 (FA Cup)
Honours – Champions: Division 3 North: 1929-30, 1953-54; Division 4: 1958-59

PRESTON NORTH END DIV. 3

Booth, Thomas A.	Houston, Graham R.	Naughton, Williams B.S.
Campbell, Anthony	Jones, David R.	Sayer, Peter A.
Clark, Jonathan	Jones, Mark T.	Twentyman, Geoffrey
Elliott, Stephen B.	Kelly, John	Walsh, Mark
Farrelly, Michael	Litchfield, Peter	Welsh, Paul W.
Houghton, Peter	McAteer, Andrew W.	

League Appearances: Bleasdale, D. 4:(1); Booth, T.A. 31; Cameron, S.J. 1; Clark, J. 31; Elliott, S.B. 44; Farrelly, M. 31; Hinningan, J.P 38(1); Houghton, P. 30(2); Houston, G.R. 23(18); Jones, D.R. 37; Jones, M.T. 4; Kelly, J. 34; Litchfield, P. 45; Lodge, P. 17(2); Murphy, A.C. 4(1); McAteer, A.W. 32(2); Naughton, W.B.S. 35(7); Sayer, P.A. 15; Telfer, G.A. (2); Twentyman, G. 25(3); Walsh, M. 25.
Goals – League (66): Elliot 16 (2 pens), Kelly 13, Houghton 10, Clark 5 (2 pens), Hinningan 5, Sayer 4, Houston 3, Naughton 3, Farrelly 2, Booth 1, Jones 1, Twentyman 1, own goals 2.
Milk Cup (5): Hinningan 2, Elliott 1, Kelly 1, Naughton 1.
FA Cup (0).
Ground: Deepdale, Preston PR1 6RU (0772 795919)
Nearest station: Preston
Manager: Alan Kelly **Secretary:** D. J. Allan
Colours: White shirts with blue collars and cuffs; blue shorts with white trim
Record home gate: 42,684 v Arsenal, April 1938 (League)
Honours – Champions: Division 1: 1888-89, 1889-90; Division 2: 1903-04, 1912-13, 1950-51; Division 3: 1970-71
FA Cup winners: 1888-89, 1937-38

QUEEN'S PARK RANGERS DIV. 1

Allen, Clive D.	Duffield, Martin J.	Micklewhite, Gary
Allen, Martin J.	Fenwick, Terence W.	Neill, Warren A.
Benstead, Graham M.	Fereday, Wayne	O'Connor, Mark A.
Burke, Steven J.	Fillery, Michael C.	Sealy, Anthony J.
Charles, Jeremy M.	Gregory, John C.	Simmons, Anthony J.
Chivers, Gary P.S.	Hucker, Peter I.	Stainrod, Simon A.
Comfort, Alan	Kerslake, David	Stewart, Ian E.
Cooper, Gary	McClure, Douglas H.	Waddock, Gary P.
Dawes, Ian R.	McDonald, Alan	Wicks. Stephen J.

League Appearances: Allen, C.D. 24(1); Burke, S.J. 1(4); Charles, J.M. 10(2); Dawes, I.R. 42; Fenwick, T.W. 41; Fereday, W. 11(6); Fillery, M.C. 29(1); Flanagan, M.A. 1(4); Gregory, J.C. 37; Hazell, R.J. 6; Hucker, P.I. 42; Micklewhite, G. 27(3); McDonald, A. 5; Neill, W.A. 41; Roeder, G.V. 1; Sealy, A.J. 6(2); Stainrod, S.A. 41; Stewart, I.E. 30(1); Waddock, G.P. 36; Wicks, S.J. 31
Goals – League (67): Allen 14, Stainrod 13, Fenwick 10 (4 pens), Gregory 7, Charles 5, Fereday 4, Waddock 3, Dawes 2, Micklewhite 2, Stewart 2, Wicks 2, Fillery 1, Neill 1, own goal 1.

Milk Cup (10): Stainrod 3, Stewart 2, Allen 1, Gregory 1, McDonald 1, Micklewhite 1, Waddock 1.
FA Cup (1): Gregory 1.
Ground: Rangers Stadium, South Africa Road, Shepherds Bush, W12 7PA (01-743 0262)
Nearest stations: Shepherds Bush (Metropolitan and Central lines); White City (Central line)
Manager: Alan Mullery M.B.E. **Secretary:** R. J. Phillips
Colours: Blue and white hooped shirts; white shorts
Record home gate: 35,353 v Leeds United, April 1974 (League)
Honours – Champions: Division 2: 1982-83; Division 3: 1966-67; Division 3 South: 1947-48
League Cup winners: 1966-67

READING — DIV. 3

Barnes, Michael F.
Beavon, Michael S.
Crown, David I.
Duncan, Colin J.
Hicks, Martin
Horrix, Dean V.
Judge, Alan G.
Price, Kenneth G.
Richardson, Steven E.
Sanchez, Lawrence P.
Senior, Trevor
White, Mark
Williams, Jeremy S.
Wood, Stephen A.

League Appearances: Barnes, M.F. 5(1); Beavon, M.S. 32(4); Crown, D.I. 45; Duncan, C.J. 33; Hicks, M. 46; Horrix, D.V. 43; Judge, A.G. 41; Matthews, M. (2); Price, K.G. 17(3); Richardson, S.E. 33(1); Sanchez, L.P. 45; Senior, T. 45; Tutty, W.K. 7; Westwood, G.M. 5; White, M. 38(1); Williams, J.S. 34(4); Wood, S.A. 37.
Goals – League (84): Senior 36, Sanchez 10, Horrix 8 (1 pen), Beavon 7 (1 pen), Crown 7, Tutty 3, Wood 3, Duncan 2, Price 2, White 2, Hicks 1, own goals 3.
Milk Cup (6): Senior 4, Barnes 1, Beavon 1.
FA Cup (3): Horrix 1, Price 1, Senior 1.
Ground: Elm Park, Norfolk Road, Reading RG3 2EF (0734 507878)
Nearest station: Reading
Manager: Ian Branfoot **Secretary:** R. Bentley
Colours: Sky blue shirts with white stripe and navy trim; shorts navy with amber stripes
Record home gate: 33,042 v Brentford, February 1927 (FA Cup)
Honours – Champions: Division 3 South: 1925-26; Divison 4: 1978-79

ROCHDALE — DIV. 4

Allatt, Vernon
Chapman, Leslie
Conroy, Steven H.
Farrell, Peter
Griffiths, Ian J.
McMahon, Ian
Williams, William R.

League Appearances: Allatt, V. 40; Blake, J.B. 2; Chapman, L. 44(1); Conroy, S.H. 46; Dean, A.G. 1; Doyle, M. 24; Ennis, M. 1; Farrell, P. 24(1); Greenhoff, B. 8(1);

Greenhoff, J. 4; Griffiths, I.J. 39(2); Hamilton, N.R. 38(1); Heaton, P.J. 2(3); Higgins, A.M. 20(2); Humphreys, J.S. 6; Johnson, S.A. 17(2); Keenan, G.P. 5; McCluskie, J.J.A. 4(1); McMahon, I. 21; O'Connor, M.J. 12(3); Oates, R.A. 42; Reid, S. 17; Thomas, G.R. 10; Thompson, D.S. 39(1); Thompson, S.C. 13(6); Williams, W.R. 27.

Goals – League (52): Allatt 8 (1 pen), Farrell 8 (3 pens), Johnson 7, Griffiths 5, S. Thompson 5, Higgins 4, D. Thompson 4, O'Connor 3, Williams 2, Doyle 1, Hamilton 1, McMahon 1, Oates 1, Scrimgeour 1, Thomas 1.
Milk Cup (2): Griffiths 1, Johnson 1.
FA Cup (4): Johnson 2, Allatt, 1, Farrell, 1.
Ground: Spotland, Sandy Lane, Rochdale OL11 5DR (0706 44648/9)
Nearest station: Rochdale
Manager: Vic Hanlon **Secretary:** W. H. Kenyon
Colours: Royal blue shirts; white shorts with blue stripe
Record home gate: 24,231 v Notts County, December 1949 (FA Cup)
Honours – Champions: Nil

ROTHERHAM UNITED DIV. 3

Birch, Alan
Crosby, Philip A.
Donovan, Terence C.
Dungworth, John H.
Durham, Jonathan S.
Forrest, Gerald
Gooding, Michael C.
Johnson, Nigel M.
Kilmore, Kevin
Mimms, Robert A.
Mitchell, Robert
O'Dell, Andrew
Pickering, Michael J.
Raynes, William
Rhodes, Mark N.
Stevenson, Alan
Stone, John G.
Trusson, Michael S.
Walker, Philip A.

League Appearances: Birch, A. 14; Brown, G.A. 1; Crosby, P.A. 39; Donovan, T.C. 5(1); Dungworth, J.H. 22; Durham, J.S. 3(3); Eley, K. (1); Forrest, G. 45; Friar, J.P. 5; Gooding, M.C. 24(2); Green, J.R. 1; Henson, P.M. 4; Johnson, N.M. 43; Kilmore, K. 45; Mimms, R.A. 22; Mitchell, R. 36(7); Moore, R.D. 4; McBride, J. 3; McEwan, W.M.J. 17(1); McFadzean, J.P. (1); McInnes, I. 1(1); O'Dell, A. 15(2); Pickering, M.J. 24; Raynes, W. 11(3); Rhodes, M.N. 28(8); Seasman, J. 7(1); Simmons, A.J. 18; Stevenson, A. 24; Stone, J.G. 10; Trusson, M.S. 25; Walker, P.A. 10(5).
Goals – League (57): Kilmore 13, Birch 10 (5 pens), Simmons 8, Gooding 7 (3 pens), Dungworth 3, Mitchell 2, Moore 2, Rhodes 2, Trusson 2, Durham 1, Johnson 1, McBride 1, Raynes 1, Stone 1, Walker 1, own goals 2.
Milk Cup (10): Kilmore 5, Gooding 2, Mitchell 1, Rhodes 1, Walker 1.
FA Cup (3): Kilmore 3.
Ground: Millmoor, Rotherham S60 1HR (0709 562434)
Nearest station: Rotherham
Manager: George Kerr **Secretary:** J. E. Bennison F.A.A.I.
Colours: Red shirts with white trim; white shorts
Record home gate: 25,000 v Sheffield United, December 1952 and Sheffield Wednesday, January 1952 (League)
Honours – Champions: Division 3: 1980-81; Division 3 North: 1950-51

SCUNTHORPE UNITED DIV. 4

Bell, Derek M.
Broddle, Julian R.
Brolly, Michael J.
Cammack, Stephen R.
Cowling, Christopher
Dey, Geoffrey
Green, John R.
Lester, Michael J.
Longden, David P.
Matthews, Michael
Neenan, Joseph P.
Pointon, Neil G.
Whitehead, Alan

League Appearances: Bell, D.M. 19; Botham, I.T. 3; Boxall, A.R. 4; Broddle, J.R. 9(4); Brolly, M.J. 40(1); Cammack, S.R. 39; Cowling, C. 21(1); Dey, G. 12; Graham, T. 25(2); Green, J.R. 45; Hill, D.M. 1(1); Holden, R.6(1); Hunter, L. 15; Leman, D. 2; Lester, M.J. 33; Longden, D.P. 43; Matthews, M. 25; Neenan, J.P. 41; O'Berg, P.J. 22(3); Parkinson, N.D. 9(1); Pointon, N.G. 45; Pratley, R.G. 10; Richardson, R. 2; Snow, S.G. 1; Steele, S.P. 5; Webster, I.A. 8(1); Whitehead, A. 15, Wilson, D. 6.
Goals – League (54): Cammack 18 (4 pens), Bell 5 (1 pen), Brolly 4, Cowling 4, Graham 4, Lester 3, O'Berg 3, Wilson 3 (1 pen), Green 2, Broddle 1, Dey 1, Holden 1 (pen), Leman 1, Matthews 1, Parkinson 1, Pointon 1, own goal 1.
Milk Cup (1): Cammack 1.
FA Cup (9): Cammack 4 (1 pen), Brolly 1, Dey 1, Graham 1, Lester 1, own goal 1.
Ground: Old Show Ground, Scunthorpe DN15 7RH (0724 848077)
Nearest station: Scunthorpe
Manager: Allan Clarke **Secretary:** A.D. Rowing
Colours: Blue shirts with claret 'v'; blue shorts with claret trim
Record home gate: 23,935 v Portsmouth, January 1954 (FA Cup)
Honours – Champions: Division 3 North: 1957-58

SHEFFIELD UNITED DIV. 2

Arnott, Kevin W.
Atkins, Robert G.
Bolton, Joseph
Brazil, Gary N.
Charles, Stephen
Cockerill, Glenn
Cooper, Richard D.
Edwards, Keith
Garner, Paul
Heffernan, Thomas P.
Henderson, Michael R.
Kenworthy, Anthony D.
McHale, Raymond
Morris, Colin
Philliskirk, Anthony
Smith, Paul M.
Stancliffe, Paul I.
Stanley, Paul S.
Tomlinson, Paul
Waugh, Keith
West, Gary

League Appearances: Arnott, K.W. 46; Atkins, R.G. 13(3); Bolton, J. 45; Brazil, G.N. 8(11); Charles, S. 11; Cockerill, G. 10; Edwards, K. 44; Garner, P. 24; Heffernan, T.P. 42; Henderson, M.R. 21(1); Kenworthy, A.D. Morris, C. 42; McHale, R. 42; Philliskirk, A. 20(1); Ross, T.W. 4; Smith, P.M. 2(1); Stancliffe, P.I. 43; Tomlinson, P. 30; Trusson, M.S. 11; Waugh, K. 16; West, G. 24.
Goals – League (86): Edwards 33, Morris 20 (10 pens), Philliskirk 8, Arnott 6, Atkins 3, Trusson 3, Brazil 2, Heffernan 2, Bolton 1, Charles 1, Cockerill 1, Garner 1, Kenworthy 1, McHale 1, Stancliffe 1, own goals 2.
Milk Cup (5): Stancliffe 2, Arnott 1, Edwards 1, Podd 1.
FA Cup (7): Edwards 4, Arnott 1, Brazil 1, Stancliffe 1.
Ground: Bramhall Lane, Sheffield S2 4SU (0742 738955)

Nearest station: Sheffield
Manager: Ian Porterfield **Secretary:** G. E. Smith
Colours: Red and white striped shirts; red shorts with white stripe down seam
Record home gate: 68,287 v Leeds, February 1936 (FA Cup)
Honours – Champions: Division 1: 1897-98; Division 2: 1952-53; Division 3 North: 1945-46; Division 4: 1981-82
FA Cup winners: 1898-99, 1901-02, 1914-15, 1924-25

SHEFFIELD WEDNESDAY DIV. 1

Bailey, Ian C.
Bannister, Gary
Cunningham, Anthony E.
Heard, Timothy P.
Hesford, Iain
Hodge, Martin J.
Lyons, Michael
Madden, Lawrence D.
Megson, Gary J.
Mills, Simon A.
Morris, Christopher B.
Mossman, David J.
Oliver, Gavin R.
Pearson, John S.
Redfern, David
Shelton, Gary
Shirtliff, Peter A.
Smith, Mark C.
Sterland, Melvyn
Taylor, Kevin
Varadi, Imre
Williamson, Charles H.
Worthington, Nigel

League Appearances: Bannister, G. 36(1); Cunningham, A.E. 26(2); Heard, T.P. 2(3); Hodge, M.J. 42; Lyons, M. 42; Madden, L.D. 38; Megson, G.J. 42; Mills, S.A. 1(1); Morris, C.B. 8(5); Oliver, G.R. 3(3); Pearson, J.S. 21(6); Shelton, G. 40; Shirtliff, P.A. 36; Smith, M.C. 27; Sterland, M. 39; Taylor, K. 1(4); Varadi, I. 35(3); Williamson, C.H. 9(1); Worthington, N. 14.
Goals – League (62): Varadi 17, Bannister 14, Sterland 8 (5 pens), Cunningham 5, Lyons 5, Shelton 5, Megson 4, Pearson 4, Smith 2, Heard 1, Madden 1, Morris 1, Shirtliff 1, Worthington 1, own goals 3.
Milk Cup (12): Bannister 4, Madden 2, Shelton 2, Megson 1, Morris 1, Varadi 1, own goal 1.
FA Cup (8): Bannister 3, Lyons 1, Pearson 1, Shirtliff 1, Sterland 1 (pen), Varadi 1.
Ground: Hillsborough, Sheffield S6 1SW (0742 343123, Box Office 343122)
Nearest station: Sheffield
Manager: Howard Wilkinson **Secretary:** R. H. Chester
Colours: Royal blue and white striped shirts; royal blue shorts
Record home gate: 72,841 v Manchester City, February 1934 (FA Cup)
Honours – Champions: Division 1: 1902-03, 1903-04, 1928-29, 1929-30; Division 2: 1899-1900, 1925-26, 1951-52, 1955-56, 1958-59
FA Cup winners: 1895-96, 1906-07, 1934-35

SHREWSBURY TOWN DIV. 2

Bates, Philip D.
Collins, Kevin
Cross, Stephen C.
Griffin, Colin R.
Hackett, Gary S.
Johnson, Paul
Kerr, Andrew A.
McNally, Bernard A.
Maclaren, Ross
Nardiello, Gerardo
Ogrizovic, Steven
Pearson, Nigel G.
Perks, Stephen J.
Petts, Paul A.
Robinson, Colin R.
Stevens, Gary M.
Tester, Paul L.
Turner, Graham J.
Williams, Wayne

League Appearances: Bates, P.D. 14(2); Brown, A. 29; Collins, K. 1; Cross, S.C. 40(1); Griffin, C.R. 27; Hackett, G.S. 29(2); Johnson, P. 15; Maclaren, R. 40; McNally, B.A. 41; Nardiello, G. 11; Ogrizovic, S. 42; Pearson, N.G. 26; Petts, P.A. 35; Robinson, C.R. 20(10); Stevens, G.M. 34(4); Tester, P.L. 6 (2); Turner, G.J. 10(1); Williams, W. 40.
Goals – League (49): Cross 9, Petts 8, Maclaren 7 (2 pens), Brown 5, Nardiello 5, McNally 4, Robinson 4, Bates 3 (1 pen), Hackett 3, Stevens 1.
Milk Cup (5): Bates 1, Brown 1, Hackett 1, Stevens 1, Williams 1.
FA Cup (5): Robinson 2, Hackett 1, Maclaren 1 (pen), Stevens 1.
Ground: Gay Meadow, Shrewsbury SY2 6AB (0743 60111)
Nearest station: Shrewsbury
Manager: **Secretary:** M. J. Starkey
Colours: Royal blue shirts with gold sleeves, gold shorts with blue trim
Record home gate: 18,917 v Walsall, April 1961 (League)
Honours – Champions: Division 3: 1978-79

SOUTHAMPTON DIV. 1

Agboola, Reuben O.F.
Armstrong, David
Armstrong, Kenneth C.
Baird, Ian J.
Baker, Stephen
Blankley, Barry S.
Burns, Duncan A.
Collins, Eamonn A.S.
Curtis, Alan T.
Dennis, Mark E.
Dixon, Timothy P.
Foyle, Martin J.
Holmes, Nicholas C.
Juryeff, Ian M.
Mills, Michael D.
Moran, Stephen J.
Puckett, David C.
Rofe, Dennis
Shilton, Peter L.
Sperring, Alastair
Wallace, David L.
Whitlock, Mark
Williams, Steven C.
Wright, Mark

League Appearances: Agboola, R.O.F. 33; Armstrong, D. 42; Armstrong, K.C. 26; Baird, I.J. 6; Baker, S. 8; Curtis, A.T. 8(1); Dennis, M.E. 20; Foyle, M.J. 2(3); Golac, I. 11; Holmes, N.C. 42; Juryeff, I.M. (2); Mills, M.D. 34; Moran, S.J. 33(1); Puckett, D.C. 7(11); Rofe, D. 2(1); Shilton, P.L. 42; Wallace, D.L. 41; Whitlock, M. 15(1); Williams, S.C. 27; Worthington, F.S. 34; Wright, M. 29.
Goals – League (66): Moran 21 (2 pens), D. Armstrong 15, Wallace 11, Worthington 4, Holmes 3, Puckett 3, Williams 3, Mills 2, Baird 1, Wright 1 own goals 2.
Milk Cup (4): D. Armstrong 2, Foyle 2.
FA Cup (9): Moran 4, D. Armstrong 2, Williams 1, Wright 1, own goal 1.
Ground: The Dell, Milton Road, Southampton SO9 4XX (0703 39633/5)
Nearest station: Southampton
Manager: Lawrie McMenemy **Secretary:** B. Truscott
Colours: Red and white vertical striped shirts; black shorts
Record home gate: 31,044 v Manchester United, October 1969 (League)
Honours – Champions: Division 3 South: 1921-22; Division 3: 1959-60
FA Cup winners: 1975-76

SOUTHEND UNITED DIV. 4

Angus, Michael A.
Clark, Paul P.
Collins, Stephen M.
Ferguson, James B.
Fuccillo, Pasquale
Keeley, John H.

Kellock, William
May, Warren D.
Owers, Adrian R.
Pennyfather, Glenn J.
Phillips, Stephen E.
Pountney, Ronald A.
Rogers, Alan J.
Shepherd, Jamie G.
Stead, Michael J.
Turner, Christopher J.
Whymark, Trevor J.

League Appearances: Cartwright, L. 2(2); Cawston, M.W. 11; Clark, P.P. 20; Collins, S.M. 36; Ferguson, J.B. 28(1); Fuccillo, P. 19(4); Greaves, D.T. (1); Gymer, J.P. 2(3); Keeley, J.H. 16; Kellock, W. 40; May, W.D. 14(8); Moody, A. 23; McDonough, R. 22; Owers, A.R. (1); Pennyfather, G.J. 33; Peyton, G.J. 10; Phillips, S.E. 41; Pountney, R.A. 27(4); Pritchard, P.J. 9; Rogers, A.J. 13; Shepherd, J.G. 36(3); Skivington, G. 2(2); Stead, M.J. 44; Steggles, K.P. 3; Turner, C.J. 22; Whymark, T.J. 19; Wilkins, G.G. 3; Yates, S. 11.
Goals – League (55): Phillips 16, Shepherd 8, Kellock 6 (1 pen), Ferguson 5, McDonough 4, Pennyfather 4, Whymark 3, Fuccillo 2, May 2, Gymer 1, Pountney 1, Stead 1, Turner 1, own goal 1.
Milk Cup (5): Shepherd 3, Kellock 1, Phillips 1.
FA Cup (0):
Ground: Roots Hall Ground, Victoria Avenue, Southend SS2 6NQ (0702 40707)
Nearest stations: Prittlewell or Southend Central
Manager: Bobby Moore **Secretary:** K. Holmes F.A.A.I.F. Inst. M.
Colours: White shirts with blue sleeves and blue V neck; blue shorts
Record home gate: 31,033 v Liverpool, January 1979 (FA Cup)
Honours – Champions: Division 4: 1980-81

STOCKPORT COUNTY — DIV. 4

Bowles, Paul M.
Coyle, Anthony
Emerson, Dean
Evans, Andrew C.
Kerr, John
Power, Michael D.
Rutter, John T.
Salmon, Michael B.
Sherlock, Stephen E.
Sword, Thomas W.
Taylor, Steven J.
Thorpe, Andrew
Williams, Oshor J.

League Appearances: Bowles, P.M. 38; Coyle, A. 38; Emerson, D. 44; Evans, A.C. 31; Jones, G. 32(3); Kerr, J. 21; Leigh, M.B. (1); Parker, S.J. (1); Power, M.D. 5; Quinn, M. 24; Rutter, J.T. 41; Ryan, J.G. 1(1); Salmon, M.B. 46; Sherlock, S.E. 24(2); Smith, N.G. 19(1); Sutcliffe, P.D. (1); Sword, T.W. 45; Taylor, S.J. 12; Thorpe, A. 45; White E.W. 4; Williams, O.J. 36(1).
Goals – League (60): Quinn 15 (1 pen), Sword 10 (2 pens), Evans 7 (1 pen), Kerr 6, Taylor 6, Williams 6, Coyle 5, Jones 2, Emerson 1, Rutter 1, Thorpe 1.
Milk Cup (7): Emerson 2, Quinn 2, Williams 2, Sword 1.
FA Cup (0):
Ground: Edgeley Park, Stockport SK3 9DD (061-480 8888/9)
Nearest station: Stockport
Manager: Eric Webster **Secretary:** T. R. McCreery F.A.A.I.
Colours: Sky blue shirts with white stripes; black shorts with blue trim
Record home gate: 27,833 v Liverpool, February 1950 (FA Cup)
Honours – Champions: Division 3 North: 1921-22, 1936-37; Division 4: 1966-67

STOKE CITY — DIV. 1

Berry, George F.
Bould, Stephen A.
Cawston, Mervyn W.
Chamberlain, Mark V.
Chamberlain, Neville P.
Chapman, Jonathan D.
Dyson, Paul I.
Fox, Peter D.
Heath, Philip A.
Hemming, Christopher A.
Howells, Neil
Hudson, Alan A.
James, Robert M.
McIlroy, Samuel B.
Maguire, Paul B.
Maskery, Christopher P.
O'Callaghan, Brendan R.
Painter, Ian J.
Parkin, Stephen J.
Saunders, Carl S.

League Appearances: Berry, G.F. 8; Bould, S.A. 38; Chamberlain, M.V. 39(1); Chamberlain, N.P. 3; Dyson, P.I. 38; Fox, P.D. 42; Griffiths, P.J. 3(1); Hampton, P.J. 31(1); Heath, P.A. 3(1); Hemming, C.A.J. 3; Hudson, A.A. 16; James, R.M. 40; Maguire, P.B. 24(9); Maskery, C.P. 16(3); McAughtrie, D. 17; McIlroy, S.B. 39(1); O'Callaghan, B.R. 37(1); Painter, I.J. 30(4); Parkin, S.J. 1; Russell, C. 11; Savage, R.J. 5(2); Thomas, R.M. 16; Tueart, D. 2(1).
Goals – League (44): Maguire 9 (3 pens), Painter 9, Chamberlain 7, R. James 6, Thomas 3, Bould 2, Dyson 2, Russell 2, Hampton 1, Heath 1, McIlroy 1, O'Callaghan 1.
Milk Cup (4): Bould 1, R. James 1, Maguire 1, O'Callaghan 1.
FA Cup (0).
Ground: Victoria Ground, Stoke-on-Trent ST4 4EG (0782 413511)
Nearest station: Stoke-on-Trent
Manager: Bill Asprey **Secretary:** M. J. Potts
Colours: White shirts with red vertical stripes; red shorts
Record home gate: 51,380 v Arsenal, March 1937 (League)
Honours – Champions: Division 2: 1932-33, 1962-63; Divison 3 North: 1926-27
League Cup winners: 1971-72

SUNDERLAND — DIV. 1

Atkins, Ian L.
Atkinson, Paul
Bracewell, Paul W.
Chapman, Lee R.
Chisholm, Gordon W.
Cooke, John
Corner, David E.
Elliot, Shaun
Hindmarch, Robert
Lemon, Paul A.
O'Hagan, Paul
Pickering, Nicholas
Proctor, Mark G.
Prudhoe, Mark
Turner, Christopher R.
Venison, Barry
West, Colin

League Appearances: Atkins, I.L. 40; Atkinson, P. 7(1); Bracewell, P.W. 38; Chapman, L.R. 14(1); Chisholm, G.W. 36; Cooke, J. 1(3); Elliot, S. 33; Hindmarch, R. 12(1); James, L. 32(2); Munro, A.I.F. 9; Murray, J.G. 1; Pickering, N. 42; Proctor, M.G. 40(1); Robson, B.S. 7(5); Rowell, G. 31(3); Turner, C.R. 42; Venison, B. 41; Walker, N.S. (1); West, C. 36(2).
Goals – League (42): West 9, Rowell 8 (3 pens), Bracewell 4, Chisholm 4, Chapman 3, Robson 3, Atkins 2, James 2 (2 pens), Proctor 2, Atkinson 1, Pickering 1, own goals 3.
Milk Cup (8): Rowell 4 (1 pen), West 2, Cooke 1, Proctor 1.
FA Cup (4): West 2, Chapman 1, Rowell 1.

Ground: Roker Park, Grantham Road, Sunderland SR6 9SW (0783 40332 and 58638)
Nearest stations: Sunderland or Seaburn
Manager: Len Ashurst **Secretary:** G. Davidson F.C.A.
Colours: Red shirts with white vertical stripes and white sleeves; black shorts with red and white seams
Record home gate: 75,118 v Derby, March 1933 (FA Cup)
Honours – Champions: Division 1: 1891-92, 1892-93, 1894-95, 1901-02, 1912-13, 1935-36; Division 2: 1975-76
FA Cup winners: 1936-37, 1972-73

SWANSEA CITY — DIV. 3

Gale, Darren
Hadziabdic, Dzemal
Hough, David J.
Hughes, Michael R.
Lewis, Dudley K.
Loveridge, James C.
McQuillan, Patrick G.
Marustik, Christopher
Mullen, Roger C.
Pascoe, Colin J.
Rajkovic, Anto
Richards, Gary V.
Rimmer, John J.
Robinson, Neil
Sander, Christopher A.
Saunders, Dean N.
Stevenson, Nigel C.A.
Walsh, In P.

League Appearances: Charles, J.M. 10; Chivers, G.P.S. 10; Curtis, A.T. 9; Evans, W.E. 17; Gale, D. 16(4); Guard, A.F. 1; Holtham, D.M. 6; Hough, D.J. 1(1); Hughes, E.W. 7; Hughes, M.R. 21; Irwin, C.T. 3; Kennedy, R. 3; Lake, H.G.T. 14(4); Latchford, R.D. 18; Lewis, D.K. 37; Loveridge, J.C. 16(2); Maddy, P.M. 18(2); Marustik, C. 38; Morgan, H. 5(2); Mullen, R.C. (1); McQuillan, P.G. 19; Pascoe, C.J. 29(3); Rajkovic, A. 3; Richards, G.V. 32(2); Rimmer, J.J. 14; Robinson, N. 18(1); Sander, C.A. 7; Saunders, D.N. 14(5); Stanley, G.E. 14(1); Stevenson, N.C.A. 37; Toshack, J.B. (M.B.E.) 3; Walsh, I.P. 22(2); Williams, P.D. (1).
Goals – League (36): Walsh 6, Marustik 4 (1 pen), Gale 3, Latchford 3, Maddy 3, Saunders 3, Stevenson 3, Lake 2, Loveridge 2, Pascoe 2, Curtis 1, Richards 1, Stanley 1 (pen), Toshack 1, own goal 1.
Milk Cup (1): Gale 1.
FA Cup (0).
Ground: Vetch Field, Swansea SA1 3SU (0792 474114)
Nearest station: Swansea
Manager: Colin Appleton **Secretary/Chief Executive:** M. Struel
Colours: White shirts with black trim; white shorts with black trim
Record home gate: 32,796 v Arsenal, February 1968 (FA Cup)
Honours – Champions: Divison 3 South: 1924-25, 1948-49

SWINDON TOWN — DIV. 4

Allan, James
Bailie, Colin J.
Barnard, Leigh K.
Batty, Paul W.
Emmanuel, John G.
Endersby, Scott A.
Gibson, Simon J.
Gray, Nigel R.
Henry, Charles A.
Hockaday, David
Mayes, Alan
Nelson, Garry
Quinn, James M.
Richardson, Paul
Rowland, Andrew A.

League Appearances: Allan, J. 8; Andrews, I.E. 1; Baddeley, K. 24(1); Bailie, C.J. 37(1); Barnard, L.K. 35(1); Batty, P.W. 40(1); Emmanuel, J.G. 41(1); Endersby, S.A.G. 37; Gardiner, M.C. 1; Gibson, S.J. 29; Graham, M.A. 36; Gray, N.R. 15; Henry, C.A. 29; Hockaday, D. 32 (4); Hughes, M.C. (1); Mayes, A.K. 34(5); Nelson, G.P. 35(1); Quinn, J.M. 28(4); Richardson, P. 7; Rowland, A.A. 36(1); Woodruff, R.J. 1(1).
Goals – League (58): Mayes 17 (6 pens), Barnard 7, Quinn 7, Rowland 6, Batty 4, Emmanuel 4, Nelson 4, Bailie 3, Gibson 3, Hockaday 3.
Milk Cup (2): Hockaday 1, Nelson 1.
FA Cup (15): Quinn 6, Batty 3, Rowland 3, Barnard 1, Gibson 1, Henry 1.
Ground: County Ground, Swindon SN1 2ED (0793 22118 and 36170)
Nearest station: Swindon
Manager: Ken Beamish **Secretary:** R. J. Jeffries
Colours: Red shirts; white shorts
Record home gate: 32,000 v Arsenal, January 1972 (FA Cup)
Honours – League Cup winners: 1968-69
Anglo-Italian Cup winners: 1970

TORQUAY UNITED DIV. 4

Allen, Kenneth
Anderson, Colin R.
Barnes, Colin
Compton, Paul D.
Dawkins, Derek A.
Fowler, Derek W.
Impey, John E.
Pugh, Steven J.
Squire, Michael R.
Wakefield. David

League Appearances: Allen, K. 11; Anderson, C.R. 37(2); Arkwright, I. 2; Bailey, D.S. 1; Barnes, C. 35; Berry, J.A. 1; Bishop, R.J. 11(4); Carr, D. 34; Carter, R.W. 5; Collins, J.D. 6; Compton, P.D. 16; Cooper, S.M. 27(4); Curle, K. 16; Currie, A.W. 9; Dawkins, D.A. 14(2); Fifield, D. (1); Fowler, D.W. 7(1); Hall, D.R. 10; Holmes, J. 15; Horn, G.R. 1; Hughes, B. 33(5); Impey, J.E. 41; Laryea, B.M. 1; Lennox, S.J.M. 11; Little, A. 14; Pugh, S.J. 37(1); Rioch, B. D. 1(1); Rollings, A.N. 2; Sheridan, F.M. 8(1); Sims, J. 30; Smith, M. 1; Squire, M.R. 12(1); Turner, J.G. 34; Wakefield, D. 8; Wharton, A. 10; Young, K. 3.
Goals – League (59): Barnes 8 (2 pens), Cooper 8, Sims 8, Curle 5 (2 pens), Hughes 5, Anderson 4, Holmes 3 (2 pens), Squires 3, Bishop 2, Compton 2, Hall 2, Sheridan 2, Fowler 1, Little 1, Pugh 1, Wakefield 1, Young 1, own goals 2.
Milk Cup (0)
FA Cup (0)
Ground: Plainmoor, Torquay, Devon TQ1 3PS (0803 38666/7)
Nearest stations: Torquay or Torre
Manager: Dave Webb **Secretary:** D. J. Easton
Colours: Yellow shirts with blue trim; blue shorts
Record home gate: 21,908 v Huddersfield, January 1955 (FA Cup)
Honours: Nil

TOTTENHAM HOTSPUR DIV. 1

Archibald, Steven
Ardiles, Osvaldo C.
Bowen, Mark R.
Brazil, Alan B.
Brooke, Garry J.
Clemence, Raymond N.
Cockram, Allan C.
Cooke, Richard E.
Crook, Ian S.
Crooks, Garth A.
Culverhouse, Ian B.
Dick, Alistair J.
Falco, Mark P.
Galvin, Anthony
Hazard, Michael
Hoddle, Glenn
Hughton, Christopher W.G.
Mabbutt, Gary V.
Miller, Paul R.
O'Reilly, Gary M.
Parks, Anthony
Perryman, Steven J.
Roberts, Graham P.
Stevens, Gary A.
Thomas, Daniel
Webster, Simon P.

League Appearances: Archibald, S. 31(1); Ardiles, O.C. 8(1); Bowen, M.R. 6(1); Brace, R.L. (1); Brazil, A.B. 17(2); Brooke, G.J. 7(5); Clemence, R.N. 26; Cockram, A.C. 2; Cooke, R.E. 9; Crook, I.S. 3; Crooks, G.A. 6(4); Culverhouse, I.B. 1(1); Dick, A.J. 10(1); Falco, M.P. 32(4); Galvin, A. 30; Hazard, M. 9(2); Hoddle, G. 24; Hughton, C.W.G. 34; Mabbutt, G.V. 21; Miller, P.R. 20(1); O'Reilly, G.M. 9(3); Parks, A. 16; Perryman, S.J. 41; Price, P.T. 1(1); Roberts, G.P. 35; Stevens, G.A. 37(3); Thomas, D.J. 26;(1); Webster, S.P. 1.
Goals – League (64): Archibald 21, Falco 13 (1 pen), Roberts 6 (1 pen), Hoddle 4 (3 pens), Stevens 4, Brazil 3 (1 pen), Hughton 3, Dick 2, Hazard 2, Mabbutt 2, Cook 1, Crooks 1, Galvin 1, Perryman 1
Milk Cup (5): Archibald 1, Falco 1, Galvin 1, Hoddle 1 (pen), own goal 1.
FA Cup (3): Archibald 1, Falco 1, Roberts 1.
Ground: White Hart Lane, 748 High Road, Tottenham, N17 0AP (01-801-3411)
Nearest stations: White Hart Lane (ER), Northumberland Park (ER) or Seven Sisters (Victoria line) thence by bus
Manager: Peter Shreeves **Secretary:** P. Day
Colours: White shirts, navy blue shorts
Record home gate: 75,038 v Sunderland, March 1938 (FA Cup)
Honours – Champions: Division 1: 1950-51, 1960-61; Division 2: 1919-20, 1949-50
FA Cup winners: 1900-01, 1920-21, 1960-61, 1961-62, 1966-67, 1980-81
League Cup winners: 1970-71, 1972-73, 1981-82
European Cup-Winners' Cup winners: 1962-63
UEFA Cup winners: 1971-72,1983-84

TRANMERE ROVERS DIV. 4

Adkins, Nigel H.
Aspinall, John J.
Burgess, David J.
Davies, William D.
Ferguson, Mark
Goodlass, Ronald
Higgins, David N.
Hilditch, Mark
Hutchinson, Robert
Mungall, Steven H.
Palios, Markos
Philpotts, David R.
Powell, Neville D.
Williams, Gary
Williams, William J.
Woods, Raymond G.

League Appearances: Adkins, N.H. 4; Allen, M.S. 6(4); Aspinall, J.J. 40; Brown, O.J. 15(6); Burgess, D.J. 44; Davies, W.D. 42; Ferguson, M. 21(6); Goodlass, R. 18(2); Greenwood, R.T. 3; Hamilton, B. 6(5); Higgins, D.A. 20; Hilditch, M. 39; Hutchinson, R. 21; Mathias, R. 6(1); Mungall, S.H. 25(1); McMahon, J. 39(1); Palios, M. 25(1); Parry, L.I. 9; Philpotts, D.R. 34; Powell, N.D. 22(3); Wellings, B. 9; Williams, G. 37; Williams, W.J. 18(2); Woods, R.G. 3(3).
Goals – League (53): Aspinall 14 (1 pen), Hilditch 8, Philpotts 6 (2 pens), Ferguson 4, Hutchinson 4, Palios 4, G. Williams 3, Woods 2, Brown 1, Mathias 1, Powell 1, J. Williams 1, own goals 4.
Milk Cup (0).
FA Cup (3): Allen 1, Aspinall 1, Powell 1.
Ground: Prenton Park, Birkenhead, Merseyside, L42 9PN (051-608 3677/4194)
Nearest station: Central Station Birkenhead, Rock Ferry.
Manager: Bryan Hamilton **General Manager/Secretary:** J. Butterfield
Colours: Royal blue shirts with white trim; white shorts
Record home gate: 24,424 v Stoke, February 1972 (FA Cup)
Honours – Champions: Division 3 North: 1937-38

WALSALL — DIV. 3

Bamber, John D.
Brazier, Colin J.
Caswell, Brian L.
Childs, Gary P.C.
Green, Ronald R.
Handysides, Ian R.
Hart, Peter O.
Hawker, Phillip N.
Jones, Paul A.
Kelly, David T.
Mower, Kenneth M.
O'Kelly, Richard F.
Preece, David W.
Rees, Mark
Shakespeare, Craig R.

League Appearances: Bamber, J.D. 9(1); Bates, M. 2; Brazier, C. J. 45; Brown, A. 37(1); Buckley, A. P. 4(9); Caswell,B. L. 32; Childs, G.P.C. 27(3); Godden, A.L. 12; Green, R.R. 9; Handysides, I.R. 17(1); Hart, P.O. 45; Hawker, P.N. 11; Jones, P.A. 2(2); Kearns, M. 10; Kelly, D.T. 5(1); Mower, K.M. 44; O'Kelly, R.F. 39(1); Preece, D.W. 41; Rees, M. 29(4); Shakespeare, G.R. 46; Sinnott, L. 4; Summerfield, K.21(12);.
Goals – League (68): Brown 13 (4 pens), O'Kelly 12 (1 pen), Summerfield 8, Rees 6, Shakespeare 6, Handysides 4, Bamber 3, Hart 3, Kelly 3, Preece 3, Brazier 2, Buckley 2, Childs 2, Mower 1.
Milk Cup (17): Rees 5, Preece 3, Brown 2, O'Kelly 2, Summerfield 2, Buckley 1 (pen), Childs 1, own goal 1.
FA Cup (0).
Ground: Fellows Park, Walsall WS2 9DB (0922-22791)
Nearest station: Walsall or Bescott (15 min walk–no public transport)
Manager: Alan Buckley **Secretary:** H. J. Westmancoat, F.A.A.I.
Colours: Shirts: red; shorts: white
Record home gate: 25,453 v Newcastle, August 1961 (League)
Honours–Champions: Division 4: 1959-60

WATFORD DIV. 1

Atkinson, Paul G.
Bardsley, David J.
Barnes, John C.B.
Callaghan, Nigel
Franklin, Paul L.
Gibbs, Nigel J.
Gilligan, James M.
Jackett, Kenneth F.
Jobson, Richard
Johnston, Maurice
Lohman, Johaanas H.P.
Paris, Alan D.
Porter, Gary
Price, Neil
Reilly, George G.
Rice, Patrick J.
Richardson, Ian P.
Rostron, John W.
Sherwood, Stephen
Sims, Steven F.
Sinnott, Lee
Steele, Eric G.
Sterling, Worrell R.
Taylor, Leslie
Terry, Steve G.
Williams, Derick H.

League Appearances: Atkinson, P.G. 8(3); Bardsley, D.J. 25; Barnes, J.C.B. 39; Bolton, I.R. 7(1); Callaghan, N. 41; Franklin, P.L. 24; Gibbs, N.J. 2(1); Gilligan, J.M. 9(3); Jackett, K.F. 31; Jobson, R.I. 11(2); Johnson, D.N. 2; Jonston, M. 28(1); Lohman, J.H.P. 7; Palmer, C.A. 10; Patching, M. 1; Porter, G. 1(1); Price, N. 7(1); Reilly, G.G. 27; Rice, P.J. 6; Richardson, I.P. 4(3); Rostron, J.W. 39; Sherwood, S. 40; Sims, S.F. 22; Sinnott, L. 19(1); Steele, E.G. 2; Sterling, W.R. 7(3); Taylor, L. 26(1); Terry, S.G. 17.
Goals – League (68): Johnston 20, Barnes 11, Callaghan 10 (1 pen), Reilly 8, Gilligan 4, Rostron 4, Jobson 2, Lohman 2, Richardson 2, Jackett 1, Palmer 1, Sherwood 1, Sterling 1, Terry 1.
Milk Cup (3): Barnes 1, Gilligan 1, Sims 1.
FA Cup (15): Barnes 4, Johnston 4 (1 pen), Reilly 4, Callaghan 1, Jackett 1, Taylor 1.
Ground: Vicarage Road Stadium, Watford WD1 8ER (0923 30933)
Nearest station: Watford Junction or Watford High Street
Manager: Graham Taylor **Secretary:** E. Plumley, F.A.A.I.
Colours: Yellow shirts with black/red trim, red shorts
Record home gate: 34,099 v Manchester United, February 1969 (FA Cup)
Honours—Champions: Division 3: 1968-69; Division 4: 1977-78

WEST BROMWICH ALBION DIV. 1

Barron, Paul G.
Bennett, Martyn
Cowdrill, Barry J.
Cross, Nicholas J.R.
Eastoe, Peter R.
Ebanks, Michael W.A.
Forsyth, Michael E.
Godden, Anthony L.
Grealish, Anthony P.
Hunt, Stephen K.
Leonard, Gary A.
Lewis, Michael
Luke, Noel E.
McNaught, Kenneth
MacKenzie, Stephen
Morley, William A.
Owen, Gary A.
Perry, Michael A.
Regis, Cyrille
Robertson, Alistair
Robson, Gary
Statham, Derek
Thompson, Garry L.
Whitehead, Clive R.

League Appearances: Barron, P.G. 42; Bennett, M. 29; Childs, G.P.C. (1); Cowdrill, B.J. 22; Cross, N.J.R. 16(9); Ebanks, M.W.A. 6(1); Forsyth, M.E. 8; Grealish, A.P. 11; Hunt, S.K. 12; Jol, M. 15(1); Kent, K.J. 1(1); Lewis, M. 14; Luke, N.E. 8; Monaghan, D.J. 2(1); Morley, W.A. 26; MacKenzie, S. 18(1); McNaught, K. 42;

Owen, G.A. 20; Perry, M.A. 8(5); Regis, C. 30; Robertson, A. 6; Robson, G. 5(2); Statham, D. 16; Thompson, G.L. 37; Webb, A.R. 5; Whitehead, C.R. 34; Zondervan, R. 29.
Goals – League (48): Thompson 13 (1 pen), Regis 10, MacKenzie 4, Morley 4, Perry 4, Cross 3, Zondervan 3, Hunt 2, Luke 1, McNaught 1, Monaghan 1, Owen 1, Whitehead 1.
Milk Cup (7): Regis 3, Thompson 3, Owen 1 (pen).
FA Cup (4): Morley 2, Luke 1, Thompson 1.
Ground: The Hawthorns, West Bromwich B7 4LF (021-533 8888)
Nearest station: Smethwick Rolfe Street or Birmingham New Street
Manager: Johnny Giles **Secretary:** Tony Rance
Colours: Navy blue and white striped shirts; white shorts
Record home gate: 64,815 v Arsenal, March 1937 (FA Cup)
Honours–Champions: Division 1: 1919-20; Division 2: 1901-02, 1910-11
FA Cup winners: 1887-88, 1891-92, 1930-31, 1953-54, 1967-68
League Cup winners: 1965-66

WEST HAM UNITED — DIV. 1

Allen, Paul K.
Ampofo, Christopher J.K.
Barnes, David O.
Bonds, William A.
Brush, Paul
Campbell, Gregory R.
Cottee, Antony R.
Devonshire, Alan E.
Dickens, Alan W.
Donald, Warren R.
Goddard, Paul
Hilton, Paul
Keen, Kevin I.
Lampard, Frank R.G.
McAlister, Thomas G.
McGiven, Michael
McPherson, Keith A.
Martin, Alvin E.
Matthews, David
Orr, Neil I.
Parkes, Philip B.F.
Parris, George
Pike, Geoffrey A.
Potts, Steven J.
Skinner, Andrew J.
Stewart, Raymond S.M.
Swindlehurst, David
Vaughan, John
Walford, Stephen J.
Whitton, Stephen P.

League Appearances: Allen, P.K. 19; Barnes, D.O. 11(2); Bonds, W.A. 27; Brooking, T.D. 35; Brush, P. 10; Cottee, A.R. 37(2); Devonshire, A.E. 22; Dickens, A.W. 7(3); Donald, W.R. 1(1); Goddard, P. 3(2); Hilton, P. 7(1); Lampard, F.R.G. 17(1); Martin, A.E. 29; Orr, N.I. 28(1); Parkes, P.B.F. 42; Pike, G.A. 27(1); Stewart, R.S. 42; Swindlehurst, D. 35(1); Walford, S.J. 41; Whitton, S.P. 22.
Goals – League (60): Cottee 15, Swindlehurst 13, Stewart 7 (6 pens), Whitton 5, Brooking 4, Martin 3, Barnes 2, Hilton 2, Pike 2, Walford 2, Devonshire 1, Goddard 1, own goals 3.
Milk Cup (15): Cottee 4, Brooking 3, Devonshire 2, Goddard 1, Martin 1, Orr 1, Pike 1, Stewart 1 (pen), Swindlehurst 1.
FA Cup (4): Barnes 1, Stewart 1 (pen), Swindlehurst 1, own goal 1.
Ground: Boleyn Ground, Green Street, Upton Park, E13 9AZ (01-472 2740)
Nearest station: Upton Park (District line)
Manager: John Lyall **Secretary:** Eddie Chapman F.A.A.I.
Colours: Claret shirts with blue sleeves; white shorts
Record home gate: 42,322 v Tottenham, October 1970 (League)
Honours – Champions: Division 2: 1957-58, 1980-81
FA Cup winners: 1963-64, 1974-75, 1979-80
European Cup-winners' Cup winners: 1964-65

WIGAN ATHLETIC — DIV. 3

Aspinall, Wayne	Comstive, Paul T.	Lowe, David A.
Bailey, Neil	Cribley, Alexander	Methven, Colin J.
Barrow, Graham	Johnson, Stephen A.	Newell, Michael C.
Bruce, Alexander R.	Kelly, Anthony G.	Tunks, Roy W.
Butler, John E.	Langley, Kevin J.	Walsh, Steven

League Appearances: Aspinall, W. 7; Bailey, N 16(7); Barrow, G. 42; Bruce, A.R. 32(4); Butler, J.E. 41; Comstive, P.T. 29; Cribley, A. 44; Houghton, P. 5(1); Johnson, S.A. 21; Kelly, A.G. 27(2); Kilner, J.I. 4; Langley, K.J. 44; Lowe, D.A. 37(3); Methven, C.J. 39; Newell, M.C. 5(4); Schofield, M.A. (1); Taylor, S.J. 29(1); Tunks, R.W. 42; Walsh, S. 42; Williams, P.J. (1).

Goals–League: (46): Lowe 8, Bruce 7, Johnson 7, Taylor 7(3 pens), Barrow 5, Butler 3, Comstive 2, Kelly 2, Bailey 1, Cribley 1, Houghton 1, Langley 1, Walsh 1.

Milk Cup (1): Methven 1.

FA Cup (5): Taylor 3 (1 pen), Bruce 2.

Ground: Springfield Park, Wigan, WNT 7BAS (0942 44433)

Nearest stations: Wigan Wallgate and Wigan North West

Manager: H. McNally **Secretary:** J. A. Bennett.

Colours: Blue shirts; blue shorts

Record home gate: 27,500 v Hereford United, December 1953 (FA Cup)

Honours – Champions: Northern Premier League 1970-71, 1974-75

Northern Premier League Cup: 1972

WIMBLEDON — DIV. 2

Beasant, David	Fishenden, Paul	Ketteridge, Stephen J.
Cork, Alan G.	Gage, Kevin W.	Morris, Mark J.
Downes, Walter J.	Galliers, Steven	Smith, Michael
Driver, Philip A.	Hatter, Stephen J.	Winterburn, Nigel
Evans, Stewart J.	Hodges, Glyn P.	

League Appearances: Beasant, D. 46; Cork, A.G. 41(1); Dibble, C. (1); Downes, W.J. 32; Driver, P.A. (2); Evans, S. 44(1); Fishenden, P. 12(11); Gage, K.W. 14(10); Galliers, S. 36; Hatter, S.J. 39(1); Hodges, G.P 39(3); Ketteridge, S.J. 43; Morris, M.J. 39; Peters, G.D. 37; Sayer, A.C. 2; Shanks, D. 1; Smith, M. 23(1); Thomas, D. 15; Thompson, K.A. (3); Winterburn, N. 43.

Goals – League (97): Cork 29, (1 pen), Hodges 15, Evans 12, Fishenden 8, Ketteridge 7, Downes 5, Gage 4, Morris 3, Peters 3, Smith 3, Thomas 3, Hatter 2 (1 pen) Galliers 1, Winterburn 1, own goals 1.

Milk Cup (12): Hodges 3, Cork 2, Evans 2, Galliers 2, Ketteridge 2, Fishenden 1.

FA Cup (4): Cork 2, Downes 1, Peters 1.

Ground: Plough Lane Ground, Durnsford Road, Wimbledon, SW19 (01-946-6311)

Nearest stations: Wimbledon or Haydons Road (BR) South Wimbledon (Northern Line)

Manager: Dave Bassett **Secretary:** Adrian Cook

Colours: Shirts blue with yellow trim; shorts blue with yellow trim

Record home gate: 18,000 v HMS Victory, 1934-35 (FA Amateur Cup)
Honours – Champions: Division 4: 1982-83

WOLVERHAMPTON WANDERERS DIV. 2

Buckland, Mark C.
Burridge, John
Butler, Paul J.
Cartwright, Ian J.
Clarke, Wayne
Crainie, Daniel
Dodd, Alan
Dougherty, Paul
Eves, Melvyn J.
Hibbitt, Kenneth
Humphrey, John
Jackson, Joseph G.
Palmer, Geoffrey
Pender, John P.
Towner, Antony J.
Troughton, Samuel E.

League Appearances: Bayly, M.J. 7; Bennett, M. 6; Blair, A. 10; Bradshaw, P.W. 10; Buckland, M.C. 13(2); Burridge, J. 32; Butler, P.J. (3); Cartwright, I.J. 16; Clarke, W. 29(2); Coy, R.A. 5; Crainie, D. 27(1); Daniel, P.W. 19; Dodd, A. 41; Daughty, P. 5; Eves, M.J. 14(1); Gray, A.M. 9; Hibbitt, K. 19(4); Humphrey, J. 28; Jackson, J.G. 1; Kellock, W. 3; Livingstone, W. 11(2); Mardenborough, S.A. 9; Matthews, M. 2(1); McGarvey, S.T. 13; Palmer, G. 27(3); Pender, J.P. 34; Rodger, G. 1; Rudge, D.A. 15(4); Smith, G.M. 11; Towner, A.J. 25(6); Troughton, S. E. 17; Watkiss, S.P. 2; Wintersgill, D. 1(1).
Goals – League (27): Clarke 6 (1 pen), Crainie 3, Eves 3, Gray 2, McGarvey 2, Towner 2, Troughton 2, Livingstone 1, Mardenborough 1, Palmer 1 (pen), Pender 1, Smith 1, own goals 2.
Milk Cup (2): Clarke 2.
FA Cup (2): Clarke 1, Eves 1.
Ground: Molineux Grounds, Wolverhampton WV1 4QR (0902 712181)
Nearest station: Wolverhampton
Manager: Tommy Docherty **Secretary:** P. G. Redfern
Colours: Old gold shirts with black trim; black shorts
Record home gate: 61,315 v Liverpool, February 1939 (FA Cup)
Honours – Champions: Division 1: 1953-54, 1957-58, 1958-59; Division 2: 1931-32, 1976-77; Division 3 North: 1923-24
FA Cup winners: 1892-93, 1907-08, 1948-49, 1959-60
League Cup winners: 1973-74, 1979-80

WREXHAM DIV. 4

Cunnington, Shaun G.
Edwards, Andrew J.
Gregory, David H.
Hunt, Simon
Keay, John P.
King, John
Muldoon, John P.
Parker, Stuart E.
Salathiel, David N.
Steel, William J.
Wright, Stephen P.

League Appearances: Arkwright, I. 28(1); Baker, D.S. 8(1); Buxton, S.C. 18(2); Coleman, P. 17; Cunnington, S.G. 42; Edwards, A.J. 22(7); Evans, M.J. 7(3); Gregory, D.H. 43(1); Heath, S.M.J.P. 32; Hunt, S. 42(2); Jones, S.W. 4; Keay, J.P. 38; King, J. 44; Millington, G.R. 13; Muldoon, J.P. 25(7); Parker, S.K. 9; Salathiel, D.N. 29; Sinclair, R.M. 11; Steel, W.J. 21; Sturridge, M.A. 3(1); Wardle, R.I. 13; Wright, S.P. 37.

Goals – League (59): Gregory 19 (4 pens), Hunt 8, Edwards 7, Arkwright 4, King 4, Muldoon 4, Buxton 3, Keay 3, Coleman 2, Heath 1, Hume 1, Jones 1, own goals 2.
Milk Cup (2): Evans 1, King 1.
FA Cup (1): Coleman 1.
Ground: The Racecourse, Mold Road, Wrexham LL1 2AN (0978 262129)
Nearest station: Wrexham General
Manager: Bobby Roberts **Secretary:** Miss M. Pike
Colours: Red shirts with white trimmings; white shorts with red trim
Record home gate: 34,445 v Manchester United, January 1957 (FA Cup)
Honours – Champions: Division 3: 1977-78

YORK CITY — DIV. 3

Astbury, Michael J.
Byrne, John F.
Chippendale, Brian A.
Crosby, Malcolm
Evans, Christopher B.
Ford, Gary
Haslegrave, Sean M.
Hay, Alan B.
Hood, Derek
Houchen, Keith M.
Jones, Roger
McPhail, John
Pearce, Alan
Sbragia, Richard
Senior, Stephen
Walwyn, Keith I.

League Appearances: Astbury, M.J. 5; Busby, V. (3); Byrne, J.F. 46; Chippendale, B.A. (4); Crosby, M. 31; Evans, C.B. 16(3); Ford, G. 46; Haslegrave, S.M. 24(2); Hay, A.B. 42; Hood, D. 33(1); Houchen, K.M. 1(6); Jones, R. 41; McPhail, J. 46, Pearce, A. 17(1); Pollard, B.E. 29(1); Sbragia, R. 45; Senior, S. 39; Walwyn, K.I. 45.
Goals – League (96): Byrne 27, Walwyn 25, Ford 11, McPhail 10, Pollard 6 (3 pens), Pearce 5, Hood 4 (1 pen), Sbragia 4, Hay 1, Houchen 1, Senior 1, own goal 1.
Milk Cup (2): Ford 1, Pollard 1.
FA Cup (2): Byrne 1, Sbragia 1.
Ground: Bootham Crescent, York YO3 7AQ (0904 24447)
Nearest station: York
Manager: Denis Smith **Secretary:** T.D.Hughes
Colours: Shirts: red with white trim; shorts navy
Record home gate: 28,123 v Huddersfield, March 1938 (FA Cup)
Honours – Champions: Division 4: 1983-84

THE LEAGUE – DIVISION I

HOME TEAM	Arsenal	Aston Villa	Birmingham C.	Coventry C.	Everton	Ipswich T.	Leicester C.	Liverpool
Arsenal	—	1–1	1–1	0–1	2–1	4–1	2–1	0–2
Aston Villa	2–6	—	1–0	2–0	0–2	4–0	3–1	1–3
Birmingham C.	1–1	2–1	—	1–2	0–2	1–0	2–1	0–0
Coventry C.	1–4	3–3	0–1	—	1–1	1–2	2–1	4–0
Everton	0–0	1–1	1–1	0–0	—	1–0	1–1	1–1
Ipswich T	1–0	2–1	1–2	3–1	3–0	—	0–0	1–1
Leicester C.	3–0	2–0	2–3	1–1	2–0	2–0	—	3–3
Liverpool	2–1	2–1	1–0	5–0	3–0	2–2	2–2	—
Luton T.	1–2	1–0	1–1	2–4	0–3	2–1	0–0	0–0
Manchester U.	4–0	1–2	1–0	4–1	0–1	1–2	2–0	1–0
Norwich C.	1–1	3–1	1–1	0–0	1–1	0–0	3–1	0–1
Nottingham F.	0–1	2–2	5–1	3–0	1–0	2–1	3–2	0–1
Notts Co.	0–4	5–2	2–1	2–1	0–1	0–2	2–5	0–0
Q.P.R.	2–0	2–1	2–1	2–1	2–0	1–0	2–0	0–1
Southampton	1–0	2–2	2–1	8–2	3–1	3–2	2–2	2–0
Stoke C.	1–0	1–0	2–1	1–3	1–1	1–0	0–1	2–0
Sunderland	2–2	0–1	2–1	1–0	2–1	1–1	1–1	0–0
Tottenham H.	2–4	2–1	0–1	1–1	1–2	2–0	3–2	2–2
Watford	2–1	3–2	1–0	2–3	4–4	2–2	3–3	0–2
W.B.A.	1–3	3–1	1–2	1–1	1–1	2–1	1–0	1–2
West Ham U.	3–1	0–1	4–0	5–2	0–1	2–1	3–1	1–3
Wolverhampton W.	1–2	1–1	1–1	0–0	3–0	0–3	1–0	1–1

1983-84 RESULTS

Luton T.	Manchester U.	Norwich C.	Nottingham F.	Notts Co.	Q.P.R.	Southampton	Stoke C.	Sunderland	Tottenham H.	Watford	W.B.A.	West Ham U.	Wolverhampton W.
2–1	2–3	3–0	4–1	1–1	0–2	2–2	3–1	1–2	3–2	3–1	0–1	3–3	4–1
0–0	0–3	1–0	1–0	3–1	2–1	1–0	1–1	1–0	0–0	2–1	4–3	1–0	4–0
1–1	2–2	0–1	1–2	0–0	0–2	0–0	1–0	0–1	0–1	2–0	2–1	3–0	0–0
2–2	1–1	2–1	2–1	2–1	1–0	0–0	2–3	2–1	2–4	1–2	1–2	1–2	2–1
0–1	1–1	0–2	1–0	4–1	3–1	1–0	1–0	0–0	2–1	1–0	0–0	0–1	2–0
3–0	0–2	2–0	2–2	1–0	0–2	0–3	5–0	1–0	3–1	0–0	3–4	0–3	3–1
0–3	1–1	2–1	2–1	0–4	2–1	2–1	2–2	0–2	0–3	4–1	1–1	4–1	5–1
6–0	1–1	1–1	1–0	5–0	2–0	1–1	1–0	0–1	3–1	3–0	3–0	6–0	0–1
—	0–5	2–2	2–3	3–2	0–0	3–1	0–1	4–1	2–4	1–2	2–0	0–1	4–0
2–0	—	0–0	1–2	3–3	3–1	3–2	1–0	2–1	4–2	4–1	3–0	0–0	3–0
0–0	3–3	—	2–3	0–1	0–3	1–0	2–2	3–0	2–1	6–1	2–0	1–0	3–0
1–0	2–0	3–0	—	3–1	3–2	0–1	0–0	1–1	2–2	5–1	3–1	3–0	5–0
0–3	1–0	1–1	0–0	—	0–3	1–3	1–1	6–1	0–0	3–5	1–1	2–2	4–0
0–1	1–1	2–0	0–1	1–0	—	4–0	6–0	3–0	2–1	1–1	1–1	1–1	2–1
2–1	3–0	2–1	0–1	0–2	0–0	—	3–1	1–1	5–0	1–0	1–0	2–0	1–0
2–4	0–1	2–0	1–1	1–0	1–2	1–1	—	2–1	1–1	0–4	3–1	3–1	4–0
2–0	0–1	1–1	1–1	0–0	1–0	0–2	2–2	—	1–1	3–0	3–0	0–1	3–2
2–1	1–1	2–0	2–1	1–0	3–2	0–0	1–0	3–0	—	2–3	0–1	0–2	1–0
1–2	0–0	1–3	3–2	3–1	1–0	1–1	2–0	2–1	2–3	—	3–1	0–0	0–0
3–0	2–0	0–0	0–5	2–0	1–2	0–2	3–0	3–1	1–1	2–0	—	1–0	1–3
3–1	1–1	0–0	1–2	3–0	2–2	0–1	3–0	0–1	4–1	2–4	1–0	—	1–1
1–2	1–1	2–0	1–0	0–1	0–4	0–1	0–0	0–0	2–3	0–5	0–0	0–3	—

THE LEAGUE – DIVISION II

HOME TEAM	Barnsley	Blackburn R.	Brighton & H. A.	Cambridge U.	Cardiff C.	Carlisle U.	Charlton Ath.	Chelsea	Crystal Palace	Derby Co.
Barnsley	—	0–0	3–1	2–0	2–3	2–1	2–0	0–0	1–1	5–1
Blackburn R.	1–1	—	2–2	1–0	1–1	4–1	1–1	0–0	2–1	5–1
Brighton & H. A.	1–0	1–1	—	3–0	3–1	1–1	7–0	1–2	3–1	1–0
Cambridge U.	0–3	2–0	3–4	—	0–2	0–2	2–2	0–1	1–3	0–1
Cardiff C.	0–3	0–1	2–2	5–0	—	2–0	2–1	3–3	0–2	1–0
Carlisle U.	4–2	0–1	1–2	0–0	1–1	—	3–0	0–0	2–2	2–1
Charlton Ath.	3–2	2–0	2–0	5–2	2–0	1–0	—	1–1	1–0	1–0
Chelsea	3–1	2–1	1–0	2–1	2–0	0–0	3–2	—	2–2	5–0
Crystal Palace	0–1	0–2	0–2	1–1	1–0	1–2	2–0	0–1	—	0–1
Derby Co.	0–2	1–1	0–3	1–0	2–3	1–4	0–1	1–2	3–0	—
Fulham	1–0	0–1	3–1	1–0	0–2	0–0	0–1	3–5	1–1	2–2
Grimsby T.	1–0	3–2	5–0	0–0	1–0	1–1	2–1	0–1	2–0	2–1
Huddersfield T.	0–1	0–2	0–1	3–0	4–0	0–0	0–0	2–3	2–1	3–0
Leeds U.	1–2	1–0	3–2	3–1	1–0	3–0	1–0	1–1	1–1	0–0
Manchester C.	3–2	6–0	4–0	5–0	2–1	3–1	0–1	0–2	3–1	1–1
Middlesbrough	2–1	1–2	0–0	1–1	2–0	0–1	1–0	2–1	1–3	0–0
Newcastle U.	1–0	1–1	3–1	2–1	3–1	5–1	2–1	1–1	3–1	4–0
Oldham Ath.	1–0	0–0	1–0	0–0	2–1	2–3	0–0	1–1	3–2	3–0
Portsmouth	2–1	2–4	5–1	5–0	1–1	0–1	4–0	2–2	0–1	3–0
Sheffield W.	2–0	4–2	2–1	1–0	5–2	2–0	4–1	2–1	1–0	3–1
Shrewsbury T.	3–2	1–0	2–1	1–0	1–0	0–0	1–1	2–4	1–1	3–0
Swansea C.	1–0	0–1	1–3	2–1	3–2	0–0	1–0	1–3	1–0	2–0

1983-84 RESULTS

Fulham	Grimsby T.	Huddersfield T.	Leeds U.	Manchester C.	Middlesborough	Newcastle U.	Oldham Ath.	Portsmouth	Sheffield W.	Shrewsbury T.	Swansea C.
3–0	3–1	2–2	0–2	1–1	0–2	1–1	0–1	0–3	0–1	3–0	3–2
0–1	1–1	2–2	1–1	2–1	1–0	1–1	3–1	2–1	0–0	1–1	4–1
1–1	2–0	3–1	3–0	1–1	3–0	0–1	4–0	0–1	1–3	2–2	1–1
1–1	2–2	0–3	2–2	0–0	0–0	1–0	2–1	1–3	1–2	1–0	1–1
0–4	3–1	3–1	0–1	2–1	2–1	0–2	2–0	0–0	0–2	2–0	3–2
2–0	1–1	0–0	1–0	2–0	1–1	3–1	2–0	0–0	1–1	1–0	2–0
3–4	3–3	1–2	2–0	1–0	2–0	1–3	2–1	2–1	1–1	2–4	2–2
4–0	2–3	3–1	5–0	0–1	0–0	4–0	3–0	2–2	3–2	3–0	6–1
1–1	0–1	0–0	0–0	0–2	1–0	3–1	2–1	2–1	1–0	1–1	2–0
1–0	1–2	1–1	1–1	1–0	1–0	3–2	2–2	2–0	1–1	1–0	2–1
—	1–1	0–2	2–1	5–1	2–1	2–2	3–0	0–2	1–1	3–0	5–0
2–1	—	2–1	2–0	1–1	0–0	1–1	3–0	3–4	1–0	1–1	3–0
2–0	0–0	—	2–2	1–3	2–2	2–2	0–1	2–1	0–1	1–0	1–0
1–0	2–1	1–2	—	1–2	4–1	0–1	2–0	2–1	1–1	3–0	1–0
0–0	2–1	2–3	1–1	—	2–1	1–2	2–0	2–1	1–2	1–0	2–1
0–2	1–1	0–0	2–2	0–0	—	1–2	3–2	0–0	2–0	4–0	1–0
3–2	0–1	5–2	1–0	5–0	3–1	—	3–0	4–2	0–1	0–1	2–0
3–0	2–1	0–3	3–2	2–2	2–1	1–2	—	3–2	1–3	0–1	3–3
1–4	4–0	1–1	2–3	1–2	0–1	1–4	3–4	—	0–1	4–1	5–0
1–1	1–0	0–0	3–1	0–0	0–2	4–2	3–0	2–0	—	1–1	6–1
0–0	1–2	1–0	5–1	1–3	1–0	2–2	2–0	2–0	2–1	—	2–0
0–3	0–1	2–2	2–2	0–2	2–1	1–2	0–0	1–2	0–1	0–2	—

THE LEAGUE – DIVISION III

HOME TEAM	Bolton W.	Bournemouth	Bradford C.	Brentford	Bristol R.	Burnley	Exeter C.	Gillingham	Hull C.	Lincoln C.
Bolton W.	—	0–1	0–2	1–0	3–0	0–0	1–0	0–1	0–0	0–2
Bournemouth	2–2	—	0–1	0–3	0–1	1–0	3–1	2–0	2–3	3–0
Bradford C.	0–2	5–2	—	1–1	0–1	2–1	1–3	3–2	0–0	0–0
Brentford	3–0	1–1	1–4	—	2–2	0–0	3–0	2–3	1–1	3–0
Bristol R.	1–1	1–3	1–0	3–1	—	2–1	2–0	3–0	1–3	3–1
Burnley	2–2	5–1	1–2	2–2	0–0	—	4–0	2–3	0–2	4–0
Exeter C.	2–2	0–2	0–2	1–2	1–2	1–1	—	0–0	2–1	0–3
Gillingham	2–0	2–1	0–0	4–2	1–2	0–1	3–1	—	1–2	2–0
Hull C.	1–1	3–1	1–0	2–0	0–0	4–1	1–0	0–0	—	2–0
Lincoln C.	0–0	3–0	2–3	2–0	4–0	3–1	1–1	4–0	1–3	—
Millwall	3–0	3–1	0–0	1–2	1–0	2–0	3–0	2–2	1–0	0–2
Newport Co.	2–3	2–1	4–3	1–1	2–1	1–0	1–0	1–0	1–1	1–0
Orient	2–1	2–0	2–0	2–0	0–1	1–2	2–2	1–1	3–1	1–1
Oxford U.	5–0	3–2	2–0	2–1	3–2	2–2	1–1	0–1	1–1	3–0
Plymouth Arg.	2–0	1–0	3–0	1–1	1–1	1–1	2–2	1–1	2–0	2–2
Port Vale	1–2	2–1	1–2	4–3	2–0	2–3	2–2	0–1	1–0	0–1
Preston N. E.	2–1	2–0	1–2	3–3	1–0	4–2	2–1	2–2	0–0	1–2
Rotherham U	1–1	1–0	1–0	4–0	2–2	1–1	1–0	3–0	0–1	1–1
Scunthorpe U.	1–0	1–2	2–1	4–4	2–2	4–0	3–1	2–0	2–0	0–0
Sheffield U.	5–0	2–0	2–0	0–0	4–0	0–0	2–2	4–0	2–2	0–0
Southend U.	0–1	0–0	2–1	6–0	1–2	2–2	0–3	3–1	2–2	2–0
Walsall	1–0	3–1	1–2	1–0	2–1	1–1	4–1	3–1	2–1	0–1
Wigan Ath.	0–1	1–3	0–1	2–1	0–0	1–0	1–1	1–2	1–1	2–0
Wimbledon	4–0	3–2	4–1	2–1	1–1	1–4	2–1	1–3	1–4	3–1

1983-84 RESULTS

Millwall	Newport Co.	Orient	Oxford U.	Plymouth Arg.	Port Vale	Preston N.E.	Rotherham U.	Scunthorpe U.	Sheffield U.	Southend U.	Walsall	Wigan Ath.	Wimbledon
2–0	2–3	3–2	1–0	2–1	2–0	2–2	2–0	0–0	3–1	2–0	8–1	0–1	2–0
1–1	1–1	3–2	2–1	2–1	1–1	0–1	4–2	1–1	0–1	1–0	3–0	0–1	2–3
3–3	1–0	4–1	2–2	2–0	2–2	3–2	1–0	2–2	2–1	1–1	0–0	6–2	5–2
2–2	2–0	1–1	1–2	2–2	3–1	4–1	2–1	3–0	1–3	0–0	1–1	0–1	3–4
3–2	4–0	0–0	1–1	2–0	0–0	3–1	2–0	4–1	1–1	2–1	4–2	2–1	1–1
1–0	2–0	2–3	1–1	2–1	7–0	2–1	2–2	5–0	2–1	3–0	0–2	3–0	0–2
3–2	1–2	3–4	3–1	1–1	1–1	2–1	0–1	1–1	1–2	3–3	0–1	1–1	0–3
3–3	4–1	3–1	2–3	2–1	1–1	2–0	4–2	1–1	4–2	5–1	1–3	3–0	0–1
5–0	0–0	2–1	0–1	1–2	1–0	3–0	5–0	1–0	4–1	2–1	2–2	1–0	1–0
2–2	2–3	2–0	2–2	3–1	3–2	2–1	0–1	2–1	0–2	1–2	2–1	0–1	1–2
—	1–1	4–3	2–1	1–0	3–2	1–0	2–0	2–1	1–2	4–0	2–0	2–0	1–1
1–1	—	0–0	1–1	2–0	2–1	1–1	1–4	1–1	0–2	1–1	3–1	5–3	1–1
5–3	2–2	—	1–2	3–2	3–0	2–1	2–1	1–0	2–0	1–0	0–1	0–0	2–6
4–2	2–0	5–2	—	5–0	2–0	2–0	3–2	1–0	2–2	2–1	6–3	0–0	2–0
0–1	0–1	3–1	2–1	—	3–0	1–0	1–1	4–0	0–1	4–0	3–1	0–0	1–2
1–0	4–2	2–0	1–3	0–1	—	1–1	2–3	0–0	2–0	2–1	0–2	1–1	2–0
0–0	2–0	3–1	1–2	2–1	4–0	—	1–0	1–0	2–2	4–1	0–1	2–3	2–3
1–0	0–1	0–1	1–2	2–0	2–1	0–1	—	3–0	0–1	0–0	0–1	4–1	1–2
0–1	3–3	3–1	0–0	3–0	1–1	1–5	1–2	—	1–1	1–6	0–0	0–0	5–1
2–0	2–0	6–3	1–2	2–0	3–1	1–1	3–0	5–3	—	5–0	2–0	2–2	1–2
3–2	3–1	3–0	0–1	1–1	1–2	1–1	2–2	0–0	3–1	—	0–0	1–0	1–1
1–1	3–2	0–1	0–1	3–2	2–0	2–1	2–2	1–1	1–2	4–0	—	3–0	4–0
0–0	1–0	0–1	0–2	1–1	3–0	1–0	2–1	2–0	3–0	1–0	0–1	—	3–2
4–3	6–0	2–2	3–1	1–0	4–2	2–2	3–1	1–1	3–1	3–2	2–0	2–2	—

THE LEAGUE – DIVISION IV

HOME TEAM	Aldershot	Blackpool	Bristol C.	Bury	Chester C.	Chesterfield	Colchester U.	Crew Alex.	Darlington	Doncaster R.
Aldershot	—	3–2	1–0	1–2	5–2	2–1	5–1	0–0	0–0	2–1
Blackpool	5–1	—	1–0	1–1	3–3	1–0	3–2	3–0	3–1	3–1
Bristol C.	2–1	1–1	—	3–2	4–2	2–0	4–1	2–1	1–0	1–2
Bury	0–3	0–0	2–1	—	2–1	2–0	1–1	1–1	0–3	2–3
Chester C.	1–2	0–2	1–2	2–1	—	0–2	1–4	0–1	2–1	1–0
Chesterfield	3–1	1–1	1–1	1–5	1–1	—	1–1	1–3	1–1	0–0
Colchester U.	4–1	2–1	0–0	1–0	1–0	2–0	—	2–0	2–1	1–1
Crew Alex.	0–0	2–1	2–2	2–1	1–1	2–1	1–1	—	2–1	1–1
Darlington	0–1	2–0	0–1	1–2	2–1	2–1	0–2	2–0	—	1–2
Doncaster R.	3–1	2–1	1–0	3–1	0–0	2–1	3–3	1–0	3–2	—
Halifax T.	1–0	1–0	1–2	0–0	2–2	2–1	4–1	1–0	0–2	1–2
Hartlepool U.	0–1	0–1	2–2	1–3	1–1	2–2	0–0	2–1	2–1	1–0
Hereford U.	2–1	1–2	0–2	1–2	2–1	3–1	1–1	0–1	1–0	0–3
Mansfield T.	5–2	1–1	0–1	1–1	3–1	0–1	0–0	3–3	1–0	1–2
Northampton T.	1–4	1–5	1–0	1–0	2–1	1–1	3–1	2–0	2–0	1–4
Peterborough U.	1–2	4–0	4–1	2–1	1–0	2–0	2–0	1–0	2–2	1–1
Reading	1–0	2–0	2–0	1–1	1–0	1–1	1–0	5–0	1–0	3–2
Rochdale	3–1	1–0	0–1	0–2	1–1	2–4	0–0	1–0	2–0	3–3
Stockport Co.	2–2	1–2	0–0	1–1	2–1	2–0	0–0	2–3	2–0	0–2
Swindon T.	0–2	0–0	1–1	0–0	4–0	1–2	2–1	1–0	1–0	2–1
Torquay U.	0–1	1–0	1–0	2–0	1–0	1–1	2–1	3–1	0–1	4–1
Tranmere R.	3–0	3–2	2–0	1–1	2–2	0–3	2–1	2–3	0–1	1–1
Wrexham	1–1	0–1	3–1	3–0	2–0	4–2	0–2	0–1	1–1	1–2
York C.	2–0	4–0	1–1	3–0	4–1	1–0	3–0	5–2	2–0	1–1

1983-84 RESULTS

Halifax T.	Hartlepool U.	Hereford U.	Mansfield T.	Northampton T.	Peterborough U.	Reading	Rochdale	Stockport Co.	Swindon T.	Torquay U.	Tranmere R.	Wrexham	York C.
5–2	2–1	1–4	7–1	1–0	3–2	0–0	2–1	1–1	2–1	3–1	1–1	1–1	1–4
4–0	1–0	3–1	2–0	2–3	1–2	1–0	0–2	1–1	1–1	1–0	0–1	4–0	3–0
3–0	2–0	1–0	4–0	4–1	0–1	3–1	1–1	3–1	1–0	5–0	1–1	1–1	1–0
3–0	3–0	1–4	2–2	1–2	2–2	2–3	3–1	2–1	2–1	0–0	0–0	2–0	1–3
1–1	4–1	0–1	0–4	1–1	1–1	2–1	1–0	2–4	0–3	1–2	0–0	1–0	1–1
0–0	4–1	0–0	0–0	2–1	1–0	2–1	3–0	2–0	1–0	3–2	3–3	1–1	2–1
4–1	6–0	3–0	1–0	2–2	1–1	3–0	4–0	1–1	0–0	3–0	0–1	1–1	1–3
6–1	2–0	1–1	1–3	3–2	0–1	1–1	0–1	0–3	2–0	2–1	3–0	1–1	0–3
3–2	2–0	0–0	3–0	5–3	1–0	1–1	1–0	1–0	1–0	0–1	1–0	2–2	0–0
3–2	0–1	3–0	3–1	1–0	1–1	2–3	3–0	2–1	3–0	1–1	1–1	3–0	2–2
—	3–2	2–1	0–0	2–2	2–1	0–1	5–0	2–0	2–1	2–2	1–2	1–1	1–2
3–0	—	0–0	4–1	2–0	1–1	3–3	1–2	1–2	0–1	2–1	0–1	1–1	2–3
0–0	5–0	—	0–0	0–0	2–1	1–1	2–1	2–0	2–1	1–1	0–1	3–0	2–1
7–1	5–0	1–1	—	3–1	0–0	2–0	3–0	1–2	2–2	1–3	1–0	3–4	0–1
1–1	1–1	0–3	2–1	—	2–1	2–2	1–1	0–0	2–0	2–1	0–0	3–3	1–2
4–0	3–1	1–1	3–0	6–0	—	3–3	2–0	2–0	1–1	5–0	2–0	0–1	0–2
1–0	5–1	3–1	4–0	3–0	1–1	—	0–0	6–2	2–2	2–2	1–0	4–1	1–0
1–1	2–0	3–3	0–0	1–1	2–1	4–1	—	2–2	3–3	1–0	2–3	1–2	0–2
4–0	1–0	1–0	0–4	1–0	4–1	3–0	2–1	—	1–3	2–1	2–1	1–1	0–2
2–3	3–2	3–0	1–1	0–0	2–0	1–1	2–1	2–1	—	2–3	1–1	0–1	3–2
1–1	0–0	1–1	1–0	2–1	1–0	2–2	4–2	1–1	1–0	—	1–1	1–0	1–3
3–2	0–1	0–1	1–0	1–0	0–0	2–3	2–2	1–0	2–1	3–0	—	2–1	0–1
1–0	1–4	0–0	2–3	0–1	2–2	0–3	5–1	1–2	0–3	2–2	5–1	—	0–0
4–1	2–0	4–0	2–1	3–0	2–0	2–2	2–0	3–1	2–0	2–3	1–1	3–2	—

FOOTBALL LEAGUE

FINAL TABLES 1983-84

First Division		Home			Goals		Away			Goals			
	P	*W*	*D*	*L*	*F*	*A*	*W*	*D*	*L*	*F*	*A*	*Pt*	*Dif*
Liverpool	42	14	5	2	50	12	8	9	4	23	20	80	41
Southampton	42	15	4	2	44	17	7	7	7	22	21	77	28
Nottingham F.	42	14	4	3	47	17	8	4	9	29	28	74	31
Manchester U.	42	14	3	4	43	18	6	11	4	28	23	74	30
QPR	42	14	4	3	37	12	8	3	10	30	25	73	30
Arsenal	42	10	5	6	41	29	8	4	9	33	31	63	14
Everton	42	9	9	3	21	12	7	5	9	23	30	62	2
Tottenham H.	42	11	4	6	31	24	6	6	9	33	41	61	−1
West Ham U.	42	10	4	7	39	24	7	5	9	21	31	60	5
Aston Villa	42	14	3	4	34	22	3	6	12	25	39	60	−2
Watford	42	9	7	5	36	31	7	2	12	32	46	57	−9
Ipswich T.	42	11	4	6	34	23	4	4	13	21	34	53	−2
Sunderland	42	8	9	4	26	18	5	4	12	16	35	52	−11
Norwich C.	42	9	8	4	34	20	3	7	11	14	29	51	−1
Leicester C.	42	11	5	5	40	30	2	7	12	25	38	51	−3
Luton T.	42	7	5	9	30	33	7	4	10	23	33	51	−13
WBA	42	10	4	7	30	25	4	5	12	18	37	51	−14
Stoke C.	42	11	4	6	30	23	2	7	12	14	40	50	−19
Coventry C.	42	8	5	8	33	33	5	6	10	24	44	50	−20
Birmingham C.	42	7	7	7	19	18	5	5	11	20	32	48	−11
Notts Co	42	6	7	8	31	36	4	4	13	19	36	41	−22
Wolverhampton W.	42	4	8	9	15	28	2	3	16	12	52	29	−53

Second Division		Home			Goals		Away			Goals			
	P	*W*	*D*	*L*	*F*	*A*	*W*	*D*	*L*	*F*	*A*	*Pt*	*Dif*
Chelsea	42	15	4	2	55	17	10	9	2	35	23	88	50
Sheffield W.	42	16	4	1	47	16	10	6	5	25	18	88	38
Newcastle U.	42	16	2	3	51	18	8	6	7	34	35	80	32
Manchester C.	42	13	3	5	43	21	7	7	7	23	27	70	18
Grimsby T.	42	13	6	2	36	15	6	7	8	24	32	70	13
Blackburn R.	42	9	11	1	35	19	8	5	8	22	27	67	11
Carlisle U.	42	10	9	2	29	13	6	7	8	19	28	64	7
Shrewsbury T.	42	13	5	3	34	18	4	5	12	15	35	61	−4
Brighton & H. A.	42	11	6	4	42	17	6	3	12	27	43	60	9
Leeds U.	42	13	4	4	33	16	3	8	10	22	40	60	−1
Fulham	42	9	6	6	35	24	6	6	9	25	29	57	7
Huddersfield T.	42	8	6	7	27	20	6	9	6	29	29	57	7
Charlton Ath.	42	13	4	4	40	26	3	5	13	13	38	57	−11
Barnsley	42	9	6	6	33	23	6	1	14	24	30	52	4
Cardiff C.	42	11	3	7	32	27	4	3	14	21	39	51	−13
Portsmouth	42	8	3	10	46	32	6	4	11	27	32	49	9
Middlesbrough	42	9	8	4	26	18	3	5	13	15	29	49	−6
Crystal Palace	42	8	5	8	18	18	4	6	11	24	34	47	−10
Oldham Ath.	42	10	6	5	33	27	3	2	16	14	46	47	−26
Derby C.	42	9	5	7	26	26	2	4	15	10	46	42	−36
Swansea C.	42	7	4	10	20	28	0	4	17	16	57	29	−49
Cambridge U.	42	4	7	10	20	33	0	5	16	8	44	24	−49

Third Division		Home			Goals		Away			Goals			
	P	*W*	*D*	*L*	*F*	*A*	*W*	*D*	*L*	*F*	*A*	*Pt*	*Dif*
Oxford U.	46	17	5	1	58	22	11	6	6	33	28	95	41
Wimbledon	46	15	5	3	58	35	11	4	8	39	41	87	21
Sheffield U.	46	14	7	2	56	18	10	4	9	30	35	83	33
Hull C.	46	16	5	2	42	11	7	9	7	29	27	83	33
Bristol R.	46	16	5	2	47	21	6	8	9	21	33	79	14
Walsall	46	14	4	5	44	22	8	5	10	24	39	75	7
Bradford C.	46	11	9	3	46	30	9	2	12	27	35	71	8
Gillingham	46	13	4	6	50	29	7	6	10	24	40	70	5
Millwall	46	16	4	3	42	18	2	9	12	29	47	67	6
Bolton W.	46	13	4	6	36	17	5	6	12	20	43	64	−4
Orient	46	13	5	5	40	27	5	4	14	31	54	63	−10
Burnley	46	12	5	6	52	25	4	9	10	24	36	62	15
Newport Co.	46	11	9	3	35	27	5	5	13	23	48	62	−17
Lincoln C.	46	11	4	8	42	29	6	6	11	17	33	61	−3
Wigan Ath.	46	11	5	7	26	18	5	8	10	20	38	61	−10
Preston N.E.	46	12	5	6	42	27	3	6	14	24	39	56	0
Bournemouth	46	11	5	7	38	27	5	2	16	25	46	55	−10
Rotherham U.	46	10	5	8	29	17	5	4	14	28	47	54	− 7
Plymouth Arg.	46	11	8	4	38	17	2	4	17	18	45	51	− 6
Brentford	46	8	9	6	41	30	3	7	13	28	49	49	−10
Scunthorpe U.	46	9	9	5	40	31	0	10	13	14	42	46	−19
Southend U.	46	8	9	6	34	24	2	5	16	21	52	44	−21
Port Vale	46	10	4	9	33	29	1	6	16	18	54	43	−32
Exeter C.	46	4	8	11	27	39	2	7	14	23	45	33	−34

Fourth Division		Home			Goals		Away			Goals			
	P	*W*	*D*	*L*	*F*	*A*	*W*	*D*	*L*	*F*	*A*	*Pt*	*Dif*
York C.	46	18	4	1	58	16	13	4	6	38	23	101	57
Doncaster R.	46	15	6	2	46	22	9	7	7	36	32	85	28
Reading	46	17	6	0	51	14	5	10	8	33	42	82	28
Bristol C.	46	18	3	2	51	17	6	7	10	19	27	82	26
Aldershot	46	14	6	3	49	29	8	3	12	27	40	75	7
Blackpool	46	15	4	4	47	19	6	5	12	23	33	72	18
Peterborough	46	15	5	3	52	16	3	9	11	20	32	68	24
Colchester U.	46	14	7	2	45	14	3	9	11	24	39	67	16
Torquay U.	46	13	7	3	32	18	5	6	12	27	46	67	−5
Tranmere R.	46	11	5	7	33	26	6	10	7	20	27	66	0
Hereford U.	46	11	6	6	31	21	5	9	9	23	32	63	1
Stockport Co.	46	12	5	6	34	25	5	6	12	26	39	62	−4
Chesterfield	46	10	11	2	34	24	5	4	14	25	37	60	−2
Darlington	46	13	4	6	31	19	4	4	15	18	31	59	−1
Bury	46	9	7	7	34	32	6	7	10	27	32	59	− 3
Crewe Alex.	46	10	8	5	35	27	6	3	14	21	40	59	−11
Swindon T.	46	11	7	5	34	23	4	6	13	24	33	58	2
Northampton T.	46	10	8	5	32	32	3	6	14	21	46	53	−25
Mansfield T.	46	9	7	7	44	27	4	6	13	22	43	52	− 4
Wrexham	46	7	6	10	34	33	4	9	10	25	41	48	−15
Halifax T.	46	11	6	6	36	25	1	6	16	19	64	48	−34
Rochdale	46	8	9	6	35	31	3	4	16	17	49	46	−28
Hartlepool U.	46	7	8	8	31	28	3	2	18	16	57	40	−38
Chester C.	46	7	5	11	23	35	0	8	15	22	47	34	−37

DIVISION ONE LEAGUE POSITIONS (1951-84)

	1983–84	1982–83	1981–82	1980–81	1979–80	1978–79	1977–78	1976–77	1975–76	1974–75	1973–74	1972–73	1971–72	1970–71	1969–70	1968–69	1967–68
Arsenal	6	10	5	3	4	7	5	8	17	16	10	2	5	1	12	4	9
Aston Villa	10	6	11	1	7	8	8	4	16	—	—	—	—	—	—	—	—
Birmingham City	20	17	16	13	—	21	11	13	19	17	19	10	—	—	—	—	—
Blackburn Rovers	—	—	—	—	—	—	—	—	—	—	—	—	—	—	—	—	—
Blackpool	—	—	—	—	—	—	—	—	—	—	—	—	—	22	—	—	—
Bolton Wanderers	—	—	—	—	22	17	—	—	—	—	—	—	—	—	—	—	—
Brighton & H.A.	—	22	13	19	16	—	—	—	—	—	—	—	—	—	—	—	—
Bristol City	—	—	—	—	20	13	17	18	—	—	—	—	—	—	—	—	—
Burnley	—	—	—	—	—	—	—	—	21	10	6	—	—	21	14	14	13
Cardiff City	—	—	—	—	—	—	—	—	—	—	—	—	—	—	—	—	—
Carlisle United	—	—	—	—	—	—	—	—	—	22	—	—	—	—	—	—	—
Charlton Athletic	—	—	—	—	—	—	—	—	—	—	—	—	—	—	—	—	—
Chelsea	—	—	—	—	—	22	16	—	—	21	17	12	7	6	3	5	6
Coventry City	19	19	14	16	15	10	7	19	14	14	16	19	18	10	6	20	20
Crystal Palace	—	—	—	22	13	—	—	—	—	—	—	21	20	18	20	—	—
Derby County	—	—	—	—	21	19	12	15	4	1	3	7	1	9	4	—	—
Everton	—	7	8	15	19	4	3	9	11	4	7	17	15	14	1	3	5
Fulham	—	—	—	—	—	—	—	—	—	—	—	—	—	—	—	—	22
Huddersfield Town	—	—	—	—	—	—	—	—	—	—	—	—	22	15	—	—	—
Ipswich Town	12	9	2	2	3	6	18	3	6	3	4	4	13	19	18	12	—
Leeds United	—	—	20	9	11	5	9	10	5	9	1	3	2	2	2	1	4
Leicester City	15	—	—	21	—	—	22	11	7	18	9	16	12	—	—	21	12
Liverpool	1	1	1	5	1	1	2	1	1	2	2	1	3	5	5	2	3
Luton Town	16	18	—	—	—	—	—	—	—	20	—	—	—	—	—	—	—
Manchester City	—	20	10	12	17	15	4	2	8	8	14	11	4	11	10	13	1
Manchester United	4	3	3	8	2	9	10	6	3	—	21	18	8	8	8	11	2
Middlesbrough	—	—	22	14	9	12	14	12	13	7	—	—	—	—	—	—	—
Newcastle United	—	—	—	—	—	—	21	5	15	15	15	9	11	12	7	9	10
Northampton Town	—	—	—	—	—	—	—	—	—	—	—	—	—	—	—	—	—
Norwich City	14	14	—	20	12	16	13	16	10	—	22	20	—	—	—	—	—
Nottingham F.	3	5	12	7	5	2	1	—	—	—	—	—	21	16	15	18	11
Notts Co.	21	15	15	—	—	—	—	—	—	—	—	—	—	—	—	—	—
Orient	—	—	—	—	—	—	—	—	—	—	—	—	—	—	—	—	—
Portsmouth	—	—	—	—	—	—	—	—	—	—	—	—	—	—	—	—	—
Preston North End	—	—	—	—	—	—	—	—	—	—	—	—	—	—	—	—	—
Queen's Park Rangers	5	—	—	—	—	20	19	14	2	11	8	—	—	—	—	22	—
Sheffield United	—	—	—	—	—	—	—	—	22	6	13	14	10	—	—	—	21
Sheffield Wednesday	—	—	—	—	—	—	—	—	—	—	—	—	—	—	22	15	19
Southampton	2	12	7	6	8	14	—	—	—	—	20	13	19	7	19	7	15
Stoke City	18	13	18	11	18	—	—	21	12	5	5	15	17	13	9	19	18
Sunderland	13	16	19	17	—	—	—	20	—	—	—	—	—	—	21	17	16
Swansea City	—	21	6	—	—	—	—	—	—	—	—	—	—	—	—	—	—
Tottenham Hotspur	8	4	4	10	14	11	—	22	9	19	11	8	6	3	11	6	7
Watford	11	2	—	—	—	—	—	—	—	—	—	—	—	—	—	—	—
West Bromwich A.	17	11	17	4	10	3	6	7	—	—	—	22	16	17	16	10	8
West Ham United	9	8	9	—	—	19	20	17	18	13	18	6	14	30	17	8	14
Wolverhampton W.	22	—	21	18	6	—	15	—	20	12	12	5	9	4	13	16	17

1966–67	1965–66	1964–65	1963–64	1962–63	1961–62	1960–61	1959–60	1958–59	1957–58	1956–57	1955–56	1954–55	1953–54	1952–53	1951–52	
7	14	13	8	7	10	11	13	3	12	5	5	9	12	1	3	Arsenal
21	16	16	19	15	7	9	—	21	14	10	20	6	13	11	6	Aston Villa
—	—	22	20	20	17	18	19	9	13	12	6	—	—	—	—	Birmingham City
—	22	10	7	11	16	8	17	10	—	—	—	—	—	—	—	Blackburn Rovers
22	13	17	18	13	13	20	11	8	7	4	2	19	6	7	9	Blackpool
—	—	—	21	18	11	18	6	4	15	9	8	18	5	14	5	Bolton Wanderers
—	—	—	—	—	—	—	—	—	—	—	—	—	—	—	—	Brighton & H.A.
—	—	—	—	—	—	—	—	—	—	—	—	—	—	—	—	Bristol City
14	3	12	9	3	2	4	1	7	6	7	7	10	7	6	14	Burnley
—	—	—	—	21	15	—	—	—	21	17	20	10	12	—	—	Cardiff City
—	—	—	—	—	—	—	—	—	—	—	—	—	—	—	—	Carlisle United
—	—	—	—	—	—	—	—	—	—	22	14	15	9	5	10	Charlton Athletic
9	5	3	5	—	22	12	18	14	11	13	16	1	8	19	19	Chelsea
—	—	—	—	—	—	—	—	—	—	—	—	—	—	—	—	Coventry City
—	—	—	—	—	—	—	—	—	—	—	—	—	—	—	—	Crystal Palace
—	—	—	—	—	—	—	—	—	—	—	—	—	—	22	17	Derby County
6	11	4	3	1	4	5	15	16	16	15	15	11	—	—	—	Everton
19	20	20	15	16	20	17	10	—	—	—	—	—	—	—	22	Fulham
—	—	—	—	—	—	—	—	—	—	—	21	12	3	—	21	Huddersfield Town
—	—	—	22	17	1	—	—	—	—	—	—	—	—	—	—	Ipswich Town
4	2	2	—	—	—	—	21	15	17	8	—	—	—	—	—	Leeds United
8	7	18	11	4	14	6	12	19	18	—	—	21	—	—	—	Leicester City
5	1	7	1	8	—	—	—	—	—	—	—	—	22	17	11	Liverpool
—	—	—	—	—	—	—	22	17	8	16	10	—	—	—	—	Luton Town
15	—	—	—	21	12	13	16	20	5	18	4	7	17	20	15	Manchester City
1	4	1	2	19	15	7	7	2	9	1	1	5	4	8	1	Manchester United
—	—	—	—	—	—	—	—	—	—	—	—	—	21	13	18	Middlesbrough
20	15	—	—	—	—	21	8	11	19	17	11	8	15	16	8	Newcastle United
—	21	—	—	—	—	—	—	—	—	—	—	—	—	—	—	Northampton Town
—	—	—	—	—	—	—	—	—	—	—	—	—	—	—	—	Norwich City
2	18	5	13	9	19	14	20	13	10	—	—	—	—	—	—	Nottingham Forest
—	—	—	—	—	—	—	—	—	—	—	—	—	—	—	—	Notts County
—	—	—	—	22	—	—	—	—	—	—	—	—	—	—	—	Orient
—	—	—	—	—	—	—	—	22	20	19	12	3	14	15	4	Portsmouth
—	—	—	—	—	—	22	9	12	2	3	19	14	11	2	7	Preston North End
—	—	—	—	—	—	—	—	—	—	—	—	—	—	—	—	Queen's Park R.
10	9	19	12	10	5	—	—	—	—	—	22	13	20	—	—	Sheffield United
11	17	8	6	6	6	2	5	—	22	14	—	22	19	18	—	Sheffield Wednesday
19	—	—	—	—	—	—	—	—	—	—	—	—	—	—	—	Southampton
12	10	11	17	—	—	—	—	—	—	—	—	—	—	21	20	Stoke City
17	19	15	—	—	—	—	—	—	21	20	9	4	18	9	12	Sunderland
—	—	—	—	—	—	—	—	—	—	—	—	—	—	—	—	Swansea City
3	8	6	4	2	3	1	3	18	3	2	18	16	16	10	2	Tottenham Hotspur
—	—	—	—	—	—	—	—	—	—	—	—	—	—	—	—	Watford
13	6	14	10	14	9	10	4	5	4	11	13	17	2	4	13	West Bromwich Albion
16	12	9	14	12	8	16	14	6	—	—	—	—	—	—	—	West Ham United
—	—	21	16	5	18	3	2	1	1	6	3	2	1	3	16	Wolverhampton W.

DIVISION TWO LEAGUE POSITIONS (1951-84)

	1983–84	1982–83	1981–82	1980–81	1979–80	1978–79	1977–78	1976–77	1975–76	1974–75	1973–74	1972–73	1971–72	1970–71	1969–70	1968–69	1967–68
Aston Villa	—	—	—	—	—	—	—	—	—	2	14	3	—	—	21	18	17
Barnsley	14	10	6	—	—	—	—	—	—	—	—	—	—	—	—	—	—
Birmingham City	—	—	—	—	3	—	—	—	—	—	—	—	2	9	18	7	4
Blackburn Rovers	6	11	10	4	—	22	5	12	15	—	—	—	—	21	8	19	9
Blackpool	—	—	—	—	—	—	20	5	10	7	5	7	6	—	2	8	3
Bolton Wanderers	—	22	19	18	—	—	1	4	4	10	11	—	—	22	16	17	12
Brentford	—	—	—	—	—	—	—	—	—	—	—	—	—	—	—	—	—
Brighton & H.A.	9	—	—	—	—	2	4	—	—	—	—	22	—	—	—	—	—
Bristol City	—	—	—	21	—	—	—	—	2	5	16	5	8	19	14	16	19
Bristol Rovers	—	—	—	22	19	16	18	15	18	19	—	—	—	—	—	—	—
Burnley	—	21	—	—	21	13	11	16	—	—	—	1	7	—	—	—	—
Bury	—	—	—	—	—	—	—	—	—	—	—	—	—	—	—	21	—
Cambridge United	22	12	14	13	8	12	—	—	—	—	—	—	—	—	—	—	—
Cardiff City	15	—	20	19	15	9	19	18	—	21	17	20	19	3	7	5	13
Carlisle United	7	14	—	—	15	—	—	20	19	—	3	18	10	4	12	12	10
Charlton Athletic	13	17	13	—	22	19	17	7	9	—	—	—	21	20	20	3	15
Chelsea	1	18	12	12	4	—	—	2	11	—	—	—	—	—	—	—	—
Chesterfield	—	—	—	—	—	—	—	—	—	—	—	—	—	—	—	—	—
Coventry City	—	—	—	—	—	—	—	—	—	—	—	—	—	—	—	—	—
Crystal Palace	18	15	15	—	—	1	9	—	—	—	20	—	—	—	—	2	11
Derby County	20	13	16	6	—	—	—	—	—	—	—	—	—	—	—	1	18
Doncaster Rovers	—	—	—	—	—	—	—	—	—	—	—	—	—	—	—	—	—
Everton	—	—	—	—	—	—	—	—	—	—	—	—	—	—	—	—	—
Fulham	11	4	—	—	20	10	10	17	12	9	13	9	20	—	—	22	—
Grimsby	5	19	17	7	—	—	—	—	—	—	—	—	—	—	—	—	—
Hereford United	—	—	—	—	—	—	—	22	—	—	—	—	—	—	—	—	—
Huddersfield Town	12	—	—	—	—	—	—	—	—	—	—	21	—	—	1	6	14
Hull	—	—	—	—	—	—	22	14	14	8	9	13	12	5	13	11	16
Ipswich Town	—	—	—	—	—	—	—	—	—	—	—	—	—	—	—	—	1
Leeds United	10	8	—	—	—	—	—	—	—	—	—	—	—	—	—	—	—
Leicester City	—	3	8	—	1	17	—	—	—	—	—	—	—	1	3	—	—
Lincoln City	—	—	—	—	—	—	—	—	—	—	—	—	—	—	—	—	—
Liverpool	—	—	—	—	—	—	—	—	—	—	—	—	—	—	—	—	—
Luton Town	—	—	1	5	6	18	13	6	7	—	2	12	13	6	—	—	—

1966–67	1965–66	1964–65	1963–64	1962–63	1961–62	1960–61	1959–60	1958–59	1957–58	1956–57	1955–56	1954–55	1953–54	1952–53	1951–52	1950–51	
—	—	—	—	—	—	—	1	—	—	—	—	—	—	—	—	—	Aston Villa
—	—	—	—	—	—	—	—	22	14	19	18	—	—	22	20	15	Barnsley
10	10	—	—	—	—	—	—	—	—	—	—	1	7	6	3	4	Birmingham City
4	—	—	—	—	—	—	—	—	2	4	4	6	3	9	14	6	Blackburn Rovers
—	—	—	—	—	—	—	—	—	—	—	—	—	—	—	—	—	Blackpool
9	9	3	—	—	—	—	—	—	—	—	—	—	—	—	—	—	Bolton Wanderers
—	—	—	—	—	—	—	—	—	—	—	—	—	21	17	10	9	Brentford
—	—	—	—	—	22	16	14	12	—	—	—	—	—	—	—	—	Brighton & H. A.
15	5	—	—	—	—	—	22	10	17	13	11	—	—	—	—	—	Bristol City
—	—	—	—	—	21	17	9	6	10	9	6	9	9	—	—	—	Bristol Rovers
—	—	—	—	—	—	—	—	—	—	—	—	—	—	—	—	—	Burnley
22	19	16	18	8	18	—	—	—	—	21	16	13	17	20	17	20	Bury
—	—	—	—	—	—	—	—	—	—	—	—	—	—	—	—	—	Cambridge United
20	20	13	15	10	—	—	2	9	15	—	—	—	—	—	2	3	Cardiff City
3	14	—	—	—	—	—	—	—	—	—	—	—	—	—	—	—	Carlisle United
19	16	18	4	20	15	10	7	8	3	—	—	—	—	—	—	—	Charlton Athletic
—	—	—	—	1	—	—	—	—	—	—	—	—	—	—	—	—	Chelsea
—	—	—	—	—	—	—	—	—	—	—	—	—	—	—	—	21	Chesterfield
1	3	10	—	—	—	—	—	—	—	—	—	—	—	—	21	7	Coventry City
7	11	7	—	—	—	—	—	—	—	—	—	—	—	—	—	—	Crystal Palace
17	8	9	13	18	16	12	18	7	16	—	—	22	18	—	—	—	Derby County
—	—	—	—	—	—	—	—	—	22	14	17	18	12	13	16	11	Doncaster Rovers
—	—	—	—	—	—	—	—	—	—	—	—	—	2	16	7	—	Everton
—	—	—	—	—	—	—	—	2	5	11	9	14	8	8	—	—	Fulham
—	—	—	21	19	—	—	—	21	13	16	—	—	—	—	—	22	Grimsby
—	—	—	—	—	—	—	—	—	—	—	—	—	—	—	—	—	Hereford United
6	4	8	12	6	7	20	6	14	9	12	—	—	—	2	—	—	Huddersfield Town
12	—	—	—	—	—	—	21	—	—	—	22	19	15	18	18	10	Hull City
5	15	5	—	—	—	1	11	16	8	—	—	21	—	—	—	—	Ipswich Town
—	—	—	1	5	19	14	—	—	—	—	2	4	10	10	6	5	Leeds United
—	—	—	—	—	—	—	—	—	—	1	5	—	1	5	5	14	Leicester City
—	—	—	—	—	—	22	13	19	20	18	8	16	16	15	—	—	Lincoln City
—	—	—	—	—	1	3	3	4	4	3	3	11	—	—	—	—	Liverpool
—	—	—	—	22	3	13	—	—	—	—	—	2	6	3	8	19	Luton Town

DIVISION TWO LEAGUE POSITIONS (1951-84)

	1983–84	1982–83	1981–82	1980–81	1979–80	1978–79	1977–78	1976–77	1975–76	1974–75	1973–74	1972–73	1971–72	1970–71	1969–70	1968–69	1967–68
Manchester City	4	—	—	—	—	—	—	—	—	—	—	—	—	—	—	—	—
Manchester United .	—	—	—	—	—	—	—	—	—	1	—	—	—	—	—	—	—
Mansfield Town	—	—	—	—	—	—	21	—	—	—	—	—	—	—	—	—	—
Middlesbrough	17	16	—	—	—	—	—	—	—	—	1	4	9	7	4	4	6
Millwall	—	—	—	—	—	21	16	10	—	20	12	11	3	8	10	10	7
Newcastle United ...	3	5	9	11	9	8	—	—	—	—	—	—	—	—	—	—	—
Northampton Town	—	—	—	—	—	—	—	—	—	—	—	—	—	—	—	—	—
Norwich City	—	—	3	—	—	—	—	—	—	3	—	—	1	10	11	13	8
Nottingham F.	—	—	—	—	—	—	—	8	16	7	14	—	—	—	—	—	—
Notts County	—	—	—	2	17	6	15	8	5	14	10	—	—	—	—	—	—
Oldham Athletic	19	7	11	15	11	14	8	13	17	18	—	—	—	—	—	—	—
Orient	—	—	22	17	14	11	14	19	13	12	4	15	17	17	—	—	—
Oxford United	—	—	—	—	—	—	—	—	20	11	18	8	15	14	15	20	—
Plymouth Argyle	—	—	—	—	—	—	—	21	16	—	—	—	—	—	—	—	22
Portsmouth	16	—	—	—	—	—	—	—	22	17	15	17	16	16	17	15	5
Port Vale	—	—	—	—	—	—	—	—	—	—	—	—	—	—	—	—	—
Preston North End ..	—	—	—	20	10	7	—	—	—	—	21	19	18	—	22	14	20
Queen's Park R.	—	1 1	5	8	5	—	—	—	—	—	—	2	4	11	9	—	2
Rotherham United	—	20	7	—	—	—	—	—	—	—	—	—	—	—	—	—	21
Scunthorpe	—	—	—	—	—	—	—	—	—	—	—	—	—	—	—	—	—
Sheffield United	—	—	—	—	—	20	12	11	—	—	—	—	—	2	6	9	—
Sheffield Wed.	2	6	4	10	—	—	—	—	—	22	19	10	14	15	—	—	—
Shrewsbury Town ...	8	9	18	14	13	—	—	—	—	—	—	—	—	—	—	—	—
Southampton	—	—	—	—	—	—	2	9	6	13	—	—	—	—	—	—	—
Stoke City	—	—	—	—	—	3	7	—	—	—	—	—	—	—	—	—	—
Sunderland	—	—	—	—	2	4	6	—	1	4	6	6	5	13	—	—	—
Swansea City	21	—	—	3	12	—	—	—	—	—	—	—	—	—	—	—	—
Swindon Town	—	—	—	—	—	—	—	—	—	—	22	16	11	12	5	—	—
Tottenham Hotspur	—	—	—	—	—	—	3	—	—	—	—	—	—	—	—	—	—
Walsall	—	—	—	—	—	—	—	—	—	—	—	—	—	—	—	—	—
Watford	—	—	2	9	18	—	—	—	—	—	—	—	22	18	19	—	—
West Bromwich Alb.	—	—	—	—	—	—	—	—	3	6	8	—	—	—	—	—	—
West Ham United ...	—	—	—	1	7	5	—	—	—	—	—	—	—	—	—	—	—
Wolverhampton W.	—	2	—	—	—	—	—	1	—	—	—	—	—	—	—	—	—
Wrexham	—	—	21	16	16	15	—	—	—	—	—	—	—	—	—	—	—
York City	—	—	—	—	—	—	—	—	21	—	—	—	—	—	—	—	—

1966–67	1965–66	1964–65	1963–64	1962–63	1961–62	1960–61	1959–60	1958–59	1957–58	1956–57	1955–56	1954–55	1953–54	1952–53	1951–52	1950–51	
—	1	11	6	—	—	—	—	—	—	—	—	—	—	—	—	2	Manchester City
—	—	—	—	—	—	—	—	—	—	—	—	—	—	—	—	—	Manchester United
—	—	—	—	—	—	—	—	—	—	—	—	—	—	—	—	—	Mansfield Town
—	21	17	10	4	12	5	5	13	7	6	14	12	—	—	—	—	Middlesbrough
8	—	—	—	—	—	—	—	—	—	—	—	—	—	—	—	—	Millwall
—	—	1	8	7	11	—	—	—	—	—	—	—	—	—	—	—	Newcastle United
21	—	2	11	—	—	—	—	—	—	—	—	—	—	—	—	—	Northampton Town
11	13	6	17	13	17	4	—	—	—	—	—	—	—	—	—	—	Norwich City
—	—	—	—	—	—	—	—	—	—	2	7	15	4	7	4	—	Nottingham Forest
—	—	—	—	—	—	—	—	—	21	20	20	7	14	19	15	17	Notts County
—	—	—	—	—	—	—	—	—	—	—	—	—	22	—	—	—	Oldham Athletic
—	22	19	16	—	2	19	10	17	12	15	—	—	—	—	—	—	Orient
—	—	—	—	—	—	—	—	—	—	—	—	—	—	—	—	—	Oxford United
16	18	15	20	12	5	11	19	—	—	—	21	20	19	4	—	—	Plymouth Argyle
14	12	20	9	17	—	21	20	—	—	—	—	—	—	—	—	—	Portsmouth
—	—	—	—	—	—	—	—	—	—	22	12	17	—	—	—	—	Port Vale
13	17	12	3	16	10	—	—	—	—	—	—	—	—	—	—	1	Preston North End
—	—	—	—	—	—	—	—	—	—	—	—	—	—	—	22	16	Queen's Park R.
18	7	14	7	14	9	15	8	20	18	17	19	3	5	12	9	—	Rotherham United
—	—	—	22	9	4	9	15	18	—	—	—	—	—	—	—	—	Scunthorpe
—	—	—	—	—	—	2	—	—	6	7	—	—	—	1	11	8	Sheffield United
—	—	—	—	—	—	—	—	1	—	—	1	—	—	—	1	—	Sheffield Wednesday
—	—	—	—	—	—	—	—	—	—	—	—	—	—	—	—	—	Shrewsbury Town
—	2	4	5	11	6	8	—	—	—	—	—	—	—	21	13	12	Southampton
—	—	—	—	1	8	18	17	5	11	5	13	5	11	—	—	—	Stoke City
—	—	—	2	3	3	6	16	15	—	—	—	—	—	—	—	—	Sunderland
—	—	22	19	15	20	7	12	11	19	10	10	10	20	11	19	18	Swansea City
—	—	21	14	—	—	—	—	—	—	—	—	—	—	—	—	—	Swindon Town
—	—	—	—	—	—	—	—	—	—	—	—	—	—	—	—	—	Tottenham Hotspur
—	—	—	—	21	14	—	—	—	—	—	—	—	—	—	—	—	Walsall
—	—	—	—	—	—	—	—	—	—	—	—	—	—	—	—	—	Watford
—	—	—	—	—	—	—	—	—	—	—	—	—	—	—	—	—	West Bromwich Albion
—	—	—	—	—	—	—	—	—	1	8	16	8	13	14	12	13	West Ham United
2	6	—	—	—	—	—	—	—	—	—	—	—	—	—	—	—	Wolverhampton W.
—	—	—	—	—	—	—	—	—	—	—	—	—	—	—	—	—	Wrexham
—	—	—	—	—	—	—	—	—	—	—	—	—	—	—	—	—	York City

DIVISION THREE LEAGUE POSITIONS (1962-84)

	1983–84	1982–83	1981–82	1980–81	1979–80	1978–79	1977–78	1976–77	1975–76	1974–75	1973–74	1972–73	1971–72	1970–71	1969–70	1968–69	1967–68	1966–67	1965–66	1964–65	1963–64	1962–63	
Aldershot	—	—	—	—	—	—	—	—	21	20	8	—	—	—	—	—	—	—	—	—	—	—	Aldershot
Aston Villa	—	—	—	—	—	—	—	—	—	—	—	—	1	4	—	—	—	—	—	—	—	—	Aston Villa
Barnsley	—	—	—	2	11	—	—	—	—	—	—	—	22	12	7	10	—	—	—	24	20	18	Barnsley
Barrow	—	—	—	—	—	—	—	—	—	—	—	—	—	—	23	19	8	—	—	—	—	—	Barrow
Blackburn Rovers	—	—	—	—	2	—	—	—	—	1	13	3	10	—	—	—	—	—	—	—	—	—	Blackburn Rovers
Blackpool	—	—	—	23	18	12	—	—	—	—	—	—	—	—	—	—	—	—	—	—	—	—	Blackpool
Bolton Wanderers	10	—	—	—	—	—	—	—	—	—	—	1	7	—	—	—	—	—	—	—	—	—	Bolton Wanderers
AFC Bournemouth	17	14	—	—	—	—	—	—	—	21	11	7	3	—	21	4	13	20	18	11	4	5	AFC Bournemouth
Bradford	—	—	—	—	—	—	—	—	—	—	—	—	—	—	—	—	—	—	—	—	—	21	Bradford
Bradford City	7	12	—	—	—	—	22	—	—	—	—	—	24	19	10	—	—	—	—	—	—	—	Bradford City
Brentford	20	9	8	9	19	10	—	—	—	—	—	22	—	—	—	—	—	—	23	5	16	—	Brentford
Brighton & Hove Alb.	—	—	—	—	—	—	—	2	4	19	19	—	2	14	5	12	11	19	15	—	—	22	Brighton & Hove Alb.
Bristol City	—	—	23	—	—	—	—	—	—	—	—	—	—	—	—	—	—	—	—	2	5	14	Bristol City
Bristol Rovers	—	7	15	—	—	—	—	—	—	—	2	5	6	6	3	16	16	5	16	6	12	19	Bristol Rovers
Burnley	5	—	1	8	—	—	—	—	—	—	—	—	—	—	—	—	—	—	—	—	—	—	Burnley
Bury	12	—	—	—	21	19	15	7	13	14	—	—	—	22	19	—	2	—	—	—	—	—	Bury
Cambridge United	—	—	—	—	—	—	2	—	—	—	21	—	—	—	—	—	—	—	—	—	—	—	Cambridge United
Cardiff City	—	2	—	—	—	—	—	—	2	—	—	—	—	—	—	—	—	—	—	—	—	—	Cardiff City
Carlisle United	—	—	2	19	6	6	13	—	—	—	—	—	—	—	—	—	—	—	—	—	—	23	Carlisle United
Charlton Athletic	—	—	—	3	—	—	—	—	—	3	14	11	—	—	—	—	—	—	—	—	—	—	Charlton Athletic
Chester	—	—	24	18	9	16	5	13	17	—	—	—	—	—	—	—	—	—	—	—	—	—	Chester
Chesterfield	—	24	11	5	4	20	9	18	14	15	5	16	13	5	—	—	—	—	—	—	—	—	Chesterfield
Colchester United	—	—	—	22	5	7	8	—	22	11	—	—	—	—	—	—	23	13	—	23	17	12	Colchester United
Coventry City	—	—	—	—	—	—	—	—	—	—	—	—	—	—	—	—	—	—	—	—	1	4	Coventry City
Crewe Alexandra	—	—	—	—	—	—	—	—	—	—	—	—	—	—	—	23	—	—	—	—	22	—	Crewe Alexandra
Crystal Palace	—	—	—	—	—	—	—	3	5	5	—	—	—	—	—	—	—	—	—	—	2	11	Crystal Palace
Darlington	—	—	—	—	—	—	—	—	—	—	—	—	—	—	—	—	—	22	—	—	—	—	Darlington
Doncaster Rovers	—	23	19	—	8	—	—	—	—	—	—	—	—	23	11	—	—	23	—	—	—	—	Doncaster Rovers
Exeter City	24	19	18	11	8	8	17	—	—	—	—	—	—	—	—	—	—	—	22	17	—	—	Exeter City
Fulham	—	—	3	13	—	—	—	—	—	—	—	—	—	2	4	—	—	—	—	—	—	—	Fulham
Gillingham	8	13	6	15	16	5	7	12	15	10	—	—	—	24	20	20	12	11	6	7	—	—	Gillingham
Grimsby Town	—	—	—	—	1	—	—	23	18	16	6	9	—	—	—	—	22	17	11	10	—	—	Grimsby Town
Halifax Town	—	—	—	—	—	—	—	—	24	17	9	20	17	3	18	—	—	—	—	—	—	24	Halifax Town
Hartlepool United	—	—	—	—	—	—	—	—	—	—	—	—	—	—	—	22	—	—	—	—	—	—	Hartlepool United

Hereford United	—	—	—	—	—	—	—	23	—	1	12	18	—	—	—	—	—	—	—	—	—	—	Hereford United
Huddersfield Town	—	3	17	4	—	—	—	—	—	24	10	—	—	—	—	—	—	—	—	—	—	—	Huddersfield Town
Hull City	4	—	—	24	20	9	—	—	—	—	—	—	—	—	—	—	—	—	1	4	8	10	Hull City
Lincoln City	14	6	4	—	—	24	16	9	—	—	—	—	—	—	1	—	—	—	—	—	—	—	Lincoln City
Luton Town	—	—	—	—	—	—	—	—	—	—	—	—	—	—	2	3	—	—	—	21	18	—	Luton Town
Mansfield Town	—	—	—	—	23	18	—	1	11	—	—	—	21	7	6	15	21	9	19	3	7	—	Mansfield Town
Middlesbrough	—	—	—	—	—	—	—	—	—	—	—	—	—	—	—	—	1	2	—	—	—	—	Middlesbrough
Millwall	9	17	9	16	14	—	—	—	3	—	—	—	—	—	—	—	—	—	2	—	21	16	Millwall
Newport County	13	4	16	12	—	—	—	—	—	—	—	—	—	—	—	—	—	—	—	—	—	—	Newport County
Northampton Town	—	—	—	—	—	—	—	22	—	—	—	—	—	—	—	21	18	—	—	—	—	1	Northampton Town
Notts County	—	—	—	—	—	—	—	—	—	—	—	2	4	—	—	—	—	—	—	—	24	7	Notts County
Oldham Athletic	—	—	—	—	—	—	—	—	—	—	1	4	11	—	—	24	17	10	20	20	20	9	Oldham Athletic
Orient	11	20	—	—	—	—	—	—	—	—	—	—	—	—	1	18	19	14	—	—	—	—	Orient
Oxford United	1	5	5	14	17	11	18	17	—	—	—	—	—	—	—	—	1	15	14	—	—	—	Oxford United
Peterborough United	—	—	—	—	—	21	4	16	10	7	—	—	—	—	—	—	9*	15	13	8	10	6	Peterborough United
Plymouth Argyle	19	8	10	7	15	15	19	—	—	2	17	8	8	15	17	5	—	—	—	—	—	—	Plymouth Argyle
Portsmouth	—	1	13	6	—	—	24	20	—	—	—	—	—	—	—	—	—	—	—	—	—	—	Portsmouth
Port Vale	23	—	—	—	—	—	21	19	12	6	20	6	15	17	—	—	—	—	22	13	3	12	Port Vale
Preston North End	16	16	14	—	—	—	3	6	8	9	—	—	—	1	—	—	—	—	—	—	—	—	Preston North End
Queen's Park Rangers	—	—	—	—	—	—	—	—	—	—	—	—	—	—	—	—	—	1	3	14	15	13	Queen's Park Rangers
Reading	—	21	12	10	7	—	—	21	—	—	—	—	—	21	8	14	5	4	8	13	6	20	Reading
Rochdale	—	—	—	—	—	—	—	—	—	—	24	13	18	16	9	—	—	—	—	—	—	—	Rochdale
Rotherham United	18	—	—	1	13	17	20	4	16	—	—	21	5	8	14	11	—	—	—	—	—	—	Rotherham United
Scunthorpe United	21	—	—	—	—	—	—	—	—	—	—	24	—	—	—	—	24	18	4	18	—	—	Scunthorpe United
Sheffield United	3	11	—	21	12	—	—	—	—	—	—	—	—	—	—	—	—	—	—	—	—	—	Sheffield United
Sheffield Wednesday	—	—	—	—	3	14	14	8	20	—	—	—	—	—	—	—	—	—	—	—	—	—	Sheffield Wednesday
Shrewsbury Town	—	—	—	—	—	1	11	10	9	—	22	15	12	13	15	17	3	6	10	16	11	15	Shrewsbury Town
Southend United	22	15	7	—	22	13	—	—	23	18	12	14	—	—	—	—	—	—	21	12	14	8	Southend United
Southport	—	—	—	—	—	—	—	—	—	—	23	—	—	—	22	8	15	—	—	—	—	—	Southport
Stockport County	—	—	—	—	—	—	—	—	—	—	—	—	—	—	24	9	14	—	—	—	—	—	Stockport County
Swansea City	—	—	—	—	—	3	—	—	—	—	—	23	14	11	—	—	—	21	17	—	—	—	Swansea City
Swindon Town	—	—	22	17	10	4	10	11	19	4	—	—	—	—	—	2	10	8	7	—	—	2	Swindon Town
Torquay United	—	—	—	—	—	—	—	—	—	—	—	—	23	10	13	6	4	7	—	—	—	—	Torquay United
Tranmere Rovers	—	—	—	—	—	23	12	14	—	22	16	10	20	18	16	7	20	—	—	—	—	—	Tranmere Rovers
Walsall	6	10	20	20	—	22	6	15	7	8	15	17	9	20	12	13	7	12	9	19	19	—	Walsall
Watford	—	—	—	—	—	2	—	—	—	23	7	19	—	—	—	1	6	3	12	9	3	17	Watford
Wigan Athletic	15	18	—	—	—	—	—	—	—	—	—	—	—	—	—	—	—	—	—	—	—	—	Wigan Athletic
Wimbledon	2	—	21	—	24	—	—	—	—	—	—	—	—	—	—	—	—	—	—	—	—	—	Wimbledon
Workington	—	—	—	—	—	—	—	—	—	—	—	—	—	—	—	—	—	24	5	15	—	—	Workington
Wrexham	—	22	—	—	—	—	—	—	—	3	18	19	—	—	—	—	—	24	—	—	—	—	Wrexham
York City	—	—	—	—	—	—	[illegible]	6	13	4	12	16	9	—	—	—	—	—	—	23	9	—	York City

*Relegated by order of the Football League

DIVISION FOUR LEAGUE POSITIONS (1962-84)

	1983–84	1982–83	1981–82	1980–81	1979–80	1978–79	1977–78	1976–77	1975–76	1974–75	1973–74	1972–73	1971–72	1970–71	1969–70	1968–69	1967–68	1966–67	1965–66	1964–65	1963–64	1962–63	
Aldershot	5	18	16	6	10	5	5	17	—	—	—	4	17	13	6	15	9	10	17	18	9	11	Aldershot
Barnsley	—	—	—	—	—	4	7	6	12	15	13	14	—	—	—	—	2	16	16	—	—	—	Barnsley
Barrow	—	—	—	—	—	—	—	—	—	—	—	—	22	24	—	—	—	3	12	21	24	9	Barrow
Blackpool	6	21	12	—	—	—	—	—	—	—	—	—	—	—	—	—	—	—	—	—	—	—	Blackpool
AFC Bournemouth	—	—	5	13	11	18	17	13	6	—	—	—	—	2	—	—	—	—	—	—	—	—	AFC Bournemouth
Bradford	—	—	—	—	—	—	—	—	—	—	—	—	—	—	24	24	24	23	11	7	13	—	Bradford
Bradford City	—	—	2	14	5	15	—	4	17	10	8	16	—	—	—	4	5	11	23	19	5	23	Bradford City
Brentford	—	—	—	—	—	—	4	15	18	8	19	—	3	14	5	11	14	9	—	—	—	1	Brentford
Brighton & Hove Alb.	—	—	—	—	—	—	—	—	—	—	—	—	—	—	—	—	—	—	—	1	8	—	Brighton & Hove Alb.
Bristol City	4	14	—	—	—	—	—	—	—	—	—	—	—	—	—	—	—	—	—	—	—	—	Bristol City
Bury	14	5	9	12	—	—	—	—	—	—	4	12	9	—	—	—	—	—	—	—	—	—	Bury
Cambridge United	—	—	—	—	—	—	—	1	13	6	—	3	10	20	—	—	—	—	—	—	—	—	Cambridge United
Carlisle United	—	—	—	—	—	—	—	—	—	—	—	—	—	—	—	—	—	—	—	—	2	—	Carlisle United
Chester City	24	13	—	—	—	—	—	—	—	4	7	15	20	5	11	14	22	19	7	8	12	21	Chester City
Chesterfield	13	—	—	—	—	—	—	—	—	—	—	—	—	—	1	20	7	15	20	12	16	15	Chesterfield
Colchester United	8	6	6	—	—	—	—	3	—	—	3	22	11	6	10	6	—	—	4	—	—	—	Colchester United
Crewe Alexandra	17	23	24	18	23	24	15	12	16	18	21	21	24	15	15	—	4	5	14	10	—	3	Crewe Alexandra
Darlington	16	17	13	8	22	21	19	11	20	21	20	24	19	12	22	5	16	—	2	17	19	12	Darlington
Doncaster Rovers	2	—	—	3	22	12	12	8	10	17	22	17	22	—	—	1	10	—	1	9	14	16	Doncaster Rovers
Exeter	—	—	—	—	—	—	—	2	7	9	10	8	15	9	18	17	20	14	—	—	4	17	Exeter
Gillingham	—	—	—	—	—	—	—	—	—	—	2	9	13	—	—	—	—	—	—	—	1	5	Gillingham
Grimsby Town	—	—	—	—	—	2	6	—	—	—	—	—	1	19	16	23	—	—	—	—	—	—	Grimsby Town
Halifax Town	21	11	19	23	18	23	20	21	—	—	—	—	—	—	—	2	11	12	15	23	10	—	Halifax Town
Hartlepool United	23	22	14	9	19	13	21	22	14	13	11	20	18	23	23	—	3	8	18	15	23	24	Hartlepool United
Hereford United	11	24	10	22	21	14	—	—	—	—	—	2	—	—	—	—	—	—	—	—	—	—	Hereford United
Huddersfield Town	—	—	—	—	1	10	11	9	5	—	—	—	—	—	—	—	—	—	—	—	—	—	Huddersfield Town
Hull City	—	2	8	—	—	—	—	—	—	—	—	—	—	—	—	—	—	—	—	—	—	—	Hull City

Lincoln City	—	—	—	2	7	—	—	—	1	5	12	10	5	21	8	8	13	24	22	22	11	22	Lincoln City
Luton Town	—	—	—	—	—	—	—	—	—	—	—	—	—	—	—	—	1	17	6	—	—	—	Luton Town
Mansfield Town	19	10	20	7	—	—	—	—	—	1	17	6	—	—	—	—	—	—	—	—	—	4	Mansfield Town
Millwall	—	—	—	—	—	—	—	—	—	—	—	—	—	—	—	—	—	—	2	—	—		Millwall
Newport County	—	—	—	—	3	8	16	19	22	12	9	5	14	22	21	22	12	18	9	16	15	20	Newport County
Northampton Town	18	15	22	10	13	19	10	—	2	16	5	23	21	7	14	—	—	—	—	—	—	—	Northampton Town
Notts County	—	—	—	—	—	—	—	—	—	—	—	—	—	1	7	19	17	20	8	13	—	—	Notts County
Oldham Athletic	—	—	—	—	—	—	—	—	—	—	—	—	—	3	19	—	—	—	—	—	—	2	Oldham Athletic
Oxford United	—	—	—	—	—	—	—	—	—	—	—	—	—	—	—	—	—	—	—	4	18	18	Oxford United
Peterborough United	7	9	4	5	8	—	—	—	—	—	1	19	8	16	9	18	—	—	—	—	—	—	Peterborough United
Portsmouth	—	—	—	—	4	7	—	—	—	—	—	—	—	—	—	—	—	—	—	—	—	—	Portsmouth
Port Vale	—	3	7	19	20	16	—	—	—	—	—	—	—	—	4	13	18	13	19	—	—	—	Port Vale
Reading	3	—	—	—	—	1	8	—	3	7	6	7	16	—	—	—	—	—	—	—	—	—	Reading
Rochdale	22	20	21	15	24	20	24	18	15	19	—	—	—	—	—	3	19	21	21	6	20	7	Rochdale
Rotherham United	—	—	—	—	—	—	—	—	—	3	15	—	—	—	—	—	—	—	—	—	—	—	Rotherham United
Scunthorpe United	—	4	23	16	14	12	14	20	19	24	18	—	4	17	12	16	—	—	—	—	—	—	Scunthorpe United
Sheffield United	—	—	1	—	—	—	—	—	—	—	—	—	—	—	—	—	—	—	—	—	—	—	Sheffield United
Shrewsbury Town	—	—	—	—	—	—	—	—	—	2	—	—	—	—	—	—	—	—	—	—	—	—	Shrewsbury Town
Southend United	—	—	—	1	—	—	2	10	—	—	—	—	2	18	17	7	6	6	—	—	—	—	Southend United
Southport	—	—	—	—	—	—	23	23	23	11	—	1	7	8	—	—	—	2	10	20	21	13	Southport
Stockport County	12	16	18	20	16	17	18	14	21	20	24	11	23	—	—	—	—	1	13	24	17	19	Stockport County
Swansea City	—	—	—	—	—	—	3	5	11	22	14	—	—	—	3	10	15	—	—	—	—	—	Swansea City
Swindon Town	15	8	—	—	—	—	—	—	—	—	—	—	—	—	—	—	—	—	—	—	—	—	Swindon Town
Torquay United	9	12	15	17	9	11	9	16	9	14	16	18	—	—	—	—	—	—	3	11	6	6	Torquay United
Tranmere Rovers	10	19	11	21	15	—	—	—	4	—	—	—	—	—	—	—	—	4	5	5	7	8	Tranmere Rovers
Walsall	—	—	—	—	2	—	—	—	—	—	—	—	—	—	—	—	—	—	—	—	—	—	Walsall
Watford	—	—	—	—	—	—	1	7	8	—	—	—	—	—	—	—	—	—	—	—	—	—	Watford
Wigan Athletic	—	—	3	11	6	6	—	—	—	—	—	—	—	10	—	—	—	—	—	—	—	—	Wigan Athletic
Wimbledon	—	1	—	4	—	3	13	—	—	—	—	—	—	—	—	—	—	—	—	—	—	—	Wimbledon
Workington	—	—	—	—	—	—	—	24	24	23	23	13	6	10	20	12	23	—	—	—	3	10	Workington
Wrexham	20	—	—	—	—	—	—	—	—	—	—	—	—	—	2	9	8	7	24	13	—	—	Wrexham
York City	1	7	17	24	17	9	22	—	—	—	—	—	—	4	13	21	21	22	—	3	22	14	York City

LEADING LEAGUE SCORERS 1983-84

Division One: 32 – Rush (Liverpool); 22 – Lineker (Leicester C.); 21 – Archibald (Tottenham H.), Moran (Southampton), Woodcock (Arsenal); 20 – Johnston (Watford); 19 – Christie (Notts Co.), Mariner (Arsenal, inc. 12 for Ipswich T.); 17 – Gibson (Coventry C.); 16 – Withe (Aston Villa); 15 – Armstrong (Southampton), Birtles (Nottingham F.), Cottee (West Ham U.), Davenport (Nottingham F.), Deehan (Norwich C.), A. Smith (Leicester C.); 14 – Allen (Q.P.R.); 13 – Falco (Tottenham H.), Gates (Ipswich T.), Stainrod (Q.P.R.), Stapleton (Manchester U.), Swindlehurst (West Ham U.), Thompson (W.B.A.), Walsh (Nottingham F.); 12 – Heath (Everton), Lynex (Leicester C.), Robson (Manchester U.); 11 – Barnes (Watford), Nicholas (Arsenal), Wallace (Southampton), Walsh (Luton T.); 10 – Callaghan (Watford), Fenwick (Q.P.R.), Hodge (Nottingham F.), Regis (W.B.A.), Whiteside (Manchester U.); 9 – Chiedozie (Notts Co.), Maguire (Stoke C.), Stein (Luton T.), West (Sunderland).

Division Two: 28 – Dixon (Chelsea); 27 – Keegan (Newcastle U.); 22 – Hateley (Portsmouth); 21 – Davies (Fulham); 20 – Beardsley (Newcastle U.), Quinn (Oldham Ath, inc. 15 for Stockport Co.); 19 – Garner (Blackburn R.); 18 – Waddle (Newcastle U.); 17 – Poskett (Carlisle U.), Varadi (Sheffield W.); 16 – Biley (Portsmouth), Parlane (Manchester C.); 15 – Currie (Middlesbrough), Drinkell (Grimsby T.); 14 – Bannister (Sheffield W.), Davison (Derby Co.), Geddis (Barnsley), Owen (Cardiff C.); 13 – Connor (Brighton & H.A.), Nevin (Chelsea), Palmer (Oldham Ath.), Speedie (Chelsea), Tolmie (Manchester C.), Wilson (Brighton & H.A., inc. 3 for Scunthorpe U.); 12 – Wilkinson (Grimsby T.), A. Young (Brighton & H.A.); 11 – Glavin (Barnsley), Lillis (Huddersfield T.); 10 – Hales (Charlton Ath.), Moore (Charlton Ath. inc. 2 for Rotherham U.), Webb (Portsmouth); 9 – Cross (Shrewsbury T.), Dillon, Morgan, Webb (all Portsmouth).

Division Three: 33 – Edwards (Sheffield U.); 28 – Cork (Wimbledon); 24 – Aldridge (Oxford U., inc. 20 for Newport Co.); 22 – Hawley (Bradford C.); 20 – Morris (Sheffield U.), Biggins (Oxford U.), Caldwell (Bolton W.); 18 – Cammack (Scunthorpe U.), Hamilton (Burnley), Joseph (Brentford); 16 – Elliot (Preston N.E.), Hodges (Wimbledon), Marwood (Hull C.), Mehmet (Gillingham), Phillips (Southend U.), Pratt (Exeter C.); 15 – Birch (Rotherham U., inc. 5 for Chesterfield), Bremner (Millwall); 14 – Chandler (Bolton W.), Johnson (Wigan Ath., inc. 7 for Rochdale); 13 – Brown (Walsall), Campbell (Bradford C., inc. 4 for Derby Co.), Haire (Bradford C.), Kelly (Preston N.E.), Kilmore (Rotherham U.), D. Neal (Millwall), Stephens (Bristol R.), Thomas (Lincoln C.); 12 – Cascarino (Gillingham), Evans (Wimbledon), Kitchen (Orient), O'Kelly (Walsall), Reeves (Burnley), Thompson (Bournemouth), Tynan (Plymouth Arg.); 11 – Hebberd (Oxford U.), Houghton (Preston N.E., inc. 1 for Wigan Ath.), Staniforth (Plymouth Arg.), Vinter (Oxford U.); 10 – Godfrey (Orient), O'Keefe (Port Vale), Roberts (Brentford), Whitehurst (Hull C.), Williams (Bristol R.); 9 – Barrett (Bristol R.), Bright (Port Vale), Brooks (Orient), Campbell (Bradford C.), Cassells (Brentford), Flounders (Hull C.), Flynn (Burnley), Houchen (Orient), Jack (Lincoln C.), Lawrence (Oxford U.), Leslie (Gillingham), McEwan (Exeter C.), Neville (Exeter C.), G. Roberts (Hull C.), Weatherly (Gillingham), White (Bristol R.).

Division Four: 36 – Senior (Reading); 27 – Byrne (York C.); 26 – Adcock (Colchester U.); 25 – Walwyn (York C.); 23 – Lawrence (Aldershot); 21 Caldwell (Mansfield T.); 19 – Banton (Aldershot), Gregory (Wrexham); 18 – Morgan (Bristol C., inc. 2 for Bournemouth); 17 – Madden (Bury), Mayes (Swindon T.), Phillips (Hereford U.); 16 – Newton (Chesterfield, inc. 2 for Port Vale, Riley (Bristol C.); 15 –

Crawford (Bristol C.), Douglas (Doncaster R.), Moss (Doncaster R.); 14 – Aspinall (Tranmere R.), Gallagher (Halifax T.), Waddle (Peterborough U., inc. 2 for Hartlepool); 13 – G. Snodin (Doncaster R.), Taylor (Stockport Co., inc. 7 for Wigan Ath.); 12 – Bowen (Colchester U.), Burvill (Aldershot), Dobson (Hartlepool U.), Ritchie (Bristol C.); 11 – Entwistle (Bury), Ford (York C.), Jakub (Bury), McDonald (Aldershot); 10 – Austin (Northampton T.), Barrowclough (Mansfield T.), Kearns (Hereford U.), Kerr (Stockport Co., inc. 4 for Bristol C.), Leonard (Crewe Alex.), McPhail (York C.); Pritchard (Bristol C.), Sanchez (Reading), Stewart (Blackpool), Waller (Crewe Alex.), Walsh (Darlington); 9 – Belfon (Northampton T.), Britton (Blackpool), Harvey (Hereford U.), Hayes (Northampton T.), Kendal (Chesterfield), Mercer (Blackpool), I. Snodin (Doncaster R.), Sword (Stockport Co.), Todd (Darlington).

TOP LEAGUE SCORERS SINCE 1946-47

1983-84	T. Senior (Reading	36
1982-83	L. Blissett (Watford)	27
1981-82	K. Edwards (Sheffield U., inc. 1 for Hull C.)	36
1980-81	T. Kellow (Exeter C.) and D. Kemp (Plymouth Arg.)	24
1979-80	C. Allen (Queen's Park Rangers)	28
1978-79	R. Jenkins (Watford)	29
1977-78	A. Curtis (Swansea City) and S. Phillips (Brentford)	32
1976-77	P. Ward (Brighton & Hove Albion)	32
1975-76	R. McNeil (Hereford United)	35
1974-75	R. McNeil (Hereford United)	31
1973-74	B. Yeo (Gillingham)	31
1972-73	B. Robson (West Ham United) and F. Binney (Exeter)	28
1971-72	E. MacDougall (Bournemouth) and A. Wood (Shrewsbury)	35
1970-71	E. MacDougall (Bournemouth)	42
1969-70	G. Jones (Bury) and A. Kinsey (Wrexham)	26
1968-69	J. Greaves (Tottenham Hotspur)	27
1967-68	G. Best (Manchester United) and R. Davies (Southampton)	28
1966-67	R. Davies (Southampton)	37
1965-66	K. Hector (Bradford)	44
1964-65	A. Jeffrey (Doncaster Rovers)	36
1963-64	H. MacIlmoyle (Carlisle United)	39
1962-63	J. Greaves (Tottenham Hotspur)	37
1961-62	R. Hunt (Liverpool) and B. Thomas (Scunthorpe and Newcastle United)	41
1960-61	T. Bly (Peterborough)	52
1959-60	C. Holton (Watford)	48
1958-59	B. Clough (Middlesbrough)	43
1957-58	T. Johnston (Blackburn Rovers and Leyton Orient)	44
1956-57	A. Rowley (Leicester City)	44
1955-56	R. Collins (Torquay United)	40
1954-55	T. Briggs (Blackburn Rovers)	33
1953-54	J. Charles (Leeds United)	42
1952-53	G. Rowley (Leicester City)	39
1951-52	D. Dooley (Sheffield W.)	46
1950-51	J. Shaw (Rotherham U.)	37
1949-50	T. Briggs (Grimsby T.)	35
1948-49	C. Wyman (Southampton)	32
1947-48	R. Rooke (Arsenal)	33
1946-47	C. Jordan (Doncaster R.)	42

LEAGUE CHAMPIONSHIP HONOURS

Division I

	First	Pt	Second	Pt	Third	Pt
1888–9 *a*	Preston NE	40	Aston Villa	29	Wolverhampton W	28
1889–90	Preston NE	33	Everton	31	Blackburn R	27
1890–1	Everton	29	Preston NE	27	Wolverhampton W / Notts County	26
1891–2 *b*	Sunderland	42	Preston NE	37	Bolton W	36
1892–3 *c*	Sunderland	48	Preston NE	37	Everton	36
1893–4	Aston Villa	44	Sunderland	38	Derby C	36
1894–5	Sunderland	47	Everton	42	Aston Villa	39
1895–6	Aston Villa	45	Derby C	41	Everton	39
1896–7	Aston Villa	47	Sheffield U	36	Derby C	36
1897–8	Sheffield U	42	Sunderland	37	Wolverhampton W	35
1898–9 *d*	Aston Villa	45	Liverpool	43	Burnley	39
1899–1900	Aston Villa	50	Sheffield U	48	Sunderland	41
1900–1	Liverpool	45	Sunderland	43	Notts C	40
1901–2	Sunderland	44	Everton	41	Newcastle U	37
1902–3	Sheffield W	42	Aston Villa	41	Sunderland	41
1903–4	Sheffield W	47	Manchester C	44	Everton	43
1904–5	Newcastle U	48	Everton	47	Manchester C	46
1905–6 *e*	Liverpool	51	Preston NE	47	Sheffield W	44
1906–7	Newcastle U	51	Bristol C	38	Everton	45
1907–8	Manchester U	52	Aston Villa	43	Manchester C	43
1908–9	Newcastle U	53	Everton	46	Sunderland	44
1909–10	Aston Villa	53	Liverpool	48	Blackburn R.	45
1910–11	Manchester U	52	Aston Villa	51	Sunderland	45
1911–12	Blackburn R	49	Everton	46	Newcastle U	44
1912–13	Sunderland	54	Aston Villa	50	Sheffield W	49
1913–14	Blackburn R	51	Aston Villa	44	Middlesbrough	43
1914–15	Everton	46	Oldham A	45	Blackburn R	43
1919–20 *f*	WBA	60	Burnley	51	Chelsea	49
1920–21	Burnley	59	Manchester C	54	Bolton W	52
1921–22	Liverpool	57	Tottenham H	51	Burnley	49
1922–23	Liverpool	60	Sunderland	54	Huddersfield T	53
1923–24	*Huddersfield T	57	Cardiff C	57	Sunderland	43
1924–25	Huddersfield T	58	WBA	56	Bolton W	55
1925–26	Huddersfield T	57	Arsenal	52	Sunderland	48
1926–27	Newcastle U	56	Huddersfield T	51	Sunderland	49
1927–28	Everton	53	Huddersfield T	51	Leicester C	48
1928–29	Sheffield W	52	Leicester C	51	Aston Villa	50
1929–30	Sheffield W	60	Derby C	50	Manchester C	47
1930–31	Arsenal	66	Aston Villa	59	Sheffield W	52
1931–32	Everton	56	Arsenal	54	Sheffield W	50
1932–33	Arsenal	58	Aston Villa	54	Sheffield W	51
1933–34	Arsenal	59	Huddersfield T	56	Tottenham H	49
1934–35	Arsenal	58	Sunderland	54	Sheffield W	49
1935–36	Sunderland	56	Derby C	48	Huddersfield T	48
1936–37	Manchester C	57	Charlton A	54	Arsenal	52
1937–38	Arsenal	52	Wolverhampton W	51	Preston NE	49
1938–39	Everton	59	Wolverhampton W	55	Charlton A	50
1946–47	Liverpool	57	Manchester U	56	Wolverhampton W	56
1947–48	Arsenal	59	Manchester U	52	Burnley	52
1948–49	Portsmouth	58	Manchester U	53	Derby C	53

	First	Pt	Second	Pt	Third	Pt
1949–50	*Portsmouth	53	Wolverhampton W	53	Sunderland	52
1950–51	Tottenham H	60	Manchester U	56	Blackpool	50
1951–52	Manchester U	57	Tottenham H	53	Arsenal	53
1952–53	*Arsenal	54	Preston NE	54	Wolverhampton W	51
1953–54	Wolverhampton W	57	WBA	53	Huddersfield T	51
1954–55	Chelsea	52	Wolverhampton W	48	Portsmouth	48
1955–56	Manchester U	60	Blackpool	49	Wolverhampton W	49
1956–57	Manchester U	64	Tottenham H	56	Preston NE	56
1957–58	Wolverhampton W	64	Preston NE	59	Tottenham H	51
1958–59	Wolverhampton W	61	Manchester U	55	Arsenal	50
1959–60	Burnley	55	Wolverhampton W	54	Tottenham H	53
1960–61	Tottenham H	66	Sheffield W	58	Wolverhampton W	57
1961–62	Ipswich T	56	Burnley	53	Tottenham H	52
1962–63	Everton	61	Tottenham H	55	Burnley	54
1963–64	Liverpool	57	Manchester U	53	Everton	52
1964–65	Manchester U	61	Leeds U	61	Chelsea	56
1965–66	Liverpool	61	Leeds U	55	Burnley	55
1966–67	Manchester U	60	Nottingham F	56	Tottenham H	56
1967–68	Manchester C	58	Manchester U	56	Liverpool	55
1968–69	Leeds U	67	Liverpool	61	Everton	57
1969–70	Everton	66	Leeds U	57	Chelsea	55
1970–71	Arsenal	65	Leeds U	64	Tottenham H	52
1971–72	Derby C	58	Leeds U	57	Liverpool	57
1972–73	Liverpool	60	Arsenal	57	Leeds U	53
1973–74	Leeds U	62	Liverpool	57	Derby C	48
1974–75	Derby C	53	Liverpool	51	Ipswich T	51
1975–76	Liverpool	60	QPR	59	Manchester U	56
1976–77	Liverpool	57	Manchester C	56	Ipswich T	52
1977–78	Nottingham F	64	Liverpool	57	Everton	55
1978–79	Liverpool	68	Nottingham F	60	WBA	59
1979–80	Liverpool	60	Manchester U	58	Ipswich T	53
1980–81	Aston Villa	60	Ipswich T	56	Arsenal	53
1981–82	*g*Liverpool	87	Ipswich T	83	Manchester U	78
1982–83	Liverpool	82	Watford	71	Manchester U	70

* Won on goal average. Maximum points: *a*, 44; *b*, 56; *c*, 60; *d*, 58; *e*, 76; *f*, 84, *g*, 126.

Division II

1892–3	*a*Small Heath	36	Sheffield U	35	Darwen	30
1893–4	*b*Liverpool	50	Small Heath	42	Notts County	39
1894–5	*c*Bury	48	Notts C	39	Newton Heath	38
1895–6	*Liverpool	46	Manchester C	46	Grimsby T	42
1896–7	Notts C	42	Newton Heath	39	Grimsby T	38
1897–8	Burnley	48	Newcastle	45	Manchester C	39
1898–9	*d*Manchester C	51	Glossop NE	46	Leicester Fosse	45
1899–1900	Sheffield W	54	Bolton W	52	Small Heath	46
1900–1	Grimsby T	49	Small Heath	48	Burnley	44
1901–2	WBA	55	Middlesbrough	51	Preston NE	42
1902–3	Manchester C	54	Small Heath	51	W'lwich Arsenal	48
1903–4	Preston NE	50	W'lwich Arsenal	49	Manchester U	48
1904–5	Liverpool	58	Bolton W	56	Manchester U	53
1905–6	*e*Bristol C	66	Manchester U	62	Chelsea	53
1906–7	Nottingham F	60	Chelsea	57	Leicester Fosse	48
1907–8	Bradford C	54	Leicester Fosse	52	Oldham	50
1908–9	Bolton W	52	Tottenham H	51	WBA	51
1909–10	Manchester C	54	Oldham A	53	Hull C	53

	First	Pt	Second	Pt	Third	Pt
1910–11	WBA	53	Bolton W	51	Chelsea	49
1911–12	*Derby C	54	Chelsea	54	Burnley	52
1912–13	Preston NE	53	Burnley	50	Birmingham	46
1913–14	Notts County	53	Bradford	49	W'lwich Arsenal	49
1914–15	Derby C	53	Preston NE	50	Barnsley	47
1919–20	*f*Tottenham H	70	Huddersfield T	64	Birmingham C	56
1920–21	*Birmingham	58	Cardiff C	58	Bristol C	51
1921–22	Nottingham F	56	Stoke C	52	Barnsley	52
1922–23	Notts C	53	West Ham U	51	Leicester C	51
1923–24	Leeds U	54	Bury	51	Derby C	51
1924–25	Leicester C	59	Manchester U	57	Derby C	55
1925–26	Sheffield W	60	Derby C	57	Chelsea	52
1926–27	Middlesbrough	62	Portsmouth	54	Manchester C	54
1927–28	Manchester C	59	Leeds U	57	Chelsea	54
1928–29	Middlesbrough	55	Grimsby T	53	Bradford C	48
1929–30	Blackpool	58	Chelsea	55	Oldham A	53
1930–31	Everton	61	WBA	55	Tottenham H	51
1931–32	Wolverhampton W	56	Leeds U	54	Stoke C	52
1932–33	Stoke C	56	Tottenham H	55	Fulham	50
1933–34	Grimsby	59	Preston NE	52	Bolton W	51
1934–35	Brentford	61	Bolton W	56	West Ham U	56
1935–36	Manchester U	56	Charlton A	55	Sheffield U	52
1936–37	Leicester C	56	Blackpool	55	Bury	52
1937–38	Aston Villa	57	Manchester U	53	Sheffield U	53
1938–39	Blackburn R	55	Sheffield U	54	Sheffield W	53
1946–47	Manchester C	62	Burnley	58	Birmingham	55
1947–48	Birmingham	59	Newcastle U	56	Southampton	52
1948–49	Fulham	57	WBA	56	Southampton	55
1949–50	Tottenham H	61	Sheffield W	52	Sheffield U	52
1950–51	Preston NE	57	Manchester C	52	Cardiff C	50
1951–52	Sheffield W	53	Cardiff C	51	Birmingham C	51
1952–53	Sheffield U	60	Huddersfield T	58	Luton T	52
1953–54	Leicester C	56	Everton	56	Blackburn R	55
1954–55	*Birmingham C	54	Luton	54	Rotherham U	54
1955–56	Sheffield W	55	Leeds U	52	Liverpool	48
1956–57	Leicester C	61	Nottingham F	54	Liverpool	53
1957–58	West Ham U	57	Blackburn R	56	Charlton A	55
1958–59	Sheffield W	62	Fulham	60	Sheffield U	53
1959–60	Aston Villa	59	Cardiff C	58	Liverpool	50
1960–61	Ipswich T	59	Sheffield U	58	Liverpool	52
1961–62	Liverpool	62	Leyton O	54	Sunderland	53
1962–63	Stoke C	53	Chelsea	52	Sunderland	52
1963–64	Leeds U	63	Sunderland	61	Preston NE	56
1964–65	Newcastle U	57	Northampton T	56	Bolton W	50
1965–66	Manchester C	59	Southampton	54	Coventry C	53
1966–67	Coventry C	59	Wolverhampton W	58	Carlisle U	52
1967–68	Ipswich T	59	QPR	58	Blackpool	58
1968–69	Derby C	63	Crystal P	56	Charlton A	50
1969–70	Huddersfield T	60	Blackpool	53	Leicester C	51
1970–71	Leicester C	59	Sheffield U	56	Cardiff C	53
1971–72	Norwich C	57	Birmingham C	56	Millwall	55
1972–73	Burnley	62	QPR	61	Aston Villa	50
1973–74	Middlesbrough	65	Luton	50	Carlisle	49
1974–75	Manchester U	61	Aston Villa	58	Norwich C	53
1975–76	Sunderland	56	Bristol C	53	WBA	53

*Won on goal average.

	First	Pt	Second	Pt	Third	Pt
1976–77	Wolverhampton	57	Chelsea	55	Nottingham F	52
1977–78	Bolton W	58	Southampton	57	Tottenham H	56
1978–79	Crystal P	57	Brighton & HA	56	Stoke C	56
1979–80	Leicester C	55	Sunderland	54	Birmingham C	53
1980–81	West Ham U	66	Notts Co	53	Swansea C	50
1981–82	*g*Luton T	88	Watford	80	Norwich C	71
1982–83	Q.P.R.	85	Wolverhampton W	75	Leicester C	70
1983–84	*Chelsea	88	Sheffield W	88	Newcastle U	80

Maximum points: *a*, 44; *b*, 56; *c*, 60; *d*, 58; *e*, 76; *f*, 84; *g*, 126

*Won on goal difference

Division III

1958–59	*a*Plymouth Argyle	62	Hull C	61	Brentford	57
1959–60	Southampton	61	Norwich C	59	Shrewsbury	52
1960–61	Bury	68	Walsall	62	QPR	60
1961–62	Portsmouth	65	Grimsby T	62	Bournemouth	59
1962–63	Northampton T	62	Swindon T	58	Port Vale	54
1963–64	*Coventry C	60	Crystal P	60	Watford	58
1964–65	Carlisle U	60	Bristol C	59	Mansfield T	59
1965–66	Hull C	69	Millwall	65	QPR	57
1966–67	QPR	67	Middlesbrough	55	Watford	54
1967–68	Oxford U	57	Bury	56	Shrewsbury T	55
1968–69	*Watford	64	Swindon T	64	Luton T	61
1969–70	Orient	62	Luton T	60	Bristol R	56
1970–71	Preston NE	61	Fulham	60	Halifax	56
1971–72	Aston Villa	70	Brighton & HA	65	Bournemouth	62
1972–73	Bolton W	61	Notts C	57	Blackburn R	55
1973–74	Oldham A	62	Bristol R	61	York C	61
1974–75	Blackburn R	60	Plymouth A	59	Charlton A	55
1975–76	Hereford U	63	Cardiff C	57	Millwall	56
1976–77	Mansfield T	64	Brighton & HA	61	Crystal P	59
1977–78	Wrexham	61	Cambridge U	58	Preston NE	56
1978–79	Shrewsbury T	61	Watford	60	Swansea C	60
1979–80	Grimsby T	62	Blackburn R	59	Sheffield W	58
1980–81	Rotherham U	61	Barnsley	59	Charlton Ath	59
1981–82	*b*Burnley	80	Carlisle U	80	Fulham	78
1982–83	Portsmouth	91	Cardiff C	86	Huddersfield T	82
1983–84	Oxford U	95	Wimbledon	87	Sheffield U	83

*Won on goal average. Maximum points *a* 92; *b* 138

Division III (Southern Section)

1920–21	*a*Crystal P	59	Southampton	54	QPR	53
1921–22	*Southampton	61	Plymouth A	61	Portsmouth	53
1922–23	Bristol C	59	Plymouth A	53	Swansea	53
1923–24	Portsmouth	59	Plymouth A	55	Millwall	54
1924–25	Swansea C	57	Plymouth A	56	Bristol C	53
1925–26	Reading	57	Plymouth A	56	Millwall	53
1926–27	Bristol C	62	Plymouth A	60	Millwall	56
1927–28	Millwall	65	Northampton T	55	Plymouth A	53
1928–29	*Charlton A	54	Crystal P	54	Northampton T	52
1929–30	Plymouth A	68	Brentford	61	QPR	51
1930–31	Notts C	59	Crystal P	51	Brentford	50
1931–32	Fulham	57	Reading	55	Southend U	53
1932–33	Brentford	62	Exeter	58	Norwich C	57
1933–34	Norwich C	61	Coventry C	54	Reading	54

*Won on goal average. Maximum points: *a*, 84; *b*, 92

	First	Pt	Second	Pt	Third	Pt
1934–35	Charlton A	61	Reading	53	Coventry C	51
1935–36	Coventry C	57	Luton T	56	Reading	54
1936–37	Luton T	58	Notts C	56	Brighton & HA	53
1937–38	Millwall	56	Bristol C	55	QPR	53
1938–39	Newport C	55	Crystal P	52	Brighton & HA	49
1946–47	Cardiff	66	QPR	57	Bristol C	51
1947–48	QPR	61	Bournemouth	57	Walsall	51
1948–49	Swansea	62	Reading	55	Bournemouth	52
1949–50	Notts C	58	Northampton T	51	Southend U	51
1950–51*b*	Nottingham F	70	Norwich C	64	Reading	57
1951–52	Plymouth A	66	Reading	61	Norwich C	61
1952–53	Bristol R	64	Northampton T	62	Millwall	62
1953–54	Ipswich T	64	Brighton & HA	61	Bristol C	56
1954–55	Bristol C	70	Leyton O	61	Southampton	59
1955–56	Leyton O	66	Brighton & HA	65	Ipswich T	64
1956–57	*Ipswich T	59	Torquay U	59	Colchester U	58
1957–58	Brighton & HA	60	Brentford	58	Plymouth A	58

Division III (Northern Section)

	First	Pt	Second	Pt	Third	Pt
1921–22*a*	Stockport C	56	Darlington	50	Grimsby	50
1922–23	Nelson	51	Bradford	47	Walsall	46
1923–24*b*	Wolverhampton W	63	Rochdale	62	Chesterfield	54
1924–25	Darlington	58	Nelson	53	New Brighton	53
1925–26	Grimsby T	61	Bradford	60	Rochdale	59
1926–27	Stoke C	63	Rochdale	58	Bradford	55
1927–28	Bradford	63	Lincoln C	55	Stockport C	54
1928–29	Bradford C	63	Stockport C	62	Wrexham	52
1929–30	Port Vale	67	Stockport C	63	Darlington	50
1930–31	Chesterfield	58	Lincoln C	57	Wrexham	54
1931–32*c*	*Lincoln C	57	Gateshead	57	Chester	50
1932–33*b*	Hull C	59	Wrexham	57	Stockport C	54
1933–34	Barnsley	62	Chesterfield	61	Stockport C	59
1934–35	Doncaster R	57	Halifax T	55	Chester	54
1935–36	Chesterfield	60	Chester	55	Tranmere R	55
1936–37	Stockport C	60	Lincoln C	57	Chester	53
1937–38	Tranmere R	56	Doncaster R	54	Hull C	53
1938–39	Barnsley	67	Doncaster R	56	Bradford C	52
1946–47	Doncaster R	72	Rotherham U	64	Chester	56
1947–48	Lincoln C	60	Rotherham U	59	Wrexham	50
1948–49	Hull C	65	Rotherham U	62	Doncaster R	50
1949–50	Doncaster R	55	Gateshead	53	Rochdale U	51
1950–51*d*	Rotherham U	71	Mansfield T	64	Carlisle U	62
1951–52	Lincoln C	69	Grimsby T	66	Stockport C	59
1952–53	Oldham A	59	Port Vale	58	Wrexham	56
1953–54	Port Vale	69	Barnsley	58	Scunthorpe	57
1954–55	Barnsley	65	Accrington S	61	Scunthorpe	58
1955–56	Grimsby T	68	Derby C	63	Accrington S	59
1956–57	Derby C	63	Hartlepool	59	Accrington S	58
1957–58	Scunthorpe U	66	Accrington S	59	Bradford C	57

*Won on goal average. Maximum points: *a*, 70; *b*, 84; *c*, 80; *d*, 90.
No championship during the World Wars.

Division IV

	First	Pt	Second	Pt	Third	Pt
1958–59*a*	Port Vale	64	Coventry C	60	York C	60
1959–60	Walsall	65	Notts C	60	Torquay	60

	First	Pt	Second	Pt	Third	Pt
1960–61	Peterborough	66	Crystal P	64	Northampton T	60
1961–62	Millwall	56	Colchester U	55	Wrexham	53
1962–63	Brentford	62	Oldham A	59	Crewe A	59
1963–64	*Gillingham	60	Carlisle U	60	Workington T	59
1964–65	Brighton & HA	63	Millwall	62	York C	62
1965–66	*Doncaster R	59	Darlington	59	Torquay	58
1966–67	Stockport C	64	Southport C	59	Barrow	59
1967–68	Luton T	66	Barnsley	61	Hartlepool	60
1968–69	Doncaster R	59	Halifax T	57	Rochdale	56
1969–70	Chesterfield	64	Wrexham	61	Swansea T	60
1970–71	Notts C	69	Bournemouth	60	Oldham A	59
1971–72	Grimsby T	63	Southend U	60	Brentford	59
1972–73	Southport	62	Hereford U	58	Cambridge U	57
1973–74	Peterborough U	65	Gillingham	62	Colchester	60
1974–75	Mansfield T	68	Shrewsbury T	62	Rotherham U	59
1975–76	Lincoln C	74	Northampton T	68	Reading	60
1976–77	Cambridge U	65	Exeter C	62	Colchester	59
1977–78	Watford	71	Southend U	60	Swansea C	56
1978–79	Reading	65	Grimsby T	61	Wimbledon	61
1979–80	Huddersfield T	66	Walsall	64	Newport Co	61
1980–81	Southend U	67	Lincoln C	65	Doncaster R	56
1981–82	*b*Sheffield U	96	Bradford C	91	Wigan Ath	91
1982–83	Wimbledon	98	Hull C	90	Port Vale	88
1983–84	York C	101	Doncaster R	85	Reading	82

Maximum points *a*, 92; *b*, 138
* Won on goal average.

RELEGATED CLUBS

(Since inception of automatic promotion and relegation in 1898–99)

Season	Division I to Division II	Division II to Division III
1983–84	Birmingham C., Notts Co., Wolverhampton W.	Derby Co., Swansea C., Cambridge U.
1982–83	Manchester C., Swansea C., Brighton & H.A.	Rotherham U., Burnley Bolton W.
1981–82	Leeds U., Middlesbrough, Wolverhampton W.	Cardiff, Wrexham, Orient.
1980–81	Norwich C., Leicester C., Crystal P.	Preston N.E., Bristol C., Bristol R.
1979–80	Bristol C., Derby Co., Bolton W.	Fulham, Burnley, Charlton Ath.
1978–79	QPR, Birmingham, Chelsea	Sheffield U., Millwall, B'burn
1977–78	West Ham, Newcastle, Leicester	Blackpool, Mansfield, Hull C.
1976–77	Sunderland, Stoke, Tottenham	Carlisle, Plymouth, Hereford
1975–76	Wolves, Burnley, Sheffield U.	Oxford, York, Portsmouth
1974–75	Luton, Chelsea, Carlisle	Millwall, Cardiff, Sheff. W.
1973–74	So'ton, Man. U., Norwich	C. Palace, Preston, Swindon
1972–73	Crystal P. and WBA	Huddersfield and Brighton
1971–72	Huddersfield and Nottingham F.	Charlton and Watford
1970–71	Burnley and Blackpool	Blackburn and Bolton
1969–70	Sunderland and Sheffield W.	Aston Villa and Preston
1968–69	Leicester and QPR	Bury and Fulham
1967–68	Sheffield U. and Fulham	Rotherham and Plymouth
1966–67	Aston Villa and Blackpool	Northampton and Bury
1965–66	Blackburn and Northampton	Leyton O. and Middlesbrough
1964–65	Birmingham and Wolverh'pton	Swindon and Swansea
1963–64	Bolton and Ipswich	Grimsby and Scunthorpe

1962–63	Manchester C. and Leyton O.	Walsall and Luton
1961–62	Cardiff and Chelsea	Bristol R. and Brighton
1960–61	Newcastle and Preston	Portsmouth and Lincoln
1959–60	Leeds and Luton	Hull and Bristol C.
1958–59	Aston V. and Portsmouth	Grimsby and Barnsley
1957–58	Sunderland and Sheffield W.	Notts Co. and Doncaster
1956–57	Cardiff and Charlton	Bury and Port Vale
1955–56	Huddersfield and Sheffield U.	Plymouth and Hull
1954–55	Leicester and Sheffield W.	Ipswich and Derby
1953–54	Middlesbrough and Liverpool	Brentford and Oldham
1952–53	Stoke and Derby	Southampton and Barnsley
1951–52	Fulham and Huddersfield	Coventry and QPR
1950–51	Sheffield W. and Everton	Chesterfield and Grimsby
1949–50	Manchester C. and Birmingham	Plymouth and Bradford
1948–49	Preston and Sheffield U.	Lincoln and Nottingham F.
1947–48	Blackburn and Grimsby	Doncaster and Millwall
1946–47	Brentford and Leeds	Swansea and Newport
1938–39	Birmingham and Leicester	Norwich and Tranmere
1937–38	Manchester C. and WBA	Barnsley and Stockport
1936–37	Manchester U. and Sheffield W.	Doncaster and Bradford C.
1935–36	Aston Villa and Blackburn	Port Vale and Hull
1934–35	Leicester and Tottenham	Oldham and Notts Co.
1933–34	Newcastle and Sheffield U.	Millwall and Lincoln
1932–33	Bolton and Blackpool	Chesterfield and Charlton
1931–32	Grimsby and West Ham	Barnsley and Bristol City
1930–31	Leeds and Manchester U.	Reading and Cardiff
1929–30	Burnley and Everton	Hull and Notts Co.
1928–29	Bury and Cardiff	Port Vale and Clapton O.
1927–28	Tottenham and Middlesbro'	Fulham and South Shields
1926–27	Leeds and WBA	Darlington and Bradford C.
1925–26	Manchester C. and Notts Co.	Stoke and Stockport
1924–25	Preston and Nottingham F.	Crystal Palace and Coventry
1923–24	Chelsea and Middlesbro'	Nelson and Bristol City
1922–23	Stoke and Oldham	Rotherham and W'ham'ton
1921–22	Bradford C. and Manchester U.	Bradford and Bristol City
1920–21	Derby and Bradford	Stockport
1919–20	Notts Co. and Sheffield W.	

1916–18 During the War the Football League competition was suspended. Previously the clubs relegated from Div. I to Div. II were:

1914–15 Tottenham and Chelsea
1913–14 Preston North End and Derby County
1912–13 Notts County and Woolwich Arsenal
1911–12 Preston North End and Bury
1910–11 Bristol City and Nottingham Forest
1909–10 Bolton Wanderers and Chelsea
1908–09 Manchester City and Leicester Fosse
1907–08 Bolton Wanderers and Birmingham
1906–07 Derby County and Stoke
1905–06 Nottingham Forest and Wolverhampton
1904–05 League extended. Bury and Notts County, two bottom clubs in First Division, re-elected.
1903–04 Liverpool and West Bromwich Albion
1902–03 Grimsby and Bolton
1901–02 Small Heath and Manchester City
1900–01 Preston North End and West Bromwich
1899–1900 Burnley and Glossop
1898–99 Bolton and Sheffield Wednesday

Season	Relegation from Third to Fourth Division
1983–84	Scunthorpe U., Southend U., Port Vale, Exeter C.
1982–83	Reading, Doncaster R., Wrexham, Chesterfield.
1981–82	Wimbledon, Swindon T., Bristol C., Chester
1980–81	Sheffield U., Colchester U., Hull C., Blackpool
1979–80	Bury, Southend U., Mansfield T. and Wimbledon
1978–79	Peterborough, Walsall, Tranmere and Lincoln
1977–78	Port Vale, Bradford, Hereford and Portsmouth
1976–77	Reading, Northampton, Grimsby and York
1975–76	Aldershot, Colchester, Southend U., and Halifax T.
1974–75	Bournemouth, Tranmere, Watford and Huddersfield
1973–74	Cambridge, Shrewsbury, Southport and Rochdale
1972–73	Rotherham, Brentford, Swansea and Scunthorpe
1971–72	Mansfield, Barnsley, Bradford C. and Torquay
1970–71	Reading, Bury, Doncaster and Gillingham
1969–70	Bournemouth, Southport, Barrow and Stockport
1968–69	Northampton, Hartlepool, Crewe and Oldham
1967–68	Grimsby, Colchester, Scunthorpe and Peterborough*
1966–67	Swansea, Darlington, Workington and Doncaster
1965–66	Southend, Exeter, Brentford, and York
1964–65	Luton, Port Vale, Colchester and Barnsley
1963–64	Millwall, Crewe, Wrexham and Notts County
1962–63	Bradford, Brighton, Carlisle and Halifax
1961–62	Torquay, Lincoln, Brentford and Newport
1960–61	Tranmere, Bradford C., Colchester and Chesterfield
1959–60	York, Mansfield, Wrexham and Accrington
1958–59	Stockport, Doncaster, Notts County and Rochdale

*Expelled to Fourth Division by League

APPLICATION FOR RE-ELECTION TO THIRD DIVISION UNTIL 1957-58

Seven times: Walsall.
Six: Exeter, Halifax, Newport.
Five: Accrington, Barrow, Gillingham, New Brighton, Southport.
Four: Norwich, Rochdale.
Three: Crewe, Crystal Palace, Darlington, Hartlepool, Merthyr Town, Swindon.
Two: Aberdare Athletic, Aldershot, Ashington, Bournemouth, Brentford, Chester, Colchester, Millwall, Durham City, Nelson, Queen's Park Rangers, Rotherham, Southend, Tranmere, Watford, Workington.
One: Bradford, Bradford City, Brighton, Bristol Rovers, Cardiff, Carlisle, Charlton, Gateshead, Grimsby, Mansfield, Shrewsbury, Thames, Torquay, York.

APPLICATION FOR RE-ELECTION TO FOURTH DIVISION

Eleven times: Hartlepool.
Seven: Crewe.
Six: Barrow, Rochdale, Southport and York.
Five: Chester C., Darlington, Halifax T., Lincoln, and Workington.
Four: Bradford, Newport and Stockport.
Three: Doncaster, Hereford U., Northampton.

Two: Bradford City, Oldham and Scunthorpe.
One: Aldershot, Blackpool, Colchester, Exeter, Gateshead, Grimsby, Port Vale, Swansea City, Tranmere R., and Wrexham.
Gateshead not re-elected, their place being taken by Peterborough in the 1960–61 season.
Accrington resigned March 1962, and Oxford United elected to replace them in 1962–63 season.
Bradford not re-elected, their place being taken by Cambridge United in the 1970–71 season.
Barrow not re-elected, their place being taken by Hereford United in the 1972–73 season.
Workington not re-elected, their place being taken by Wimbledon in the 1977–78 season.
Southport not re-elected, their place being taken by Wigan in the 1978–79 season.

LEAGUE TITLE WINS

League Division I–15–Liverpool; 8–Arsenal; 7–Aston Villa, Everton, Manchester U.; 6–Sunderland; 4–Newcastle, Sheffield Wed.; 3–Huddersfield, Wolves; 2–Blackburn, Burnley, Derby, Leeds, Manchester City, Portsmouth, Preston, Tottenham; 1–Chelsea, Ipswich, Nottingham Forest, Sheffield United, West Bromwich Albion.

League Division II–6–Manchester City, Leicester; 5–Sheffield Wed.; 4–*Birmingham, Liverpool; 3–Derby, Middlesbrough, Notts Co., Preston; 2–Aston Villa, Bolton, Burnley, Grimsby, Ipswich, Leeds, Manchester U., Nottingham Forest, Stoke, Tottenham, West Bromwich, West Ham, Wolverhampton; 1–Blackburn, Blackpool, Bradford City, Brentford, Bristol City, Bury, Chelsea, Coventry, Crystal Palace, Everton, Fulham, Huddersfield, Luton, Newcastle, Norwich, Q.P.R., Sheffield United, Sunderland.
*Once as Small Heath.

League Division III–2–Oxford U., Portsmouth, 1–Aston Villa, Blackburn R., Bolton, Burnley, Bury, Carlisle, Coventry, Grimsby T., Hereford U., Hull, Mansfield, Northampton, Oldham Ath., Orient, Plymouth, Preston, Queen's Park Rangers, Rotherham U., Shrewsbury T., Southampton, Watford, Wrexham.

League Division IV–Doncaster 2, Peterborough 2; Brentford, Brighton, Cambridge, Chesterfield, Gillingham, Grimsby, Huddersfield T., Lincoln C., Luton, Mansfield T., Millwall, Notts Co., Port Vale, Reading, Sheffield U., Southend U., Southport, Walsall, Watford, Wimbledon, York C.

To 1957-58
Division III (South): Bristol City, three times; Charlton, Ipswich, Millwall, Notts Co., Plymouth, Swansea, twice; Brentford, Brighton, Bristol R., Cardiff, Coventry, Crystal P., Fulham, Leyton Orient, Luton, Newport, Nottingham Forest, Norwich, Portsmouth, Queen's Park Rangers, Reading, Southampton, once.
Division III (North): Barnsley, Doncaster, Lincoln, three times; Chesterfield, Grimsby, Hull, Port Vale, Stockport, twice; Bradford, Bradford City, Darlington, Derby, Nelson, Oldham, Rotherham, Scunthorpe, Stoke, Tranmere, Wolverhampton, once.

TRANSFER TRAIL
(players with British Clubs)

First four-figure transaction
Alf Common: Sunderland to Middlesbrough £1,000 February 1905.
First five-figure transaction
David Jack: Bolton Wanderers to Arsenal £10,340 October 1928.
First six-figure transaction
Alan Ball: Blackpool to Everton £112,000, August 1966.
First £200,000 transaction
Martin Peters: West Ham United to Tottenham Hotspur £200,000, March 1970.
First seven-figure transaction
Trevor Francis: Birmingham City to Nottingham Forest £1,000,000, February 1979.

Bryan Robson: West Bromwich Albion to Manchester United £1,500,000, October 1981.
Andy Gray: Aston Villa to Wolverhampton W. £1,469,000, September 1979.
Steve Daley: Wolverhampton W. to Manchester City £1,450,000, September 1979.
Kenny Sansom: Crystal Palace to Arsenal £1,350,000, August 1980.
Clive Allen: Queen's Park Rangers to Arsenal £1,250,000, June 1980.
Clive Allen: Arsenal to Crystal Palace, £1,250,000, August 1980.
Gary Birtles: Nottingham Forest to Manchester United £1,250,000, October 1980
Trevor Francis: Birmingham City to Nottingham Forest £1,000,000, February 1979.
Kevin Reeves: Norwich City to Manchester City £1,000,000, March 1980.
Justin Fashanu: Norwich City to Nottingham Forest £1,000,000, August 1981.
Trevor Francis: Nottingham Forest to Manchester City £1,000,000, September 1981.
Peter Barnes: West Bromwich Albion to Leeds United £930,000, August 1981.
Mark Lawrenson: Brighton & Hove Albion to Liverpool £900,000, August 1981.
Frank Stapleton: Arsenal to Manchester United £900,000, August 1981.
Steve Archibald. Aberdeen to Tottenham Hotspur £800,000, May 1980.
Paul Goddard: Queen's Park Rangers to West Ham United £800,000 August 1980.
Jesper Olsen: Ajax Amsterdam to Manchester United £800,000 June 1984.
Mick Robinson: Preston North End to Manchester City £756,000, July 1979.
Ray Wilkins: Chelsea to Manchester United £750,000, August 1979.
Charlie Nicholas: Celtic to Arsenal £750,000, July 1983
Gordon Strachan: Aberdeen to Manchester United £750,000, May 1984
Mike Flanagan: Charlton Athletic to Crystal Palace £722,000 August 1979.
Adrian Heath: Stoke City to Everton £700,000, January 1982.
Paul Walsh: Luton Town to Liverpool £700,000, May 1984
Steve Wicks: Queen's Park Rangers to Crystal Palace £670,000, June 1981.
Peter Barnes: Manchester City to West Bromwich Albion £650,000, July 1979.
John Gidman: Aston Villa to Everton £650,000, October 1979.
Garth Crooks: Stoke City to Tottenham Hotspur £600,000, July 1980.
David Armstrong: Middlesbrough to Southampton £600,000, August 1981.
John Chiedozie: Orient to Notts County £600,000, August 1981.
Craig Johnston: Middlesbrough to Liverpool £575,000, April 1981.
Phil Parkes: Queen's Park Rangers to West Ham United £565,000, February 1979.
David Mills: Middlesbrough to West Bromwich Albion £516,000, January 1979.
Asa Hartford: Manchester City to Nottingham Forest £500,000, July 1979.
Asa Hartford: Nottingham Forest to Everton £500,000, August 1979.
Peter Withe: Newcastle United to Aston Villa £500,000, May 1980.

Andrew Ritchie: Manchester U. to Brighton & Hove A. £500,000, October 1980.
Steve McKenzie: Manchester C. to West Bromwich A. £500,000, August 1981.
Remi Moses: West Bromwich A. to Manchester U. £500,000, September 1981.
Tony Woodcock: FC Cologne to Arsenal £500,000, July 1982.
Lee Chapman: Stoke City to Arsenal £500,000, August 1982.
Gerry Francis: Queen's Park Rangers to Crystal Palace £465,000, July 1979.
Gordon McQueen: Leeds United to Manchester United £450,000, February 1978.
Brian Talbot: Ipswich Town to Arsenal £450,000, January 1979.
Garry Owen: Manchester City to West Bromwich Albion £450,000, June 1979.
David Hodgson: Middlesbrough to Liverpool £450,000, August 1982
Vladimir Petrovic: Red Star Belgrade to Arsenal £450,000, December 1982
Alan Brazil: Ipswich Town to Tottenham Hotspur £450,000, March 1983
John Wark: Ipswich Town to Liverpool £450,000, March 1984
Kenny Dalglish: Celtic to Liverpool £440,000, May 1979.
Mick Baxter: Preston North End to Middlesbrough £425,000, August 1981.
Paul Proctor: Middlesbrough to Nottingham Forest £425,000, August 1981.
Osvaldo Ardiles: Huracan to Tottenham Hotspur £400,000, July 1978.
Charlie George: Derby County to Southampton £400,000, December 1978.
Tony Currie: Leeds United to Queen's Park Rangers £400,000, August 1979.
Frank Gray: Leeds United to Nottingham Forest £400,000, August 1979.
John Deehan: Aston Villa to West Bromwich Albion £400,000, September 1979.
Gordon Smith: Rangers to Brighton & Hove Albion £400,000, May 1980.
Ray Stewart: Dundee United to West Ham United £400,000, September 1979.
Dave Thomas: Everton to Wolverhampton Wanderers £400,000, October 1979.
Dave Swindlehurst: Crystal Palace to Derby County £400,000, April 1980.
Alex Sabella: Sheffield United to Leeds United £400,000, May 1980.
Kevin Keegan: Hamburg to Southampton £400,000, July 1980.
Michael Robinson: Manchester C. to Brighton & Hove Albion £400,000, July 1980.
Paul Barron: Arsenal to Crystal Palace £400,000, August 1980.
Thomas Langley: Chelsea to Queen's Park Rangers £400,000, August 1980.
Andrew King: Everton to Queen's Park Rangers £400,000, September 1980.
Peter Ward: Brighton & Hove A. to Nottingham Forest £400,000, October 1980.
Peter Nicholas: Crystal Palace to Arsenal £400,000, March 1981.
Clive Allen: Crystal Palace to Queen's Park Rangers £400,000, June 1981.
Jimmy Case: Liverpool to Brighton & Hove Albion £400,000, August 1981.
Andy King: Queen's Park Rangers to West Bromwich Albion £400,000 September 1981.
Kenny Burns: Nottingham Forest to Leeds United £400,000, October 1981.
Neil Orr: Greenock Morton to West Ham United £400,000, January 1982.
Paul Walsh: Charlton Athletic to Luton Town £400,000, July 1982
Alan Curtis: Swansea City to Leeds United £375,000, May 1979.
Irving Nattrass: Newcastle United to Middlesbrough £375,000, August 1979.
Kevin Hird: Blackburn Rovers to Leeds United £360,000, March 1979.
Graeme Souness: Middlesbrough to Liverpool £352,000, January 1978.
Bob Latchford: Birmingham City to Everton £350,000, February 1974
Joe Jordan: Leeds United to Manchester United £350,000, January 1978.
Paul Futcher: Luton Town to Manchester City £350,000, June 1978.
Richardo Villa: Racing Club to Tottenham Hotspur £350,000, July 1978.
Len Cantello: West Bromwich Albion to Bolton Wanderers £350,000, June 1979.
Garry Collier: Bristol City to Coventry City £350,000, July 1979.
Brian Greenhoff: Manchester United to Leeds United £350,000, August 1979.
Alan Biley: Cambridge United to Derby County £350,000, January 1980.
David Langan: Derby County to Birmingham City £350,000, July 1980.
Joe Gallagher: Birmingham City to Wolverhampton Wanderers £350,000, August 1981.
Colin Irwin: Liverpool to Swansea City £350,000, August 1981.
Kevin Bond: Seattle Sounders to Manchester City £350,000, September 1981.
Chris Kamara: Portsmouth to Brentford £350,000, October 1981.

Peter Shilton: Nottingham Forest to Southampton £350,000, August 1982
Tommy Caton: Manchester City to Arsenal £350,000, December 1983
Malcolm Macdonald: Newcastle United to Arsenal £333,333, August 1976
Richard Money: Fulham to Liverpool £333,000, May 1980.
Paul Hart: Blackpool to Leeds United £330,000, March 1978.
Colin Todd: Derby County to Everton £330,000, September 1978.
Mick Walsh: Blackpool to Everton £325,000, August 1978.
John Gidman: Everton to Manchester United £325,000, August 1981.
Gary Gillespie: Coventry City to Liverpool £325,000, July 1983
Claudio Marangoni: San Lorenzo (Arg.) to Sunderland £320,000, December 1979.
Allan Simonsen: Barcelona to Charlton Athletic £320,000, November 1982
Alan Kennedy: Newcastle United to Liverpool £300,000, August 1978.
Mike Thomas: Wrexham to Manchester United £300,000, November 1978.
Frank McGarvey: St Mirren to Liverpool £300,000, May 1979.
John Gregory: Aston Villa to Brighton & Hove Albion £300,000, July 1979.
Bobby Shinton: Wrexham to Manchester City £300,000, July 1979.
Garry Stanley: Chelsea to Everton £300,000, August 1979.
Terry Yorath: Coventry City to Tottenham Hotspur £300,000, August 1979.
David Geddis: Ipswich Town to Aston Villa £300,000, September 1979.
Steve Wicks: Derby County to Queen's Park Rangers £300,000, September 1979.
Barry Powell: Coventry City to Derby County £300,000, October 1979.
Stan Cummins: Middlesbrough to Sunderland £300,000, November 1979.
Ian Rush: Chester to Liverpool £300,000, May 1980.
Gerrard Daly: Derby County to Coventry City £300,000, August 1980.
Drazen Muzinic: Hadjuk Split to Norwich City £300,000, September 1980.
Alexander Munro: St. Mirren to Stoke City £300,000, October 1980.
Frank Gray: Nottingham Forest to Leeds United £300,000, May 1981.
John Gregory: Brighton & Hove Albion to Queen's Park Rangers £300,000, June 1981.
Alan Biley: Derby Co. to Everton £300,000, July 1981.
Andy Blair: Coventry City to Aston Villa £300,000, August 1981.
Ray Clemence: Liverpool to Tottenham Hotspur £300,000, August 1981.
Ally McCoist: St Johnstone to Sunderland £300,000, August 1981.
Neil Whatmore: Bolton Wanderers to Birmingham City £300,000, August 1981.
Steve Nicol: Ayr United to Liverpool £300,000, October 1981.
Ray Hankin: Vancouver Whitecaps to Arsenal £300,000 November 1981.
Peter Beardsley: Vancouver Whitecaps to Manchester United £300,000, September 1982
Steve McMahon: Everton to Aston Villa £300,000, May 1983
Gary Stevens: Brighton & Hove Albion to Tottenham Hotspur £300,000 June 1983
Trevor Steven: Burnley to Everton £300,000, July 1983
Peter Eastoe: Queen's Park Rangers to Everton £280,000, March 1979.
Mick Walsh: Everton to Queen's Park Rangers £280,000, March 1979.
Mick Ferguson: Coventry City to Everton £280,000, August 1981.
Steve Wicks: Chelsea to Derby County £275,000, January 1979.
Des Bremner: Hibernian to Aston Villa £275,000, September 1979.
Frank McGarvey: Liverpool to Celtic £275,000, March 1980.
Simon Stainrod: Oldham Athletic to Q.P.R. £275,000, November 1980.
Martin O'Neill: Norwich City to Manchester City £275,000, June 1981.
Micky Thomas: Manchester United to Everton, £275,000, August 1981.
Paul Maguire: Shrewsbury Town to Stoke City £262,000, September 1980.

FA CUP 1983-84

Everton at last

When Henry VIII's flagship the Mary Rose was raised from Southampton water, the joke going around Merseyside was that the Everton trophy room had been found on board. Actually it had been 14 years since Everton's last major trophy – the 1970 League Championship – and the 1984 FA Cup Final provided the Goodison club with a fresh chance to hold their heads high in Liverpool. Having lost the Milk Cup final to their neighbours a couple of months earlier, the victory was all the sweeter – and in a competition where Liverpool have had the least success.

For Watford, there was all the glamour of their first-ever Wembley appearance – a remarkable achievement for a club who had been in the Fourth Division as recently as 1978. Manager Graham Taylor could be justly proud of his own personal success, having built an attractive young team with limited resources, and the experience would have stood the club in good stead for the future.

The earlier rounds of the competition had provided all the thrills and spills for which it is famous. In the Third Round, the most notable exit was that of Manchester United at the hands of Bournemouth, and in the next round Brighton knocked Liverpool out for the second consecutive season. At the same stage, eventual winners Everton needed three attempts to remove Gillingham, and by the Fifth Round there were only eight First Division teams left out of the sixteen clubs still in the running.

Perhaps the most exciting prospect in the Semi-finals was lowly Plymouth Argyle's chance for glory. They had battled through against Southend, Barking, Newport, Darlington, West Bromwich Albion and Derby County to reach a Semi-final tie against Watford at Villa Park, and suffered no disgrace by losing only 1-0. They spent the rest of the season in a grim struggle to avoid relegation from the Third Division – a feat which they finally pulled off with victories in their last two League games of the season.

The final produced an exciting first half, with plenty of action in both penalty areas, and Watford's Jamaican-born star forward, John Barnes, could have had two goals in the first quarter of an hour, but the slightly more experienced Everton side held steady, and in the 38th minute Graeme Sharp turned on a loose ball ten yards out and fired home off the inside of a post. Within six minutes of the start of the second half, Andy Gray rose to challenge Watford 'keeper Steve Sherwood for a far-post cross, and appeared to head the ball at the same moment that Sherwood's hands made contact. Sherwood's handling had been slightly suspect all afternoon, and he had shown a tendency to punch the ball out a little too often for comfort. In any event, Everton held their deserved lead until the end, and the FA Cup was off on one of its rare trips to Merseyside.

FA CUP

First Round

Aldershot	1 1	Worcester C	1 2
AP Leamington	0	Gillingham	1
Barking	2	Farnborough	1
Barnet	0 1	Bristol R	0 3
Boston U	0	Bury	3
AFC Bournemouth	4	Walsall	0
Bradford C	0 2	Wigan Ath	0 4
Burton A	1	Windsor	2

Chelmsford	0 2	Wycombe W	0 1
Chester C	1	Chesterfield	2
Corinthian Casuals	0 0	Bristol C	0 4
Dagenham	2 1	Brentford	2 2
Darlington	5	Mossley	0
Exeter C	1 1	Maidstone	1 2
Frickley	0	Altrincham	1
Gainsborough Tr	0	Blackpool	2
Halifax T	2	Whitby	3
Hyde	0	Burnley	2
Kettering	0	Swindon T	7
Macclesfield	0 0	York C	0 2
Mansfield T	3	Doncaster R	0
Millwall	2	Dartford	1
Northampton T	1 1 2	Waterlooville	1 1 0
Northwich Vic	1 0	Bangor	1 1
Oxford U	2	Peterborough U	0
Penrith	0	Hull C	2
Poole	0 1	Newport Co	0 3
Port Vale	1	Lincoln C	2
Reading	2	Hereford U	0
Rochdale	1	Crewe Alex	0
Rotherham U	0 1	Hartlepool U	0 0
Scunthorpe U	1	Preston NE	0
Southend U	0 0	Plymouth Arg	0 2
Telford	3	Stockport Co	0
Torquay U	1	Colchester U	2
Tranmere R	2 1	Bolton W	2 4
Wealdstone	1 2 2	Enfield	1 2 0
Wimbledon	2	Orient	1
Wrexham	1	Sheffield U	5
Yeovil T	0	Harrow	1

Second round

Bangor	1 1	Blackpool	1 2
Bolton W	2	Mansfield T	0
Brentford	3	Wimbledon	2
Bristol R	1	Bristol C	2
Chesterfield	2 2	Burnley	2 3
Colchester U	4	Wealdstone	0
Darlington	0 2	Altrincham	0 0
Gillingham	6	Chelmsford	1
Harrow	1	Newport Co	3
Lincoln C	0 0	Sheffield U	0 1
Maidstone	3	Worcester C	2
Millwall	2	Swindon T	3
Northampton T	1 2	Telford	1 3
Plymouth Arg	2	Barking	1
Reading	1 0	Oxford U	1 3
Rotherham U	2	Hull C	1
Scunthorpe U	2	Bury	0
Wigan Ath	1	Whitby	0
Windsor	0 0	AFC Bournemouth	0 2
York C	0	Rochdale	2

Third round	Fourth round	Fifth round	Quarter-finals	Semi-finals	Final
Burnley 0 1	Oxford U. 2	Oxford U. 0	Sheffield W. . .0 1	Southampton 0	**EVERTON (1) 2** *Scorers:* Sharp, Gray:
Oxford U. 0 2					
Blackpool 2 0	Blackpool 1				
Manchester C. 1					
Sheffield Wednesday .1	Sheffield W. 3	Sheffield W. 3			
Barnsley 0					
Coventry C. 1 1 3	Coventry C. 2				
Wolverhampton. .1 1 0					
Carlisle U. 1 1	Swindon T. 1	Blackburn R. 0	Southampton .0 5		
Swindon T. 1 3					
Blackburn R. 1	Blackburn R. 2				
Chelsea 0					
Portsmouth 2	Portsmouth 0	Southampton 1			
Grimsby T. 1					
Nottingham F. 1	Southampton 1				
Southampton 2					
Huddersfield T. 2	Huddersfield T. 1	Notts Co. 1	Notts Co. 1	Everton 1	
Q.P.R. 1					
Notts Co. 2 2	Notts Co. 2				
Bristol C. 2 0					
Middlesbrough 3	Middlesbrough 2	Middlesbrough 0			
Arsenal 2					
AFC Bournemouth . . .2	AFC Bournemouth . . .0				
Manchester U. 0					
Stoke C. 0	Everton 0 0 3	Everton 3	Everton 2		
Everton 2					
Gillingham 5	Gillingham 0 0 0				
Brentford 3					
Shrewsbury T. 3	Shrewsbury T. 2	Shrewsbury T. 0			
Oldham Ath. 0					
Cardiff C. 0	Ipswich T. 0				
Ipswich T. 3					

Rotherham U 0 0	W.B.A. 1	W.B.A. 0	Plymouth Arg. .0 1	Plymouth Arg. . . .0	**WATFORD (0) 0** Wembley, att. 100,000
W.B.A. 0 3					
Leeds U. 1 1 2	Scunthorpe U. 0				
Scunthorpe U. . . .1 1 4					
Plymouth Arg. 2 1	Plymouth Arg. 2	Plymouth Arg. 1			
Newport Co. 2 0					
Darlington 4	Darlington 1				
Maidstone 1					
Cambridge U. 0	Derby Co. 3	Derby Co. 2	Derby Co. 0 0		
Derby Co. 3					
Rochdale 1	Telford 2				
Telford 4					
Fulham 0 0	Tottenham H. 0 1	Norwich C. 1			
Tottenham H. 0 2					
Aston Villa 1 0	Norwich C. 0 2				
Norwich C. 1 3					
Bolton W. 0	Sunderland 1	Birmingham C. 3	Birmingham C. . . .1	Watford 1	
Sunderland 3					
Sheffield U. 1 0	Birmingham C. 2				
Birmingham C. 1 2					
Crystal Palace 1	Crystal Palace 1 0	West Ham U. 0			
Leicester C. 0					
West Ham U. 1	West Ham U. 1 2				
Wigan Ath. 0					
Colchester U. 0	Charlton Ath. 0	Watford 3	Watford 3		
Charlton Ath. 1					
Luton T. 2 3	Watford 2				
Watford 2 4					
Brighton & Hove A. . .2	Brighton & Hove A. . .2	Brighton & Hove A. . .1			
Swansea C. 0					
Liverpool 4	Liverpool 0				
Newcastle U. 0					

PAST FA CUP FINALS

1872	The Wanderers	1	Royal Engineers	0
	Betts			
1873	The Wanderers	2	Oxford University	0
	Kinnaird, Wollaston			
1874	Oxford University	2	Royal Engineers	0
	Mackarness, Patton			
1875	Royal Engineers	1	Old Etonians	1
	Unknown		*Unknown*	
	Royal Engineers	2	Old Etonians	0
	Scorers in replay: Renny-Tailyour and one from a rush			
1876	The Wanderers	0	Old Etonians	0
	The Wanderers	3	Old Etonians	0
	Wollaston, Hughes 2			
1877	The Wanderers	2	Oxford University	0
	Kenrick, Lindsay		*(After extra time)*	
1878	The Wanderers	3	Royal Engineers	1
	Kenrick 2, unknown		*Unknown*	
1879	Old Etonians	1	Clapham Rovers	0
	Clerke			
1880	Clapham Rovers	1	Oxford University	0
	Lloyd-Jones			
1881	Old Carthusians	3	Old Etonians	0
	Page, Wynard, Tod			
1882	Old Etonians	1	Blackburn Rovers	0
	Anderson			
1883	Blackburn Olympic	2	Old Etonians	1
	Costley, unknown		*Goodhart (After extra time)*	
1884	Blackburn Rovers	2	Queen's Park	1
	Forrest, Brown		*Christie*	
1885	Blackburn Rovers	2	Queen's Park	0
	Forrest, Brown			
1886	Blackburn Rovers	0	West Bromwich Albion	0
	Blackburn Rovers	2	West Bromwich Albion	0
	Brown, Sowerbutts			
1887	Aston Villa	2	West Bromwich Albion	0
	Hunter, Hodgetts			
1888	West Bromwich Albion	2	Preston North End	1
	Woodall, Bayliss		*Goodall*	
1889	Preston North End	3	Wolverhampton W.	0
	Ross, Dewhurst, Thomson			
1890	Blackburn Rovers	6	Sheffield Wednesday	1
	Dewar, Lofthouse, John, Townley 3		*Bennett*	
1891	Blackburn Rovers	3	Notts County	1
	Dewar, John, Townley		*Oswald*	
1892	West Bromwich Albion	3	Aston Villa	0
	Reynolds, Nicholls, Geddes			
1893	Wolverhampton W.	1	Everton	0
	Allen			
1894	Notts County	4	Bolton Wanderers	1
	Watson, Logan 3		*Cassidy*	
1895	Aston Villa	1	West Bromwich Albion	0
	Unknown			
1896	Sheffield Wednesday	2	Wolverhampton W.	1
	Spiksley 2		*Black*	

1897	Aston Villa	3	Everton	2
	Crabtree, Campbell, Wheldon		*Boyle, Bell*	
1898	Nottingham Forest	3	Derby County	1
	McPherson, Capes 2		*Bloomer*	
1899	Sheffield United	4	Derby County	1
	Bennett, Beer, Almond, Priest		*Boag*	
1900	Bury	4	Southampton	0
	Wood, McLuckie 2, Plant			
1901	Tottenham Hotspur	2	Sheffield United	2
	Brown 2		*Bennett, Priest*	
	Tottenham Hotspur	3	Sheffield United	1
	Cameron, Smith, Brown		*Priest*	
1902	Sheffield United	1	Southampton	1
	Common		*Brown*	
	Sheffield United	2	Southampton	1
	Hedley, Barnes		*Brown*	
1903	Bury	6	Derby County	0
	Wood, Sagar, Ross, Plant, Leeming 2			
1904	Manchester City	1	Bolton Wanderers	0
	Meredith			
1905	Aston Villa	2	Newcastle United	0
	Hampton 2			
1906	Everton	1	Newcastle United	0
	Young			
1907	Sheffield Wednesday	2	Everton	1
	Stewart, Simpson		*Sharp*	
1908	Wolverhampton W.	3	Newcastle United	1
	Hunt, Harrison, Hedley		*Howie*	
1909	Manchester United	1	Bristol City	0
	A. Tyrnbull			
1910	Newcastle United	1	Barnsley	1
	Rutherford		*Tuffnell*	
	Newcastle United	2	Barnsley	0
	Shepherd 2 (1 pen)			
1911	Bradford City	0	Newcastle United	0
	Bradford City	1	Newcastle United	0
	Spiers			
1912	Barnsley	2	West Bromwich Albion	0
	Tuffnell 2		*(After extra time)*	
1913	Aston Villa	1	Sunderland	0
	Barber			
1914	Burnley	1	Liverpool	0
	Freeman			
1915	Sheffield United	3	Chelsea	0
	Simmons, Fazackerley, Kitchen			
1920	Aston Villa	1	Huddersfield Town	0
	Kirton			
1921	Tottenham Hotspur	1	Wolverhampton W.	0
	Dimmock			
1922	Huddersfield Town	1	Preston North End	0
	Smith (pen)			
1923	Bolton Wanderers	2	West Ham United	0
	Jack, J.R. Smith			
1924	Newcastle United	2	Aston Villa	0
	Harris, Seymour			
1925	Sheffield United	1	Cardiff City	0
	Tunstall			

1926	Bolton Wanderers *Jack*	1	Manchester City	0
1927	Cardiff City *Ferguson*	1	Arsenal	0
1928	Blackburn Rovers *Roscamp 2, M'Lean*	3	Huddersfield Town *A. Jackson*	1
1929	Bolton Wanderers *Butler, Blackmore*	2	Portsmouth	0
1930	Arsenal *Lambert, James*	2	Huddersfield Town	0
1931	West Bromwich Albion *W.G Richardson 2*	2	Birmingham City *Bradford*	1
1932	Newcastle United *Allen 2*	2	Arsenal *John*	1
1933	Everton *Dunn, Dean, Stein*	3	Manchester City	0
1934	Manchester City *Tilson 2*	2	Portsmouth *Rutherford*	1
1935	Sheffield Wednesday *Hooper, Palethorpe, Rimmer 2*	4	West Bromwich Albion *Sandford, Boyes*	2
1936	Arsenal *Drake*	1	Sheffield United	0
1937	Sunderland *Carter, Gurney, Burbanks*	3	Preston North End *F. O'Donnell*	1
1938	Preston North End *Mutch (pen)*	1	Huddersfield Town	0
1939	Portsmouth *Anderson, Barlow, Parker 2*	4	Wolverhampton W *Dorsett*	1
1946	Derby County *H. Turner (og), Stamps 2, Doherty*	4	Charlton Athletic *H. Turner (After extra time)*	1
1947	Charlton Athletic *Duffy*	1	Burnley	0
1948	Manchester United *Anderson, Rowley 2, Pearson*	4	Blackpool *Shimwell (pen), Mortensen*	2
1949	Wolverhampton W *Smyth, Pye 2*	3	Leicester City *Griffiths*	1
1950	Arsenal *Lewis 2*	2	Liverpool	0
1951	Newcastle *Milburn 2*	2	Blackpool	0
1952	Newcastle *G. Robledo*	1	Arsenal	0
1953	Blackpool *Mortensen 3, Perry*	4	Bolton Wanderers *Bell, Moir, Lofthouse*	3
1954	West Bromwich Albion *Griffin, Allen 2*	3	Preston North End *Wayman, Morrison*	2
1955	Newcastle United *Milburn, Hannah, Mitchell*	3	Manchester City *Johnstone*	1
1956	Manchester City *Johnstone, Hayes, Dyson*	3	Birmingham City *Kinsey*	1
1957	Aston Villa *McParland 2*	2	Manchester United *T. Taylor*	1
1958	Bolton Wanderers *Lofthouse 2*	2	ManchekyUnited	0

1959	Nottingham Forest	2	Luton Town	1
	Dwight, Wilson		*Pacey*	
1960	Wolverhampton W	3	Blackburn Rovers	0
	Deeley 2, McGrath (og)			
1961	Tottenham Hotspur	2	Leicester City	0
	Smith, Dyson			
1962	Tottenham Hotspur	3	Burnley	1
	Blanchflower (p), Smith, Greaves		*Robson*	
1963	Manchester United	3	Leicester City	1
	Herd 2,W		*Keyworth*	
1964	West Hnited	3	Preston North End	2
	Boyce, Hurst, Sissons		*Dawson, Holden*	
1965	Liverpool	2	Leeds United	1
	Hunt, St John		*Bremner*	
1966	Everton	3	Sheffield Wednesday	2
	Trebilcock 2, Temple		*McCalliog, Ford*	
1967	Tottenham Hotspur	2	Chelsea	1
	Robertson, Saul		*Tambling*	
1968	West Bromwich Albion	1	Everton	0
	Astle			
1969	Manchester City	1	Leicester City	0
	Young			
1970	Chelsea	2	Leeds United	2
	Houseman, Hutchinson		*Charlton, Jones*	
	Chelsea	2	Leeds United	1
	Webb, Osgood		*Jones (After extra time)*	
1971	Arsenal	2	Liverpool	1
	Kelly, George		*Heighway (After extra time)*	
1972	Leeds United	1	Arsenal	0
	Clarke			
1973	Sunderland	1	Leeds United	0
	Porterfield			
1974	Liverpool	3	Newcastle United	0
	Keegan 2, Heighway			
1975	West Ham United	2	Fulham	0
	A. Taylor			
1976	Southampton	1	Manchester United	0
	Stokes			
1977	Manchester United	2	Liverpool	1
	Pearson, J. Greenhoff		*Case*	
1978	Ipswich Town	1	Arsenal	0
	Osborne			
1979	Arsenal	3	Manchester United	2
	Talbot, Stapleton, Sunderland		*McQueen, McIlroy*	
1980	West Ham United	1	Arsenal	0
	Brooking			
1981	Tottenham Hotspur	1	Manchester City	1
	Hutchinson (og)		*Hutchinson*	
	Tottenham Hotspur	3	Manchester City	2
	Crooks, Villa 2		*Mackenzie, Reeves (pen)*	
1982	Tottenham Hotspur	1	Q.P.R.	1
	Hoddle		*Fenwick*	
	Tottenham Hotspur	1	Q.P.R.	0
	Hoddle (pen)			
1983	Manchester United	2	Brighton & Hove Albion	2
	Stapleton, Wilkins		*Smith, Stevens*	
	Brighton & Hove Albion	0	Manchester United	4
			Robson 2, Whiteside, Muhren (pen)	

FA CUP WINNERS SINCE 1871

Aston Villa	7
Tottenham Hotspur	7
Blackburn Rovers	6
Newcastle United	6
Arsenal	5
Manchester United	5
Wanderers	5
West Bromwich Albion	5
Bolton Wanderers	4
Everton	4
Manchester City	4
Sheffield United	4
Wolverhampton Wanderers	4
Sheffield Wednesday	3
West Ham United	3
Bury	2
Liverpool	2
Nottingham Forest	2
Old Etonians	2
Preston North End	2
Sunderland	2
Barnsley	1
Blackburn Olympic	1
Blackpool	1
Bradford City	1
Burnley	1
Cardiff City	1
Charlton Athletic	1
Chelsea	1
Clapham Rovers	1
Derby County	1
Huddersfield Town	1
Ipswich Town	1
Leeds United	1
Notts County	1
Old Carthusians	1
Oxford University	1
Portsmouth	1
Royal Engineers	1
Southampton	1

APPEARANCES IN FA CUP FINAL

Arsenal	11
Newcastle United	11
West Bromwich Albion	10
Aston Villa	9
Manchester United	9
Blackburn Rovers	8
Everton	8
Manchester City	8
Wolverhampton Wanderers	8
Bolton Wanderers	7
Preston North End	7
Tottenham Hotspur	7
Liverpool	6
Old Etonians	6
Sheffield United	6
Huddersfield Town	5
Sheffield Wednesday	5
Wanderers	5
Derby County	4
Leeds United	4
Leicester City	4
Oxford University	4
Royal Engineers	4
West Ham United	4
Blackpool	3
Burnley	3
Chelsea	3
Portsmouth	3
Southampton	3
Sunderland	3
Barnsley	2
Birmingham City	2
Bury	2
Cardiff City	2
Charlton Athletic	2
Clapham Rovers	2
Nottingham Forest	2
Notts County	2
Queen's Park (Glasgow)	2
Blackburn Olympic	1
Bradford City	1
Brighton & Hove Albion	1
Bristol City	1
Fulham	1
Ipswich Town	1
Luton Town	1
Old Carthusians	1
Queen's Park Rangers	1
Watford	1

FOOTBALL LEAGUE MILK CUP

First prize for Fagan

The Milk Marketing Board will have to commission a new trophy for this competition after Liverpool's third consecutive Milk Cup victory – their fourth consecutive League Cup win – ensured that they keep the cup in the Anfield trophy room in perpetuity. The 1983-84 competition also provided the first-ever all-Merseyside Wembley final, and it was – despite the 0-0 scoreline – an enthralling match worthy of the occasion.

Liverpool's progress to the final, however, had been far from straight forward as they had needed at least one replay in every tie from the third round onwards. After disposing of Brentford in predictably easy fashion in the second round, they had to play Fulham three times and Birmingham and Sheffield Wednesday twice to earn their semi-final place against Walsall, and even then they managed to contrive no better than a 2-2 draw at Anfield in the first leg before running out 2-0 winners at Fellows Park.

Walsall had earlier been responsible for repeating a little bit of history by knocking out Arsenal at Highbury in the fourth round – 50 years after their historic FA Cup win over the Gunners – but the real story of the fourth round was Oxford's victory over Manchester United after two replays.

The high-scoring feat of the competition was performed at Upton Park in the second round when West Ham added to a 2-1 first leg win over Bury by wiping them out 10-0. At the time the Hammers were still in contention for the League title, but later faded in both competitions. The longest drawn-out battle was between Birmingham City and Notts County in the third round – a tie which needed four matches to settle it.

By the quarter-final stages, only four First Division clubs were left, but any ideas that the tournament might end in anti-climax at Wembley were dispersed on a rainy afternoon in front of 100,000 noisy but well-behaved Merseyside fans. Not all goal-less draws lack excitement, and certainly on this occasion there were thrills enough for everyone. Perhaps the biggest disappointment of the afternoon was a personal one for the prolific Liverpool striker Ian Rush, who missed an open goal when it would have been easier to score, but he was cheered up that same evening when his fellow professionals voted him the Professional Footballers' Association Player of the Year at a dinner in London.

His team-mate Graeme Souness came second in the poll, but had the satisfaction of scoring the winner in the replayed final at Maine Road three days later, thus making sure that not only did Liverpool win the cup outright, but also that manager Joe Fagan chalked up his first major trophy in his first season in charge of the club.

PAST LEAGUE CUP FINALS

Played as two legs up to 1966

1961	Rotherham United	2	Aston Villa	0
	Webster, Kirkman			
	Aston Villa	3	Rotherham Utd	0
	O'Neill, Burrows, McParland			
1962	Rochdale	0	Norwich City	3
			Lythgoe 2, Punton	
	Norwich City	1	Rochdale	0
	Hill			
1963	Birmingham City	3	Aston Villa	1
	Leek 2, Bloomfield		*Thomson*	
	Aston Villa	0	Birmingham City	0
1964	Stoke City	1	Leicester City	1
	Bebbington		*Gibson*	
	Leicester City	3	Stoke City	2
	Stringfellow, Gibson, Riley		*Viollett, Kinnell*	
1965	Chelsea	3	Leicester City	2
	Tambling, Venables (pen), McCreadie		*Appleton, Goodfellow*	
	Leicester City	0	Chelsea	0
1966	West Ham United	2	West Bromwich Albion	1
	Moore, Byrne		*Astle*	
	West Bromwich Albion	4	West Ham United	1
	Kaye, Brown, Clark, Williams		*Peters*	
1967	Queens Park Rangers	3	West Bromwich Albion	2
	Morgan R., Marsh, Lazarus		*Clark C. 2*	
1968	Leeds United	1	Arsenal	0
	Cooper			
1969	Swindon Town	3	Arsenal	1
	Smart, Rogers 2		*Gould*	
1970	Manchester City	2	West Bromwich Albion	1
	Doyle, Pardoe		*Astle*	
1971	Aston Villa	0	Tottenham Hotspur	2
			Chivers 2	
1972	Chelsea	1	Stoke City	2
	Osgood		*Conroy, Eastham*	
1973	Tottenham Hotspur	1	Norwich City	0
	Coates			
1974	Wolverhampton W.	2	Manchester City	1
	Hibbitt, Richards		*Bell*	
1975	Aston Villa	1	Norwich City	0
	Graydon			
1976	Manchester City	2	Newcastle United	1
	Barnes, Tueart		*Gowling*	
1977	Aston Villa	0	Everton	0
Replay	Aston Villa	1	Everton	1
	Kenyon (og)		*Latchford*	
Replay	Aston Villa	3	Everton	2
	Little 2, Nicholl		*Latchford, Lyons*	
1978	Nottingham Forest	1	Liverpool	0
	Robertson (pen)			
1979	Nottingham Forest	3	Southampton	2
	Birtles 2, Woodcock		*Peach, Holmes*	

1980	Nottingham Forest 0	Wolverhampton W 1	
		Gray	
1981	Liverpool 1	West Ham U 1	
	Kennedy, A	*Stewart (pen)*	
Replay	Liverpool 2	West Ham U 1	
	Dalglish, Hansen	*Goddard*	
1982	Liverpool 3	Tottenham 1	
	Whelan 2, Rush	*Archibald*	
1983	Liverpool 3	Manchester U 1	
	Kennedy, Whelan	*Whiteside*	

LEAGUE MILK CUP 1983-84

First Round *(2 legs)*

Aldershot	3	3	Orient	1	3
Blackpool	2	1	Walsall	1	3
Bolton W	3	0	Chester C*	0	3
Bournemouth	1	2	Bristol R	2	2
Bradford C	0	1	Sheffield U.	1	1
Brentford	3	1	Charlton Ath	0	2
Colchester U**	3	3	Reading	2	4
Crewe Alex	1	4	Burnley	0	3
Crystal Palace	3	0	Peterborough U*	0	3
Exeter C	2	1	Cardiff C	3	2
Gillingham	1	0	Chelsea	2	4
Halifax T	0	2	Darlington	1	3
Hereford U	3	1	Portsmouth	2	3
Hull C	0	1	Lincoln C	0	3
Mansfield T	1	1	Huddersfield T	2	5
Middlesbrough	0	1	Chesterfield*	1	0
Millwall	3	2	Northampton	0	1
Newport Co	2	0	Torquay U	3	1
Oxford U	1	1	Bristol C	1	0
Port Vale	3	5	Wrexham	1	1
Preston N.E.	1	0	Tranmere R.	0	0
Rochdale	0	2	Stockport Co	3	2
Rotherham U	0	1	Hartlepool U	0	0
Scunthorpe U	1	0	Doncaster R	1	3
Southend U	1	4	Wimbledon	0	6
Swindon T	1	1	Plymouth Arg	0	4
Wigan Ath	1	0	Bury	2	2
York C	2	0	Grimsby T	1	2

**Won on penalties*
***Won on away goals*

Second round
(2 legs)

Leeds U.	0	4
Chester C.	1	1
Newcastle U.	1	1
Oxford U.	1	2
Swansea C.	1	0
Colchester U.	1	1
Port Vale	0	0
Manchester U.	1	2
Bury	1	0
West Ham U.	2	10
Brighton & H.A.	4	1
Bristol R.	2	2
Chesterfield	0	2
Everton	1	2
Grimsby T.	0	1
Coventry C.	0	2
Ipswich T.	4	2
Blackburn R.	3	1
Q.P.R.	8	0
Crewe Alex.	1	3
Cardiff C.	0	0
Norwich C.	0	3
Cambridge U.	2	3
Sunderland	3	4
Leicester C.	0	2
Chelsea*	2	0
Millwall	3	1
W.B.A.	0	5
Portsmouth	2	2
Aston Villa	2	3
Torquay U.	0	0
Manchester C.	0	6

Third round

Leeds U.	1	1
Oxford U.	1	4
Colchester U.	0	
Manchester U.	2	
West Ham U.	1	
Brighton & H.A.	0	
Everton	2	
Coventry C.	1	
Ipswich T.	3	
Q.P.R.	2	
Norwich C.	0	2
Sunderland	0	1
Chelsea	0	
W.B.A.	1	
Aston Villa	3	
Manchester C.	0	

Fourth round

Oxford U.	1	1	2
Manchester U.	1	1	1
West Ham U.	2	0	
Everton	2	2	
Ipswich T.	0		
Norwich C.	1		
W.B.A.	1		
Aston Villa	2		

Fifth round

Oxford U.	1	1
Everton	1	4
Norwich C.	0	
Aston Villa	2	

Semi-finals
(2 legs)

Everton	2	0
Aston Villa	0	1

EVERTON 0 *replay* 0

Wembley att: 100,000

* *won on penalties*

LIVERPOOL 0 *replay* 1

Maine Road att: 52,089

Scorer: Souness

Round 1

Stoke C.	0	2
Peterborough U.	0	1
Huddersfield T.	2	2
Watford	1	2
Wolverhampton W.	2	0
Preston N.E.	3	1
Sheffield W.	3	4
Darlington	0	2
Derby Co.	0	0
Birmingham C.	3	4
Aldershot	2	1
Notts Co.	4	4
Doncaster R.	1	1
Fulham	3	3
Brentford	1	0
Liverpool	4	4
Rotherham U.	2	2
Luton T.	3	0
Carlisle U.	2	0
Southampton	0	3
Wimbledon	2	1
Nottingham F.	0	1
Stockport Co.	0	2
Oldham Ath.	2	2
Tottenham H.	3	1
Lincoln C.	1	2
Plymouth Arg.	1	0
Arsenal	1	1
Walsall	1	2
Barnsley	0	0
Shrewsbury T.	3	2
Sheffield U.	2	2

Round 2

Stoke C.	0	2		
Huddersfield	0	0		
Preston N.E.	0			
Sheffield W.	2			
Birmingham C.	2	0	0	3
Notts Co.	2	0	0	1
Fulham	1	1	0	
Liverpool	1	1	1	
Rotherham U.	2			
Southampton	1			
Wimbledon	3			
Oldham Ath.	1			
Tottenham H.	1			
Arsenal	2			
Walsall	2			
Shrewsbury T.	1			

Round 3

Stoke C.	0	
Sheffield W.	1	
Birmingham C.	1	0
Liverpool	1	3
Rotherham U.	1	
Wimbledon	0	
Arsenal	1	
Walsall	2	

Round 4

Sheffield W.	2	0
Liverpool	2	3
Rotherham U.	2	
Walsall	4	

Semi-final

Liverpool	2	2
Walsall	2	0

FOOTBALL LEAGUE ASSOCIATE MEMBERS' CUP

The twelve winners of the Second Round ties were joined by the four highest-scoring losers to form the northern and southern quarter-final groupings.

First Round (N. Section)
Bradford C. 3, Hartlepool U. 2
Burnley 2, Bolton W. 1
Bury 1, Wigan Ath. 0
Chester C. 2, Blackpool 1
Lincoln C. 0, Doncaster R. 2
Mansfield T. 1, Darlington 3
Rochdale 0, Preston N.E. 3
Rotherham U. 0, Sheffield U. 1
Scunthorpe U. 2, Chesterfield 1
Stockport Co. 2, Crewe Alex.* 2
Tranmere R. 2, Halifax T. 0
York C. 1, Hull C. 2

First Round (S. Section)
Bournemouth 4, Aldershot 0
Brentford 3, Orient 2
Colchester U. 2, Wimbledon 1
Exeter C. 3, Bristol C. 1
Hereford U. 0, Port Vale 1
Millwall 4, Gillingham 3
Newport Co. 0, Bristol R. 1
Oxford U. 1, Swindon T. 3
Plymouth Arg. 5, Torquay U. 1
Southend U. 5, Reading 0
Walsall 3, Northampton T. 1
Wrexham 3, Peterborough U. 2

**won on penalties*

Second Round (N. Section)
Burnley 2, Darlington 1
Doncaster R. 2, Preston N.E. 1
Hull C. 1, Bury 0
Scunthorpe U.* 4, Crewe Alex. 4
Sheffield U. 2, Bradford C. 1
Tranmere R. 4, Chester C. 1

Second Round (S. Section)
Bristol R. 2, Port Vale 0
Colchester U. 0, Southend U. 2
Millwall 2, Bournemouth* 2
Plymouth Arg. 2, Brentford 0
Swindon T. 3, Walsall 0
Wrexham 2, Exeter C. 0

Quarter-finals (N. Section)
Doncaster R. 1, Burnley 3
Hull C. 3, Preston N.E. 0
Scunthorpe U. 2, Sheffield U. 3
Tranmere R.* 0, Crewe Alex. 0

Quarter-finals (S. Section)
Bournemouth 2, Wrexham 0
Millwall 3, Swindon T. 1
Plymouth Arg. 2, Exeter C. 1
Southend U. 1, Bristol R. 0

Semi-finals (N. Section)
Hull C. 1, Sheffield U. 0
Tranmere R. 2, Burnley 0

Final (N. Section)
Hull C. 4, Tranmere R. 1

Semi-finals (S. Section)
Bournemouth 1, Bristol R. 0
Plymouth Arg. 0, Millwall 1

Final (S. Section)
Bournemouth 2, Millwall 1

Final
Hull C. 1, Bournemouth 2
McNeil; Graham, Morrell.

SCOTTISH CLUBS

ABERDEEN — PREM. DIV.

Ground: Pittodrie Stadium, Aberdeen (Aberdeen 21428)
Colours: All scarlet.
Goals – League (78): McGhee 13, Strachan 13 (8 pens), Hewitt 12, Black 6, Stark 6 (1 pen), Weir 5, Rougvie 4, Bell 3, Porteous 3, Falconer 2, McLeish 2, Miller 2, Simpson 2, Mckimmie 1, own goals 4.
League Cup (23): Black 5, (1 pen), Stark 5, Hewitt 4, McGhee 3, Porteous 2, Bell 1, Miller 1, Simpson 1, own goal 1.
Cup: (11): McGhee 2, Strachan 2, Weir 2, Angus 1, Black 1, Cooper 1, Miller 1, Porteous 1.

AIRDRIEONIANS — DIV. 1

Ground: Broomfield Park, Gatlea Road, Airdrie (Airdrie 62067)
Colours: White shirts with red diamond, white shorts.
Goals – League (45): Flood 11 (2 pens), McGuire 7, Black 4 (3 pens), Gordon 4, Rodger 4, McCabe 3, Yule 3, Anderson N. 2, Anderson G. 1, Fairlie 1, Jarvie 1, Lawrie 1, McLauchlan 1 (pen), March 1, Sinclair 1.
League Cup (5): Black 1, McKeown 1, McLauchlan 1 (pen), Millar B. 1, Walker 1.
Cup (2): Flood 1, McGuire 1.

ALBION ROVERS — DIV. 2

Ground: Clifton Hill Park, Coatbridge (Coatbridge 21865)
Colours: Yellow shirts with white sleeves, white shorts with red trim.
Goals – League (46): McGorm 11 (3 pens), Gallagher 8, McAteer 6, Conn 5, Greene 5, Kasule 3, Burgess 2, Deakin 1, Evans 1, McCusker 1, Ritchie 1, Rodgers 1, own goal 1.
League Cup (1): Gray 1.
Cup (1): McGorm 1.

ALLOA — DIV. 2

Ground: Recreation Park, Alloa (Alloa 2695)
Colours: Gold shirts with black trim, black shorts.
Goals – League (41): Lloyd 10 (1 pen), Paterson 6, Cole 4, McComb 4, Harris 3, Garner 2, Houston 2, Martin 2, Purdie 2, Munro 1, Shearer 1, Sorbie 1, Thompson G. 1, Weir 1, own goal 1.
League Cup (16): Garner 5 (2 pens), Cole 2, McComb 2, Thompson G. 2, Haggart 1, Houston 1, Jobson 1, Lloyd 1, Paterson 1.
Cup (1): Munro 1.

ARBROATH DIV. 2

Ground: Gayfield Park, Arbroath (Arbroath 2157)
Colours: Maroon shirts, white shorts.
Goals – League (51): Harley 18, Lees 5, kennedy 4, Shaw 4, Steele 4 (1 pen), Gavine 3, Hill, H. 3, Davie 2, Dawson 1, Dunlop 1, Forsyth 1, payne 1 (pen), Rendall 1, Robb 1, Taylor 1, Young 1.
League Cup (1): Shaw 1..
Cup: (6): Lees 4, Gavine 2.

AYR UNITED DIV. 1

Ground: Somerset Park, Ayr (Ayr 63435)
Colours: White shirts with black trim, black shorts.
Goals – League (56): McInally 15, Murphy 8 (1 pen), Connor 7, Collins 5, McNaughton 5, Buchan 3 (2 pens), Charnley 3 (1 pen), Evans 3, Smart 2, Armour 1, Christie 1, McAllister 1, own goals 2.
League Cup (1): McInally 1.

BERWICK RANGERS DIV. 2

Ground: Shiefield Park, Berwick-on-Tweed (Berwick 7424)
Colours: Black and gold striped shirts, black shorts.
Goals – League (60): Davidson 9, O'Hara 9, Steedman 7 (2 pens), Tomassi 5, Cannell 4, Bassett 3, Marshall 3, Morgan 3, Romaines 3, Smith 3, Armstrong 2, McCann 2 (2 pens), Millar 2, Rodier 2, Flavell 1, Mason 1, Ross 1.
League Cup (3): McCann 1 (pen), O'Hara 1, Romaines 1.
Cup (2): O'Hara 1, Tait 1.

BRECHIN CITY DIV. 1

Ground: Glebe Park, Brechin (Brechin 2856)
Colours: All red.
Goals – League (56): Campbell 19 (2 pens), Fleming I. 10, Eadie 5, Elvin 4, Hyslop 4, Mackie 4, Paterson 3, Mitchell 2, Scott 2, Brown 1, Harte 1, Stewart 1.
League Cup : Nil.

CELTIC PREM. DIV.

Ground: Celtic Park, Glasgow (041-554 2710)
Colours: Green and white hooped shirts, white shorts.
Goals – League (80): McClair 23, McGarvey 10, Burns 9, MacLeod, Melrose 7, Aitken 5, McStay, P. 3, Colquhoun 2, Dobbin 2, Provan 2, Reid 2 (2 pens), Whittaker 2, Archdeacon 1, McAdam 1, McStay, W. 1, Sinclair 1, own goals 2.
League Cup (17): Reid 4 (3 pens), Melrose 3, McGarvey 2, MacLeod 2 (2 pens), McStay, P. 2, McClair 1, Provan 1, Whittaker 1, own goal 1.
Cup (19): McClair 6, Burns 3, McGarvey 3, MacLeod 2, McStay, P. 2, Colquhoun 1, Melrose 1, Reid 1.

CLYDE DIV. 1

Ground: Shawfield Stadium, Glasgow (041-647 6329)
Colours: White shirts with red trim, black shorts.
Goals – League (53): Frye 17, Masterton 11, Dean 7, Doherty, J. 4, Ahern 3 (3 pens), Docherty, D. 2, Evans 2, O'Neill 2, Willock 2, Flexney 1, McQueen 1, Reilly 1.
League Cup (1): Doherty, J. 1.
Cup (2): O'Neill 1, Reilly 1.

CLYDEBANK DIV. 1

Ground: Kilbowie Park, Clydebank (041-952 2887)
Colours: Red shirts with broad white vertical stripe on front, black shorts.
Goals – League (62): Coyne 10 (2 pens), Given 9 (6 pens), Ferguson 7, Larnach 7, McGhie 7, Ronald 6, McCabe 4 (1 pen), Williamson 4, Hughes 3, McKeown 1, Murray 1, Shanks 1, Treanor 1 (pen), own goal 1.
League Cup (9): Williamson 4, Coyne 2, Hughes 2, McKeown 1.
Cup (4): McCabe 2, Ferguson 1, Hughes 1.

COWDENBEATH DIV. 2

Ground: Central Park, Cowdenbeath (Cowdenbeath 511205)
Colours: Royal blue shirts with white stripes, white shorts.
Goals – League (44): Paterson 7, Christie 6, Mitchell 6 (2 pens), Ward 5, Graham 4, Miller 3 (1 pen), Oliver 3, Stevenson 3, Shanks 2, Dunlop 1, Henderson 1, Tierney 1, Williamson 1, Wilson, D. 1.
League Cup (4): Christie 3, Shanks 1.
Cup (5): Gavin 1, Miller 1, Shanks 1, Ward 1, own goal 1.

DUMBARTON PREM. DIV.

Ground: Boghead Par, Dumbarton (Dumbarton 2569)
Colours: White shirts with gold and black trim, white shorts
Goals – League (66): Coyle, J. 15 (8 pens), Ashwood 13 (1 pen), Bourke 13, Coyle, T. 7, Craig 4, Robertson 4, McCaig 3, McNeil 3, Crawley 1, McGowan, M. 1, Montgomerie 1, Walsh 1.
League Cup (1): McGrogan 1.
Cup (5): Ashwood 2, Bourke 1, Coyle, J. 1, Craig 1.

DUNDEE PREM. DIV.

Ground: Dens Park, Dundee (Dundee 86104)
Colours: White shirts, dark blue shorts.
Goals – League (50): McCall 13, Ferguson 12 (5 pens), Fraser 3, Mackie 3, McKinlay 3, Stephen 3, Geddes, A. 2, Glennie 2, Harris 2, McInally 2, Kidd 1, MacDonald 1, McGlashan 1, own goals 2.
League Cup (15): Ferguson 4 (1 pen), McCall 4, MacDonald 3, Fraser 2, Kidd 1, Mackie 1.
Cup (9): Ferguson 4, McCall 2, Kidd 1, Smith 1, Stephen 1.

DUNDEE UNITED — PREM. DIV.

Ground: Tannadice Park, Dundee (Dundee 86289)
Colours: Tangerine shirts with black trim, black shorts.
Goals – League (67): Dodds 15, Kirkwood 9, Bannon 7 (3 pens), Reilly 7, Milne 5, Hegarty 4, Sturrock 4, Coyne 3, Gough 3, Stark 3, Holt 2, Malpas 2, Clark 1, Narey 1, Taylor 1.
League Cup (29): Dodds 7, Gough 5, Reilly 5, Bannon 3 (1 pen), Milne 3, Johnstone 2, Holt 1, McGinnis 1, Taylor 1, own goal 1.
Cup (3): Sturrock 2, Dodds 1.

DUNFERMLINE ATHLETIC — DIV. 2

Ground: East End Park, Dunfermline (Dunfermline 24295)
Colours: Black and white striped shirts, black shorts.
Goals – League (44): Stephen Morrison 9, Jenkins 6, McCathie 5, Stewart 4, Forrest 3, Perry 3, Watson 3, Bowie 2, Tait 2, Dall 1, Donnelly 1, Forsyth 1, Lapsley 1, Robertson 1, Smith, T. 1, own goal 1.
League Cup (1): Stephen Morrison 1.
Cup (2): Stewart 2.

EAST FIFE — DIV. 1

Ground: Bayview Park, Methil, Fife (Leven 2323)
Colours: Old gold shirts with black trim, black shorts.
Goals – League (57): Durie 16 (8 pens), Hutt 7, Burt 6, Kirk 5, O'Brien 4, Russell 4, Pryde 3, Caithness 2, Jenkins 2, Kirkwood 2, McCafferty 2, Allan 1, Inglis 1, Scott 1, Stalker 1.
League Cup (6): Hutt 3, Forrest 2, Scott 1.
Cup (7): McCafferty 2, Burt 1, Durie 1 (pen), Kirk 1, Pryde 1, Stalker 1.

EAST STIRLINGSHIRE — DIV. 2

Ground: Firs Park, Falkirk (Falkirk 23583)
Colours: White shirts with black pinstripe, black shorts, red stockings.
Goals – League (51): Gibson 13, Wilson 10 (5 pens), Rennie 6 (1 pen), McIntosh 5, Meakin 4, Doig 3, Marshall 3, Russell 2, Buchanan 1, Gilchrist 1, Hamilton 1, Murray, S. 1, Steel 1.
League Cup (1): Gibson 1.
Cup (4): Wilson 2 (1 pen), Gibson 1, Meakin 1.

FALKIRK — DIV. 1

Ground: Brockville Park, Falkirk (Falkirk 24121)
Colours: Navy blue shirts with white trim, white shorts.
Goals – League (46): McAllister 11, Houston 10, Grant 6, Mackin 4, O'Hara 3 (1 pen), Brown 2, Irvine A. 2, Kemp 2, McGonnigal 2, Stevenson W. 2, Bell 1, own goal 1.
League Cup (4): Brown 2, Herd 1, Irvine 1.
Cup (1): O'Hara 1.

FORFAR ATHLETIC — DIV. 1

Ground: Station Park, Forfar, Angus (Forfar 3576)
Colours: Sky blue shadow stripe, sky blue shorts and stockings.
Goals – League (73): Liddle 22, McDonald 13 (2 pens), Clark 12 (2 pens), Farningham 6, McPhee 5 (1 pen), Gallacher 3, Leitch 3, Brash 2, Cormack 2, Lorimer 2, Graham 1, Scott 1, Weir 1.
League Cup (5): McPhee 2 (1 pen), Clark 1, Liddle 1, McDonald 1.
Cup (4): Liddle 2, McDonald 2.

HAMILTON ACADEMICALS — DIV. 1

Ground: Douglas Park, Hamilton (Hamilton 23108)
Colours: Red and white striped shirts, white shorts.
Goals – League (43): Somner 9, Phillips 8, Kean 7, McCurdy 5, Forsyth 3, McNaught 3, Hutchison 2 (1 pen), Donnelly 1, Mitchell 1, Paton 1, Pelosi 1, Speirs 1, own goal 1.
League Cup (3): Mitchell 1, Phillips 1, Wright 1.
Cup (4): McNaught 1, Paton 1, Phillips 1, Somner 1.

HEART OF MIDLOTHIAN — PREM. DIV.

Ground: Tynecastle Park, Gorgie Road, Edinburgh (031-337 6132)
Colours: White shirts with maroon centre panel at front, maroon trim, white shorts.
Goals – League (38): Robertson 14 (2 pens), Bone 7, Mackay 4 (2 pens), Park 4, Johnston 2, MacDonald, R. 2, Cowie 1, Kidd 1, Macdonald, A. 1, O'Connor 1, own goal 1.
League Cup (10): Robertson 4 (1 pen), Mackay 2 (1 pen), Bone 1, Johnston 1, O'Connor 1, Park 1.
Cup (3): Bone 1, Cowie 1, Robertson 1.

HIBERNIAN — PREM. DIV.

Ground: Easter Road Park, Edinburgh (031-661 2159)
Colours: Green shirts with white sleeves and collar, white shorts.
Goals – League (45): Irvine 18 (4 pens), Rice 5 (1 pen), Callachan 4, Jamieson 4, Thomson 4, Duncan 2, Harvey 2, Brazil 1, Conroy 1, Kane 1, McGachie 1, Sneddon 1, own goal 1.
League Cup (14): Irvine 5, Conroy 2, Harvey 2, Murray 1, Rice 1, Schaedler 1, Thomson 1, own goal 1.

KILMARNOCK — DIV. 1

Ground: Rugby Park, Kilmarnock (Kilmarnock 25184)
Colours: Royal blue shirts with white trim, royal blue shorts.
Goals – League (57): Clark, R. 11 (5 pens), Gallagher 11, McKinna 8, McDicken 7, McGivern 7, Bryson 4, McClurg 2, MacLeod 2, Brown 1, Clarke, P. 1, Cuthbertson 1, own goals 2.
League Cup (14): Gallagher 4, McDickern 3, Clark, J. 2, Clarke, P. 2, McGivern 2, Robertson 1.
Cup (2): Gallagher 1, McKinna 1.

MEADOWBANK THISTLE — DIV. 1

Ground: Meadowbank Stadium, Edinburgh (031-661 5351)
Colours: Amber with black trim.
Goals – League (49): Robertson 10, Smith 7, Sprott 6, Armstrong 5 (2 pens), Lawson 5, Hendrie 4, Boyd 3, Godfrey 3, Korotkich 2, Campbell 1, Stewart 1, Tomassi 1, own goal 1.
League Cup (8): Hendrie 3, Sprott 2 (1 pen), Godfrey 1, Smith 1, Tomassi 1.
Cup (3): Sprott 2, Hendrie 1.

MONTROSE — DIV. 2

Ground: Links Park, Montrose (Montrose 498)
Colours: All royal blue.
Goals – League (36): Burke 7, Bennett, M. 6, Barbour 5, Copeland 5, Allan 4, Barr 3 (2 pens), Street 2, Loch 2, Duffy 1, Forbes 1.
League Cup (5): Loch 3, Barbour 1, Barr 1.
Cup (1): McManus 1.

MORTON — PREM. DIV.

Ground: Cappielow Park, Greenock (Greenock 23571)
Colours: Blue and white hooped shirts, white shorts.
Goals – League (75): McNeil 17 (5 pens), Robertson 16 Pettigrew 9, Rooney 8, Clinging 7, Docherty 4, Houston 3, Sullivan 3, Doak 2, Duffy 2, McNab 2, Miller 1, Welsh 1.
League Cup (11): Robertson 6, McNeil 2, Sullivan 2, Miller 1 (pen).
Cup (7): Pettigrew 3, Robertson 3, Sullivan 1.

MOTHERWELL — DIV. 1

Ground: Fir Park, Motherwell (Motherwell 63229)
Colours: All amber with claret trim.
Goals – League (31): Gahagan 5, Harrow 6, Edvaldsson 4, Rafferty 4, Dornan 2, Lyall 2, McFadden 2, Alexander 1, Burns 1, Forbes 1, Ritchie 1 (pen).
League Cup (15): Gillespie 5, Ritchie 3 (1 pen), Gahagan 2, Alexander 1, Carson 1, Edvaldsson 1, Harrow 1. Mauchlen 1.
Cup (6): Harrow 4, Gillespie 1, Rafferty 1.

PARTICK THISTLE — DIV. 1

Ground: Firhill Park, Glasgow (041-946 2673)
Colours: Yellow shirts with red trim, red shorts.
Goals – League (67): McDowall 13, Johnston 10, O'Hara 8, Watson 7 (1 pen), McDonald 5, Buckley 4, Doyle, J. 4, Dunlop 4, Herd 4, Kay 3, Jardine 2 (2 pens), Fleck 1, Scott 1, own goal 1.
League Cup (2): Docherty 1, Jardine 1.

QUEEN OF THE SOUTH DIV. 2

Ground: Palmerston Park, Dumfries (Dumfries 4853)
Colours: Royal blue shirts with white trim, white shorts.
Goals – League (51): Robertson, J. 9, Robertson, G. 8, Cloy 5 (1 pen), Cochrane, S. 5, Dunlop 5, Busby 4, McMinn 3, (2 pens), Cochrane, I. 2, Gordon 2, Gray 2, Hyslop 2, McCluskey 1, McLaren 1, Russell 1, Young 1.
League Cup (7): Cloy 2, Cochrane, S. 1, Dunlop 1, Faulds 1, Gray 1, own goal 1.

QUEEN'S PARK DIV. 2

Ground: Hampden Park, Glasgow (041-632 1275)
Colours: Black and white hooped shirts, white shorts.
Goals – League (58): Grant 17 (2 pens), Gilmour 10 (2 pens), McNiven 9, Quinn 6, Fraser 3, Brannigan 2, McKay 2, Smith 2, Walker 2, Ward 2, Cook 1, McCall 1, own goal 1.
League Cup (4): Gilmour 3, Grant 1.
Cup (4): Gilmour 2, McNiven 1, Walker 1.

RAITH ROVERS DIV. 2

Ground: Stark's Park, Pratt Street, Kirkcaldy (Kirkcaldy 3514)
Colours: All royal blue.
Goals – League (53): Kerr 16 (10 pens), Smith 8, Marshall 6, Wright 5, Harris 4, Ramsay 4, Robertson 3, Craig 3, Spence 2, Urquhart 2, Forsyth 1, Ritchie 1, Sweeney 1.
League Cup : Nil.
Cup (1): Smith 1.

RANGERS PREM. DIV.

Ground: Ibrox Stadium, Glasgow (041-427 0159)
Colours: Royal blue shirts, white shorts.
Goals – League (53): Clark 9, McCoist 9 (1 pen), Cooper 6 (1 pen), Williamson 6, Prytz 4 (4 pens), Redford 4, Russell 4, McClelland 2, McPherson 2, Mitchell 2, Burns 1, Davies 1, McAdam 1, Macdonald 1, Paterson 1.
League Cup (32): McCoist 9 (2 pens), Clark 5, Cooper 3, Mitchell 3, Prytz 3 (1 pen), MacDonald 2, McClelland 1, MacKinnon 1, McPherson 1, Paterson 1, Redford 1, Russell 1, own goal 1.
Cup (12): McCoist 3, Russell 2, Williamson 2, McAdam 1, McClelland 1, McPherson 1, Redford 1, own goal 1.

ST JOHNSTONE DIV. 1

Ground: Muirton Park, Perth (Perth 26961)
Colours: Royal blue shirts, white shorts.
Goals – League (36): Brogan 9, Lyons 5, Blair 4, Gibson 3, Reid 3, Scott 3, Barron 2, Beedie 2, Morton 2 (2 pens), Brannigan 1, Kilgour 1, own goal 1.
League Cup (10): Brogan 4, Gibson 3, Morton 2, Blair 1.
Cup: Nil.

ST MIRREN PREM. DIV.

Ground: St Mirren Park, Paisley (Paisley 2558)
Colours: White shirts with black vertical stripes, black shorts.
Goals – League (55): McDougall 13, McAvennie 12, Scanlon 12 (5 pens), Abercromby 4, Alexander 3, McCormack 3, Clarke 2, Jarvie 2, Fulton 1, Logan 1, McEachran 1, McGregor 1.
League Cup (9): McAvennie 2, Scanlon 2 (1 pen), Spiers 2, Fitzpatrick 1, Logan 1, McDougall 1.
Cup (11): Scanlon 3 (2 pens), Cooper 2, McAvennie 2, McDougall 2, Fitzpatrick 1, Fulton 1.

STENHOUSEMUIR DIV. 2

Ground: Ochilview Park, Stenhousemuir (Larbert 2992)
Colours: Maroon shirts with white trim, white shorts.
Goals – League (47): Forrest 14 (1 pen), Murray, G. 13 (1 pen), Thompson 7, Murray, S. 3, Larnach 2, Rae 2, Sinclair 2, Erwin 1, Gillen 1, Quinn 1, own goal 1.
League Cup (2): Larnach 1, Reid 1.
Cup: Nil.

STIRLING ALBION DIV. 2

Ground: Annfield Stadium, Stirling (Stirling 3584)
Colours: All red.
Goals – League (51): Irvine 12, Colquhoun 11 (1 pen), Watt 7 (2 pens), Torrance 4, Cavanagh 3, Grant 3, Dawson 2, Leetion 2, McNeil 2, Ormond 2, Allison 1, McDaid 1, Ward 1.
League Cup (1): Irvine 1.
Cup (3): Dawson 1, Philliben 1, Shirra 1.

STRANRAER DIV. 2

Ground: Stair Park, Stranraer (Stranraer 3271)
Colours: Royal blue shirts, white shorts.
Goals – League (47): McGuire 11, McDonald 8 (6 pens), Knox 7, Sweeney 6, Docherty, L. 5, Bryce 3, McBride 3, Logan 1, Murphy 1, Neil 1, O'Donnell 1.
League Cup (1): McGuire 1.
Cup (1): McDonald 1 (pen).

SCOTTISH LEAGUE – PREMIER DIVISION RESULTS 1983-84

	Aberdeen	Celtic	Dundee	Dundee U.	Hearts	Hibernian	Motherwell	Rangers	St Johnstone	St Mirren
Aberdeen	—	3–1 1–0	3–0 5–2	1–2 5–1	2–0 1–1	2–1 2–2	3–1 2–1	3–0 0–0	5–0 1–0	5–0 2–0
Celtic	0–0 1–0	—	1–0 2–0	1–1 1–1	1–1 4–1	5–1 3–2	4–0 4–2	2–1 3–0	5–2 5–2	1–1 2–0
Dundee	1–3 0–1	2–6 3–2	—	1–4 2–5	1–2 4–1	0–3 1–2	2–0 1–0	3–2 1–3	0–1 2–0	2–2 2–5
Dundee United	0–2 0–0	2–1 3–1	0–1 1–1	—	1–0 3–1	5–0 2–0	4–0 2–1	0–2 1–2	7–0 3–0	2–0 2–2
Heart of Midlothian	0–2 0–1	1–3 1–1	1–3 1–1	0–0 0–0	—	3–2 8–1	0–0 2–1	3–1 2–2	2–0 2–2	2–2 2–1
Hibernian	2–1 0–2	0–2 0–1	2–1 3–1	0–2 1–0	1–1 0–0	—	2–1 4–2	0–2 0–0	4–1 1–2	3–1 1–1
Motherwell	1–1 0–4	2–2 2–2	2–4 2–4	1–3 1–3	0–1 0–1	2–3 2–3	—	0–3 0–3	1–0 1–0	1–0 1–0
Rangers	0–2 1–1	1–2 1–0	2–1 2–2	0–0 2–2	3–0 0–0	1–0 0–0	1–2 2–1	—	6–3 2–0	1–1 1–1
St Johnstone	0–5 0–2	0–3 0–0	0–2 1–0	1–2 1–2	0–1 1–2	0–3 1–0	3–1 3–1	0–1 1–4	—	3–2 4–2
St Mirren	0–3 3–2	4–2 2–4	0–0 4–0	4–0 2–2	0–1 1–1	2–1 3–1	1–1 2–1	3–0 1–1	1–2 1–1	—

SCOTTISH LEAGUE – DIVISION I RESULTS 1983-84

	Airdrieonians	Alloa	Ayr U.	Brechin C.	Clyde	Clydebank	Dumbarton	Falkirk	Hamilton A.	Kilmarnock	Meadowbank Th.	Morton	Partick Th.	Raith Rovers
Airdrieonians	—	1–0	2–0 1–0	1–0 1–2	0–4	1–0 3–3	1–1 1–4	0–1	1–0 0–1	1–0 3–0	1–2	0–3	0–0 1–0	1–0
Alloa	1–0 0–0	—	0–0	4–1	1–1 0–0	0–2	1–0	0–1 3–1	2–1 3–1	0–4	0–1	1–3	3–4 2–2	1–2 2–0
Ayr U.	2–2	4–2 3–1	—	1–1	1–0 1–1	2–2	1–2	0–1 1–2	1–1 1–1	0–2	2–2	2–2 1–2	1–5 2–1	2–2
Brechin C.	3–1	1–0 1–1	2–1 4–1	—	3–0 3–2	0–2 2–2	2–3 0–3	1–0	1–0	3–2	0–0	3–1 1–2	2–0	1–1
Clyde	1–1 1–1	2–2	1–1	2–2	—	2–2 1–1	0–0	1–2 1–0	1–0 0–1	0–1 2–1	2–1	2–3 3–2	1–2	5–0
Clydebank	2–4	2–7 1–0	4–1 1–2	1–0	1–0	—	0–2	3–1 1–2	1–1	4–0 3–0	3–0 1–1	3–3 1–1	1–0	1–1 4–3
Dumbarton	4–2	1–1 2–0	2–1 0–3	1–2	1–0 2–2	2–0 2–1	—	3–0 2–0	2–0	4–3	0–0 3–0	1–1	0–1	2–1 3–1
Falkirk	2–0 1–1	1–1	2–1	0–1 0–0	0–2	1–1	4–1	—	4–1	1–3 2–1	2–1 1–4	0–2 0–1	2–2 1–2	2–1 1–0
Hamilton A.	1–1	1–0	0–0	3–3 3–2	1–2	1–0 0–1	4–1 3–3	1–2 2–0	—	0–1 1–1	1–1 1–2	1–1	3–1	0–0
Kilmarnock	4–1	2–0 2–0	1–0 3–0	4–1 1–1	0–1	0–1	2–2 0–0	2–1	2–1	—	3–1 1–1	0–1	1–2	2–1 1–2
Meadowbank Th.	1–0 0–4	4–0 2–1	1–5 2–2	2–1 2–2	1–1 3–1	1–3	0–2	0–1	2–0	2–1	—	1–4 1–1	2–1	1–3 1–2
Morton	3–2 2–1	1–0 3–0	2–3	0–0	2–1	1–2	2–2 2–0	3–1	1–1 0–0	2–2 3–2	4–0	—	1–2 4–2	0–0
Partick Th.	2–1	5–0	4–3	2–2 1–1	1–2 1–2	1–0 1–1	1–0 0–0	3–1	0–0 1–2	2–0 1–2	4–1 2–1	3–1	—	2–0
Raith R.	0–0 2–3	1–1	1–3 5–0	1–1 6–0	2–1 2–2	0–0	1–3	2–2	1–2 0–2	2–1	3–1	1–3 0–2	1–2 2–1	—

Note: In the Scottish League Divisions I and II, each team plays each other twice and then after a draw made at the beginning of the season, half of the fixtures are repeated once.

SCOTTISH LEAGUE – DIVISION II RESULTS 1983-84

	Albion R.	Arbroath	Berwick R.	Cowdenbeath	Dunfermline	East Fife	East Stirling	Forfar Ath.	Montrose	Queen of the S.	Queens Park	Stenhousemuir	Stirling A.	Stranraer
Albion R.	—	3–0	4–4	2–0	1–1	1–2	2–3 0–1	2–2	0–2 0–4	1–1 1–4	1–4 0–0	1–2 1–1	1–1 1–4	2–1
Arbroath	3–0 0–1	—	1–1	3–2 1–0	3–0	0–2 0–1	3–2	0–1	2–1 1–1	1–2 6–3	2–0 0–5	1–1	2–1	3–1
Berwick R.	4–3 0–0	0–0 2–0	—	0–0	1–1 2–0	1–0 2–1	1–2	1–2 0–1	4–0	2–0	3–0	3–0 6–1	1–1	0–1 2–0
Cowdenbeath	0–1 2–3	0–1	2–1 0–1		0–1 1–2	0–0 1–5	2–1	0–1 1–2	5–2 1–0	0–0	3–1	1–1	0–4 0–0	2–2
Dunfermline	1–2 5–0	0–1 2–0	1–0	0–0	—	1–1 0–1	1–1 1–2	1–2 3–1	1–1	1–0	2–2	2–0	1–1	1–1 1–0
East Fife	1–0 1–4	0–1	1–2	2–1	3–1	—	2–1 2–0	2–3 0–0	1–0	1–2 0–0	3–1 3–0	0–1 3–1	1–1 4–2	1–0
East Stirling	2–2	0–3 0–1	0–2 1–1	3–1 3–4	0–2	1–4	—	3–1	1–3	1–0	1–2	1–3 2–1	0–1 1–3	1–1 2–2
Forfar Ath.	2–1 1–0	4–1 1–1	4–1	1–0	1–0	3–1	0–0 4–3	—	4–0 2–0	2–0 3–0	4–1 0–0	1–0	1–1	2–0 5–3
Montrose	3–1	0–4	0–1 2–1	1–2	0–1 2–0	0–1 1–1	0–2 0–4	0–1	—	1–0 2–1	1–2 2–1	0–0	1–0 0–0	1–5
Queen of The S.	4–0	2–1	1–1 5–1	1–0 0–2	2–1 1–0	0–0	2–1 1–1	1–1	1–2	—	2–1 2–0	2–0	2–2	3–1 0–0
Queen's Park	1–1	2–1	1–0 1–1	4–3 0–4	3–1 1–2	5–2	5–4 1–1	0–1	3–0	0–2	—	1–1 3–1	0–1 3–1	0–1 1–0
Stenhousemuir	1–1	0–0 1–0	3–2	2–0 0–1	2–1 2–1	3–1	1–1	2–1 0–4	1–2 0–0	0–3 2–2	4–2	—	4–3	2–0
Stirling A.	3–1	2–1 0–1	0–2 0–0	4–1	2–1 1–2	0–1	0–0	0–0 1–1	2–0	2–0 3–1	1–0	0–0 0–3	—	2–1 0–2
Stranraer	3–1 2–0	0–1 2–1	1–0	1–1 1–1	1–1	1–0 1–2	1–1	1–3	2–1 0–0	2–1	1–1	2–0 2–0	1–1	—

Note: In the Scottish League Divisions I and II, each team plays each other twice and then after a draw made at the beginning of the season, half of the fixtures are repeated once

SCOTTISH FOOTBALL LEAGUE
FINAL TABLES 1983-84

Premier Division		Home			Goals		Away			Goals			
	P	*W*	*D*	*L*	*F*	*A*	*W*	*D*	*L*	*F*	*A*	*Pt*	*Dif*
Aberdeen	36	14	3	1	46	12	11	4	3	32	9	57	57
Celtic	36	13	5	0	46	15	8	3	7	34	26	50	39
Dundee U.	36	11	3	4	38	14	7	8	3	29	25	47	28
Rangers	36	7	8	3	26	18	8	4	6	27	23	42	12
Hearts	36	5	9	4	23	23	5	7	6	15	24	36	−9
St Mirren	36	8	6	4	34	23	1	8	9	21	36	32	− 4
Hibernian	36	7	4	7	21	21	5	3	10	24	34	31	−10
Dundee	36	6	1	11	28	42	5	4	9	22	32	27	−24
St Johnstone	36	6	1	11	19	33	4	2	12	17	48	23	−45
Motherwell	36	2	5	11	15	36	2	2	14	16	39	15	−44

First Division		Home			Goals		Away			Goals			
	P	*W*	*D*	*L*	*F*	*A*	*W*	*D*	*L*	*F*	*A*	*Pt*	*Dif*
Morton	39	10	6	3	36	21	11	6	3	39	25	54	29
Dumbarton	39	13	4	3	37	19	7	7	5	29	25	51	22
Partick Th.	39	11	5	4	37	20	8	3	8	30	30	46	17
Clydebank	39	10	5	5	38	29	6	8	5	24	21	45	12
Brechin C.	39	11	4	4	33	22	3	10	7	23	36	42	− 2
Kilmarnock	39	10	4	5	31	17	6	2	12	26	36	38	4
Falkirk	39	8	5	7	27	25	8	1	10	19	29	38	−8
Clyde	39	6	8	5	28	23	6	5	9	25	27	37	3
Hamilton A.	39	6	8	5	27	22	5	6	9	16	24	36	−3
Airdrieonians	39	10	3	7	20	21	3	7	9	25	32	36	− 8
Meadowbank Th.	39	8	4	8	29	35	4	6	9	20	34	34	−20
Ayr U.	39	5	8	6	29	32	5	4	11	27	38	32	−14
Raith R.	39	6	6	8	33	30	4	5	10	20	32	31	− 9
Alloa	39	7	5	7	24	24	1	5	14	17	40	26	−23

Second Division		Home			Goals		Away			Goals			
	P	*W*	*D*	*L*	*F*	*A*	*W*	*D*	*L*	*F*	*A*	*Pt*	*Dif*
Forfar Ath.	39	16	4	0	45	13	11	5	3	28	18	63	42
East Fife	39	11	3	6	31	21	9	4	6	26	21	47	15
Berwick R.	39	11	5	4	35	13	5	6	8	22	25	43	19
Stirling A.	39	9	5	6	23	18	5	9	5	28	24	42	9
Arbroath	39	10	3	6	32	25	8	3	9	19	21	42	5
Queen of the S.	39	11	6	2	29	15	5	4	11	22	31	42	5
Stenhousemuir	39	10	5	4	30	25	4	6	10	17	32	39	−10
Stranraer	39	9	7	3	25	16	4	5	11	22	31	38	0
Dunfermline Ath.	39	7	7	5	25	16	6	3	11	19	29	36	− 1
Queen's Park	39	10	4	6	35	28	4	4	11	23	35	36	− 5
East Stirling	39	4	4	11	23	37	6	7	7	31	29	31	−12
Montrose	39	7	3	10	17	28	5	4	10	19	31	31	−23
Cowdenbeath	39	5	5	10	21	29	5	4	10	23	29	29	−14
Albion R.	39	3	7	9	24	37	5	4	11	22	39	27	−30

SCOTTISH LEAGUE HONOURS LIST

Premier Division (Maximum points: 72)

	First	Pt	Second	Pt	Third	Pt
1975–76	Rangers	54	Celtic	48	Hibernian	43
1976–77	Celtic	55	Rangers	46	Aberdeen	43
1977–78	Rangers	55	Aberdeen	53	Dundee United	40
1978–79	Celtic	48	Rangers	45	Dundee United	44
1979–80	Aberdeen	48	Celtic	47	St Mirren	42
1980–81	Celtic	56	Aberdeen	49	Rangers	44
1981–82	Celtic	55	Aberdeen	53	Rangers	43
1982–83	Dundee United	56	Celtic	55	Aberdeen	55
1983–84	Aberdeen	57	Celtic	50	Dundee United	47

First Division (Maximum points: 78)

	First	Pt	Second	Pt	Third	Pt
1975–76	Partick Thistle	41	Kilmarnock	35	Montrose	30
Maximum points: 52						
1976–77	St Mirren	62	Clydebank	58	Dundee	51
1977–78	*Morton	58	Hearts	58	Dundee	57
1978–79	Dundee	55	Kilmarnock	54	Clydebank	54
1979–80	Hearts	53	Airdrieonians	51	Ayr United	44
1980–81	Hibernian	57	Dundee	52	St Johnstone	51
1981–82	Motherwell	61	Kilmarnock	51	Hearts	50
1982–83	St Johnstone	55	Hearts	54	Clydebank	50
1983–84	Morton	54	Dumbarton	51	Partick Thistle	46

Second Division (Maximum points: 78)

	First	Pt	Second	Pt	Third	Pt
1975–76	*Clydebank	40	Raith Rovers	40	Alloa	35
Maximum points: 52						
1976–77	Stirling Albion	55	Alloa	51	Dunfermline	50
1977–78	*Clyde	53	Raith Rovers	53	Dunfermline	48
1978–79	Berwick	54	Dunfermline	52	Falkirk	50
1979–80	Falkirk	50	East Stirlingshire	49	Forfar Athletic	46
1980–81	Queen's Park	50	Queen of the S	46	Cowdenbeath	45
1981–82	Clyde	59	Alloa	50	Arbroath	50
1982–83	Brechin	55	Meadowbank	54	Arbroath	49
1983–84	Forfar Athletic	63	East Fife	47	Berwick Rangers	43

First Division to 1974-75

	First	Pt	Second	Pt	Third	Pt
1890–1	*a*††Dumbarton	29	Rangers	29	Celtic	24
1891–2	*b*Dumbarton	37	Celtic	35	Hearts	30
1892–3	*a*Celtic	29	Rangers	28	St Mirren	23
1893–4	*a*Celtic	29	Hearts	26	St Bernards	22
1894–5	*a*Hearts	31	Celtic	26	Rangers	21
1895–6	*a*Celtic	30	Rangers	26	Hibernian	24
1896–7	*a*Hearts	28	Hibernian	26	Rangers	25
1897–8	*a*Celtic	33	Rangers	29	Hibernian	22
1898–9	*a*Rangers	36	Hearts	26	Celtic	24
1899–1900	*a*Rangers	32	Celtic	25	Hibernian	24
1900–1	*c*Rangers	35	Celtic	29	Hibernian	25
1901–2	*a*Rangers	28	Celtic	26	Hearts	22
1902–3	*b*Hibernian	37	Dundee	31	Rangers	29
1903–4	*d*Third Lanark	43	Hearts	39	*Rangers	38
1904–5	*d*‡Celtic	41	Rangers	41	Third Lanark	35
1905–6	*e*Celtic	49	Hearts	43	Airdrieonians	38
1906–7	*f*Celtic	55	Dundee	48	Rangers	45
1907–8	*f*Celtic	55	Falkirk	51	Rangers	50
1908–9	*f*Celtic	51	Dundee	50	Clyde	48

	First	Pt	Second	Pt	Third	Pt
1909–10	*f*Celtic	54	Falkirk	52	Rangers	46
1910–11	*f*Rangers	52	Aberdeen	48	Falkirk	44
1911–12	*f*Rangers	51	Celtic	45	Clyde	42
1912–13	*f*Rangers	53	Celtic	49	*Hearts	41
1913–14	*g*Celtic	65	Rangers	59	*Hearts	54
1914–15	*g*Celtic	65	Hearts	61	Rangers	50
1916–17	*g*Celtic	64	Morton	54	Rangers	53
1917–18	*f*Rangers	56	Celtic	55	Kilmarnock	43
1918–19	*f*Celtic	58	Rangers	57	Morton	47
1919–20	*h*Rangers	71	Celtic	68	Motherwell	57
1920–21	*h*Rangers	76	Celtic	66	Hearts	56
1921–22	*h*Celtic	67	Rangers	66	Raith Rovers	56
1922–23	*g*Rangers	55	Airdrieonians	50	Celtic	46
1923–24	*g*Rangers	59	Airdrieonians	50	Celtic	41
1924–25	*g*Rangers	60	Airdrieonians	57	Hibernian	52
1925–26	*g*Celtic	58	*Airdrieonians	50	Hearts	50
1926–27	*g*Rangers	56	Motherwell	51	Celtic	49
1927–28	*g*Rangers	60	*Celtic	55	Motherwell	55
1928–29	*g*Rangers	67	Celtic	51	Motherwell	50
1929–30	*g*Rangers	60	Motherwell	55	Aberdeen	53
1930–31	*g*Rangers	60	Celtic	58	Motherwell	56
1931–32	*g*Motherwell	66	Rangers	61	Celtic	48
1932–33	*g*Rangers	62	Motherwell	59	Hearts	50
1933–34	*g*Rangers	66	Motherwell	62	Celtic	47
1934–35	*g*Rangers	55	Celtic	52	Hearts	50
1935–36	*g*Celtic	66	*Rangers	61	Aberdeen	61
1936–37	*g*Rangers	61	Aberdeen	54	Celtic	52
1937–38	*g*Celtic	61	Hearts	58	Rangers	49
1938–39	*g*Rangers	59	Celtic	48	Aberdeen	46
1946–47	*f*Rangers	46	Hibernian	44	Aberdeen	39
1947–48	*j*Hibernian	48	Rangers	46	Partick Thistle	36
1948–49	*j*Rangers	46	Dundee	45	Hibernian	39
1949–50	*j*Rangers	50	Hibernian	49	Hearts	43
1950–51	*j*Hibernian	48	*Rangers	38	Dundee	38
1951–52	*j*Hibernian	45	Rangers	41	East Fife	37
1952–53	*j**Rangers	43	Hibernian	43	East Fife	39
1953–54	*j*Celtic	43	Hearts	38	Partick Thistle	35
1954–55	*j*Aberdeen	49	Celtic	46	Rangers	41
1955–56	*f*Rangers	52	Aberdeen	46	*Hearts	45
1956–57	*f*Rangers	55	Hearts	53	Kilmarnock	42
1957–58	*f*Hearts	62	Rangers	49	Celtic	46
1958–59	*f*Rangers	50	Hearts	48	Motherwell	44
1959–60	*f*Hearts	54	Kilmarnock	50	*Rangers	42
1960–61	*f*Rangers	51	Kilmarnock	50	Third Lanark	42
1961–62	*f*Dundee	54	Rangers	51	Celtic	46
1962–63	*f*Rangers	57	Kilmarnock	48	Partick Thistle	46
1963–64	*f*Rangers	55	Kilmarnock	49	*Celtic	47
1964–65	*f**Kilmarnock	50	Hearts	50	Dunfermline Ath.	49
1965–66	*f*Celtic	57	Rangers	55	Kilmarnock	45
1966–67	*f*Celtic	58	Rangers	55	Clyde	46
1967–68	*f*Celtic	63	Rangers	61	Hibernian	45
1968–69	*f*Celtic	54	Rangers	49	Dunfermline Ath.	45
1969–70	*f*Celtic	57	Rangers	45	Hibernian	44
1970–71	*f*Celtic	56	Aberdeen	54	St Johnstone	44
1971–72	*f*Celtic	60	Aberdeen	50	Rangers	44

Maximum points: *a*, 36; *b*, 44; *c*, 40; *d*, 52; *e*, 60; *f*, 68; *g*, 76; *h*, 84; *j*, 60.

	First	Pt	Second	Pt	Third	Pt
1972–73	*f*Celtic	57	Rangers	56	Hibernian	45
1973–74	*f*Celtic	53	Hibernian	49	Rangers	48

Second Division to 1974-75

	First	Pt	Second	Pt	Third	Pt
1921–22	*a*†Alloa	60	Cowdenbeath	47	Armadale	48
1922–23	*a*Queen's Park	57	Clydebank	**50	St Johnstone	**45
1923–24	*a*St Johnstone	56	Cowdenbeath	55	Bathgate	44
1924–25	*a*Dundee United	50	Clydebank	48	Clyde	47
1925–26	*a*Dunfermline A.	59	Clyde	53	Ayr United	52
1926–27	*a*Bo'ness	56	Raith Rovers	49	Clydebank	45
1927–28	*a*Ayr United	54	Third Lanark	45	King's Park	44
1928–29	*b*Dundee United	51	Morton	50	Arbroath	47
1929–30	*a**Leith Athletic	57	East Fife	57	Albion Rovers	54
1930–31	*a*Third Lanark	61	Dundee United	50	Dunfermline A.	47
1931–32	*a**East Stirling	55	St Johnstone	55	*Raith Rovers	46
1932–33	*c*Hibernian	54	Queen of the S.	49	Dunfermline A.	47
1933–34	*c*Albion Rovers	45	*Dunfermline A.	44	Arbroath	44
1934–35	*c*Third Lanark	52	Arbroath	50	St Bernard's	47
1935–36	*c*Falkirk	59	St Mirren	52	Morton	48
1936–37	*c*Ayr United	54	Morton	51	St Bernard's	48
1937–38	*c*Raith Rovers	59	Albion Rovers	48	Airdrieonians	47
1938–39	*c*Cowdenbeath	60	*Alloa	48	East Fife	48
1946–47	*d*Dundee	45	Airdrieonians	42	East Fife	31
1947–48	*e*East Fife	53	Albion Rovers	42	Hamilton A	40
1948–49	*e**Raith Rovers	42	Stirling Albion	42	*Airdrieonians	41
1949–50	*e*Morton	47	Airdrieonians	44	*St Johnstone	36
1950–51	*e**Queen of the S.	45	Stirling Albion	45	*Ayr United	36
1951–52	*e*Clyde	43	Falkirk	33	Ayr United	39
1952–53	*e*Stirling Albion	44	Hamilton A.	43	Queen's Park	37
1953–54	*e*Motherwell	45	Kilmarnock	42	*Third Lanark	36
1954–55	*e*Airdrieonians	46	Dunfermline A.	42	Hamilton A.	39
1955–56	*b*Queen's Park	54	Ayr United	51	St Johnstone	49
1956–57	*b*Clyde	64	Third Lanark	51	Cowdenbeath	45
1957–58	*b*Stirling Albion	55	Dunfermline A.	53	Arbroath	47
1958–59	*b*Ayr United	60	Arbroath	51	Stenhousemuir	46
1959–60	*b*St Johnstone	53	Dundee United	50	Queen of the S.	49
1960–61	*b*Stirling Albion	55	Falkirk	54	Stenhousemuir	50
1961–62	*b*Clyde	54	Queen of the S.	53	Morton	44
1962–63	*b*St Johnstone	55	East Stirling	49	Morton	48
1963–64	*b*Morton	67	Clyde	53	Arbroath	46
1964–65	*b*Stirling Albion	59	Hamilton A	50	Queen of the S.	45
1965–66	*b*Ayr United	53	Airdrieonians	50	Queen of the S.	49
1966–67	*b*Morton	69	Raith Rovers	58	Arbroath	57
1967–68	*b*St Mirren	62	Arbroath	53	East Fife	40
1968–69	*b*Motherwell	64	Ayr United	53	*East Fife	47
1969–70	*b*Falkirk	56	Cowdenbeath	55	Queen of the S.	58
1970–71	*b*Partick Thistle	56	East Fife	51	Arbroath	46
1971–72	*b*†Dumbarton	52	Arbroath	52	Stirling Albion	50
1972–73	*b*Clyde	56	Dunfermline A.	52	*Raith Rovers	47
1973–74	*b*Airdrieonians	60	Kilmarnock	59	Hamilton A.	55
1974–75	*b*Falkirk	54	*Queen of the S.	53	Montrose	53

Maximum points: *a*, 76; *b*, 72; *c*, 68; *d*, 52; *e*, 60.

*On goal average. †Held jointly after indecisive play-off. ‡Won on deciding match. ††Held jointly. **Two points deducted for fielding ineligible player. Competition suspended 1940–45.

RELEGATED CLUBS

From Premier Division

1975–76	Dundee, St Johnstone
1976–77	Hearts, Kilmarnock
1977–78	Ayr United, Clydebank
1978–79	Hearts, Motherwell
1979–80	Dundee, Hibernian
1980–81	Kilmarnock, Hearts
1981–82	Partick Th., Airdrieonians
1982–83	Morton, Kilmarnock
1983–84	St Johnstone, Motherwell

From Division 1

1975–76	Dunfermline A., Clyde
1976–77	Raith Rovers, Falkirk
1977–78	Alloa, East Fife
1978–79	Montrose, Queen of the S.
1979–80	Arbroath, Clyde
1980–81	Stirling A., Berwick R.
1981–82	East Stirling, Queen of the S.
1982–83	Dunfermline, Queen's Park
1983–84	Raith Rovers, Alloa

Relegated from Division 1 to 1973-74

1921–22*	Queen's Park, Dumbarton, Clydebank
1922–23	Albion Rovers, Alloa
1923–24	Clyde, Clydebank
1924–25	Third Lanark, Ayr United
1925–26	Raith R., Clydebank
1926–27	Morton, Dundee United
1927–28	Dunfermline Athletic, Bo'ness
1928–29	Third Lanark, Raith R.
1929–30	St Johnstone, Dundee United
1930–31	Hibernian, East Fife
1931–32	Dundee United, Leith Athletic
1932–33	Morton, East Stirling
1933–34	Third Lanark, Cowdenbeath
1934–35	St Mirren, Falkirk
1935–36	Airdrieonians, Ayr United
1936–37	Dunfermline Athletic, Albion Rovers
1937–38	Dundee, Morton
1938–39	Queen's Park, Raith R.
1946–47	Kilmarnock, Hamilton Academicals
1947–48	Airdrieonians, Queen's Park
1948–49	Morton, Albion Rovers
1949–50	Queen of the South, Stirling Albion
1950–51	Clyde, Falkirk
1951–52	Morton, Stirling Albion
1952–53	Motherwell, Third Lanark
1953–54	Airdrieonians, Hamilton Academicals
1954–55	No clubs relegated
1955–56	Stirling Albion, Clyde
1956–57	Dunfermline Athletic, Ayr United
1957–58	East Fife, Queen's Park
1958–59	Queen of the S., Falkirk
1959–60	Arbroath, Stirling Albion
1960–61	Ayr United, Clyde
1961–62	St Johnstone, Stirling Albion
1962–63	Clyde, Raith Rovers
1963–64	Queen of the South, East Stirling
1964–65	Airdrieonians, Third Lanark
1965–66	Morton, Hamilton A.
1966–67	St Mirren, Ayr United
1967–68	Motherwell, Stirling Albion
1968–69	Falkirk, Arbroath
1969–70	Raith Rovers, Partick Thistle
1970–71	St Mirren, Cowdenbeath
1971–72	Clyde, Dunfermline Athletic
1972–73	Kilmarnock, Airdrieonians
1973–74	East Fife, Falkirk
1974–75	League re-organised at end of season

*Season 1921–22—only 1 club promoted, 3 clubs relegated.

SCOTTISH CUP 1983-84

Third round

Team	Score
Falkirk	1
Clyde	2
Aberdeen	1 3
Kilmarnock	1 1
Dundee U.	1
Ayr U.	0
Hearts	2
Partick Th.	0
Cowdenbeath	0
Dundee	2
Airdrieonians	1
St Johnstone	0
Inverness C.	0 2
Stirling A.	0 1
Rangers	2
Dunfermline Ath	1
Meadowbank Th.	0 2 1
St Mirren	0 2 2
Hamilton A.	3
Alloa	1
Morton	2
East Stirling	0
Raith R.	1
Dumbarton	4
Motherwell	3
Queen's Park	0
Clydebank	0 3
Brechin C.	0 0
Hibernian	0 0
East Fife	0 2
Berwick R.	0
Celtic	4

Fourth round

Team	Score
Clyde	0
Aberdeen	2
Dundee U.	2
Hearts	1
Dundee	2
Airdrie	1
Inverness C.	0
Rangers	6
St Mirren	2
Hamilton	1
Morton	2
Dumbarton	1
Motherwell	3
Clydebank	1
East Fife	0
Celtic	6

Fifth round

Team	Score
Aberdeen	0 1
Dundee U.	0 0
Dundee	2 3
Rangers	2 2
St Mirren	4
Morton	3
Motherwell	0
Celtic	6

Semi-finals

Team	Score
Aberdeen	2
Dundee	0
St Mirren	1
Celtic	2

Final

Aberdeen **2**
Black, McGhee
At Hampden Park
Attendance: 58,900

Celtic **1**
McStay
After extra time
90 mins: 1-1

SCOTTISH CUP PAST FINALS

1874	Queens Park	2	Clydesdale	0
1875	Queens Park	3	Renton	0
1876	Queens Park	1 2	Third Lanark	1 0
1877	Vale of Leven	0 1 3	Rangers	0 1 2
1878	Vale of Leven	1	Third Lanark	0
1879	Vale of Leven	1	Rangers	1
	Vale of Leven awarded cup, Rangers did not appear for replay			
1880	Queens Park	3	Thornlibank	0
1881	Queens Park	2 3	Dumbarton	1 1
	Replayed because of protest			
1882	Queens Park	2 4	Dumbarton	2 1
1883	Dumbarton	2 2	Vale of Leven	2 1
1884	*Queens Park awarded cup when Vale of Leven did not appear for the final.*			
1885	Renton	0 3	Vale of Leven	0 1
1886	Queens Park	3	Renton	1
1887	Hibernian	2	Dumbarton	1
1888	Renton	6	Cambuslang	1
1889	Third Lanark	3 2	Celtic	0 1
	Replayed because of protest			
1890	Queens Park	1 2	Vale of Leven	1 1
1891	Hearts	1	Dumbarton	0
1892	Celtic	1 5	Queens Park	0 1
	Replayed because of protest			
1893	Queens Park	2	Celtic	1
1894	Rangers	3	Celtic	1
1895	St Bernards	2	Renton	1
1896	Hearts	3	Hibernian	1
1897	Rangers	5	Dumbarton	1
1898	Rangers	2	Kilmarnock	0
1899	Celtic	2	Rangers	0
1900	Celtic	4	Queens Park	3
1901	Hearts	4	Celtic	3
1902	Hibernian	1	Celtic	0
1903	Rangers	1 0 2	Hearts	1 0 0
1904	Celtic	3	Rangers	2
1905	Third Lanark	0 3	Rangers	0 1
1906	Hearts	1	Third Lanark	0
1907	Celtic	3	Hearts	0
1908	Celtic	5	St Mirren	1
1909	*After two drawn games between Celtic and Rangers, 2-2, 1-1, there was a riot and the cup was withheld.*			
1910	Dundee	2 0 2	Clyde	2 0 1
1911	Celtic	0 2	Hamilton	0 0
1912	Celtic	2	Clyde	0
1913	Falkirk	2	Raith Rovers	0
1914	Celtic	0 4	Hibernian	0 1
1920	Kilmarnock	3	Albion Rovers	2
1921	Partick Thistle	1	Rangers	0
1922	Morton	1	Rangers	0
1923	Celtic	1	Hibernian	0
1924	Airdrieonians	2	Hibernian	0
1925	Celtic	2	Dundee	1
1926	St Mirren	2	Celtic	0
1927	Celtic	3	East Fife	1
1928	Rangers	4	Celtic	0

1929	Kilmarnock	2	Rangers	0
1930	Rangers	0 2	Partick Thistle	0 1
1931	Celtic	2 4	Motherwell	2 2
1932	Rangers	1 3	Kilmarnock	1 0
1933	Celtic	1	Motherwell	0
1934	Rangers	5	St Mirren•	0
1935	Rangers	2	Hamilton Academicals	1
1936	Rangers	1	Third Lanark	0
1937	Celtic	2	Aberdeen	1
1938	East Fife	1 4	Kilmarnock	1 2
1939	Clyde	4	Motherwell	0
1947	Aberdeen	2	Hibernian	1
1948	Rangers	1 1	Morton	1 0
1949	Rangers	4	Clyde	1
1950	Rangers	3	East Fife	0
1951	Celtic	1	Motherwell	0
1952	Motherwell	4	Dundee	0
1953	Rangers	1 1	Aberdeen	1 0
1954	Celtic	2	Aberdeen	1
1955	Clyde	1 1	Celtic	1 0
1956	Hearts	3	Celtic	1
1957	Falkirk	1 2	Kilmarnock	1 1
1958	Clyde	1	Hibernian	0
1959	St Mirren	3	Aberdeen	1
1960	Rangers	2	Kilmarnock	0
1961	Dunfermline Athletic	0 2	Celtic	0 0
1962	Rangers	2	St Mirren	0
1963	Rangers	1 3	Celtic	1 0
1964	Rangers	3	Dundee	1
1965	Celtic	3	Dunfermline Athletic	2
1966	Rangers	0 1	Celtic	0 0
1967	Celtic	2	Aberdeen	0
1968	Dunfermline Athletic	3	Hearts	1
1969	Celtic	4	Rangers	0
1970	Aberdeen	3	Celtic	1
1971	Celtic	1 2	Rangers	1 1
1972	Celtic	6	Hibernian	1
1973	Rangers	3	Celtic	2
1974	Celtic	3	Dundee United	0
1975	Celtic	3	Airdrieonians	1
1976	Rangers	3	Hearts	1
1977	Celtic	1	Rangers	0
1978	Rangers	2	Aberdeen	1
1979	Rangers	0 0 3	Hibernian	0 0 2
1980	Celtic	1	Rangers	0
1981	Rangers	0 4	Dundee United	0 1
1982	Aberdeen	4	Rangers	1
1983	Aberdeen	1	Rangers	0

SCOTTISH LEAGUE CUP 1983-84

No quarter-final ties were played in 1983-84. The winners of the four preliminary sections qualified directly for the semi-finals.

Semi-finals *(2 legs)*			**Final**	
Dundee U	1	0	Rangers	3
Rangers	1	2	*McCoist 3 (2 pens)*	
Aberdeen	0	0	Celtic	2
Celtic	0	1	*McClair, Reid (pen)*	

PAST SCOTTISH LEAGUE CUP FINALS

1946-47	Hampden Park	Rangers	4		Aberdeen	0	
1947-48	Hampden Park	East Fife	0	4	Falkirk	0	1
1948-49	Hampden Park	Rangers	2		Raith Rovers	0	
1949-50	Hampden Park	East Fife	3		Dunfermline	0	
1950-51	Hampden Park	Motherwell	3		Hibernian	0	
1951-52	Hampden Park	Dundee	3		Rangers	2	
1952-53	Hampden Park	Dundee	2		Kilmarnock	0	
1953-54	Hampden Park	East Fife	3		Partick Thistle	2	
1954-55	Hampden Park	Hearts	4		Motherwell	2	
1955-56	Hampden Park	Aberdeen	2		St Mirren	1	
1956-57	Hampden Park	Celtic	0	3	Partick Thistle	0	0
1957-58	Hampden Park	Celtic	7		Rangers	1	
1958-59	Hampden Park	Hearts	5		Partick Thistle	1	
1959-60	Hampden Park	Hearts	2		Third Lanark	1	
1960-61	Hampden Park	Rangers	2		Kilmarnock	0	
1961-62	Hampden Park	Rangers	1	3	Hearts	1	1
1962-63	Hampden Park	Hearts	1		Kilmarnock	0	
1963-64	Hampden Park	Rangers	5		Morton	0	
1964-65	Hampden Park	Rangers	2		Celtic	1	
1965-66	Hampden Park	Celtic	2		Rangers	1	
1966-67	Hampden Park	Celtic	1		Rangers	0	
1967-68	Hampden Park	Celtic	5		Dundee	3	
1968-69	Hampden Park	Celtic	6		Hibernian	2	
1969-70	Hampden Park	Celtic	1		St Johnstone	0	
1970-71	Hampden Park	Rangers	1		Celtic	0	
1971-72	Hampden Park	Partick Thistle	4		Celtic	1	
1972-73	Hampden Park	Hibernian	2		Celtic	1	
1973-74	Hampden Park	Dundee	1		Celtic	0	
1974-75	Hampden Park	Celtic	6		Hibernian	3	
1975-76	Hampden Park	Rangers	1		Celtic	0	
1976-77	Hampden Park	Aberdeen	2		Celtic	1	
1977-78	Hampden Park	Rangers	2		Celtic	1	
1978-79	Hampden Park	Rangers	2		Aberdeen	1	
1979-80	Hampden Park	Aberdeen	0	0	Dundee U	0	3
1980-81	Hampden Park	Dundee	0		Dundee U	3	
1981-82	Hampden Park	Rangers	2		Dundee U	1	
1982-83	Hampden Park	Celtic	2		Rangers	1	

FOOTBALL LEAGUE ATTENDANCES 1983-84

As in the past four seasons, League attendances in 1983-84 declined compared with those of the previous season, but the percentage drop was the smallest for the period, showing, it is to be hoped,that the decline is being arrested. As usual, Manchester United were the best-supported club, even showing an average increase in their home gates, but Liverpool, despite all their success in the season, pulled in nearly 3,000 fewer spectators per home game than in 1982-83. Halifax Town had the poorest home gates, and the Second Division was the only one to display a healthy increase in spectators, thanks mainly to the crowd-pulling of the three top clubs. The divisional totals, with last year's figures in brackets and the percentage change, were:

Division One: 8,701,230 (9,295,613) –1.4%
Division Two: 5,359,757 (4,974,937) +7.7%
Division Three: 2,726,062 (2,943,568) –7.4%
Division Four: 1,555,067 (1,552,040) +0.2%
Total: 18,342,116 (18,766,158)–2.3%

DIVISION ONE

	League position	Home Average 1983-84	Home Average 1982-83	Difference
Arsenal	6	28,116	24,153	+3,963
Aston Villa	10	21,370	23,748	−2,378
Birmingham City	20	14,106	15,638	−1,532
Coventry City	19	12,572	10,552	+2,020
Everton	7	19,343	20,277	−934
Ipswich Town	12	17,464	19,503	−2,039
Leicester City	15	14,923	12,380	+2,543
Liverpool	1	31,974	34,758	−2,784
Luton Town	16	11,938	13,452	−1,514
Manchester United	4	42,534	41,552	+982
Norwich City	14	15,659	16,862	−1,203
Nottingham Forest	3	17,698	17,851	−153
Notts County	21	9,463	10,265	−802
Queen's Park Rangers	5	15,370	12,807	+2,563
Southampton	2	18,088	18,799	−711
Stoke City	18	13,900	16,622	−2,722
Sunderland	13	16,180	17,370	−1,190
Tottenham Hotspur	8	28,701	30,581	−1,880
Watford	11	16,510	19,488	−2,978
West Bromwich Albion	17	14,568	15,200	−632
West Ham United	9	21,386	22,822	−1,436
Wolverhampton W.	22	12,478	15,667	−3,189

DIVISION TWO

	League position	Home Average 1983-84	Home Average 1982-83	Difference
Barnsley	14	9,738	12,341	−2,603
Blackburn Rovers	6	7,622	7,103	+519
Brighton & Hove Albion	9	12,275	14,662	−2,387
Cambridge United	22	4,070	4,513	−443
Cardiff City	15	7,067	7,036	+31
Carlisle United	7	5,611	5,944	−333
Charlton Athletic	13	6,732	7,213	−481
Chelsea	1	21,119	12,672	+8,447
Crystal Palace	19	8,199	9,887	−1,688
Derby County	20	12,858	13,601	−743
Fulham	11	8,143	10,826	−2,683
Grimsby Town	5	7,643	7,741	−98
Huddersfield Town	12	11,044	9,261	+1,783
Leeds United	10	15,493	15,994	−501
Manchester City	4	25,604	26,789	−1,185
Middlesbrough	17	8,474	10,018	−1,544
Newcastle United	3	29,810	24,166	+5,644
Oldham Athletic	18	6,035	6,962	−927
Portsmouth	16	13,196	14,095	−899
Sheffield Wednesday	2	22,770	16,835	+5,935
Shrewsbury Town	8	4,740	5,277	−537
Swansea City	21	6,980	11,704	−4,724

DIVISION THREE

	League position	Home Average 1983-84	Home Average 1982-83	Difference
Bolton Wanderers	10	5,892	7,552	−1,660
Bournemouth	17	4,039	5,732	−1,693
Bradford City	7	4,203	4,867	−664
Brentford	20	4,735	6,184	−1,449
Bristol Rovers	5	5,550	6,221	−671
Burnley	12	6,625	9,086	−2,461
Exeter City	24	3,380	3,230	+150
Gillingham	8	3,916	4,076	−160
Hull City	4	8,135	6,586	+1,549
Lincoln City	14	3,148	4,790	−1,642
Millwall	9	4,351	4,013	+338
Newport County	13	3,135	4,714	−1,579
Orient	11	3,222	2,718	+504
Oxford United	1	7,870	5,660	+2,210
Plymouth Argyle	19	5,336	4,540	+796
Port Vale	23	4,023	4,806	−783
Preston North End	16	4,571	4,941	−370
Rotherham United	18	4,645	8,317	−3,672
Scunthorpe United	21	3,349	3,580	−231
Sheffield United	3	12,881	11,764	+1,117
Southend United	22	3,142	3,529	−387
Walsall	6	5,017	3,243	+1,774
Wigan Athletic	15	3,899	4,434	−535
Wimbledon	2	3,459	2,347	+1,112

DIVISION FOUR

	League position	Home Average 1983-84	Home Average 1982-83	Difference
Aldershot	5	2,483	1,929	+554
Blackpool	6	3,936	3,002	+934
Bristol City	4	7,287	4,799	+2,488
Bury	15	2,104	3,097	−993
Chester City	24	1,764	2,071	−307
Chesterfield	13	3,414	3,226	+188
Colchester United	8	2,220	2,552	−332
Crewe Alexandra	16	2,454	2,244	+210
Darlington	14	1,507	1,449	+58
Doncaster Rovers	2	3,778	3,541	+237
Halifax Town	21	1,412	2,032	−620
Hartlepool United	23	1,505	1,368	+137
Hereford United	11	2,984	2,217	+767
Mansfield Town	19	2,440	2,318	+122
Northampton Town	18	2,343	2,594	−251
Peterborough United	7	3,424	2,795	+629
Reading	3	4,471	3,459	+1,012
Rochdale	22	1,491	1,688	−197
Stockport County	12	2,098	2,309	−211
Swindon Town	17	3,344	4,195	−851
Torquay United	9	1,922	2,336	−414
Tranmere Rovers	10	2,138	1,921	+217
Wrexham	20	2,083	2,710	−627
York City	1	5,008	3,243	+1,765

WELSH FA CUP WINNERS (Since 1901)

1900-1 Oswestry
1901-2 Wellington
1902-3 Wrexham
1903-4 Druids
1904-5 Wrexham
1905-6 Wellington
1906-7 Oswestry
1907-8 Chester
1908-9 Wrexham
1909-10 Wrexham
1910-11 Wrexham
1911-12 Cardiff
1912-13 Swansea
1913-14 Wrexham
1914-15 Wrexham
1915-16 Abandoned
1919-20 Cardiff
1920-21 Wrexham
1921-22 Cardiff
1922-23 Cardiff
1923-24 Wrexham
1924-25 Wrexham
1925-26 Ebbw Vale
1926-27 Cardiff
1927-28 Cardiff
1928-29 Connah's Quay
1929-30 Cardiff
1930-31 Wrexham
1931-32 Swansea
1932-33 Chester
1933-34 Bristol City
1934-35 Tranmere
1935-36 Crewe
1936-37 Crewe
1937-38 Shrewsbury
1938-39 S. Liverpool
1939-40 Wellington
1940-46 No contest
1946-47 Chester
1947-48 Lovell's Ath.
1948-49 Merthyr Tydfil
1949-50 Swansea
1950-51 Merthyr Tydfil
1951-52 Rhyl
1952-53 Rhyl
1953-54 Flint
1954-55 Bury
1955-56 Cardiff
1956-57 Wrexham
1957-58 Wrexham
1958-59 Cardiff
1959-60 Wrexham
1960-61 Swansea
1961-62 Bangor
1962-63 Borough Utd
1963-64 Cardiff
1964-65 Cardiff
1965-66 Swansea
1966-67 Cardiff
1967-68 Cardiff
1968-69 Cardiff
1969-70 Cardiff
1970-71 Cardiff
1971-72 Wrexham
1972-73 Cardiff
1973-74 Cardiff
1974-75 Wrexham
1975-76 Cardiff
1976-77 Shrewsbury
1977-78 Wrexham
1978-79 Shrewsbury
1979-80 Newport County
1980-81 Swansea
1981-82 Swansea
1982-83 Swansea
1983-84 Shrewsbury

NORTHERN IRISH CUP FINALS 1881-1984

1880-81	Moyola Park	1	Cliftonville	0
1881-82	Queen's Island	2	Cliftonville	1
1882-83	Cliftonville	5	Ulster	0
1883-84	Distillery	5	Wellington Park	0
1884-85	Distillery	2	Limavady	0
1885-86	Distillery	1	Limavady	0
1886-87	Ulster	3	Cliftonville	0
1887-88	Cliftonville	2	Distillery	1
1888-89	Distillery	5	YMCA	4
1889-90	Gordon Highlanders	3	Cliftonville	1
1890-91	Linfield	4	Ulster	2
1891-92	Linfield	7	The Black Watch	0
1892-93	Linfield	5	Cliftonville	1
1893-94	Distillery	3	Linfield	2
1894-95	Linfield	10	Bohemians	1
1895-96	Distillery	3	Glentoran	1
1896-97	Cliftonville	3	Sherwood Foresters	1
1897-98	Linfield	2	St Columb's Hall Celtic	0
1898-99	Linfield	2	Glentoran	1
1899–1900	Cliftonville	2	Bohemians	1
1900-1	Cliftonville	1	Freebooters	0
1901-2	Linfield	5	Distillery	1
1902-3	Distillery	3	Bohemians	1
1903-4	Linfield	5	Derry Celtic	1
1904-5	Distillery	3	Shelbourne	0
1905-6	Shelbourne	2	Belfast Celtic	0
1906-7	Cliftonville	1	Shelbourne	0
1907-8	Bohemians	3	Shelbourne	1
1908-9	Cliftonville	2	Bohemians	1
1909-10	Distillery	1	Cliftonville	0
1910-11	Shelbourne	2	Bohemians	1
1911-12	Linfield were awarded Cup. Final not played.			
1912-13	Linfield	2	Glentoran	0
1913-14	Glentoran	3	Linfield	1
1914-15	Linfield	1	Belfast Celtic	0
1915-16	Linfield	1	Glentoran	0
1916-17	Glentoran	2	Belfast Celtic	0
1917-18	Belfast Celtic	2	Linfield	0
1918-19	Linfield	2	Glentoran	1
1919-20	Cup awarded to Shelbourne.			
1920-21	Glentoran	2	Glenavon	0
1921-22	Linfield	2	Glenavon	0
1922-23	Linfield	2	Glentoran	0
1923-24	Queen's Island	1	Willowfield	0
1924-25	Distillery	2	Glentoran	1
1925-26	Belfast Celtic	3	Linfield	2
1926-27	Ards	3	Cliftonville	2
1927-28	Willowfield	1	Larne	0
1928-29	Ballymena United	2	Belfast Celtic	1
1929-30	Linfield	4	Ballymena United	3
1930-31	Linfield	3	Ballymena United	0
1931-32	Glentoran	2	Linfield	1

1932-33	Glentoran	3	Distillery	1
1933-34	Linfield	5	Cliftonville	0
1934-35	Glentoran	1	Larne	0
1935-36	Linfield	2	Derry City	1
1936-37	Belfast Celtic	3	Linfield	0
1937-38	Belfast Celtic	2	Bangor	0
1938-39	Linfield	2	Ballymena United	0
1939-40	Ballymena United	2	Glenavon	0
1940-41	Belfast Celtic	1	Linfield	0
1941-42	Linfield	3	Glentoran	1
1942-43	Belfast Celtic	1	Glentoran	0
1943-44	Belfast Celtic	2	Linfield	1
1944-45	Linfield	4	Glentoran	2
1945-46	Linfield	3	Distillery	0
1946-47	Belfast Celtic	1	Glentoran	0
1947-48	Linfield	3	Coleraine	0
1948-49	Derry City	3	Glentoran	1
1949-50	Linfield	2	Distillery	1
1950-51	Glentoran	3	Ballymena United	1
1951-52	Ards	1	Glentoran	0
1952-53	Linfield	5	Coleraine	0
1953-54	Derry City	1	Glentoran	0
1954-55	Dundela	3	Glenavon	0
1955-56	Distillery	1	Glentoran	0
1956-57	Glenavon	2	Derry City	0
1957-58	Ballymena United	2	Linfield	0
1958-59	Glenavon	2	Ballymena United	0
1959-60	Linfield	5	Ards	1
1960-61	Glenavon	5	Linfield	1
1961-62	Linfield	4	Portadown	0
1962-63	Linfield	2	Distillery	1
1963-64	Derry City	2	Glentoran	0
1964-65	Coleraine	2	Glenavon	1
1965-66	Glentoran	2	Linfield	0
1966-67	Crusaders	3	Glentoran	1
1967-68	Crusaders	2	Linfield	0
1968-69	Ards	4	Distillery	1
1969-70	Linfield	2	Ballymena United	1
1970-71	Distillery	3	Derry City	0
1971-72	Coleraine	2	Portadown	1
1972-73	Glentoran	3	Linfield	2
1973-74	Ards	2	Ballymena United	1
1974-75	Coleraine	1	Linfield	0
	(after 1-1 and 0-0 draws)			
1975-76	Carrick Rangers	2	Linfield	1
1976-77	Coleraine	4	Linfield	1
1977-78	Linfield	3	Ballymena United	1
1978-79	Cliftonville	3	Portadown	2
1979-80	Linfield	2	Crusaders	0
1980-81	Ballymena	1	Glenavon	0
1981-82	Linfield	2	Coleraine	1
1982-83	Glentoran	1 2	Linfield	1 1
1983-84	Ballymena	4	Carrick Rangers	1

EUROPEAN TOURNAMENTS 1983-84

British clubs dominated the European tournaments in 1983-84, with one representative in each of the six semi-finals. Liverpool and Spurs went through to win the Champions' Cup and U.E.F.A. Cup respectively, with both finals being decided on penalties.

In the Champions' Cup, it looked for a while as though we might have had a final between Liverpool and Dundee United. In their semi-final first leg, United beat AS Roma 2-0 at Tannadice Park with goals from Dodds and Stark, and thoroughly deserved the result. Unfortunately the atmosphere in Rome's Olympic Stadium, combined with a sparkling performance from the home side, was too much for them in the second leg, and they went down to goals from Pruzzo and Kickedin and a penalty from Bartolomei. If anything, Liverpool looked less certain of a place in the final after the first leg of their semi-final, taking only a 1-0 lead away with them for the second leg in Bucharest. However, two goals from Ian Rush saw them through.

The final had, fortunately for Roma, been scheduled for the Olympic Stadium in Rome, and so the Romans started as favourites; but it was Liverpool who took an early lead through an opportunist goal from Phil Neal. The Italians replied before half-time with a delightful headed goal from Pruzzo but there were few clear chances for either side after that, and the match eventually ended in a penalty competition which Liverpool won 4-2 after surprising misses from Conti and Graziani. It was Liverpool's fourth European Cup, and means that British clubs have now won the trophy more times than teams from any other nation.

In the Cup-Winners' Cup, Manchester United and Aberdeen featured in separate semi-finals, both having overturned 2-0 deficits in the first legs of their quarter-finals to win 3-2 on aggregate. For United, a 1-1 draw at home against Juventus in the first leg of their semi-final never looked enough, and they went down 2-1 in Turin. Aberdeen lost both legs of their semi-final tie against Porto by the narrowest of margins. Juventus went on to win the Cup, adding it to the Italian League Championship which they had clinched a few days earlier for the 21st time.

Nottingham Forest and Spurs were the British representatives in the semi-finals of the U.E.F.A. Cup. Forest looked a good bet for the final after their 2-0 semi-final first leg victory over Anderlecht, but the Belgians ran out 3-2 winners on aggregate to face Spurs, who reached the final on away goals against the Yugoslavian side Hadjuk Split. The first leg of the final, played in Brussels, was marred by tragedy off the field. The reputation of the Spurs fans, deserved or otherwise, went before them, and a tense situation exploded when one Spurs fan was shot dead by a bar manager after an argument over payment for some drinks. Several other Spurs fans were badly hurt in this and other incidents, and many were arrested. On the field of play, both legs of the final were drawn 1-1, and Spurs took the trophy 4-3 on penalties.

The fact that penalties settled two of the three European finals in 1983-84 highlighted this method of settling a final, and many people think that it is an unsatisfactory method of achieving a result. However, the alternatives are, if anything, less satisfactory still. Replays are often an anti-climax, and in European competitions ther is the additional problem of the expense and inconvenience involved for supporters wishing to attend the replay. On balance, it is probably better to get a result on the day, and the penalty competition themselves have an excitement and tension all of their own.

Key: A – Austria; AL – Albania; B – Bulgaria; BE – Belgium; CY – Cyprus; CZ – Czechoslovakia; D – Denmark; E – Eire; EG – East Germany; FI – Finland; F – France; G – Greece; H – Hungary; I – Italy; IC – Iceland; L – Luxembourg; N – Netherlands; NI – Northern Ireland; NO – Norway; PO – Poland; P – Portugal; R – Rumania; S – Switzerland; SP – Spain; SW – Sweden; T – Turkey; WG – West Germany; Y – Yugoslavia.

EUROPEAN CHAMPIONS' CUP 1983-84

Second round			Quarter-finals			Semi-finals			Final	
Bohemians Prague (CZ)	2	0	Rapid Vienna	2	0	Dundee United	2	0	**AS Roma**	1
Rapid Vienna* (A)	1	1	Dundee United*	1	1	AS Roma	0	3	*Pruzzo*	
Standard Liège (BE)	0	0	AS Roma	3	1	Liverpool	1	2	*Rome*	
Dundee United	0	4	Dynamo Berlin	0	2	Dinamo Bucharest	1	1	*Attendance: 69,693*	
CSKA Sofia (B)	0	0	Liverpool	1	4				**Liverpool**	1
AS Roma (I)	1	1	Benfica	0	1				*Neal*	
Dynamo Berlin (EG)	2	0	Dinamo Minsk	1	0				*After extra time*	
Partizan Belgrade (Y)	0	1	Dinamo Bucharest	1	1				*Liverpool won 4-2 on penalties*	
Liverpool	0	1								
Athletico Bilbao (SP)	0	0								
Olympiakos (G)	1	0								
Benfica (P)	0	3								
Raba Vasas Eto Györ (H)	3	1								
Dinamo Minsk (USSR)	6	3								
Dinamo Bucharest (R)	3	2								
SV Hamburg (WG)	0	3								

*won on away goals

EUROPEAN CUP-WINNERS' CUP 1983-84

Second round	Quarter-finals	Semi-finals	Final
NEC Nijmegen (N) 2 0	Barcelona 2 0		
Barcelona (S) 3 2		Manchester United 1 1	
Spartak Varna (B) 1 0	Manchester United 0 3		
Manchester United 2 2			**Juventus** 2
Hammarby IF (SW) 1 1	Valkeakosken Haka ...0 0		*Vignola, Boniek*
Valkeakosken Haka (FI) ...1 2		Juventus 1 2	*Basle*
Paris St-Germain (F) 2 0	Juventus 1 1		*Attendance: 60,000*
Juventus* (I) 2 0			
Rangers 2 0	Porto 3 1		
Porto* (P) 1 1		Porto 1 1	
Shakhter Donetsk (USSR) ..1 2	Shakhter Donetsk 2 1		
Servette (S) 0 1			**Porto** 1
Ujpesti Dozsa* (H) 3 2	Ujpesti Dozsa 2 0		*Sousa*
Cologne (WG) 1 4		Aberdeen 0 0	
SK Beveren (BE) 0 1	Aberdeen 0 3		
Aberdeen 0 4			

**won on away goals.*

UEFA CUP 1983-84

Third round

Nottingham Forest 0 2
Celtic 0 1

Sturm Graz (A) 2 0
Lokomotiv Leipzig (EG) ...0 1

RC Lens (F) 1 0
RSC Anderlecht (BE) 1 1

Sparta Rotterdam (N) 1 0
Spartak Moscow (USSR) ...1 2

Watford 2 0
Sparta Prague (CZ) 3 4

Radnicki Nis (Y) 0 0
Hajduk Split (Y) 2 2

Bayern Munich (WG) 1 0
Tottenham Hotspur 0 2

Memphis Vienna (A) 2 1
Internazionale Milan (I) 1 1

Quarter-finals

Nottingham Forest 1 1
Sturm Graz 0 1

RSC Anderlecht 4 0
Spartak Moscow 2 1

Sparta Prague 1 0
Hajduk Split 0 2

Tottenham Hotspur 2 2
Memphis Vienna 0 2

Semi-finals

Nottingham Forest 2 0
RSC Anderlecht 0 3

Hajduk Split 2 0
Tottenham Hotspur* ...1 1

Final

RSC Anderlecht 1 1
First leg in Brussels
Attendance: 40,000
Scorers: Olsen; Miller

Tottenham Hotspur 1 1
Second leg in London
Attendance: 46,205
Scorers: Roberts; Czerniatinski
Tottenham H. won 4-3 on penalties

*won on away goals.

EUROPEAN CUP PAST FINALS

1956	Real Madrid	4	Stade de Rheims	3
1957	Real Madrid	2	Florentina	0
1958	Real Madrid	3	AC Milan	2**
1959	Real Madrid	2	Stade de Rheims	0
1960	Real Madrid	7	Eintracht Frankfurt	3
1961	SL Benfica	3	Barcelona	2
1962	SL Benfica	5	Real Madrid	3
1963	AC Milan	2	SL Benfica	1
1964	Inter Milan	3	Real Madrid	1
1965	Inter Milan	1	SL Benfica	0
1966	Real Madrid	2	Partizan Belgrade	1
1967	Celtic	2	Inter Milan	1
1968	Manchester United	4	SL Benfica	1
1969	AC Milan	4	Ajax Amsterdam	1
1970	Feyenoord	2	Celtic	1**
1971	Ajax Amsterdam	2	Panathinaikos	0
1972	Ajax Amsterdam	2	Inter Milan	0
1973	Ajax Amsterdam	1	Juventus	0
1974	Bayern Munich	1 4	Atlético Madrid	1 0
1975	Bayern Munich	2	Leeds United	0
1976	Bayern Munich	1	St Etienne (Fra)	0
1977	Liverpool	3	Borussia Munchengladbach	1
1978	Liverpool	1	FC Bruges	0
1979	Nottingham Forest	1	Malmoe	0
1980	Nottingham Forest	1	SV Hamburg	0
1981	Liverpool	1	Real Madrid	0
1982	Aston Villa	1	Bayern Munich	0
1983	SV Hamburg	1	Juventus	0

EUROPEAN CUP-WINNERS' CUP PAST FINALS

1961	Fiorentina	4	Rangers	1†
1962	Atlético Madrid	3	Fiorentina	0
	(After 1–1 draw)			
1963	Tottenham Hotspur	5	Atlético Madrid	1
1964	Sporting Lisbon	1	MTK Budapest	0
	(After 3–3 draw)			
1965	West Ham United	2	Munich 1860	0
1966	Borussia Dortmund	2	Liverpool	1**
1967	Bayern Munich	1	Rangers	0**
1968	AC Milan	2	SV Hamburg	0
1969	Slovan Bratislava	3	Barcelona	2
1970	Manchester City	2	Gornik Zabrze	1
1971	Chelsea	2	Real Madrid	1
	(After 1–1 draw)			
1972	Rangers	3	Dynamo Moscow	2
1973	AC Milan	1	Leeds United	0
1974	FC Magdeburg	2	AC Milan	0
1975	Dynamo Kiev	3	Ferencvaros	0
1976	RSC Anderlecht	4	West Ham United	2
1977	SV Hamburg	2	Anderlecht	0
1978	RSC Anderlecht	4	Austria Wien	0
1979	Barcelona	4	Fortuna Dusseldorf	3

1980	Valencia ...0 *(Valencia won on penalties)*	Arsenal ...0
1981	Dinamo Tbilisi ...2	Carl Zeiss Jena ...1
1982	Barcelona ...2	Standard Liege ...1
1983	Aberdeen ...2	Real Madrid ...1

FAIRS CUP PAST FINALS

1958	Barcelona ...8	London ...2†
1960	Barcelona ...4	Birmingham City ...1†
1961	AS Roma ...4	Birmingham City ...2†
1962	Valencia ...7	Barcelona ...3†
1963	Valencia ...4	Dynamo Zagreb ...1†
1964	Real Zaragoza ...2	Valencia ...1
1965	Ferencvaros ...1	Juventus ...0
1966	Barcelona ...4	Real Zaragoza ...3†
1967	Dynamo Zagreb ...2	Leeds United ...0
1968	Leeds United ...1†	Ferencvaros ...0†
1969	Newcastle United ...6	Ujpest Dozsa ...2†
1970	Arsenal ...4	Anderlecht ...3†
1971	Leeds United ...3*	Juventus ...3†

UEFA CUP PAST FINALS

1972	Tottenham Hotspur ...3	Wolverhampton Wanderers ...2
1973	Liverpool ...3	Borussia Munchengladbach ...2
1974	Feyenoord ...4	Tottenham Hotspur ...2
1975	Borussia Munchengladbach ...5	Twente Enschede ...1
1976	Liverpool ...4	FC Bruges ...3
1977	Juventus* ...2	Athletic Bilbao ...2
1978	PSV Eindhoven ...3	SEC Bastia ...0
1979	Borussia Munchengladbach 1 1	Red Star Belgrade ...1 0
1980	Borussia Munchengladbach 3 0	Eintracht Frankfurt* ...2 1
1981	Ipswich T. ...3 2	AZ 67 Alkmaar ...0 4
1982	IFK Gothenburg ...1 3	SV Hamburg ...0 0
1983	RSC Anderlecht ...1 1	Benfica ...0 1

EUROPEAN SUPER CUP

1972	Ajax ...3 3	Glasgow Rangers ...1 2
1973	Ajax ...0 6	AC Milan ...1 0
1974	Not contested	
1975	Dynamo Kiev ...1 2	Bayern Munich ...0 0
1976	Anderlecht ...4 1	Bayern Munich ...1 2
1977	Liverpool ...1 6	SV Hamburg ...1 0
1978	Anderlecht ...1 3	Liverpool ...1 2
1979	Nottingham Forest ...1 1	Barcelona ...0 1
1980	Nottingham Forest ...2 0	Valencia* ...1 1
1981	Not contested	
1982	Not contested	
1983	Aston Villa ...0 3	Barcelona ...1 0

**Won on away goals*

***After extra time*

†Aggregate score

EUROPEAN CHAMPIONSHIP PAST FINALS

1958-60 Paris, 10 July 1960
USSR 2, Yugoslavia 1 (*after extra time*)
USSR: Yachin; Tchekeli, Kroutikov, Voinov, Maslenkin, Netto, Metreveli, Ivanov, Ponedelnik, Bubukin, Meshki.
Yugoslavia: Vidinic; Durkovic, Jusufi, Zanetic, Miladinovic, Perusic, Sekularac, Jerkovic, Galic, Matus, Kostic.
Scorers: *USSR* – Metreveli, Ponedelnik; *Yugoslavia* – Netto og.

1962-64 Madrid, 21 June 1964
SPAIN 2, USSR 1
Spain; Iribar; Rivilla, Calleja, Fuste, Olivella, Zoco, Amancio, Pereda, Marcellino, Suarez, Lapetra.
USSR: Yachin; Chustikov, Mudrik, Voronin, Shesternjev, Anitchkin, Chislenko, Ivanov, Ponedelnik, Kornaev, Khusainov.
Scorers: *Spain* – Peredal Marcellino; *USSR* – Khusainov.

1966-68 Rome, 8 June 1968
ITALY 1, YUGOSLAVIA 1
Italy: Zoff; Burgnich, Facchetti, Ferrini, Guarneri, Castano, Domenghini, Juliano, Anastasi, Lodetti, Prati.
Yugoslavia: Pantelic; Fazlagic, Damjanovic, Pavlovic, Paunovic, Holcer, Petkovic, Acimovic, Musemic, Trivic, Dzajic.
Scorers: *Italy* – Domenghini, *Yugoslavia* – Dzajic.

Replay: Rome, 10 June 1968
ITALY 2, YUGOSLAVIA 0
Italy: Zoff; Burgnich, Facchetti, Rosato, Guarneri, Salvadore, Domenghini, Mazzola, Anastasi, De Sisti, Riva.
Yugoslavia: Pantelic; Fazlagic, Damjanovic, Pavlovic, Paunovic, Holcer, Hosic, Acimovic, Musemic, Trivic, Dzajic.
Scorers: *Italy* – Riva, Anastasi.

1970-72 Brussels, 18 June 1972
WEST GERMANY 3, USSR 0
West Germany: Maier; Hottges, Schwarzenbeck, Beckenbauer, Breitner, Hoeness, Wimmer, Netzer, Heynckes, Muller, Kremers.
USSR: Rudakov; Dzodzuashvili, Khurtislava, Kaplichny, Istomin, Troshkin, Kolotov, Baidachini, Konkov (Dolmatov), Banishevski (Konzinkievits), Onishenko.
Scorers: *West Germany* – Muller 2, Wimmer.

1974-76 Belgrade, 20 June 1976
CZECHOSLOVAKIA 2, WEST GERMANY 2 (*after extra time*)
Czechoslovakia: Viktor; Dobias (Vesely, F.), Pivarnik, Ondrus, Capkovic, Gogh, Moder, Panenka, Svehlik (Jurkemik), Masny, Nehoda.
West Germany: Maier; Vogts, Beckenbauer, Schwarzenbeck, Dietz, Bonhof, Wimmer, (Flohe), Muller, D., Beer (Bongartz), Hoeness, Holzenbein.
Scorers: *Czechoslovakia* – Svehlik, Dobias; *West Germany* – Muller, Holzenbein.
Czechoslovakia won 5-3 on penalties.

1978-80 Rome, 22 June 1980
WEST GERMANY 2, BELGIUM 1
West Germany: Schumacher; Briegel, Foerster, Dietz, Schuster, Rummenigge, Hrubesch, Mueller, Allofs, Stielike, Kaltz.
Belgium: Pfaff; Gerets, Millecamps, Meeuws, Renquin, Cools, Van der Eycken, Van Moer, Mommens, Van der Elst, Ceulemans.
Scorers: *West Germany* – Hrubesch 2; *Belgium* – Van der Eycken.

THE EUROPEAN FOOTBALL CHAMPIONSHIP 1982-84

THE QUALIFYING TOURNAMENT

Note: France qualify automatically as host nation.

Group 1 (Belgium, East Germany, Scotland, Switzerland)

Belgium 3, Switzerland 0 — 6 October 1982
Scotland 2, East Germany 0 — 13 October 1982
Scotland: Leighton; Narey, F. Gray, Souness, Hansen, Miller, Strachan, Archibald, Brazil (Sturrock), Wark, Robertson.
East Germany: Rudwaleit; Kreer, Trieloff, Stahmann, Baum, Schnuphese, Pilz, Dorner (Liebers), Steich, Hafner (Pommerenke), Riediger.
Scorers: Scotland – Wark, Sturrock.
Switzerland 2, Scotland 0 — 17 November 1982
Switzerland: Burgener; Ludi, Hermann, Egli, Geiger, Wehrli, Decastel, Favre, Sulser, Ponte, Elsener.
Scotland: Leighton; Narey, F. Gray, Souness, Hansen, Miller, Strachan, Sturrock (Archibald), Brazil, Wark, Robertson.
Scorers: Switzerland – Sulser, Egli.
Belgium 3, Scotland 2 — 15 December 1982
Belgium: Pfaff; Gerets, Dearden, Meeuws, Baecke, Vercauteren (Verheyen), Van der Elst, Vandersmissen, Vandenbergh (De Schrijver), Coeck, Ceulemans.
Scotland: Leighton; McLeish, F. Gray, Aitken, Hansen, Narey, Strachan (Sturrock), Souness, Archibald, Bett (Burns), Dalglish.
Scorers: Belgium – Vandenburgh, Van der Elst; Scotland – Dalglish 2.
Scotland 2, Switzerland 2 — 30 March 1983
Scotland: Leighton; Gough, F. Gray, Souness, Hansen (McLeish), Miller, Strachan, Dalglish, Nicholas, Wark, Weir.
Switzerland: Burgener; Ludi, Hermann (Braschler), Egli, Geiger, Wehrli, Favre, Decastel, Sulser (In-Albion), Ponte, Elsener.
Scorers: Scotland – Wark, Nicholas; Switzerland – Egli, Hermann.

East Germany 1, Belgium 2 — 30 March 1983
Belgium 2, East Germany 1 — 27 April 1983
Switzerland 0, East Germany 0 — 14 May 1983
East Germany 3, Switzerland 0 — 12 October 1983
Scotland 1, Belgium 1 — 12 October 1983
Scotland: Leighton; Gough, Albiston, Wark (Aitken), McLeish, Miller, Dalglish, McStay, Nicholas (McGarvey), Bett, Robertson.
Belgium: Pfaff; Gerets, Millecamps L., Meeuws (De Wolf), Wintacq, Vercauteren, Van der Elst, Claesen, Voordeckers, Coeck, Ceulemans.
Scorers: Scotland – Nicholas; Belgium – Vercauteren.
Switzerland 3, Belgium 1 — 9 November 1983
East Germany 2, Scotland 1 — 16 November 1983
East Germany: Rudwaleit; Stahmann, Kreer, Troppa, Zotzsche, Pilz, Ernst (Raab), Backs, Steinbach, Streich, Richter.
Scotland: Thomson; Gough, Albiston, Wark, McLeish, Miller, Strachan, McStay (McGarvey), Dalglish, Archibald, Bannon.
Scorers: East Germany – Kreer, Streich; Scotland - Bannon

FINAL TABLE	P	W	D	L	F	A	Pts
Belgium	6	4	1	1	12	8	9
Switzerland	6	2	2	2	7	9	6
East Germany	6	2	1	3	7	7	5
Scotland	6	1	2	3	8	10	4

Group 2 (Poland, USSR, Portugal, Finland)

Finland 2, Poland 3	8 September 1982
Finland 0, Portugal 2	22 September 1982
Portugal 2, Poland 1	10 October 1982
USSR 2, Finland 0	13 October 1982
Poland 1, Finland 1	17 April 1983
USSR 5, Portugal 0	27 April 1983
Poland 1, USSR 1	22 May 1983
Finland 0, USSR 1	1 June 1983
Portugal 5, Finland 0	21 September 1983
USSR 2, Poland 0	9 October 1983
Poland 0, Portugal 1	28 October 1983
Portugal 1, USSR 0	13 November 1983

FINAL TABLE	P	W	D	L	F	A	Pts
Portugal	6	5	0	1	11	6	10
USSR	6	4	1	1	11	2	9
Poland	6	1	2	3	6	9	4
Finland	6	0	1	5	3	14	1

Group 3 (England, Hungary, Greece, Denmark, Luxembourg)

Denmark 2, England 2 — 22 September 1982
Denmark: T. Rasmussen; Nielsen, Busk, Rontved, O. Rasmussen, Lerby, Berteisen, Olsen, Hansen, Elkjaer, Bastrup.
England: Shilton; Neal, Sansom, Wilkins, Osman, Butcher, Morley, Robson, Mariner, Francis, Rix (Hill).
Scorers: Denmark – Hansen (pen), Olsen; England – Francis 2.

Luxembourg 0, Greece 2 — 9 October 1982
Luxembourg 1, Denmark 2 — 10 November 1982
Greece 0, England 3 — 17 November 1982
Greece: Sarganis; Gounaris, Isofides, Foiros, Kapsis, Livathinos, Mihos, Mitropoulos, Anastopoulos, Ardizoglou (Kostos), (Kofidis).
England: Shilton, Neal, Sansom, Thompson, Martin, Robson, Lee, Mabbutt, Mariner, Woodcock, Morley.
Scorers: England – Woodcock 2, Lee.

England 9, Luxembourg 0 — 15 December 1982
England: Clemence, Neal, Martin, Butcher, Sansom, Lee, Mabbutt (Hoddle), Robson, Coppell (Chamberlain), Woodcock, Blissett.
Luxembourg: Moses, Girres, Meunier, Bossi, Rohmann, Clemens, Hellers, Weis, Dresch, Reiter, Di Domenico (Nurenberg).
Scorers: England – Moses (og), Coppell, Woodcock, Blissett 3, Chamberlain, Hoddle, Neal.

Luxembourg 2, Hungary 6 — 27 March 1983
England 0, Greece 0 — 30th March 1983
England: Shilton, Neal, Sansom, Lee, Martin, Butcher, Coppell, Mabbutt, Francis, Woodcock (Rix), Devonshire (Blissett).
Greece: Sarganis; Gounaris, Karoulais, Galizios, Micos, Xanthopoulos, Kounsoulakis, Kouis, Anastopoulos (Ardizoglou), Miropoulos (Dontas), Kostikos.

Hungary 6, Luxembourg 2 — 16 April 1983
England 2, Hungary 0 — 27 April 1983
England: Shilton; Neal, Sansom, Lee, Martin, Butcher, Mabbutt, Francis, Withe, Blissett, Cowans.
Hungary: Katzirz; Martos (Burcsa), Kocis, Toth, Hannich, Garaba, Varga, Nyilasi, Kiss (Torocsik), Kardos, Hajszan
Scorers: England – Francis, White.

Denmark 1, Greece 0 27 April 1983
Hungary 2, Greece 3 15 May 1983
Denmark 3, Hungary 1 1 June 1983
England 0, Denmark 1 21 September 1983

England: Shilton; Neal, Sansom, Wilkins, Osman, Butcher, Francis, Lee (Blissett), Mariner, Gregory, Barnes (Chamberlain).
Denmark: Kjaer; Rasmussen, Busk, Olsen M. (Molby), Nielsen, Simonsen, Bertelsen, Lerby, Berggreen, Laudrup (Elkjaer-Laren), Olsen J.
Scorer: Denmark – Simonsen (pen).

Denmark 6, Luxembourg 0 12 October 1983
Hungary 0, England 3 12 October 1983
Hungary: Kovacs; Csonka, Kardos, Garaba, Varga, Hannich (Szokolai), Csongradi, Burcsa (Nagy), Dajka, Nyilasi, Hajszan.
England: Shilton; Gregory, Sansom, Lee, Martin, Butcher, Robson, Blissett (Withe), Mariner, Hoddle, Mabbutt.
Scorers: England – Hoddle, Lee, Mariner.

Hungary 1, Denmark 0 26 October 1983
Greece 0, Denmark 2 16 November 1983
Luxembourg 0, England 4 16 November 1983
Luxembourg: Defrang; Michaux, Bossi, Dresch, Meunier, Langers, Wagner, Hellers, Barboni (Jeitz), Reiter, Malget (Girres).
England: Clemence; Duxbury, Sansom, Lee, Martin, Butcher, Robson, Hoddle, Mariner, Woodcock (Barnes), Devonshire.
Scorers: England – Robson 2, Mariner, Butcher.

Greece 2, Hungary 2 3 December 1983
Greece 1, Luxembourg 0 14 December 1983

FINAL TABLE	P	W	D	L	F	A	Pts
Denmark	8	6	1	1	17	5	13
England	8	5	2	1	23	3	12
Greece	8	3	2	3	8	10	8
Hungary	8	3	1	4	18	17	7
Luxembourg	8	0	0	8	5	36	0

Group 4 (Yugoslavia, Wales, Bulgaria, Norway)
Wales 1, Norway 0 22 September 1982
Wales: Southall; Marustik, Jones, Jackett, Stevenson, Price, Curtis (Charles), Flynn, Rush, Thomas, R. James.
Norway: Nygard; Berntsen, Kojedahl, Hareide, Grondalen, Albertsen, Erlandsen (Kollsnangen), Soler, Lund, Okland, Thoresen.
Scorer: Wales – Rush.

Norway 3, Yugoslavia 1 13 October 1982
Bulgaria 2, Norway 2 27 October 1982
Bulgaria 0, Yugoslavia 1 17 November 1982
Yugoslavia 4, Wales 4 15 December 1982

Yugoslavia: Svilar; Stokovic, Cvetkovic, Trifunovic, Ferhatovic (Djurovski), Hadzibegic, Deveric (Jesic), Nicolic, Krancjar, Gudelj, Zizkovic.
Wales: Davies: Jones, Price, Jackett, Ratcliffe, Flynn, Nicholas (Vaughan), Mahoney, Thomas (Charles), R. James, Rush.
Scorers: Yugoslavia – Cvetkovic, Zizkovic, Krancjar, Jesic; Wales – Flynn, Rush, Jones, R. James.

Wales 1, Bulgaria 0 — 27 April 1983
Wales: Southall; Jones, Jackett, Nicholas, Price, Ratcliffe, R. James, Flynn, Rush (Charles), Thomas, Davies
Bulgaria: Velinov; Nikolov, Arabov, Petrov, Borisov, Zdravkov, Yontchev, Yordanov (Slavkov), Djevizov, Sadakov, Mladenov.
Scorer: Wales – Charles.

Norway 1, Bulgaria 2 — 7 September 1983
Norway 0, Wales 0 — 21 September 1983
Norway: Thorstvedt; Kojedal, Fjaelberg, Hareide, Grondalen, Albertsen, Davidsen, Soler, Thoresen, Dokken, Kollshaugen.
Wales: Southall; Hopkins, Price, Ratcliffe, Jones J., Nicholas, Flynn, Vaughan, Jackett, James R., Rush.

Yugoslavia 2, Norway 1 — 12 October 1983
Bulgaria 1, Wales 0 — 16 November 1983
Bulgaria: Mikhailov; Sirakov, Arabov, Petrov P., Dimitrov G., Zdravkov, Iskrenov, Sadakov, Danov (Gochev), Gospodinov (Borisov), Mladenov S.
Wales: Southall; Hopkins, Price, Ratcliffe, Jones J., Flynn, Nicholas (Charles), Thomas, Vaughan, James R., Rush.
Scorer: Bulgaria – Gochev.
Wales 1, Yugoslavia 1 — 14 December 1983
Wales: Southall; Hopkins, Price, Ratcliffe, Jones J., Jackett, Flynn (Charles), Vaughan, Thomas, James R., Rush.
Yugoslavia: Simovic; Peruzovic, Zoran Vujovic, Radanovic, Brobnjak, Katanec, Gudelj, Bazdarevic, Mlinaric, Susic, Zlatko Vujovic.
Scorers: Wales – James; Yugoslavia – Bazdarevic.

Yugoslavia 3, Bulgaria 2 — 21 December 1983

FINAL TABLE	P	W	D	L	F	A	Pts
Yugoslavia	6	3	2	1	12	11	8
Wales	6	2	3	1	7	6	7
Bulgaria	6	2	1	3	7	8	5
Norway	6	1	2	3	7	8	4

Group 5 (Italy, Czechoslovakia, Rumania, Sweden, Cyprus)
Rumania 3, Cyprus 1 — 1 May 1982
Rumania 2, Sweden 0 — 8 September 1982
Czechoslovakia 2, Sweden 2 — 6 October 1982
Italy 2, Czechoslovakia 2 — 13 November 1982
Cyprus 0, Sweden 1 — 13 November 1982
Italy 0, Rumania 0 — 4 December 1982
Cyprus 1, Italy 1 — 12 February 1983
Cyprus 1, Czechoslovakia 1 — 27 March 1983
Rumania 1, Italy 0 — 16 April 1983
Czechoslovakia 6, Cyprus 0 — 16 April 1983
Sweden 5, Cyprus 0 — 15 May 1983
Rumania 0, Czechoslovakia 1 — 15 May 1983
Sweden 2, Italy 0 — 26 May 1983
Sweden 0, Rumania 1 — 9 June 1983
Sweden 1, Czechoslovakia 0 — 21 September 1983
Italy 0, Sweden 3 — 15 October 1983
Cyprus 0, Rumania 1 — 12 November 1983
Czechoslovakia 2, Italy 0 — 16 November 1983
Czechoslovakia 1, Rumania 1 — 30 November 1983
Italy 3, Cyprus 1 — 22 December 1983

FINAL TABLE	P	W	D	L	F	A	Pts
Rumania	8	5	2	1	9	3	12
Sweden	8	5	1	2	14	5	11
Czechoslovakia	8	3	4	1	15	7	10
Italy	8	1	3	4	6	12	5
Cyprus	8	0	2	6	4	21	2

Group 6 (West Germany, Austria, Northern Ireland, Turkey, Albania)

Austria 5, Albania 0 — 22 September 1982
Austria 2, Northern Ireland 0 — 13 October 1982
Austria: Koncilla; Krauss, Obermayer, Peggey, Degeorgi, Prohaska, Weber, Gesselich, Schachner, Hagmayr (Pacult), Jurtin (Baumeister).
Northern Ireland: Platt; J. Nicholl, McClelland, J. O'Neill, Donaghy, M. O'Neill, McIlroy (Brotherston), McCreery, Armstrong, Hamilton, Stewart (Healy).
Scorer: Austria – Schachner 2.

Turkey 1, Albania 0 — 27 October 1982
Northern Ireland 1, West Germany 0 — 17 November 1982
Northern Ireland: Platt; J. Nicholl, J. O'Neill, McClelland, Donaghy, Brotherston, McIlroy, M. O'Neill, Stewart, Hamilton, Whiteside.
West Germany: Schumacher; Kaltz, Strack, B. Forster, Briegel, Matthaus, Schuster, Stielike, Rummenigge, Allofs, Littbarski.
Scorer: Northern Ireland – Stewart.

Austria 4, Turkey 0 — 17 November 1982
Albania 0, Northern Ireland 0 — 15 December 1982
Albania: Musta; Bino, Ahmetaj, Targaj, Ruci, Vukatana, Ragami, Balljini, Luci, Kola, Minga.
Northern Ireland: Platt; J. Nicholl, McClelland, J. O'Neill, Donaghy, M. O'Neill, McIlroy, Brotherston, Hamilton, Whiteside, Stewart.
Northern Ireland 2, Turkey 1 — 30 March 1983
Northern Ireland: Platt; J. Nicholl, McClelland, J. O'Neill, Donaghy, M. O'Neill, McIlroy, Brotherston, Whiteside, Armstrong, Stewart.
Turkey: Eser; Erdogan, Fatih, Yusuf, Hakan, Eren, Metin, Rasit, Heseyin, Hasan, Selcuk.
Scorers: Northern Ireland – Yusuf (og), McClelland; Turkey – Hasan.

Albania 1, West Germany 2 — 30 March 1983
Turkey 0, West Germany 3 — 23 April 1983
Austria 0, West Germany 0 — 27 April 1983
Northern Ireland 1, Albania 0 — 27 April 1983
Northern Ireland: Jennings; J. Nicholl, McClelland, J. O'Neill, Donaghy, M. O'Neill, McIlroy, Brotherston, Hamilton, Armstrong, Stewart.
Albania: Musta; Ruci, Ahmetagi, Targaj, Omuri, Eskaro, Muca (Mema), Lame, Minga, Bukatana, Demollari.
Scorer: Northern Ireland – Stewart.
Albania 1, Turkey 1 — 12 May 1983
Austria 2, Albania 1 — 8 June 1983
Northern Ireland 3, Austria 1 — 21 September 1983

Northern Ireland: Jennings; Ramsey, Nicholl C., McClelland, Donaghy, O'Neill M., McIlroy, Stewart, Hamilton, Armstrong, Whiteside.
Austria: Koncilia; Krauss, Pezzey, Kienast (Degeorgi), Lainer, Weber, Prohaska, Gasselich, Gisinger (Willfurth), Schachner, Krankl.
Scorers: Northern Ireland – Hamilton, Whiteside, O'Neill M.; Austria – Gasselich.
West Germany 3, Austria 0 — 5 October 1983
Turkey 1, Northern Ireland 0 — 12 October 1983
Turkey: Adem; Ismail, Fatih, Yusuf, Erdogan, Ibrahim (Riza), Sedat, Rasit, Tufekci, Hassan, Selcuk.

Northern Ireland: Jennings; Nicholl J., Donaghy, Nicholl C., McClelland, O'Neill M., Brotherston (Cleary), McIlroy, Hamilton (McCreery), Whiteside, Stewart.
Scorer: Turkey – Selcuk.

West Germany 5, Turkey 1 — 26 October 1983
Turkey 3, Austria 1 — 16 November 1983
West Germany 0, Northern Ireland 1 — 16 November 1983
West Germany: Schumacher; Dremmler, Augenthaler, Forster K-H., Briegel, Matthaus, Stielike (Strack), Rolff, Meir (Littbarski), Rummenigge K-H., Waas.
Northern Ireland: Jennings; Nicholl J., McElhinney, McClelland, Donaghy, Ramsey, O'Neill M., Armstrong, Whiteside, Hamilton, Stewart.

FINAL TABLE	P	W	D	L	F	A	Pts
West Germany	8	5	1	2	15	5	11
Northern Ireland	8	5	1	2	8	5	11
Austria	8	4	1	3	15	10	9
Turkey	8	3	1	4	8	16	7
Albania	8	0	2	6	4	14	2

Group 7 (Spain, Netherlands, Eire, Iceland, Malta)

Malta 2, Iceland 1 — 5 June 1982
Iceland 1, Netherlands 1 — 1 September 1982
Netherlands 2, Eire 1 — 22 September 1982
Netherlands: Van Breukelen; Spelbos, Van der Korput, Stevens, Metgod, Wijnstekers, Van der Kirkhof, Schoemaker, Vandenberg, Guillit, Van der Gijp.
Eire: McDonagh; Lawrenson, O'Leary, Martin, Hughton, Daly (Walsh), Grealish, Brady, Stapleton, Robinson, Galvin (Waddock).
Scorers: Netherlands – Schoemaker, Guillit; Eire – Daly.

Eire 2, Iceland 0 — 13 October 1982
Eire: McDonagh; Moran, Lawrenson, O'Leary, Walsh, Whelan, Grealish, Waddock, Brady (O'Callaghan), Robinson, Stapleton.
Iceland: Bjarnson; Oskarsson, Halldorsson, Jonsson, Giersson, Gudjohnsen, Gislarson, Ormsley (Margiersson), Edvaldsson, Gudmundsson, Pedursson.
Scorers: Eire – Stapleton, Grealish.

Spain 1, Iceland 0 — 27 October 1982
Eire 3, Spain 3 — 17 November 1982
Eire: McDonagh; Devine, Martin, Lawrenson, Hughton, Grealish (Walsh), Brady, Grimes, Robinson, Stapleton, K. O'Callaghan.
Spain: Arconada; Juan Jose, Bonnet, Maceda, Camacho, Senor, Victor, Gordillo, Pederaza, Santillana (Roberto), Marcos.
Scorers: Eire – Grimes, Stapleton 2; Spain – Maceda, Martin (og), Victor.

Malta 0, Netherlands 6 — 19 December 1982
Spain 1, Netherlands 0 — 16 February 1983
Malta 0, Eire 1 — 30 March 1983
Malta: Bonello, Emme Farrugia, Holland, Schembri, Edwin Farrugia, R. Xuereb, Fabri, M. Farrugia, Degiorgio, G. Xuereb, Demanuele.
Eire: McDonagh; Devine, Martin, Lawrenson, Hughton, Whelan, Waddock, Brady, Stapleton, Robinson, Galvin (O'Callaghan).
Scorer: Eire – Stapleton.

Spain 2, Eire 0 — 27 April 1983
Spain: Arconada; Juan Jose, Maceda, Bonet, Camacho, Victor (Gallego), Senor, Gordillo, Marcos, Santillana, Carrasco (Rincon).

Eire: McDonagh; Lawrenson, O'Leary, Martin, Hughton, Whelan, Grealish, Waddock, Grimes (O' Callaghan), Stapleton, Walsh.
Scorers: Spain – Santillana, Rincon.

Malta 2, Spain 3 — 15 May 1983
Iceland 0, Spain 1 — 29 May 1983
Iceland 1, Malta 0 — 5 June 1983
Netherlands 3, Iceland 0 — 7 September 1983
Iceland 0, Eire 3 — 21 September 1983
Iceland: Bjarnasson; Larusson, Edvaldsson J., Jonsson, Gudlaugsson, Edvaldsson A., Gudjohnsen (Eliasson), Gudmundsson, Ormslev, Petursson (Gretarsson), Halldorsson.
Eire: McDonagh; Devine, Lawrenson, Moran, Hughton, Brady, Waddock, Grealish, O'Callaghan K., Stapleton, Robinson (Walsh M.).
Scorers: Eire – Waddock, Robinson, Walsh.
Eire 2, Netherlands 3 — 12 October 1983
Eire: McDonagh; Devine, Hughton, Lawrenson, Moran, Brady, Waddock, Grealish (Sheedy), Stapleton, Robinson, O'Callaghan K. (Gilbert).
Netherlands: Schrijvers; Silooy, Ophof, Boeve, Wijnstekers, Koeman R., Gullit, Willy Van de Kerkhof, Van Basten, Vanenburg, Van Tiggelen (Brocken).
Scorers: Eire – Waddock, Brady (pen); Netherlands – Gullit 2, Van Basten.
Netherlands 2, Spain 1 — 16 November 1983
Eire 8, Malta 0 — 16 November 1983
Eire: Bonner; O'Reagan, Moran (McDonagh I.), Lawrenson, Hughton, Daly, Sheedy, Brady, Walsh, Stapleton, O'Callaghan K.
Malta: Bonello; Ed Farrugia, Holland, Buttigieg, Azzopardi, Faori, Busuttil, Em Farrugia, Degiorgio, Demanuele, Spiteri-Gonzi.
Scorers: Eire – Lawrenson 2, Stapleton (pen), O'Callaghan, Sheedy, Brady 2, Daly.
Netherlands 5, Malta 0 — 17 December 1983
Spain 12, Malta 1 — 21 December 1983

FINAL TABLE	P	W	D	L	F	A	Pts
Spain	8	6	1	1	24	8	13
Netherlands	8	6	1	1	22	6	13
Eire	8	4	1	3	20	10	9
Iceland	8	1	1	6	3	13	3
Malta	8	2					

THE EUROPEAN FOOTBALL CHAMPIONSHIP 1982-84 FINAL TOURNAMENT

GROUP ONE
(Belgium, Denmark, France, Yugoslavia)
Paris, 12 June 1984, 47,570
France (0) 1 *(Platini)*
Denmark (0) 0
France: Bats, Battiston, Le Roux (Domergue), Bossis, Amoros, Tigana, Fernandez, Giresse, Platini, Lacombe, Bellone.
Denmark: Qvist; Busk, M. Olsen, Lerby, Nielsen, Bertelsen, Arnesen (J. Olsen), Berggreen, Simonsen (Lauridsen), Elkjaer, Laudrup.

Lens, 13 June 1984, 45,000
Belgium (2) 2 *(Vandenbergh, Grun)*
Yugoslavia (0) 0
Belgium: Pfaff; Grun, De Greef, Clijsters (Lambrichts), De Wolf, Schifo, Vandereycken, Vercauteren, Ceulemans, Claesen, Vandenbergh.
Yugoslavia: Simovic; N. Stojkovic, Hadzibegic, Katanec, Zajec, Bazdarevic (D. Stojkovic), Sestic, Gudelj, Vujovic (Cvetkovic), Susic, Halilovic.

Nantes, 16 June 1984, 52,000
France (3) 5 *(Platini 3 (1 pen), Fernandez, Giresse)*
Belgium (0) 0
France: Bats; Domergue, Bossis, Battiston, Fernandez, Genghini (Tusseau), Platini, Giresse, Six, Tigana, Lacombe (Rocheteau).
Belgium: Pfaff; Grun, Lambrichts, De Greef, De Wolf, Scifo (Verheyen), Vandereycken (Coeck), Vercauteren, Ceulemans, Claesen, Vandenbergh.

Lyons, 16 June 1984, 28,000
Denmark (2) 5 *(Arnesen 2 (1 pen), Berggreen, Elkjaer, Lauridsen)*
Yugoslavia (0) 0
Denmark: Qvist; Busk, Nielsen, M. Olsen, O. Rasmussen (Sivebak), Berggreen, Bertelsen, Arnesen (Lauridsen), Lerby, Laudrup, Elkjaer.
Yugoslavia: Ivkovic; N. Stojkovic, Radanovic, Zajek, Milius, Gudelj, Katanec (Halilovic), Bazdarevic (D. Stojkovic), Vujovic, Susis, Cvetkovic.

St Etienne, 19 June 1984, 50,000
France (0) 3 *(Platini 3)*
Yugoslavia (1) 2 *(Sestic, D. Stojkovic, pen)*
France: Bats; Fernandez, Battiston, Bossis, Domergue, Tigana, Giresse, Platini, Ferreri, Rocheteau (Tusseau), Six.
Yugoslavia: Simovic; Radanovic, N. Stojkovic, Zajec, Milius, Sestic, Gudelj, Bazdarevic (Katanec), D. Stojkovic, Susic, Vujovic (Halilovic).

Strasbourg, 19 June 1984, 45,000
Denmark (1) 3 *(Arnesen (pen), Brylle, Elkjaer)*
Belgium (2) 2 *(Ceulemans, Vercauteren)*
Denmark: Qvist, O. Rasmussen (Brylle), M. Olsen, Nielsen, Busk, Arnesen, (Sivebak), Bertelsen, Berggreen, Lerby, Elkjaer, Laudrup.
Belgium: Pfaff; Grun, Clijsters, De Greef, De Wolf, Scifo, Vercauteren (Voordeckers), Vandereycken, Vandenbergh, Claesen (Coeck), Ceulemans.

FINAL TABLE

	P	W	D	L	F	A	Pt	GD
France	3	3	0	0	9	2	6	+7
Denmark	3	2	0	1	8	3	4	+5
Belgium	3	1	0	2	4	8	2	–4
Yugoslavia	3	0	0	3	2	10	0	–8

GROUP TWO
(Portugal, Rumania, Spain, West Germany)
Strasbourg, 14 June 1984, 47,950
West Germany (0) 0
(Portugal (0) 0
West Germany: Schumacher; B. Forster, Stielike, K-H. Forster, Briegel, Buchwald (Matthaus), Brehme, Rolff (Bommer), Rummenigge, Voller, Allofs.
Portugal: Bento; Joao Pinto, Lima Pereira, Eurico, Alvaro, Sousa, Frasco (Beloso), Pacheco, Carlos Manuel, Jordao (Gomes), Chalana.

St Etienne, 14 June 1984, 15,000
Spain (1) 1 *(Carrasco, pen)*
Rumania (1) 1 *(Boloni)*
Spain: Arconada; Urquiaga, Camacho, Maceda, Goicoechea, Gordillo, Senor, Victor, Santillana, Gallego (Julio Alberto), Carrasco.
Rumania: Lung, Rednic, Stefanescu, Ungureanu, Iorgulescu, Coras, Klein, Camataru, Boloni, Dragnea (Ticleanu), Gabor (Hagi).

Marseilles, 17 June 1984, 22,000
Spain (0) 1 *(Santillana)*
Portugal (0) 1 *(Sousa)*
Spain: Arconada; Urquiaga (Senor), Goicoechea, Camacho, Maceda, Victor, Gallego, Julio Alberto (Sarabia), Carrasco, Santillana.
Portugal: Bento; Joao Pinto, Lima Pereira, Eurico, Alvaro, Frasco (Diamantino), Carlos Manuel, Pacheco, Sousa, Chalana, Jordao.

Lens, 17 June 1984, 30,000
West Germany (1) 2 *(Voller 2)*
Rumania (0) 1 *(Coras)*
West Germany: Schumacher; B. Forster, Stielike, K-H. Forster (Buchwald), Briegel, Meier (Littbarski), Matthaus, Brehme, Rummenigge, Voller, Allofs.
Rumania: Lung; Rednic, Andone, Stefanescu, Ungureanu, Klein, Coras, Dragnea (Ticleanu), Boloni, Hagi (Zare), Camataru.

Paris, 20 June 1984, 40,000
West Germany (0) 0
Spain (0) 1 *(Maceda)*
West Germany: Schumacher; Briegel, B. Forster, K-H. Forster, Stielike, Matthaus, Brehme (Rolff), Meier (Littbarski), Allofs, Voller, Rummenigge.
Spain: Arconada, Camacho, Maceda, Goicoechea (Salva), Julio Alberto (Francisco), Gordillo, Senor, Victor, Santillana Carrasco, Gallego.

Nantes, 20 June 1984, 20,000
Portugal (0) 1 *(Nene)*
Rumania (0) 0
Portugal: Bento; Joao Pinto, Eurico, Lima Pereira, Alvaro, Frasco Carlos Manuel (Nene), Sousa, Jordao, Gomez, Chalana (Diamantino).
Rumania: Moraru; Rednic, Iorgulescu, Stefanescu, Ungureanu, Ticleanu, Klein, Boloni, Coras, Irimescu (Gabor), Camataru (Augustin).

FINAL TABLE

	P	W	D	L	F	A	Pt	GD
Spain	3	1	2	0	3	2	4	+1
Portugal	3	1	2	0	2	1	4	+1
West Germany	3	1	1	1	2	2	3	0
Rumania	3	0	1	2	2	4	1	–2

SEMI-FINALS

Marseilles, 23 June 1984, 56,468
France (1) 3 *(Domergue 2, Platini)*
Portugal (0) 2 *(Jordao 2) (a.e.t., 90 mins 1-1)*
France: Bats; Battiston, Le Roux, Bossis, Domergue, Tigana, Fernandez, Platini, Giresse, Lacombe (Ferreri), Six (Bellone).
Portugal: Bento; Alvaro, Lima Pereira, Eurico, Joao Pinto, Sousa (Nene), Frasco, Jaime Pahceco, Diamantino (Gomez), Chalana, Jordao.

Lyons, 24 June 1984, 47,843
Denmark (1) 1 *(Lerby)*
Spain (0) 1 *(Maceda) (a.e.t., 90 mins 1-1)*
Denmark: Qvist; Busk, M. Olsen (Brylle), Nielsen, Arnesen (J. Olsen), Bertelsen, Berggreen, Lerby, Sivebak, Elkjaer, Laudrup.
Spain: Arconada; Camacho, Maceda, Salva (Urquiaga), Senor, Gallego, Julio Alberto (Sarabia), Victor, Gordillo, Carrasco, Santillana.
Spain won 5–4 on penalties.

FINAL

Paris, 27 June 1984, 80,000
France (0) 2 *(Platini, Bellone)*
Spain (0) 0
France: Bats; Battiston (Amoros), Le Roux, Bossis, Domergue, Giresse, Platini, Tigana, Fernandez, Lacombe (Genghini), Bellone.
Spain: Arconada; Urquiaga, Salva (Roberto), Gallego, Camacho, Francisco, Julio Alberto (Sarabia), Senor, Victor, Carrasco, Santillana.

BRITISH INTERNATIONAL CHAMPIONSHIP 1983-84

The British International Championship was played for the last time in 1983-84, despite the protestations of the Welsh and Northern Irish, whose Football Associations will have to look elsewhere to supplement their meagre incomes now that three regular annual fixtures have been cancelled. Ironically, the Northern Irish won this last tournament (and the Welsh came second) – only Northern Ireland's third outright win in the 101 years of the championship – and they keep the trophy permanently.

The attendance figures for five out of the six games in 1983-84 confirm that interest in the championship is anything but great, and it is interesting to note that the gate for the game between the two countries who didn't want the championship scrapped was the lowest of all – only 7,845 people turning out to see Wales and Northern Ireland draw 1-1 at Swansea in May. As usual, the only healthy attendance figure was that for the Scotland v England fixture, and it is to be assumed that this fixture will continue on an annual basis.

England started their campaign with a dour 1-0 victory over Northern Ireland at Wembley in April in front of the smallest Wembley crowd for many years. All season manager Bobby Robson was frustrated by club commitments and injuries in his efforts to pick the strongest team, and the lack of consistent selection was reflected in the performance on the field. A month later, in Wrexham, this problem was highlighted even more when an almost unrecognisable England XI went down 1-0 to Wales, who seem to have found a new hero in Mark Hughes of Manchester United. It was Hughes who scored again when Wales drew with Northern Ireland three weeks later, and this meant that the two 'minnows' of the tournament finished in first and second place in the final table!

Scotland must have been enormously disappoined to finish in bottom position. They continue to turn out gifted players – many of whom enrich the English League – but never seem to make a real impression at international level. Jock Stein spurned Arsenal's Charlie Nicholas for this series, and indeed still tends to pick mainly players from Scottish clubs. In this championship, only five 'anglos' were used – three of them twice – and although fixture pressure in the English League makes it difficult to select players from English clubs for mid-season internationals, a Scotland team selected from a free choice of players would surely be formidable. As it was, Scotland took the field against England at Hampden Park, and either team could have won the championship by winning this match. England looked menacing for the first quarter of an hour, only to be rocked by a goal from Mark McGhee. Just before half-time Tony Woodcock scored a fine goal from the edge of the area, and that's the way it stayed right throughout a second half which lacked the excitement of the first, but in which Scotland could probably be said to have had the better of the play. The celebrations were taking place off-stage at the Northern Irish Football Association H.Q. in Belfast, where the old British Championship trophy will now find a permanent home – on goal difference!

RESULTS

Belfast, 13 December 1983, 10,000
Northern Ireland (1) 2 *(Whiteside, McIlroy)* **Scotland (0) 0**
Northern Ireland: Jennings; J. Nicholl, Donaghy, McClelland, McElhinney, Ramsey, Cochrane (J. O'Neill), McIlroy, Hamilton, Whiteside, Stewart.
Scotland: Leighton; Gough, Roughvie, Souness, McLeish, Aitken, Strachan, McStay, McGarry (McGhee), Dodds, Weir.

Hampden Park, 28 February 1984, 21,542
Scotland (1) 2 *(Cooper pen. Johnston)* **Wales (0) 1** *(R. James)*
Scotland: Leighton; Gough, Albiston, Souness, McLeish, Miller, Sturrock, McStay (Aitken), McGarry (Johnston), Bett, Cooper.
Wales: Southall; Hopkins, J. Jones, Jackett, Charles, Ratcliffe, R. James, Flynn, Rush (G. Davies), M. Thomas, Curtis (Price).

Wembley, 4 April 1984, 24,000
England (0) 1 *(Woodcock)* **Northern Ireland (0) 0**
England: Shilton; Anderson, Roberts, Butcher, Kennedy, Lee, Wilkins, Robson, Rix, Francis, Woodcock.
Northern Ireland: Platt; J. Nicholl, McClelland, McElhinney, Donaghy, Armstrong, M. O'Neill, Hamilton, Whiteside, McIlroy, Stewart.

Wrexham, 2 May 1984, 15,000
Wales (1) 1 *(Hughes)* **England (0) 0**
Wales: Southall; Phillips, J. Jones, R. James, Hopkins, Ratcliffe, G. Davies, A. Davies, Rush, M. Thomas, Hughes.
England: Shilton; Duxbury, Kennedy, Lee, Martin (Fenwick), Wright, Wilkins, Gregory, Walsh, Woodcock, Armstrong (Blissett).

Swansea, 22 May 1984, 7,845
Wales (0) 1 *(Hughes)* **Northern Ireland (0) 1** *(Armstrong)*
Wales: Southall; Phillips, J. Jones, A. Davies, Hopkins, Ratcliffe, R. James, G. Davies (Vaughan), Rush, Jackett, Hughes.
Northern Ireland: Jennings (Platt); Donaghy, Worthington, McClelland, McElhinney, M. O'Neill, McIlroy, Armstrong, Whiteside, Hamilton, Stewart.

Hampden Park, 26 May 1984 73,064
Scotland (1) 1 *(McGhee)* **England (1) 1** *(Woodcock)*
Scotland: Leighton; Gough, Albiston, Wark, McLeish, Miller, Strachan (McStay), Archibald, McGhee (Johnston), Bett, Cooper.
England: Shilton; Duxbury, Sansom, Wilkins, Roberts, Fenwick, Chamberlain (Hunt), Robson, Woodcock (Lineker), Blissett, Barnes.

FINAL TABLE	*P*	*W*	*D*	*L*	*F*	*A*	*Pts*	*Diff*
Northern Ireland	3	1	1	1	3	2	3	+1
Wales	3	1	1	1	3	3	3	0
England	3	1	1	1	2	2	3	0
Scotland	3	1	1	1	3	4	3	−1

OTHER INTERNATIONAL MATCHES 1983-84

Glasgow, 21 September 1983, 20,545
Scotland (1) 2 *(Robertson (pen), Dodds*
Uruguay (0) 0
Scotland: Leighton; Gough, Albiston, Souness, McLeish, Miller, Dalglish, McStay (Dodds), McGarvey, Wark, Robertson.
Uruguay: Rodriguez; Gutierrez, Acivedo, Diogo, Agresta, Gonzalez, Ramos (Aguilera), Barrios, Santelli (Montelongo), Saralegui, Acosta (De Los Santos).

Wrexham, 12 October 1983, 4,161
Wales (3) 5 *(Rush 2, Thomas, R. James, Curtis)*
Rumania (0) 0
Wales: Southall (Felgate); J. Jones, Hopkins, Ratcliffe, Price, Flynn, R. James (Curtis), Vaughan, Rush (G. Davies), Thomas, Jackett.
Rumania: Lung (Moraru): Rednic, Iorgulescu (Andone), Stefanescu, Ungureanu, Ticleanu (Augustin), Boloni, Klein (Irimescu), Coras, Gabor, Camataru.

Paris, 29 February 1984, 45,000
France (0) 0 *(Platini 2)*
England (0) 0
France: Bats, Battiston (Tusseau), Amoros, Le Roux, Bossis, Tigana, Fernandez, Giresse, Stopyra, Platini, Bellone (Rocheteau).
England: Shilton; Duxbury, Sansom, Lee (Barnes), Roberts, Butcher, Robson, Stein (Woodcock), Walsh, Hoddle, Williams.

Marseilles, 1 June 1984, 45,000
France (2) 2 *(Giresse, Lacombe)*
Scotland (0) 0
France: Bats, Battiston, Amoros, Le Roux, Bossis, Fernandez (Genghini), Tigana, Giresse, Lacombe (Bravo), Platini, Belloni (Six).
Scotland: Leighton; Gough (Nicholas), Stewart, Miller, McLeish, Malpas, Strachan (Simpson), Wark, Archibald, Bett, Johnston.

Wembley, 2 June 1984, 38,125
England (0) 0
USSR (0) 2 *(Gotsanov, Protasov)*
England: Shilton; Duxbury, Roberts, Fenwick, Sansom, Wilkins, Robson, Chamberlain, Francis (Hateley), Blissett, Barnes (Hunt).
USSR: Dasayev; Chivadze, Baltacha, Demyanenko, Sulakvelidze, Aleinikov (Pozdnyakov), Litovchenko, Oganesyan, Zygmantovich (Gotsanov), Rodionov (Protasov), Blokhin.

Trondheim, 6 June 1984, 13,654
Norway (0) 1 *(Oekland)*
Wales (0) 0
Norway: Thorstvet; Fjallberg (Sundby), Kojedal, Hareide, Grondalen, Herlovsen, Ahlsen, Giske (Davidsen), Brandhaug, Okland, Thorsesen (Dokken).
Wales: Southall; Phillips (Slatter), J. Jones, Ratcliffe, Hopkins, Flynn, R. James, Nicholas, Pascoe (Rees), Vaughan (Hodges), Jackett.

Rio de Janeiro, 10 June 1984, 56,126
Brazil (0) 0
England (1) 2 *(Barnes, Hateley)*
Brazil: Roberto Costa; Leandro, Mozer, Ricardo, Junior, Pires, Renato, Zenon, Roberto, Assis, Tato.
England: Shilton; Duxbury, Sansom, Wilkins, Watson, Fenwick, Chamberlain, Robson, Hateley, Woodcock (Allen), Barnes.

Tel Aviv, 10 June 1984, 3,000
Israel (0) 0
Wales (0) 0
Israel: Ginsburg; Lazry (Shlomo), Azulay, Ekhois (Malmillian), A. Cohen (Eli), Barda, Sinai, Turk, Lundau, M. Cohen, Ohana (Armeli).
Wales: Southall; Slatter, J. Jones, Ratcliffe, Hopkins, Flynn, R. James, Nicholas, Pascoe (Holden), Vaughan, Jackett (Hodges).

Montevideo, 13 June 1984, 32,800
Uruguay (1) 2 *(Acosta (pen), Cabrera)*
England (0) 0
Uruguay: Rodriguez; Gutierrez, Acivedo, Montelongo, Bossio, Martinez, Aguilera, Perdomo, Cabrera, Carrasco, Acosta (Sosa).
England: Shilton; Duxbury, Sansom, Wilkins, Watson, Fenwick, Robson, Chamberlain, Hateley, Allen (Woodcock), Barnes.

Santiago, 17 June 1984, 9,876
Chile (0) 0
England (0) 0
Chile: Rojas; Tabilo, Gomez, Hormazabal, Araya, Hisis, Toro (Copri), Soto (Luis Rodrigues), Venegas, Aravena, Covarrubias (Puebla).
England: Shilton; Duxbury, Sansom, Wilkins, Watson, Fenwick, Robson, Chamberlain (Lee), Hateley, Allen, Barnes.

BRITISH INTERNATIONAL GOALSCORERS SINCE 1946

ENGLAND

A'Court, A. 1
Allen, R. 2
Astall, G. 1
Atyeo, P.J.W. 5

Baily, E.F. 5
Baker, J.H. 4
Ball, A.J. 8
Barnes, J. 1
Barnes, P.S. 4
Beattie, T.K. 1
Bell, C. 9
Bentley, R.T.F. 9
Blissett, L. 3
Bowles, S. 1
Bradford, G.R.W. 1
Bradley, W. 2
Bridges, B.J. 1
Broadbent, P.F. 2
Broadis, I.A. 8
Brooking, T.D. 5
Brooks, J. 2
Butcher, T. 2
Byrne, J.J. 8

Carter, H.S. 7
(inc. 2 scored pre-war)
Chamberlain, M. 1
Channon, M.R. 21
Charlton, J. 6
Charlton, R. 49
Chivers, M. 13
Clarke, A.J. 10
Connelly, J.M. 7
Coppell, S.J. 7
Cowans, G. 1
Crawford, R. 1
Currie, A.W. 3

Douglas, B. 11

Eastham, G. 2
Edwards, D. 5
Elliot, W.H. 3

Finney, T. 30
Flowers, R. 10
Francis, G.C.J. 3
Francis, T. 12
Froggatt, J. 2
Froggatt, R. 2

Goddard, P. 1
Grainger, C. 3
Greaves, J. 44

Haines, J.T.W. 2
Hancocks, J. 2
Hassall, H.W. 4
Hateley, M. 1
Haynes, J.N. 17
Hinton, A.T. 1
Hitchens, G.A. 5
Hoddle, G. 6
Hughes, E.W. 1
Hunt, R. 18
Hunter, N. 2
Hurst, G.C. 24

Johnson, D.E. 5

Kay, A.H. 1
Keegan, J.K. 21
Kennedy, R. 3
Kevan, D.T. 8
Kidd, B. 1

Langton, R. 1
Latchford, R.D. 5
Lawler, C. 1
Lawton, T. 22
(inc. 6 scored pre-war)
Lee, F. 10
Lee, J. 1
Lee, S. 2
Lofthouse, N. 30

Macdonald, M. 6
Mannion, W.J. 11
Mariner, P. 14
Marsh, R.W. 1
Matthews, S. 11
(inc. 8 scored pre-war)
McDermott, T. 3
Medley, L.D. 1
Melia, J. 1
Milburn, J.E.T. 9
Moore, R.F. 2
Morris, J. 3
Mortensen, S.H. 24
Mullen, J. 6
Mullery, A.P. 1

Neal, P.G. 5
Nicholls, J. 1
Nicholson, W.E. 1

O'Grady, M. 3

Own goals 12

Paine, T.L. 7
Parry, R.A. 1
Peacock, A. 3
Pearson, J.S. 5
Pearson, S.C. 5
Perry, W. 2
Peters, M. 20
Pickering, F. 5
Pointer, R. 2

Ramsey, A.E. 3
Revie, D.G. 4
Robson, B. 12
Robson, R. 4
Rowley, J.F. 6
Royle, J. 2

Sewell, J. 3
Shackleton, L.F. 1
Smith, R. 13
Stiles, N.P. 1
Summerbee, M.G. 1

Tambling, R.V. 1
Taylor, P.J. 2
Taylor, T. 16
Thompson, P.B. 1
Tueart, D. 2

Viollet, D.S. 1

Walsh, P. 1
Watson, D.V. 4
Weller, K. 1
Wignall, F. 2
Wilkins, R.G. 3
Wilshaw, D.J. 10
Withe, P. 1

Woodcock, T. 13
Worthington, F.S. 2
Wright, W.A. 3

SCOTLAND

Archibald, S. 4
Baird, S. 2
Bannon, E. 1
Bauld, W. 2
Baxter, J.C. 3
Bone, J. 1
Brand, R. 8
Brazil, A. 1
Bremner, W.J. 3
Brown, A.D. 6
Buckley, P. 1
Burns, K. 1

Caldow, E. 4
Campbell, R. 1
Chalmers, S. 3
Collins, R.Y. 10
Combe, J.R. 1
Conn, A. 1
Cooper, D. 1
Craig, J. 1
Curran, H.P. 1

Dalglish, K. avidson,
J.A. 1
Docherty, T.H. 1
Dodds, D. 1
Duncan, D.M. 1

Fernie, W. 1
Flavell, R. 2
Fleming, C. 2

Gemmell, T. *(St Mirren)* 1
Gemmell, T. *(Celtic)* ...1
Gemmill, A. 8
Gibson, D.W. 3
Gilzean, A.J. 10
Gough, C.R. 1
Graham, A. 2
Graham, G. 3
Gray, A. 7
Gray, E. 3
Gray, F. 1
Greig, J. 5

Hamilton, G. 4
Harper, J.M. 2
Hartford, R.A. 4
Henderson, J.G. 1
Henderson, W. 5
Herd, D.G. 4
Hewie, J.D. 2
Holton, J.A. 2
Houliston, W. 2
Howie, H. 1
Hughes, J. 1
Hunter, W. 1
Hutchison, T. 1

Jackson, C. 1
Jardine, A. 1
Johnston, L.H. 1
Johnston, M. 1
Johnstone, D. 2
Johnstone, J. 4
Johnstone, R. 9
Jordan, J. 11

Law, D. 30
Leggat, G. 8
Lennox, R. 3
Liddell, W. 6
Linwood, A.B. 1
Lorimer, P 4

Macari, L. 5
MacDougall, E.J. 3
MacKay, D.C. 4
MacKenzie, J.A. 1
Mason, J. 4
Masson, D.S. 5
McCalliog, J. 1
McGhee, M. 2
McKinnon, R. 1
McLaren, A. 4
McLean, T. 1
McLintock, F. 1
McMillan, I.L. 2
McNeill, W. 3
McPhail, J. 3
McQueen, G 5
Miller, W. 1
Mitchell, R.C. 1
Morgan, W. 1
Morris, H. 3
Mudie, J.K. 9
Mulhall, G. 1
Murdoch, R. 5
Murray, J. 1

Narey, D. 1
Nicholas, C. 3

O'Hare, J. 5
Ormond, W.E. 1
Orr, T. 1
Own goals 7

Parlane, D. 1
Pettigrew, W. 2
Provan, D. 1

Quinn, P. 1

Reilly, L. 22
Ring, T. 2
Rioch, B.D. 6
Robertson, A. 2
Robertson, J. 8

Scott, A.S. 5
Smith, G. 4
Souness, G.J. 2
St John, I. 9
Steel, W. 12
Stein, C. 10
Stewart, R. 1
Strachan, G. 2
Sturrock, P. 2

Thornton, W. 1

Waddell, W. 6
Wallace, I.A. 1
Wark, J. 7
Weir, A 1
White, J.A. 3
Wilson, D. 9

Young, A. 5

WALES

Allchurch, I.J. 23

Barnes, W. 1
Bowen, D.L. 1
Boyle, T. 1
Burgess, W.A.R. 1

Charles, J. 1
Charles, M. 6
Charles, W.J. 15
Clarke, R.J. 5
Curtis, A. 6

Davies, G. 1
Davies, R.T. 7
Davies, R.W. 8
Deacy, N. 4

Durban, A. 2
Dwyer, P. 2

Edwards, G 2
Edwards, R.I. 4
England, H.M. 3
Evans, I. 1

Flynn, B. 7
Ford, T. 23
Foulkes, W.I. 1

Giles, D. 2
Godfrey, B.C. 2
Griffiths, A.T. 6
Griffiths, M.W. 2

Harris, C.S. 1
Hewitt, R. 1
Hockey, T. 1
Hughes, M. 2

James, L. 10
James, R. 7
Jones, B.S. 2
Jones, Cliff 15
Jones, D.E. 1
Jones, J.P. 1

Krzywicki, R.L. 1

Leek, K. 5
Lowrie, G. 2

Mahoney, J.F. 1
Medwin, T.C. 6
Moore, G. 1

Nicholas, P. 2

O'Sullivan, P.A. 1

Own goals 3

Palmer, D 1
Paul R. 1
Powell, A. 1
Powell, D. 1
Price, P. 1

Reece, G.I 2
Rees, R.R. 3
Roberts, P.S. 1
Rush, I. 7

Smallman, D.P. 1

Tapscott, D.R. 4
Thomas, M. 3
Toshack, J.B. 13

Vernon, T.R. 8

Walsh, I. 7
Williams, G.E. 2
Woosnam, A.P. 4

Yorath, T.C. 2

NORTHERN IRELAND

Anderson, T 4
Armstrong, G. 11

Barr, H.H. 1
Best, G. 9
Bingham, W.L. 10
Blanchflower, D. 2
Blanchflower, J. 1
Brennan, R.A. 1
Brotherston, N. 3

Campbell, W.G. 1
Casey, T. 2
Caskey, W. 1
Cassidy, T. 1
Clements, D. 2
Cochrane, T. 1
Crossan, E. 1
Crossan, J.A. 10
Cush, W.W. 5

D'Arcy, S.D. 1
Doherty, P.D. 3
(inc. 1 scored pre-war)
Dougan, A.D. 8

Elder, A.R. 1

Ferguson, W. 1
Ferris, R.O. 1
Finney, T. 2

Hamilton, B. 4
Hamilton, W. 5
Harkin, J.T. 2
Harvey, M. 3
Humphries, W. 1
Hunter, A. 1

Irvine, W.J. 8

Johnston, W.C. 1
Jones, J. 1

Lockhart, N. 3

McAdams, W.J. 7
McClelland, J. 1
McCrory, S. 1
McCurdy, C. 1
McGarry, J.K. 1
McGrath, R.C. 4
McIlroy, J. 10
McIlroy, S.B. 5
McLaughlin, J.C. 6
McMordie, A.S. 3
McMorran, E.J. 4
McParland, P.J. 10
Moreland, V. 1
Morgan, S. 3

Neill, W.J.T. 2
Nelson, S. 1
Nicholl, C.J. 3
Nicholl, J.M. 1
Nicholson, J.J. 6

O'Kane, W.J. 1
O'Neill, M.H. 8

Own goals 3

Peacock, R. 2

Simpson, W.J. 5
Smyth, S. 5
Spence, D.W. 3
Stewart, I. 2

Tully, C.P. 3

Walker, J. 1
Walsh, D.J. 5
Welsh, E. 1
Whiteside, N. 3
Wilson, S.J. 7

POST-WAR INTERNATIONAL APPEARANCES

As at 30 June, 1984

Abbreviations *A*—Albania; *Arg*—Argentina; *Aust*—Austria; *Au*—Australia; *Bel*—Belgium; *Braz*—Brazil; *Bulg*—Bulgaria; *Can*—Canada *Ch*—Chile; *Czecho*—Czechoslovakia; *Co*—Colombia; *C*—Cyprus; *D*—Denmark; *Ec*—Ecuador; *E*-England; *E/Germ*—East Germany; *F*—France; *FIFA*—Federation of International Associations; *Fin*—Finland; *G*—West Germany; *Gr*—Greece; *H*—Hungary; *Holl*—Holland; *Hon*—Honduras; *I*—N Ireland; *Ic*—Iceland; *Ir*—Iran; *Isr*—Israel; *It*—Italy; *K*—Kuwait; *Lux*—Luxembourg; *M*—Malta; *Mex*—Mexico; *N*—Norway; *NZ*—New Zealand; *P*—Paraguay; *Per*—Peru; *Pol*—Poland; *Port*—Portugal; *Ru*—Rumania; *Rus*—Russia; *S*—Scotland; *Sp*—Spain; *Swdn*—Sweden; *Switz*—Switzerland; *T*—Turkey; *U*—Uruguay; *UK*—Rest of United Kingdom; *US*—United States of America; *W*—Wales; *Y*—Yugoslavia; *Z*—Zaire.

ENGLAND

A'court, A. (5) (Liverpool) 1957/8 *I, Braz, Aust, Rus;* 1958/9 *W.*
Allen, C. (3) (Q.P.R.) 1983/4 *Braz, U, Ch.*
Allen, R. (5) (West Bromwich Albion) 1951/2 *Switz*; 1953/4 *US, Y*; 1954/5 *W, G.*
Allen, T. (3) (Stoke City) 1959/60 *W, Swdn, I.*
Anderson, S. (2) (Sunderland) 1961/2 *Aust, S.*
Anderson, V. (10) (Nottingham Forest) 1978/9 *Czecho, Swdn;* 1979/80 *Bulg, Sp;* 1980/81 *N, Ru, W, S;* 1981/82 *I, Ic;* 1983/4 *I.*
Angus, J. (1) (Burnley) 1960/1 *Aust.*
Armfield, J. (43) (Blackpool) 1958/9 *Braz, Per, Mex, US*; 1959/60 *S, Y, Sp, H*; 1960/1 *Lux, Sp, W, S, Mex, Port, It, Aust*; 1961/2 *Lux, W, Port, I, Aust, S, Switz, Per, H, Arg, Bulg, Braz*; 1962/3 *F, I, W, F, S, Braz, E/Germ, Switz*; 1963/4 *W, FIFA, I, S*; 1965/6 *Y, Fin.*
Armstrong, D. (3) (Middlesbrough) 1979/80 *Au;* (Southampton) 1982/3 *G;* 1983/4 *W.*
Armstrong, K. (1) (Chelsea) 1954/5 *S.*
Astall, G. (2) (Birmingham) 1955/6 *Fin, G.*
Astle, J. (5) (West Bromwich Albion) 1968/9 *W;* 1969/70 *Port, S, Braz, Czecho.*
Aston, J. (17) (Manchester United) 1948/9 *W, S, D, Switz, Swdn, N, F;* 1949/50 *W, I, S, Eire, It, Port, Bel, Ch, US;* 1950/1 *I.*
Atyeo, J. (6) (Bristol City) 1955/6 *Sp, Braz, Swdn;* 1956/7 *Eire, D, Eire.*

Bailey, M. (2) (Charlton) 1963/4 *US*; 1964/5 *W.*
Baily, E. (9) (Tottenham Hotspur) 1949/50 *Sp*; 1950/1 *I, W, Y*; 1951/2 *W, Aust* (2), *Switz*; 1952/3 *I.*
Baker, J. (8) (Hibernian) 1959/60 *I, S, Y, Sp, H;* 1965/6 (Arsenal) *I, Sp, Pol.*
Ball, A. (72) (Blackpool) 1964/5 *Y, G, Swdn*; 1965/6 *Sp, Pol, G, S, Fin, D, Pol, U, Arg, Port, G*; 1966/7 (Everton) *I, Czecho, W, S, Sp, Aust*; 1967/8 *W, Rus, S, Sp* (2), *G, Y*; 1968/9 *Ru* (2), *I, W, S, Mex, U, Braz*; 1969/70 *Port, Bel, W, S, Co, Ec, Ru, Braz, Czecho, G*; 1970/1 *E/Germ, M, Gr, M, I, S*; 1971/2 *Switz, Gr* (Arsenal), *G*(2), *S*; 1972/3 *Y, W* (2), *S, I, W, S, Czecho, Pol*; 1973/4 *Port*; 1974/5 *G, C* (2), *I, W, S.*
Banks, G. (73) (Leicester) 1962/3 *S, Braz, Czecho, E/Germ*; 1963/4 *W, FIFA, I, S,*

U, Port, US, Port, Arg; 1964/5 *I, S, H, Y, G, Swdn*: 1965/6 *I, Sp, Pol, G, S, Y, Fin, Pol, Y, Mex, F, Arg, Port, G;* 1966/7 *I, Czecho, W, S;* 1967/8 (Stoke) *W, I, Rus, S, Sp, G, Y, Rus*; 1968/9 *Ru* (2), *F, I, S, U, Braz*; 1969/70 *Holl, Bel, W, I, S, Co, Ec, Ru, Braz, Czecho*; 1970/1 *M, Gr, M, I, S*; 1971/2 *Switz, Gr, G* (2), *W, S.*

Banks, T. (6) (Bolton Wanderers) 1957/8 *Rus* (2), *Braz, Aust, Rus*; 1958/9 *I.*

Barham, M. (2) (Norwich C.) 1982/83 *Au* (2).

Barlow, R. (1) (West Bromwich Albion) 1954/5 *I.*

Barnes, J. (12) (Watford) 1982/3 *I, Au* (3); 1983/4 *D, Lux, F, S, Rus, Braz, U, Ch.*

Barnes, P. (22) (Manchester City) 1977/8 *It, G, Braz, W, S, H*; 1978/9 *D, Eire, Czecho, I, I, S, Bulg, Aust*; 1979/80 (West Bromwich Albion) *D, W;* 1980/81 *Sp, Braz, W, Switz;* 1981/2 (Leeds U.) *N, Holl.*

Barrass, M. (3) (Bolton Wanderers) 1951/2 *W, I*; 1952/3 *S.*

Baynham, R. (3) (Luton Town) 1955/6 *D, I, Sp.*

Beattie, T. K. (9) (Ipswich Town) 1974/5 *C* (2), *S*; 1975/6 *Switz, Port*; 1976/7 *Fin, It, Holl*; 1977/8 *Lux.*

Bell, C. (48) (Manchester City) 1967/8 *Swdn, G*; 1968/9 *Bulg, F, W, U, Braz*; 1969/70 *Holl, Port, Holl, I, Braz, Czecho, G*; 1971/2 *Gr, G* (2), *W, I, S*; 1972/3 *Y, W* (2), *S, I, W, S, Czecho, Pol*; 1973/4 *Pol, It, W, I, S, Arg, Aust, E/Germ, Bulg, Y*; 1974/5 *Czecho, Port, G, C* (2), *I, S*; 1975/6 *Switz, Czecho.*

Bentley, R. (12) (Chelsea) 1948/9 *Swdn*; 1949/50 *S, Port, Bel, Ch, US*; 1952/3 *W, Bel*; 1954/5 *W, G, Sp, Port.*

Berry, J. (4) (Manchester United) 1952/3 *Arg, Ch, U*; 1955/6 *Swdn.*

Birtles, G. (3) (Nottingham Forest) 1979/80 *Arg, It;* 1980/81 (Manchester U.) *Ru.*

Blisset, L. (14) (Watford) 1982/3 *G, Lux, W, Gr, H, I, S Au* (2); 1983/4 (AC Milan) D, *H, W, S, Rus.*

Blockley, J. (1) (Arsenal) 1972/3 *Y.*

Blunstone, F. (5) (Chelsea) 1954/5 *W, S, F, Port*; 1956/7 *Y.*

Bonetti, P. (7) (Chelsea) 1965/6 *D*; 1966/7 *Sp, Aust*; 1967/8 *Sp*; 1969/70 *Holl, Port, G.*

Bowles, S. (5) (Q.P.R.) 1973/4 *Port, W, I*; 1976/7 *It, Holl.*

Boyer, P. (1) (Norwich City) 1975/6 *W.*

Brabrook, P. (3) (Chelsea) 1957/8 *Rus*; 1959/60 *I, Sp.*

Bradford, G (1) (Bristol Rovers) 1955/6 *D.*

Bradley, W. (3) (Manchester United) 1958/9 *It, Mex, US.*

Bridges, B. (4) (Chelsea) 1964/5 *S, H, Y*; 1965/6 *Aust.*

Broadbent, P. (7) (Wolverhampton Wanderers) 1957/8 *Rus*; 1958/9 *I, W, S, It, Braz*; 1959/60 *S.*

Broadis, I. (14) (Manchester City) 1951/2 *Aust, S, It*; 1952/3 *S, Arg, Ch, U, US* (Newcastle United); 1953/4 *S, Y, H, Bel, Switz, U.*

Brooking, T. (46) (West Ham United) 1973/4 *Port, Arg, E/Germ, Bulg, Y*; 1974/5 *Czecho, Port*; 1975/6 *W, Port, Braz, It, Fin*; 1976/7 *Eire, Fin, It, Hol, I, W*; 1977/8 *It, G, W, S, H*; 1978/9 *D, Eire, I, S, Bulg, Swdn, Aust*; 1979/80 *D, I, Arg, W, I, S, Bel, Sp;* 1980/81 *Switz, Sp, Ru, H;* 1981/2 *H, S, Fin, Sp.*

Brooks, J. (3) (Tottenham Hotspur) 1956/7 *W, Y, D.*

Brown, Tony (1) (West Bromwich Albion) 1970/1 *W.*

Brown, K. (1) (West Ham United) 1959/60 *I.*

Butcher, T. (24) (Ipswich T.) 1979/80 *Au;* 1980/81 *Sp;* 1981/2 *W, S, F, Czecho, G,*

Sp; 1982/3 *D, G, Lux, W, Gr, H, I, S, Au* (3); 1983/4 *D, H, Lux, F, I.*
Byrne, G. (2) (Liverpool) 1962/3 *S*; 1965/6 *N.*
Byrne, J. (11) (Crystal Palace) 1961/2 *I*; 1962/3 (West Ham United) *Switz*; 1963/4 *S, U, Port, Eire, Braz, Arg*; 1964/5 *W, S.*
Byrne, R. (33) (Manchester United) 1953/4 *S, Y, H, Bel, Switz, U*; 1954/5 *I, W, G, S, F, Sp, Port*; 1955/6 *D, W, I, Sp, Braz, Swdn, Fin, G*; 1956/7 *I, W, Y, D, S, Eire*; 1957/8 *W, I, F.*

Callaghan, I. (4) (Liverpool) 1965/6 *Fin, F*; 1977/8 *Switz, Lux.*
Carter, H. (7) (Derby County) 1946/7 *I, W, S, Eire, Holl, F, Switz.*
Chamberlain, M. (7) (Stoke City) 1982/3 *Lux*; 1983/4 *D, S, Rus, Braz, U. Ch.*
Channon, M. (46) (Southampton) 1972/3 *Y, S, I, W, S, Czecho, Rus, It*; 1973/4 *Pol, It, Port, W, I, S, Arg, Aust, E/Germ, Bulg, Y*; 1974/5 *Czecho, Port, G, C* (2), *I, W, S*; 1975/6 *Switz, Czecho, Port, W, I, S, Braz, It, Fin*; 1976/7 *Fin, It, Lux, I, W, S, Braz, Arg, U*; 1977/8 *Switz.*
Charlton, J. (35) (Leeds United) 1964/5 *S, H, Y, G, Swdn*; 1965/6 *W, Aust, I, Sp, Pol, G, S, Y, Fin, D, Pol, U, Mex, F, Arg, Port, G*; 1966/7 *I, Czecho, W, S*; 1967/8 *W, Sp*; 1968/9 *Ru, F, W*; 1969/70 *Holl, Port, Holl, Czecho.*
Charlton, R. (106) (Manchester United) 1957/8 *S, Port, Y*; 1958/9 *I, Rus, W, S, It, Braz, Per, Mex, US*; 1959/60 *W, Swdn, S, Y, Sp, H*; 1960/1 *I, Lux, Sp, W, S, Mex, Port, It, Aust*; 1961/2 *Lux, W, Port, I, Aust, S, Switz, Per, H, Arg, Bulg, Braz*; 1962/3 *F, S, Braz, Czecho, E/Germ, Switz*; 1963/4 *W, FIFA, I, S, U, Port, Eire, US, Braz, Arg*; 1964/5 *I, Holl, S*; 1965/6 *W, Aust, I, G, S, Sp, Y, Fin, N, Pol, U, Mex, F, Arg, Port, G*; 1966/7 *I, Czecho, W, S*; 1967/8 *W, I, Rus, S, Sp* (2), *Swdn, Y, Rus*; 1968/9 *Ru, Bulg, Ru, I, W, S, Mex, Braz*; 1969/70 *Holl, Port, Holl, W, I, Co, Ec, Ru, Braz, Czecho, G.*
Charnley, R. (1) (Blackpool) 1961/2 *F.*
Cherry, T. (27) (Leeds United) 1975/6 *W, S, Braz, Fin*; 1976/7 *Eire, It, Lux, I, S, Braz, Arg, U*; 1977/8 *Switz, Lux, It, Braz, W*; 1978/9 *Czecho, W, Swdn*; 1979/80 *Eire, Arg, W, I, S, Au, Sp.*
Chilton, A. (2) (Manchester United) 1950/1 *I*; 1951/2 *F.*
Chivers, M. (24) (Tottenham Hotspur) 1970/1 *M, Gr, M, I, S*; 1971/2 *Switz* (2), *Gr, G* (2), *S*; 1972/3 *W* (2), *S, I, W, S, Czecho, Pol, Rus, It*; 1973/4 *Pol, Aust.*
Clamp, E. (4) (Wolverhampton Wanderers) 1957/8 *Rus* (2), *Braz, Aust.*
Clapton, D. (1) (Arsenal) 1958/9 *W.*
Clarke, A. (19) (Leeds United) 1969/70 *Czecho*; 1970/1 *E/Germ, M, I, W, S*; 1972/3 *S, W, S, Czecho, Pol, Rus, It*; 1973/4 *Pol, It, Aust*; 1974/5 *Port*; 1975/6 *Czecho, Port.*
Clarke, H. (1) (Tottenham Hotspur) 1953/4 *S.*
Clayton, R. (35) (Blackburn Rovers) 1955/6 *I, Sp, Braz, Swdn, Fin, G*; 1956/7 *I, W, Y, D, S, Eire*; 1957/8 *W, I, F, S, Port, Y, Rus*; 1958/9 *I, Rus, W, S, It, Braz, Per, Mex, US*; 1959/60 *W, Swdn, I, S, Y.*
Clemence, R. (61) (Liverpool) 1972/3 *W* (2); 1973/4 *E/Germ, Bulg, Y*; 1974/5 *Czecho, Port, G, C, I, W, S*; 1975/6 *Switz, Czecho, Port, U* (2), *I, S, Braz, Fin*; 1976/7 *Eire, Fin, It, Holl, Lux, S, Braz, Arg, U*; 1977/8 *Switz, Lux, It, G, I, S*; 1978/9 *D, Eire, I, I, S, Bulg, Aust*; 1979/80 *D, Bulg, Eire, Arg, W, S, Bel, Sp*; 1980/81 *Ru, Sp, Braz, Switz, H*; 1981/2 (Tottenham H.) *N, I, Fin*; 1982/3 *Lux*; 1983/4 *Lux.*
Clement, D. (5) (Queens Park Rangers) 1975/6 *W* (2), *It*; 1976/7 *It, Holl.*
Clough, B. (2) (Middlesbrough) 1959/60 *W, Swdn.*
Coates, R. (4) (Burnley) 1969/70 *I*; 1970/1 *Gr*, (Tottenham Hotspur) *M, W.*

Cockburn, H. (13) (Manchester United) 1946/7 *I, W, Eire*; 1947/8 *S, It*; 1948/9 *I, S, D, Switz*; 1950/1 *Arg, Port*; 1951/2 *F*.
Cohen, G. (37) (Fulham) 1963/4 *U, Port, Eire, US, Braz*; 1964/5 *I, Bel, W, Holl, S, H, Y, G, Swdn*; 1965/6 *W, Aust, I, Sp, Pol, G, S, N, D, Pol, U, Mex, F, Arg, Port, G*; 1966/7 *I, Czecho, W, S, Sp*; 1967/8 *W, I*.
Compton, L. (2) (Arsenal) 1950/1 *W, Y*.
Connelly J. (20) (Burnley) 1959/60 *W, Swdn, I, S*; 1961/2 *W, Port, Aust, Switz*; 1962/3 *W, F*; 1964/5 (Manchester United) *H, Y, Swdn*; 1965/6 *W, Aust, I, S, N, D, U*.
Cooper, T. (20) (Leeds United) 1968/9 *F, W, S, Mex*; 1969/70 *Holl, Bel, Co, Ec, Ru, Braz, Czecho, G*; 1970/1 *E/Germ, M, I, W, S*; 1971/2 *Switz* (2); 1974/5 *Port*.
Coppell, S. (41) (Manchester United) 1977/8 *It, G, Braz, W, I, S, H*; 1978/9 *D, Eire, Czecho, I, I, S, Bulg, Aust*; 1979/80 *D, I, Eire, Sp, Arg, W, S, Bel, It;* 1980/81 *Ru, Switz, Ru, Braz, W, S, Switz, H;* 1981/2 *H, S, Fin, F, Czecho, K, G*; 1982/3 *Lux, Gr*.
Corrigan J. (9) (Manchester City) 1975/6 *It;* 1977/8 *Braz;* 1978/9 *W*; 1979/80 *I, Au;* 1980/81 *W, S;* 1981/2 *W, Ic*.
Cowans, G. (7) (Aston Villa) 1982/3 *W, H, I, S, Au* (3).
Crawford, R. (2) (Ipswich Town) 1961/2 *I, Aust*.
Crowe, C. (1) (Wolverhampton Wanderers) 1962/3 *F*.
Cunningham, L. (6) (West Bromwich Albion) 1978/9 *W, Swdn, Aust*; (Real Madrid) 1979/80 *Eire, Sp;* 1980/81 *Ru*.
Currie, A. (17) (Sheffield United) 1971/2 *I*; 1972/3 *Rus, It*; 1973/4 *Pol, It, Aust*; 1975/6 *Switz*; (Leeds United) 1977/8 *Braz, W, I, S, H*; 1978/9 *Czecho, I, I, W, Swdn*.

Deeley, N. (2) (Wolverhampton Wanderers) 1958/9 *Braz, Per*.
Devonshire, A. (8) (West Ham United) 1979/80 *I, Au;* 1981/2 *Holl, Ic;* 1982/3 *G, W, Gr;* 1983/ *Lux*.
Dickinson, J. (48) (Portsmouth) 1948/9 *N, F*; 1949/50 *W, S, Eire, Port, Bel, Ch, US, Sp*; 1950/1 *I, W, Y*; 1951/2 *W, I, Aust* (2), *S, It, Switz*; 1952/3 *I, W, Bel, S, Arg, Ch, U, US*; 1953/4 *W, FIFA, I, H* (2), *S, Y, Bel, Switz, U*; 1954/5 *Sp, Port*; 1955/6 *D, W, I, Sp, S*; 1956/7 *W, Y, D*.
Ditchburn, E. (6) (Tottenham Hotspur) 1948/9 *Switz, Swdn*; 1952/3 *US*; 1956/7 *W, Y, D*.
Dobson, M. (5) (Burnley) 1973/4 *Port, E/Germ, Bulg, Y*; 1974/5 (Everton) *Czecho*.
Douglas, B. (36) (Blackburn Rovers) 1957/8 *W, I, F, S, Port, Y, Rus* (2), *Braz, Aust*; 1958/9 *Rus, S*; 1958/9 *Rus, S*; 1959/60 *Y, H*; 1960/1 *I, Lux, Sp, W, S, Mex, Port, It, Aust*; 1961/2 *Lux, W, Port, I, S, Per, H, Arg, Bulg, Braz*; 1962/3 *S, Braz, Switz*.
Doyle, M. (5) (Manchester City) 1975/6 *W, S, Braz, It*; 1976/7 *Holl*.
Duxbury, M. (8) (Manchester U.) 1983/4 *Lux, F, W, S, Rus, Braz, U. Ch*.

Eastham, G. (19) (Arsenal) 1962/3 *Braz, Czecho, E/Germ*; 1963/4 *W, FIFA, I, S, U, Port, Eire, US, Braz, Arg*; 1964/5 *H, G, Swdn*; 1965/6 *Sp, Pol, D*.
Eckersley, W. (17) (Blackburn Rovers) 1949/50 *Sp*; 1950/1 *Y, S, Arg, Port*; 1951/2 *Aust* (2), *Switz*; 1952/3 *I, Arg, Ch, U, US*; 1953/4 *W, FIFA, I, H*.
Edwards, D. (18) (Manchester United) 1954/5 *S, F, Sp, Port*; 1955/6 *S, Braz, Swdn, Fin, G*; 1956/7 *I, D, S, Eire, D, Eire*; 1957/8 *W, I, F*.
Ellerington, W. (2) (Southampton) 1948/9 *N, F*.
Elliott, W. H. (5) (Burnley) 1951/2 *It, Aust*; 1952/3 *I, W, Bel*.

Fantham, J. (1) (Sheffield Wednesday) 1961/2 *Lux*.
Fenwick, T. (6) (Q.P.R.) 1983/4 *W, S, Rus, Braz, U, Ch*.
Finney, T. (76) (Preston) 1946/7 *I, Eire, Holl, F, Port*; 1947/8 *W, I, S, Bel, Swdn, It*;

1948/9 *I, W, S, Swdn, N, F*; 1949/50 *W, I, S, Eire, It, Port, Bel, Ch, US, Sp*; 1950/1 *W, S, Arg, Port*; 1951/2 *F, W, I, S, It, Aust, Switz*; 1952/3 *I, W, Bel, S, Arg, Ch, U, US*; 1953/4 *D, S, Y, H, Bel, Switz, U*; 1954/5 *G*; 1955/6 *D, W, I, Sp, S*; 1956/7 *W, Y, D, S, Eire, D, Eire*; 1957/8 *W, F, S, Port, Y, Rus* (2); 1958/9 *I, Rus*.

Flowers, R. (49) (Wolverhampton Wanderers) 1954/5 *F*; 1958/9 *W, S, It, Braz, Per, Mex, US*; 1959/60 *W, S, Y, Sp, H, Swdn, I*; 1960/1 *Lux, Sp, W, S, Mex, Port, It, Aust*; 1961/2 *Lux, W, Port, I, Aust, S, Switz, Per, H, Arg, Bulg, Braz*; 1962/3 *F, I, W, F, S, Switz*; 1963/4 *Eire, US, Port*; 1964/5 *W, Holl, G*; 1965/6 *N*.

Foster, S. (3) (Brighton) 1981/2 *I, Holl, K*.

Foulkes, W. (1) (Manchester United) 1954/5 *I*.

Francis, G. (12) (Q.P.R.) 1974/5 *Czecho, Port, W, S*; 1975/6 *Switz, Czecho, Port, W, I, S, Braz, Fin*.

Francis, T. (43) (Birmingham City) 1976/7 *Holl, Lux, S, Braz*; 1977/8 *Switz, Lux, It, G, Braz, W, S, H*; 1978/9 *Bulg, Swdn, Aust*; (Nottingham Forest) 1979/80 *I, Bulg, Sp*; 1980/81 *Sp, Ru, S, Switz*; 1981/2 (Manchester C.) *N, I, W, S, Fin, F, Czecho, K, G, Sp*; 1982/3 (Sampdoria) *D, Gr, H, I, S, Au* (3); 1983/4 *D, I, Rus*.

Franklin, N. (27) (Stoke City) 1946/7 *I, W, S, Eire, Holl, F, Switz, Port*; 1947/8 *W, I, S, Bel, Swdn, It*; 1948/9 *I, W, S, D, Switz, Swdn, N, F*; 1949/50 *W, I, S, Eire, It*.

Froggatt, J. (13) (Portsmouth) 1949/50 *I, It*; 1950/1 *S*; 1951/2 *Aust* (2), *S, It, Switz*; 1952/3 *I, W, Bel, S, US*.

Froggatt, R. (4) (Sheffield Wednesday) 1952/3 *W, Bel, S, US*.

Garrett, T. (3) (Blackpool) 1951/2 *S, It*; 1953/4 *W*.

Gates, E. (2) (Ipswich T.) 1980/81 *N, Ru*.

George, F. C. (1) (Derby County) 1976/7 *Eire*.

Gidman, J. (1) (Aston Villa) 1976/7 *Lux*.

Gillard, I. (3) (Queens Park Rangers) 1974/5 *G, W*; 1975/6 *Czecho*.

Goddard, P. (1) (West Ham U.) 1981/2 *Ic*.

Grainger, C. (7) (Sheffield United) 1955/6 *Braz, Swdn, Fin, G*; 1956/7 *I, W*, (Sunderland) *S*.

Greaves, J. (57) (Chelsea) 1958/9 *Per, Mex, US*; 1959/60 *W, Swdn, Y, Sp*; 1960/1 *I, Lux, Sp, W, S, Port, It, Aust*; 1961/2 (Tottenham Hotspur) *S, Switz, Per, H, Arg, Bulg, Braz*; 1962/3 *F, I, W, F, S, Braz, Czecho, Switz*; 1963/4 *W, FIFA, I, U, Port, Eire, Braz, Port, Arg*; 1964/5 *I, Bel, Holl, S, H, Y*; 1965/6 *W, Aust, Y, N, D, Pol, U, Mex, F*; 1966/7 *S, Sp, Aust*.

Greenhoff, B. (18) (Manchester United) 1975/6 *W, I*; 1976/7 *Eire, Fin, It, Holl, I, W, S, Braz, Arg, U*; 1977/8 *Braz, W, I, S, H*; 1979/80 *Au*.

Gregory, J. (6) (Q.P.R.) 1982/3 *Au* (3); 1983/4 *D, H, W*.

Hagan, J. (1) (Sheffield United) 1948/9 *D*.

Haines, J. (1) (West Bromwich Albion) 1948/9 *Switz*.

Hall, J. (17) (Birmingham City) 1955/6 *D, I, W, Sp, S, Braz, Swdn, Fin, G*; 1956/7 *I, W, Y, D, S, Eire, D, Eire*.

Hancocks, J. (3) (Wolverhampton Wanderers) 1948/9 *Switz*; 1949/50 *W*; 1950/1 *Y*.

Hardwick, G. (13) (Middlesbrough) 1946/7 *I, W, S, Eire, Holl, F, Switz, Port*; 1947/8 *W, I, S, Bel, Swdn*.

Harris, G. (1) (Burnley) 1965/6 *Pol*.

Harris, P. (2) (Portsmouth) 1949/50 *Eire*; 1953/4 *H*.

Harvey, C. (1) (Everton) 1970/1 *M*.

Hassall, H. (5) (Huddersfield Town) 1950/1 *S, Arg, Port*; 1951/2 *F* (Bolton Wanderers); 1953/4 *I.*
Hateley, M. (4) (Portsmouth) 1983/4 *Rus, Braz, U, Ch.*
Haynes, J. (56) (Fulham) 1954/5 *I*; 1955/6 *I, Sp, S, Swdn, Fin, G*; 1956/7 *W, Y, Eire, D, Eire*; 1957/8 *W, I, F, S, Port, Y, Rus* (2), *Braz, Aust, Rus*; 1958/9 *I, Rus, S, It, Braz, Per, Mex, US*; 1959/60 *I, Y, Sp, H*; 1960/1 *I, Lux, Sp, W, S, Mex, Port, It, Aust*; 1961/2 *W, Port, I, Aust, S, Switz, H, Per, Arg, Bulg, Braz.*
Hector, K. (2) (Derby County) 1973/4 *Pol, It.*
Hellawell, M. (2) (Birmingham City) 1962/3 *F, I.*
Henry, R. (1) (Tottenham Hotspur) 1962/3 *F.*
Hill, F. (2) (Bolton Wanderers) 1962/3 *I, W.*
Hill, G. (6) (Manchester United) 1975/6 *It*; 1976/7 *Eire, Fin, Lux*; 1977/8 *Switz, Lux.*
Hill, R. (2) (Luton Town) 1982/3 *D, G.*
Hinton, A. (3) (Wolverhampton W.) 1962/3 *F*; 1964/5 (Nottingham Forest) *Bel, W.*
Hitchens, G. (7) (Aston Villa) 1960/1 *Mex, It, Aust* (Inter Milan); 1961/2 *Switz, Per, H, Braz.*
Hoddle, G. (19) (Tottenham Hotspur) 1979/80 *Bulg, W, Au, Sp;* 1980/81 *Sp, W, S;* 1981/2 *N, I, W, Ic, Czecho, K;* 1982/3 *Lux, I, S;* 1983/4 *H, Lux, F.*
Hodgkinson, A. (5) (Sheffield United) 1956/7 *S, Eire, D, Eire*; 1960/1 *W.*
Holden, D. (5) (Bolton Wanderers) 1958/9 *S, It, Braz, Per, Mex.*
Holliday, E. (3) (Middlesbrough) 1959/60 *W, Swdn, I.*
Hollins, J. (1) (Chelsea) 1966/7 *Sp.*
Hopkinson, E. (14) (Bolton Wanderers) 1957/8 *W, I, F, S, Port, Y*; 1958/9 *S, It, Braz, Per, Mex, US*; 1959/60 *W, Swdn.*
Howe, D. (23) (West Bromwich Albion) 1957/8 *W, I, E, F, S, Port, Y, Rus* (2), *Braz, Aust, Rus*; 1958/9 *I, Rus, W, S, It, Braz, Per, Mex, US*; 1959/60 *W, Swdn, I.*
Howe, J. (3) (Derby County) 1947/8 *It*; 1948/9 *I, S.*
Hudson, A. (2) (Stoke City) 1974/5 *G, C.*
Hughes, E. (61) (Liverpool) 1969/70 *Holl, Port, Bel, W, I, S*; 1970/1 *E/Germ, M, Gr, M, W*; 1971/2 *Switz, Gr, G* (2), *W, I, S*; 1972/3 *W* (2), *S, W, S, Pol, Rus, It*; 1973/4 *Pol, It, W, I, S, Arg, Aust, E/Germ, Bulg, Y*; 1974/5 *Czecho, Port, C, I*; 1976/7 *It, Lux, W, S, Braz, Arg, U*; 1977/8 *Switz, Lux, It, G, I, S, H*; 1978/9 *D, I, W, Swdn*; (Wolverhampton Wanderers) 1979/80 *Sp, I, S.*
Hughes, L. (3) (Liverpool) 1949/50 *Ch, US, Sp.*
Hunt, R. (34) (Liverpool) 1961/2 *Aust*; 1962/3 *E/Germ*; 1963/4 *S* (2), *US, Port*; 1964/5 *W*; 1965/6 *Sp, Pol, G, S, Fin, N, Pol, U, Mex, F, Arg, Port, G*; 1966/7 *I, Czecho, W, Sp, Aust*; 1967/8 *W, I, Rus, Sp* (2), *Swdn, Y, Rus*; 1968/9 *Ru* (2).
Hunt, S. (2) (W.B.A.) 1983/4 *S, Rus.*
Hunter, N. (28) (Leeds United) 1965/6 *Sp, G, Y, Fin*; 1966/7 *Aust*; 1967/8 *Sp, Swdn, G, Y, Rus*; 1968/9 *Ru, W*; 1969/70 *Holl, G*; 1970/1 *M*; 1971/2 *G* (2), *W, I, S*; 1972/3 *W* (2), *Rus*; 1973/4 *Pol, I, S, Aust*; 1974/5 *Czecho.*
Hurst, G. (49) (West Ham United) 1965/6 *G, S, Y, Fin, D, Arg, Port, G*; 1966/7 *I, Czecho, W, S, Sp, Aust*; 1967/8 *W, I, Rus, S, Swdn, G, Rus*; 1968/9 *Ru, Bulg, Ru, F, I, S, Mex, U, Braz*; 1969/70 *Holl* (2), *Bel, W, I, S, Co, Ec, Ru, Braz, G*; 1970/1 *E/Germ, Gr, W, S*; 1971/2 *Switz* (2), *Gr, G.*

Jezzard, B. (2) (Fulham) 1953/4 *H*; 1955/6 *I.*
Johnson, D. (8) (Ipswich Town) 1974/5 *W, S*; 1975/6 *Switz*; (Liverpool) 1979/80 *Eire, Arg, I, S, Bel.*

Johnston, H. (10) (Blackpool) 1946/7 *S, Holl*; 1950/1 *S*; 1952/3 *Arg, Ch, U, US*; 1953/4 *W, I, H.*
Jones, M. (3) (Sheffield United) 1964/5 *G, Swdn* (Leeds United); 1969/70 *Holl.*
Jones, W. H. (2) (Liverpool) 1949/50 *Port, Bel.*

Kay, A. (1) (Everton) 1962/3 *Switz.*
Keegan, K. (63) (Liverpool) 1972/3 *W* (2); 1973/4 *W, I, Arg, E/Germ, Bulg, Y*; 1974/5 *Czecho, G, C* (2), *I, S*; 1975/6 *Switz, Czecho, Port, W* (2), *I, S, Braz, Fin*; 1976/7 *Eire, Fin, It, Holl, Lux,* (SV Hamburg), *W, Braz, Arg, U*; 1977/8 *Switz, It, G, Braz. H*: 1978/9 *D. Eire. Czecho. I. W. S. Bulg. Swdn. Aust*; 1979/80 *D, I, Eire, Sp, Arg, Bel, It, Sp;* 1980/81 *Sp, Switz, H;* 1981/2 (Southampton) *N, H, I, S, Fin, Sp.*
Kennedy, A. (2) (Liverpool) 1983/4 *I, W.*
Kennedy, R. (17) (Liverpool) 1975/6 *W* (2), *I, S*; 1976/7 *Lux, W, S, Braz, Arg*; 1977/8 *Switz, Lux*; 1979/80 *Bulg, Sp, Arg, W, Bel, It.*
Kevan, D. (14) (West Bromwich Albion) 1956/7 *S;* 1957/8 *W, I, S, Port, Y, Rus* (2), *Braz, Aust, Rus*; 1958/9 *Mex, US*; 1960/1 *Mex.*
Kidd, B. (2) (Manchester United) 1969/70 *I, Ec.*
Knowles, C. (4) (Tottenham Hotspur) 1967/8 *Rus, Sp, Swdn, G.*

Labone, B. (26) (Everton) 1962/3 *I, W, F*; 1966/7 *Sp, Aust*; 1967/8 *S, Sp, Swdn, G, Y, Rus,* 1968/9 *Ru, Bulg, I, S, Mex, U, Braz*; 1969/70 *Bel, W, S, Co, Ec, Ru, Braz, G.*
Lampard, F. (2) (West Ham United) 1972/3 *Y*; 1979/80 *Au.*
Langley, J. (3) (Fulham) 1957/8 *S, Port, Y.*
Langton, R. (11) (Blackburn Rovers) 1946/7 *I, W, Eire, Holl, F, Switz*; 1947/8 *Swdn*; 1948/9 (Preston North End) *D, Swdn*; 1949/50 (Bolton Wanderers) *S*; 1950/1 *I.*
Latchford, R. (12) (Everton) 1977/8 *It, Braz, W*; 1978/9 *D, Eire, Czecho, I, I, W, S, Bulg, Aust.*
Lawler, C. (4) (Liverpool) 1970/1 *M, W, S*; 1971/2 *Switz.*
Lawton, T. (15) (Chelsea) 1946/7 *I, W, S, Eire, Holl, F, Switz, Port*; 1947/8 *W, I* (Notts County), *S, Bel, Swdn, It*; 1948/9 *D.*
Lee, F. (27) (Manchester City) 1968/9 *Bulg, F, I, W, S, Mex, U*; 1969/70 *Holl, Port, Holl, Bel, W, Co, Ec, Ru, Braz, G*; 1970/1 *E/Germ, Gr, M, I, W, S*; 1971/2 *Switz* (2), *Gr, G.*
Lee, J. (1) (Derby County) 1950/1 *I.*
Lee, S. (14) (Liverpool) 1982/3 *Gr, Lux, W, Gr, H, S, Au;* 1983/4 *D, H, Lux, F, I, W, Ch.*
Lindsay, A. (4) (Liverpool) 1973/4 *Arg, E/Germ, Bulg, Y.*
Lineker, G. (1) (Leicester C.) 1983/4 *S.*
Little, B. (1) (Aston Villa) 1974/5 *W.*
Lloyd, L. (4) (Liverpool) 1970/1 *W*; 1971/2 *Switz, I*; (Nottingham F.) 1979/80 *W.*
Lofthouse, N. (33) (Bolton Wanderers) 1950/1 *Y*; 1951/2 *W, I, Aust* (2), *It, Switz*; 1952/3 *I, W, Bel, S, Arg, Ch, U, US*; 1953/4 *W, FIFA, I, Bel, U*; 1954/5 *I, S, F, Sp, Port*; 1955/6 *D, W, Sp, S, Fin*; 1958/9 *Rus, W.*
Lowe, E. (3) (Aston Villa) 1946/7 *F, Switz, Port.*

Mabbutt, G. (9) (Tottenham Hotspur) 1982/3 *G, Gr, Lux, W, Gr, H, I, S;* 1983/4 *H.*
Macdonald, M. (14) (Newcastle United) 1971/2 *W, I, S*; 1972/3 *Rus;* 1973/4 *Port, S, Y*; 1974/5 *G, C* (2), *I,* (Arsenal) 1975/6 *Switz, Czecho, Port.*

Madeley, P. (24) (Leeds United) 1970/1 *I*; 1971/2 *Switz* (2), *Gr, G* (2), *W, S*; 1972/3 *S, Czecho, Pol, Rus, It*; 1973/4 *Pol, It, Aust*; 1974/5 *Czecho, Port, C*; 1975/6 *Czecho, Port, Fin*; 1976/7 *Eire, Holl.*
Mannion, W. (26) (Middlesbrough) 1946/7 *I, W, S, Eire, Holl, F, Switz, Port*; 1947/8 *W, I, Bel, Swdn, It*; 1948/9 *N, F*; 1949/50 *S, Eire, Port, Bel, Ch, US*; 1950/1 *I, W, Y, S*; 1951/2 *F.*
Mariner, P. (33) (Ipswich Town) 1976/7 *Lux, I*; 1977/8 *Lux, W, S*; 1979/80 *W, I, S, Au, It, Sp;* 1980/81 *N, Switz, Sp, Switz, H;* 1981/2 *N, H, Holl, S, Fin, F, Czecho, K, G, Sp*; 1982/3 *D, G, Gr, W;* 1983/4 *D, H, Lux.*
Marsh, R. (9) (Q.P.R.) 1971/2 *Switz,* (Manchester City), *G* (2), *W, I, S*; 1972/3 *Y, W* (2).
Martin, A. (12) (West Ham U.) 1980/81 *Braz, S;* 1981/2 *H, Fin*; 1982/3 *Gr, Lux, W, Gr, H;* 1983/4 *H, Lux, W.*
Matthews, R. (5) (Coventry City) 1955/6 *S, Braz, Swdn, G*; 1956/7 *I,* (Chelsea).
Matthews, S. (37) (Stoke City) 1946/7 *S* (Blackpool), *Switz, Port*; 1947/8 *W, I, S, Bel, It*; 1948/9 *I, W, S, D, Switz*; 1949/50 *Sp*; 1950/1 *I, S*; 1953/4 *FIFA, I, H, Bel, U*; 1954/5 *I, W, G, S, F, Sp, Port*; 1955/6 *W, Braz*; 1956/7 *I, W, Y, D, S, Eire, D.*
McDermott, T. (24) (Liverpool) 1977/8 *Switz, Lux*; 1978/9 *I, W, Swdn*; 1979/80 ,W, Holl, S, Ic.
McDonald, C. (8) (Burnley) 1957/8 *Rus* (2), *Braz, Aust, Rus*; 1958/9 *I, Rus, W.*
McFarland, R. (28) (Derby County) 1970/1 *M, Gr, M, I, S*; 1971/2 *Switz, Gr, G, W, S*; 1972/3 *W* (2), *I, W, S, Czecho, Pol, Rus, It*; 1973/4 *Pol, It, W, I, Aust*; 1975/6 *Czecho, S*; 1976/7 *Eire, It.*
McGarry, W. (4) (Huddersfield Town) 1953/4 *Switz, U*; 1955/6 *D, W.*
McGuinness, W. (2) (Manchester United) 1958/9 *I, Mex.*
McNab, R. (4) (Arsenal) 1968/9 *Ru, Bulg, Ru, I.*
McNeil, M. (9) (Middlesbrough) 1960/1 *I, Lux, Sp, W, Mex, Port, It*; 1961/2 *Lux.*
Meadows, J. (1) (Manchester City) 1954/5 *S.*
Medley, L. (6) (Tottenham Hotspur) 1950/1 *W, Y*; 1951/2 *F, W, I, Aust.*
Melia, J. (2) (Liverpool) 1962/3 *S, Switz.*
Merrick, G. (23) (Birmingham City) 1951/2 *I, Aust* (2), *S, It, Switz*; 1952/3 *I, W, Bel, S, Arg, Ch, U*; 1953/4 *W, FIFA, I, H* (2), *S, Y, Bel, Switz, U.*
Metcalfe, V. (2) (Huddersfield Town) 1950/1 *Arg, Port.*
Milburn, J. (13) (Newcastle United) 1948/9 *I, W, S, Switz*; 1949/50 *W, Port, Bel, Sp*; 1950/1 *W, Arg, Port*; 1951/2 *F*; 1955/6 *D.*
Miller, B. (1) (Burnley) 1960/1 *Aust.*
Mills, M. (44) (Ipswich Town) 1972/3 *Y;* 1975/6 *W* (2), *I, S, Braz, It, Fin*; 1976/7 *Fin, It, I, W, S*; 1977/8 *G, Braz, W, I, S, H*; 1978/9 *D, Eire, I, I, S, Bulg, Aust*; 1979/80 *D, I, Sp, I, S, Sp;* 1980/81 *Switz, Switz, H;* 1981/2 *N, H, S, Fin, F, Czecho, K, G, Sp.*
Milne, G. (14) (Liverpool) 1962/3 *Braz, Czecho, E/Germ*; 1963/4 *W, FIFA, I, S, U, Port, Eire, Braz, Arg*; 1964/5 *I, Bel.*
Milton, C. A. (1) (Arsenal) 1951/2 *Aust.*
Moore, I. (1) (Nottingham Forest) 1969/70 *Holl.*
Moore, R. (108) (West Ham United) 1961/2 *Per, H, Arg, Bulg, Braz*; 1962/3 *F, I, W, F, S, Braz, Czecho, E/Germ, Switz*; 1963/4 *W, FIFA, I, S, U, Port, Eire, Braz, Port, Arg*; 1964/5 *I, Bel, S, H, Y, G, Swdn*; 1965/6 *W, Aust, I, Sp, Pol, G, S, N, D, Pol, U, Mex, F, Arg, Port, G*; 1966/7 *I, Czecho, W, S, Sp, Aust*; 1967/8 *W, I, Rus, S, Sp* (2), *Swdn, G, Y, Rus*; 1968/9 *Ru, Bulg, F, I, W, S, Mex, U, Braz*; 1969/70 *Holl, Port, Bel, W, I, S, Co, Ec, Ru, Braz, Czecho, G*; 1970/1 *E/Germ, Gr, M, I, S*; 1971/2 *Switz* (2),

Gr, G (2), *W, S*; 1972/3 *Y, W* (3), *S* (2), *I, Czecho, Pol, Rus, It*; 1973/4 *It.*
Morley, A (6) (Aston Villa) 1981/2 *H, I, W, Ic*;1982/3 *D, Gr.*
Morris, J. (3) (Derby County) 1948/9 *N, F*; 1949/50 *Eire.*
Mortensen, S. (25) (Blackpool) 1946/7 *Port;* 1947/8 *W, I, S, Bel, Swdn, It*; 1948/9 *I, W, S, Swdn, N*; 1949/50 *W, I, S, It, Port, Bel, Ch, US, Sp*; 1950/1 *S, Arg*; 1953/4 *FIFA, H.*
Mozley, B. (3) (Derby County) 1949/50 *W, I, Eire.*
Mullen, J. (12) (Wolverhampton Wanderers) 1946/7 *S*; 1948/9 *N, F*; 1949/50 *Bel, Ch, US*; 1953/4 *W, FIFA, I, S, Y, Switz.*
Mullery, A. (35) (Tottenham Hotspur) 1964/5 *Holl*; 1966/7 *Sp, Aust*; 1967/8 *W, I, Rus, S, Sp* (2), *Swdn, Y*; 1968/9 *Ru, Bulg, F, I, S, Mex, U, Braz*; 1969/70 *Holl, Port, Holl, W, I, S, Co, Ec, Ru, Braz, Czecho, G*; 1970/1 *E/Germ, M, Gr*; 1971/2 *Switz.*

Neal, P. (50) (Liverpool) 1975/6 *W, It*; 1976/7 *W, S, Braz, Arg, U*; 1977/8 *Switz, It, G, I, S, H*; 1978/9 *D, Eire, I, I, S, Bulg, Aust*; 1979/80 *D, I, Sp, Arg, W, Bel, It;* 1980/81 *Ru, Switz, Sp, Braz, H;* 1981/2 *N, H, W, Holl, Ic, F, K*; 1982/3 *D, Gr, Lux, W, Gr, H, I, S, Au* (2); 1983/4 *D.*
Newton, K. (27) (Blackburn Rovers) 1965/6 *G, S*; 1966/7 *Sp, Aust*; 1967/8 *W, S, Sp, Swdn, G, Y*; 1968/9 *Ru, Bulg, F, I, W, S, Mex, U, Braz*; 1969/70 (Everton) *Holl, I, S, Co, Ec, Ru, Czecho, G.*
Nicholls, J. (2) (West Bromwich Albion) 1953/4 *S, Y.*
Nicholson, W. (1) (Tottenham Hotspur) 1950/1 *Port.*
Nish, D. (5) (Derby County) 1972/3 *I;* 1973/4 *Port, W, I, S.*
Norman, M. (23) (Tottenham Hotspur) 1961/2 *Per, H, Arg, Bulg, Braz*; 1962/3 *F, S, Braz, Czecho, E/Germ*; 1963/4 *W, FIFA, I, S, U, Port, US, Braz, Port, Arg*; 1964/5 *I, Bel, Holl.*

Owen, S. (3) (Luton Town) 1953/4 *H, Bel.*
O'Grady, M. (2) (Huddersfield Town) 1962/3 *I;* 1968/9 (Leeds United) *F.*
Osgood, P. (4) (Chelsea) 1969/70 *Bel, Ru, Czecho*; 1973/4 *It.*
Osman, R. (11) (Ipswich Town) 1979/80 *Au;* 1980/81 *Sp, Ru, Switz;* 1981/2 *N, Ic*; 1982/3 *D, Au* (3); 1983/4 *D.*

Paine, T. (19) (Southampton) 1962/3 *Czecho, E/Germ*; 1963/4 *W, FIFA, I, S, U, US, Port*; 1964/5 *I, H, Y, G, Swdn*; 1965/6 *W, Aust, Y, N, Mex.*
Parkes, P. (1) (Queens Park Rangers) 1973/4 *Port.*
Parry, R. (2) (Bolton Wanderers) 1959/60 *I, S.*
Peacock, A. (6) (Middlesbrough) 1961/2 *Arg, Bulg*; 1962/3 *I, W*; 1965/6 (Leeds United) *W, I.*
Pearson, Stan (8) (Manchester United) 1947/8 *S;* 1948/9 *I, S*; 1949/50 *I, It*; 1950/1 *Port*; 1951/2 *S, It.*
Pearson, Stuart (15) (Manchester United) 1975/6 *W, I, S, Braz, Fin*; 1976/7 *Eire, Holl, W, S, Braz, Arg, U*; 1977/8 *It, G, I.*
Pegg, D. (1) (Manchester United) 1956/7 *Eire.*
Pejic, M. (4) (Stoke City) 1973/4 *Port, W, I, S.*
Perry, W. (3) (Blackpool) 1955/6 *I, Sp, S.*
Perryman, S. (1) (Tottenham H.) 1981/2 *Ic.*
Peters, M. (67) (West Ham United) 1965/6 *Y, Fin, Pol, Mex, F, Arg, Port, G*; 1966/7 *I, Czecho, W, S*; 1967/8 *W, I, Rus, S, Sp* (2), *Swdn, Y, Rus*; 1968/9 *Ru, Bulg, F, I, S,*

Mex, U, Braz; 1969/70 *Holl, Port, Holl, Bel,* (Tottenham Hotspur) *W, I, S, Co, Ec, Ru, Braz, Czecho, G*; 1970/1 *E/Germ, M, Gr, M, I, W, S*; 1971/2 *Switz, Gr, G* (2), *I*; 1972/3 *S, I, W, S, Czecho, Pol, Rus, It*; 1973/4 *Pol, It, Port, S, Aust.*
Phillips, L. (3) (Portsmouth) 1951/2 *I*; 1954/5 *W, G.*
Pickering, F. (3) (Everton) 1963/4 *US*; 1964/5 *I, Bel.*
Pickering, N. (1) (Sunderland) 1982/3 *Au.*
Pilkington, B. (1) (Burnley) 1954/5 *I.*
Pointer, R. (3) (Burnley) 1961/2 *Lux, W, Port.*
Pye, J. (1) (Wolverhampton Wanderers) 1949/50 *Eire.*

Quixall, A. (5) (Sheffield Wednesday) 1953/4 *W, FIFA, I*; 1954/5 *Sp, Port.*

Radford, J. (2) (Arsenal) 1968/9 *Ru*; 1971/2 *Switz.*
Ramsey, A. (32) (Southampton) 1948/9 *Switz*; 1949/50 (Tottenham Hotspur) *S, It, Port, Bel, Ch, US, Sp*; 1950/1 *I, W, Y, S, Arg, Port*; 1951/2 *F, W, I, Aust* (2), *S, It, Switz*; 1952/3 *I, W, Bel, S, Arg, Ch, U, US*; 1953/4 *FIFA, H.*
Reaney, P. (3) (Leeds United) 1968/9 *Bulg*; 1969/70 *Port*; 1970/1 *M.*
Reeves, K. (2) (Norwich City) 1979/80 *Bulg, I.*
Regis, C. (3) (W.B.A.) 1981/2 *I, Ic*; 1982/3 *G.*
Revie, D. (6) (Manchester City) 1954/5 *I, S, F*; 1955/6 *D, W*; 1956/7 *I.*
Richards, J. (1) (Wolverhampton Wanderers) 1972/3 *I.*
Rickaby, S. (1) (West Bromwich Albion) 1953/4 *I.*
Rimmer, J. (1) (Arsenal) 1975/6 *It.*
Rix, G. (17) (Arsenal) 1980/81 *N, Ru, Switz, Braz, W, S;* 1981/2 *Holl, Fin, F, Czecho, K, G, Sp*; 1982/3 *D, G, Gr;* 1983/4 *I.*
Robb, G. (1) (Tottenham Hotspur) 1953/4 *H.*
Roberts, G. (6) (Tottenham Hotspur) 1982/3 *I, S;* 1983/4 *F, I, S, Rus.*
Robson, B. (36) (West Bromwich Albion) 1979/80 *Eire, Au;* 1980/81 *N, Ru, Switz, Sp, Ru, Braz, W, S, Switz, H;* 1981/2 *N,* (Manchester U.) *H, I, W, Holl, S, Fin, F, Czecho, G, Sp*; 1982/3 *D, Gr, Lux, S;* 1983/4 *H, Lux, F, I, S, Rus, Braz, U, Ch.*
Robson, R. (20) (West Bromwich Albion) 1957/8 *F, Rus* (2), *Braz, Aust*; 1959/60 *Sp, H*; 1960/1 *I, Lux, Sp, W, S, Mex, Port, It*; 1961/2 *Lux, W, Port, I, Switz.*
Rowley, J. (6) (Manchester United) 1948/9 *Switz, Swdn, F*; 1949/50 *I, It*; 1951/2 *S.*
Royle, J. (6) (Everton) 1970/1 *M*; 1972/3 *Y;* (Manchester City) 1975/6 *I, It*; 1976/7 *Fin, Lux.*

Sadler, D. (4) (Manchester United) 1967/8 *I, Rus*; 1969/70 *Ec*; 1970/1 *E/Germ.*
Sansom, K. (44) (Crystal Palace) 1978/9 *W;* 1979/80 *Bulg, Eire, Arg, W, I, S, Bel, It;* 1980/81 (Arsenal) *N, Ru, Switz, Sp, Ru, Braz, W, S, Switz;* 1981/2 *I, W, Holl, S, Fin, F, Czecho, G, Sp*; 1982/3 *D, G, Gr, Lux, Gr, H, I, S;* 1983/4 *D, H, Lux, F, S, Rus, Braz, U, Ch.*
Scott, L. (17) (Arsenal) 1946/7 *I, W, S, Eire, Holl, F, Switz, Port*; 1947/8 *W, I, S, Bel, Swdn, It*; 1948/9 *I, W, D.*
Sewell, J. (6) (Sheffield Wednesday) 1951/2 *I, Aust, Switz*; 1952/3 *I;* 1953/4 *H* (2).
Shackleton, L. (5) (Sunderland) 1948/9 *W, D*; 1949/50 *W;* 1954/5 *W, G.*
Shaw, G. (5) (Sheffield United) 1958/9 *Rus, W, S, It*; 1962/3 *W.*
Shellito, K. (1) (Chelsea) 1962/3 *Czecho.*
Shilton, P. (63) (Leicester City) 1970/1 *E/Germ, W*; 1971/2 *Switz, I*; 1972/3 *Y, S, I, W, S, Czecho, Pol, Rus, It*; 1973/4 *Pol, It, W, I, S, Arg, Aust*; 1974/5 (Stoke City) *C;*

1976/7 *I, W*; (Nottingham Forest) 1977/8 *W, H*; 1978/9 *Czecho, Swdn, Aust*; 1979/80 *I, Sp, It;* 1980/81 *N, Switz, Ru;* 1981/2 *H, Holl, S, F, Czecho, K, G, Sp*; 1982/3 *D, G, Gr, W, Gr, H, I, S, Au* (3); 1983/4 *D, H, F, I, W, S, Rus, Braz, U, Ch.*
Shimwell, E. (1) (Blackpool) 1948/9 *Swdn.*
Sillett, P. (3) (Chelsea) 1954/5 *F, Sp, Port.*
Slater, W. (12) (Wolverhampton Wanderers) 1954/5 *W, G*; 1957/8 *S, Port, Y, Rus* (2), *Braz, Aust, Rus*; 1958/9 *Rus*; 1959/60 *S.*
Smith, L. (6) (Arsenal) 1950/1 *W*; 1951/2 *W, I*; 1952/3 *W, Bel, S.*
Smith, Tom (1) (Liverpool) 1970/1 *W.*
Smith, Trevor (2) (Birmingham City) 1959/60 *W, Swdn.*
Smith, R. (15) (Tottenham Hotspur) 1960/1 *I, Lux, Sp, W, S, Port*; 1961/2 *S*; 1962/3 *F, S, Braz, Czecho, E/Germ*; 1963/4 *W, FIFA, I.*
Spink, N. (1) (Aston Villa) 1982/3 *Au.*
Springett, R. (33) (Sheffield Wednesday) 1959/60 *I, S, Y, Sp, H*; 1960/1 *I, Lux, Sp, Mex, Port, It, Aust*; 1961/2 *Lux, W, Port, I, Aust, S, Switz, Per, H, Arg, Bulg, Braz*; 1962/3 *F, I, W, F, Switz*; 1965/6 *W, Aust, N.*
Staniforth, R. (8) (Huddersfield Town) 1953/4 *S, Y, H, Bel, Switz, U*; 1954/5 *W, G.*
Statham, D. (3) (West Bromwich Albion) 1982/3 *W, Au* (2).
Stein, B. (1) (Luton T.) 1983/4 *F.*
Stepney, A. (1) (Manchester United) 1967/8 *Swdn.*
Stiles, N. (28) (Manchester United) 1964/5 *S, H, Y, Swdn*; 1965/6 *W, Aust, I, Sp, Pol, G, S, N, D, Pol, U, Mex, F, Arg, Port, G*; 1966/7 *I, Czecho, W, S*; 1967/8 *Rus;* 1968/9 *Ru;* 1969/70 *I, S.*
Storey, P. (19) (Arsenal) 1970/1 *Gr, I, S*; 1971/2 *Switz, G, W, I, S*; 1972/3 *Y, W* (2), *S, I, W, S, Czecho, Pol, Rus, It.*
Streten, B. (1) (Luton Town) 1949/50 *I.*
Summerbee, M. (8) (Man.C.) 1967/8 *S, Sp, G*; 1971/2 *Switz, G, W, I*; 1972/3 *Rus.*
Sunderland, A. (1) (Arsenal) 1979/80 *Au.*
Swan, P. (19) (Sheffield Wednesday) 1959/60 *Y, Sp*; 1960/1 *I, Lux, Sp, W, S, Mex, Port, It, Aust*; 1961/2 *Lux, W, Port, I, Aust, S, Switz.*
Swift, F. (19) (Manchester City) 1946/7 *I, W, S, Eire, Holl, F, Switz, Port*; 1947/8 *W, I, S, Bel, Swdn, It*; 1948/9 *I, W, S, D, N.*

Talbot, B. (6) (Ipswich Town) 1976/7 *I, S, Braz, Arg, U*; 1979/80 *Au.*
Tambling, R. (3) (Chelsea) 1962/3 *W, F*; 1965/6 *Y.*
Taylor, E. (1) (Blackpool) 1953/4 *H.*
Taylor, J. (2) (Fulham) 1950/1 *Arg, Port.*
Taylor, P. (3) (Liverpool) 1947/8 *W, I, Swdn.*
Taylor, P. (4) (Crystal Palace) 1975/6 *W* (2), *I, S.*
Taylor, T. (19) (Manchester United) 1952/3 *Arg, Ch, U*; 1953/4 *Bel, Switz*; 1955/6 *S, Braz, Swdn, Fin, G*; 1956/7 *I, Y, D, Eire, D, Eire*; 1958/9 *W, I, F.*
Temple, D. (1) (Everton) 1964/5 *G.*
Thomas, Dave. (8) (Q.P.R.) 1974/5 *Czecho, Port, C* (2), *W, S*; 1975/6 *Czecho, Port.*
Thomas, Danny (2) (Coventry C.) 1982/3 *Au* (2).
Thomson, R. (8) (Wolverhampton W.) 1963/4 *I, US, Port, Arg*; 1964/5 *I, Bel, W, Hol.*
Thompson, P. (16) (Liverpool) 1963/4 *Port, Eire, US, Braz, Port, Arg*; 1964/5 *I, Bel, W, Holl, S*; 1965/6 *I;* 1967/8 *I, G*; 1969/70 *Holl.*
Thompson, P. (42) (Liverpool) 1975/6 *W* (2), *I, S, Braz, It, Fin*; 1976/7 *Fin*; 1978/9 *Eire, Czecho, I, S, Bulg, Swdn, Aust*; 1979/80 *D, I, Bulg, Eire, Sp, Arg, W, S, Bel, It,*

Sp; 1980/81 *N, Ru, H;* 1981/2 *N, H, W, Holl, S, Fin, F, Czecho, K, G, Sp*; 1982/3 *G, Gr.*

Thompson, T. (2) (Aston Villa) 1951/2 *W* (Preston); 1956/7 *S.*

Todd, C. (27) (Derby County) 1971/2 *I;* 1973/4 *Port, W, I, S, Arg, E/Germ, Bulg, Y*; 1974/5 *Port, G, C* (2), *I, W, S*; 1975/6 *Switz, Czecho, Port, I, S, Braz, Fin*; 1976/7 *Eire, Fin, Holl, I.*

Towers, T. (2) (Sunderland) 1975/6 *W, It.*

Tueart, D. (6) (Manchester City) 1974/5 *C, I*; 1976/7 *Fin, I, W, S.*

Ufton, D. (1) (Charlton Athletic) 1953/4 *FIFA.*

Venables, T. (2) (Chelsea) 1964/5 *Bel, Holl.*

Viljoen, C. (2) (Ipswich Town) 1974/5 *I, W.*

Viollet, D. (2) (Manchester United) 1959/60 *H*; 1961/2 *Lux.*

Waiters, A. (5) (Blackpool) 1963/4 *Eire, Braz*; 1964/5 *Bel, W, Holl.*

Walsh, P. (5) (Luton T.) 1982/3 *Au* (2); 1983/4 *F, W.*

Ward, P. (1) (Brighton) 1979/80 *Au.*

Ward, T. (2) (Derby County) 1947/8 *Bel;* 1948/9 *W.*

Watson, D. (65) (Sunderland) 1973/4 *Port, S, Arg, E/Germ, Bulg, Y*; 1974/5 *Czecho, Port, G, C* (2), *I, W, S*; 1975/6 (Manchester City) *Switz, Czecho, Port*; 1976/7 *Holl, Lux, I, W, S, Braz, Arg, U*; 1977/8 *Switz, Lux, It, G, Braz, W, I, S, H*; (Southampton) 1978/9 *D, Eire, Czecho, I, I, W, S, Bulg, Swdn, Aust*; 1979/80 *D, I, Bulg, Eire, Sp, Arg, I, S, Bel, It, Sp;* 1980/81 *N, Ru, Switz, Ru, W, S, Switz, H;* 1981/2 (Stoke C.) *I, Ic.*

Watson, D. (3) (Norwich C.) 1983/4 *Braz, U, Ch.*

Watson, W. (4) (Sunderland) 1949/50 *I, It*; 1950/1 *W, Y.*

Weller, K. (4) (Leicester City) 1973/4 *W, I, S, Arg.*

West, G. (3) (Everton) 1968/9 *Bulg, W, Mex.*

Wheeler, J. (1) (Bolton Wanderers) 1954/5 *I.*

Whitworth, S. (7) (Leicester City) 1974/5 *G, C, I, W, S*; 1975/6 *Switz, Port.*

Whymark, T. (1) (Ipswich Town) 1977/8 *Lux.*

Wignall, F. (2) (Nottingham Forest) 1964/5 *W, Holl.*

Wilkins, R. (62) (Chelsea) 1975/6 *It*; 1976/7 *Eire, Fin, I, Braz, Arg, U*; 1977/8 *Switz, Lux, It, G, W, I, S, H*; 1978/9 *D, Eire, Czecho, I, W, S, Bulg, Swdn, Aust*; (Manchester United) 1979/80 *D, I, Bulg, Sp, Arg, W, I, S, Bel, It, Sp;* 1980/81 *Sp, Ru, Braz, W, S, Switz, H;* 1981/2 *I, W, Holl, S, Fin, F, Czecho, K, G, Sp*; 1982/3 *D, G;* 1983/4 *D, I, W, S, Rus, Braz, U, Ch.*

Williams, B. (24) (Wolverhampton Wanderers) 1948/9 *F*; 1949/50 *W, S, Eire, It, Port, Bel, Ch, US, Sp*; 1950/1 *I, W, Y, S, Arg, Port*; 1951/2 *F, W*; 1954/5 *G, S, F, Sp, Port*; 1955/6 *W.*

Williams, S. (3) (Southampton) 1982/3 *Au* (2); 1983/4 *F.*

Willis, A. (1) (Tottenham Hotspur) 1951/2 *F.*

Wilshaw, D. (12) (Wolverhampton Wanderers) 1953/4 *W, Switz, U*; 1954/5 *S, F, Sp, Port*; 1955/6 *W, I, Fin, G*; 1956/7 *I.*

Wilson, R. (63) (Huddersfield Town) 1959/60 *S, Y, Sp, H*; 1961/2 *W, Port, I, Aust, S, Switz, Per, H, Aust, Bulg, Braz*; 1962/3 *F, I, Braz, Czecho, E/Germ, Switz*; 1963/4 *W, FIFA, S, U, Port, Eire, Braz, Port, Arg*; 1964/5 (Everton) *S, H, Y, G, Swdn*; 1965/6 *W, Aust, I, Sp, Pol, G, Y, Fin, D, Pol, U, Mex, F, Arg, Port, G*; 1966/7 *I, Czecho, W, S,*

Aust; 1967/8 *I, Rus, S, Sp* (2), *Y, Rus.*
Withe, P. (10) (Aston Villa) 1980/81 *Braz, W, S;* 1981/2 *N, W, Ic*; 1982/3 *H, I, S;* 1983/4 *H.*
Wood, R. (3) (Manchester United) 1954/5 *I, W*; 1955/6 *Fin.*
Woodcock, A. (35) (Nottingham Forest) 1977/8 *I;* 1978/9 *Eire, Czecho, Bulg, Swdn*; (FC Cologne) 1979/80 *I, Bulg, Eire, Sp, Arg, Bel, It, Sp;* 1980/81 *N, Ru, Switz, Ru, W, S;* 1981/2 *I, Holl, Fin,* (Arsenal) *G, Sp*; 1982/3 *G, Gr, Lux, Gr;* 1983/4 *Lux, F, I, W, S, Braz, U.*
Worthington, F. (8) (Leicester City) 1973/4 *I, S, Arg, E/Germ, Bulg, Y*; 1974/5 *Czecho, Port.*
Wright M. (1) (Southampton) 1983/4 *W.*
Wright, T. (11) (Everton) 1967/8 *Rus*; 1968/9 *Ru* (2), *Mex, U, Braz*; 1969/70 *Holl, Bel, W, Ru, Braz.*
Wright, W. (105) (Wolverhampton Wanderers) 1946/7 *I, W, S, Eire, Holl, Switz, Port*; 1947/8 *W, I, S, Bel, Swdn, It*; 1948/9 *I, W, S, D, Switz, Swdn, N, F*; 1949/50 *W, I, S, Eire, It, Port, Bel, Ch, US, Sp*; 1950/1 *I, S, Arg*; 1951/2 *F, W, I, Aust* (2), *S, It, Switz*; 1952/3 *I, W, Bel, S, Arg, Ch, U, US*; 1953/4 *W, FIFA, I, H* (2), *S, Y, Bel, Switz, Y*; 1954/5 *I, W, G, S, F, Sp, Port*; 1955/6 *D, W, I, Sp, Braz, Swdn, Fin, G*; 1956/7 *I, W, Y, D, S, Eire, D, Eire*; 1957/8 *W, I, F, S, Port, Y, Rus* (2), *Braz, Aust, Rus*; 1958/9 *Rus, W, S, It, Braz, Per, Mex, US.*

Young, G. (1) (Sheffield Wednesday) 1964/5 *W.*

NORTHERN IRELAND

Aherne, T. (4) (Belfast Celtic) 1946/7 *E*; 1947/8 *S*; 1948/9 *W*; 1949/50 (Luton Town) *W.*
Anderson, T. (22) (Manchester United) 1972/3 *C, E, S, W*; 1973/4 *Bulg, Port*; 1974/5 (Swindon Town) *S*; 1975/6 *Isr*; 1976/7 *Holl, G, Bel, E, S, W, Ic*; 1977/8 *Ic, Holl, Bel, S, E, W*; 1978/9 *D.*
Armstrong, G. (53) (Tottenham Hotspur) 1976/7 *G, E, W, Ic*; 1977/8 *Bel, S, E, W*; 1978/9 *Eire, D, Bulg, E, Bulg, E, S, W, D*; 1979/80 *E, Eire, Isr, S, E, W, Au, Au, Au;* 1980/81 *Swdn* (Watford), *Port, S, Port, S, Swdn;* 1981/2 *S, Isr, F, E, W, Y, Hon, Sp, Aust, F*; 1982/3 *Aust, T, A, S, E, W;* (Real Mallorca) 1983/4 *Aust, G, E, W, Fin.*

Barr, H. (Linfield) 1961/2 *E*; 1962/3 (Coventry City) *Pol, E.*
Best, G. (37) (Manchester United) 1963/4 *W, U*; 1964/5 *E, Switz* (2), *S, Holl* (2), *A*; 1965/6 *S, E, A*; 1966/7 *E*; 1967/8 *S*; 1968/9 *T, E, S, W*; 1969/70 *Rus, S, E, W*; 1970/1 *Sp, C* (2), *E, S, W*; 1971/2 *Rus, Sp*; 1972/3 *Bulg*; 1973/4 *Port*; 1976/7 *Holl, G, Bel*; (Fulham) 1977/8 *Ic, Holl.*
Bingham, W. (56) (Sunderland) 1950/1 *F*; 1951/2 *S, E, W*; 1952/3 *E, S, F, W*; 1953/4 *S, E, W*; 1954/5 *E, S, W*; 1955/6 *S, E, W*; 1956/7 *E, S, W, It, Port* (2); 1957/8 *S, E, It, W, Czecho, Arg, G, It, Czecho, F*; 1958/9 (Luton Town) *E, S, W, Sp*; 1959/60 *S, E, W*; 1960/1 (Everton) *E, G, S, It, Gr, G*; 1961/2 *Gr, E*; 1962/3 *Pol, E, S, Pol, Sp*; 1963/4 (Port Vale) *S, Sp, E.*
Blair, R. (5) (Oldham Athletic) 1974/5 *Swdn, S, W*; 1975/6 *Swdn, Isr.*
Blanchflower, D. (54) (Barnsley) 1949/50 *S, W*; 1950/1 *E, S, F*; 1951/2 (Aston Villa) *W*; 1952/3 *E, S, F, W*; 1953/4 *S, E, W*; 1954/5 *E, S* (Tottenham Hotspur), *W;* 1955/6 *S, E, W*; 1956/7 *E, S, W, It, Port*; 1957/8 *S, E, It* (2); *W, Czecho, Arg, Czecho, F*; 1958/9 *E, S, W, Sp*; 1959/60 *S, E, W*; 1960/1 *F, G, S, W, G*; 1961/2 *S, Gr, E, W,*

Holl; 1962/3 *Pol, E, S, Pol.*
Blanchflower, J. (11) (Manchester United) 1953/4 *W*; 1954/5 *E, S*; 1955/6 *S.W*; 1956/7 *E, S*; 1957/8 *S, E, It* (2).
Bowler, G. (4) (Hull City) 1949/50 *S, E, W, G.*
Braithwaite, R. (10) (Linfield) 1961/2 *W*; 1962/3 *Pol, Sp* (Middlesbrough) 1963/4 *W, U*; 1964/5 *E, Switz* (2), *S, Holl.*
Brennan, R. (5) (Luton Town) 1948/9 *W*; 1949/50 (Birmingham City) *S, E, W,* (Fulham); 1950/1 *E.*
Briggs, R. (2) (Manchester United) 1961/2 *W*; 1964/5 (Swansea) *Holl.*
Brotherston, N. (24) (Blackburn Rovers) 1979/80 *S, E, W, Au, Au, Au;* 1980/81 *Swdn, Port;* 1981/2 *S, Isr, F, E, S, W, Hon, Aust*; 1982/3 *Aust, G, A, T, A, E, W:* 1983/4 *T.*
Bruce, W. (2) (Glentoran) 1960/1 *S*; 1966/7 *W.*

Campbell, J. (2) (Fulham) 1950/1 *E, S.*
Campbell, R. (2) (Crusaders) 1962/3 *W*; 1964/5 *Switz.*
Cambell, R.M. (2) (Bradford C) 1981/2 *S, W.*
Campbell, W. (6) (Dundee) 1967/8 *S, E*; 1968/9 *T*; 1969/70 *Rus, S, W.*
Carey, J. (7) (Manchester United) 1946/7 *E, S, W*; 1947/8 *E*; 1948/9 *E, S, W.*
Casey, T. (11) (Newcastle United) 1954/5 *W*; 1955/6 *W*; 1956/7 *E, S, W, It, Port*; 1957/8 *G, F*; 1958/9 (Portsmouth) *E, Sp.*
Caskey, A. (6) (Derby County) 1978/9 *Bulg, E, Bulg, E*; 1979/80 *E;* 1981/2 (Tulsa Roughnecks) F.
Cassidy, T. (25) (Newcastle United) 1970/1 *E*; 1971/2 *Rus*; 1973/4 *Bulg, S, E, W*; 1974/5 *N*; 1975/6 *S, E, W*; 1976/7 *G*; 1979/80 *E, Eire, Isr, S, E, W, Au, Au, Au;* 1980/81 *Swdn, Port;* 1981/2 (Burnley) *Isr, Sp.*
Cleary, J. (4) (Glentoran) 1981/2 *S, W*; 1982/3 *W;* 1983/4 *T.*
Clements, D. (48) (Coventry City) 1964/5 *Holl, W*; 1965/6 *Mex*; 1966/7 *S, W*; 1967/8 *S, E;* 1968/9 *T* (2), *S, W;* 1969/70 *Rus* (2), *S, E, W;* 1970/1 *Sp, C, E, S, W;* 1971/2 (Sheffield Wednesday) *Rus* (2), *Sp, S, E, W*; 1972/3 *Bulg, C, Port, C, E, S, W*; (Everton) 1973/4 *Bulg, Port, S, E, W*; 1974/5 *N, Y, E, D, Bulg, E, Bulg,* (Middlesbrough) *E*; 1979/80 *Isr, E, W, Au, Au, Au;* 1980/81 *Swdn, Port, S, Port, S, Swdn;* 1981/2 *F, E:* (Gillingham) 1983/4 *S, Fin.*
Cochrane, A. (22) (Coleraine) 1975/6 *S;* (Burnley) 1978/9 *Eire, D, Bulg, E, Bulg,* (Middlesbrough) *E*; 1979/80 *Isr, E, W, Au, Au, Au*; 1980/81 *Swdn, Port, S, Swdn*; 1981/2 *F, E*; (Gillingham) 1983/4 *S, Fin*.
Cochrane, D. (10) (Leeds United) 1946/7 *E, S, W*; 1947/8 *S, E, W*; 1948/9 *S, W*; 1949/50 *S, E.*
Cowan, J. (1) (Newcastle United) 1969/70 *E.*
Coyle, F. (3) (Coleraine) 1955/6 *S, E*; 1957/8 (Nottingham Forest) *Arg.*
Coyle, R. (3) (Sheffield Wednesday) 1972/3 *Port, W*; 1973/4 *Bulg.*
Craig, D. (25) (Newcastle United) 1966/7 *W*; 1967/8 *W*; 1968/9 *T* (2), *E, S, W*; 1969/70 *Rus, S, E, W*; 1970/1 *Sp, C* (2), *S*; 1971/2 *Rus, S*; 1972/3 *C* (2), *E, S, W*; 1973/4 *Bulg, Port*; 1974/5 *N.*
Crossan, E. (3) (Blackburn Rovers) 1949/50 *S*; 1950/1 *E*; 1954/5 *W.*
Crossan, J. (23) (Rotterdam Sparta) 1959/60 *E*; 1962/3 (Sunderland) *Pol, W, Sp*; 1963/4 *S, Sp, E, W, U*; 1964/5 *E, Switz* (2), *S, Holl* (2), *W*; 1965/6 (Manchester City) *S, E, A, G*; 1966/7 *E, S*; 1967/8 (Middlesbrough) *S.*
Cunningham, W. (29) (St Mirren) 1950/1 *W*; 1952/3 *E*; 1953/4 *S*; 1954/5 *S*; 1955/6

S, E, W; 1956/7 (Leicester City) *E, S, W, It, Port*; 1957/8 *S, It, W, Czecho, Arg, G, Czecho, F*; 1958/9 *E, S, W*; 1959/60 *S, E, W*; 1960/1 (Dunfermline Athletic) *W, Holl.*
Cush, W. (25) (Glentoran) 1950/1 *E, S*; 1953/4 *S, E*; 1956/7 *W, It, Port*; 1957/8 *It* (Leeds United), *W, Czecho, Arg, F, Czecho, It, F*; 1958/9 *E, S, W, Sp*; 1959/60 *S, E, W*; 1960/1 (Portadown) *Gr, G*; 1961/2 *Gr.*

D'Arcy, S. (5) (Chelsea) 1951/2 *W*; 1952/3 *E*, (Brentford), *S, F, W.*
Dickson, D. (2) (Coleraine) 1972/3 *C, Port.*
Dickson, T. (1) (Linfield) 1956/7 *S.*
Dickson, W. (12) (Chelsea) 1950/1 *W, F*; 1951/2 *S, E, W*; 1952/3 *E, S, F, W*; (Arsenal) 1953/4 *E, W*; 1954/5 *E.*
Dixon, D. (2) (Coleraine) 1969/70 *S, W.*
Doherty, P. (6) (Derby County) 1946/7 *E* (Huddersfield Town), *W*; 1947/8 *E, W*; 1948/9 *S*; 1950/1 *S.*
Donaghy, M. (31) (Luton Town) 1979/80 *S, E, W*; 1980/81 *Swdn, Port, S*; 1981/2 *S, Isr, F, E, S, W, Y, Hon, Sp, F*; 1982/3 *Aust, G, A, T, A, S, E, W*; 1983/4 *Aust, T, G, S, E, W, Fin.*
Dougan, D. (41) (Portsmouth) 1957/8 *Czecho*; 1959/60 (Blackburn Rovers) *S*; 1960/1 *W, It, Gr*; 1962/3 (Aston Villa) *Pol, S, Pol*; 1965/6 (Leicester City) *S, E, A, W, G, Mex*; 1966/7 *E* (Wolverhampton Wanderers), *W*; 1967/8 *S, W*; 1968/9 *Isr, T, T, E, S, W*; 1969/70 *Rus* (2), *S, E*; 1970/1 *Sp, C* (2), *E, S, W*; 1971/2 *Rus* (2), *S, E, W*; 1972/3 *Bulg, C.*
Douglas, S. (1) (Belfast Celtic) 1946/7 *E.*
Dowd, D. (3) (Glentoran) 1972/3 *W*; 1974/5 (Sheffield Wednesday) *N, Swdn.*

Eglington, T. (6) (Everton) 1946/7 *S, W*; 1947/8 *S, E, W*; 1948/9 *E.*
Elder, A. (39) (Burnley) 1959/60 *W*; 1960/1 *E, G, S, W, Gr*; 1961/2 *S, Gr, E*; 1962/3 *Pol, E, S, Pol, W, Sp*; 1963/4 *W, U*; 1964/5 *W, Switz* (2), *S, Holl* (2), *W*; 1965/6 *S, E, A, W, Mex*; 1966/7 *E, S, W*; (Stoke City) 1967/8 *E, W*; 1968/9 *E, S, W*; 1969/70 *Rus.*

Farrell, P. (7) (Everton) 1946/7 *S, W*; 1947/8 *S, E, W*; 1948/9 *E, W.*
Feeney, A. (1) (Glentoran) 1975/6 *Isr.*
Feeney, J. (2) (Linfield) 1946/7 *S* (Swansea City); 1949/50 *E.*
Ferguson, W. (2) (Linfield) 1965/6 *Mex*; 1966/7 *E.*
Ferris, R. (3) (Birmingham City) 1949/50 *S*; 1950/1 *F*; 1951/2 *S.*
Finney, T. (14) (Sunderland) 1974/5 *N, E, S, W*; 1975/6 *N, Y, S*; (Cambridge United) 1979/80 *E, Isr, S, E, W, Au, Au.*
Forde, T. (4) (Ards) 1958/9 *Sp*; 1960/1 *E, G, S.*

Gaston, R. (1) (Coleraine) 1968/9 *Isr.*
Gallogly, C. (2) (Huddersfield Town) 1950/1 *E, S.*
Gorman, W. (4) (Brentford) 1946/7 *E, S, W*; 1947/8 *W.*
Graham, R. (13) (Doncaster Rovers) 1950/1 *W, F*; 1951/2 *S, E, W*; 1952/3 *S, F*; 1953/4 *E, W*; 1954/5 *S, W*; 1955/6 *E*; 1958/9 *E.*
Gregg, H. (24) (Doncaster Rovers) 1953/4 *W*; 1956/7 *E, S, W, It, Port*; 1957/8 *E* (Manchester United) *W, Czecho, Arg, G, F, It*; 1958/9 *E, W*; 1959/60 *S, E, W*; 1960/1 *E, S*; 1961/2 *S, Gr*; 1963/4 *S, E.*

Hamilton, B. (50) (Linfield) 1968/9 *T*; 1970/1 *C* (2), *E, S, W*; 1971/2 (Ipswich Town) *Rus* (2), *Sp*; 1972/3 *Bulg, C, Port, C, E, S, W*; 1973/4 *Bulg, S, E, W*; 1974/5 *N, Swdn, Y, E*; 1975/6 *Swdn, N, Y,* (Everton) *Isr, S, E, W*; 1976/7 *Holl, G, Bel, E, S, W, Ic*; 1977/8 *S, E, W*; (Millwall) 1978/9 *Eire, Bulg, Bulg,* (Swindon) *S, E, W, D, Au, Au.*

Hamilton, W. (35) (Q.P.R.) 1977/8 *S*; 1979/80 (Burnley) *S, E, W, Au, Au;* 1980/81 *Swdn, Port, S, Port, S, Swdn;* 1981/2 *S, Isr, E, W, Y, Hon, Sp, Aust, F*; 1982/3 *Aust, G, A, A, S, E, W;* 1983/4 *Aust, T, G, S, E, W, Fin.*

Harkin, T. (5) (Southport) 1967/8 *W*; 1968/9 *T, W*; 1969/70 *Rus*; 1970/1 *Sp.*

Harvey, M. (34) (Sunderland) 1960/1 *It*; 1961/2 *Holl*; 1962/3 *W, Sp*; 1963/4 *S, Sp, E, W, U*; 1964/5 *W, Switz* (2), *E, S, Holl* (2), *A*; 1965/6 *S, E, A, W, G, Mex*; 1966/7 *E, S*; 1967/8 *E, W*; 1968/9 *Isr, T, T, E*; 1969/70 *Rus*; 1970/1 *C, W.*

Hatton, S. (2) (Linfield) 1962/3 *Pol, S.*

Healy, P. (3) (Coleraine) 1981/2 *S, W, Hon*; 1982/3 *Aust.*

Hegan, D. (7) (West Bromwich Albion) 1969/70 *Rus*; 1971/2 (Wolverhampton Wanderers) *Rus, S, E, W*; 1972/3 *Bulg, C.*

Hill, J. (6) (Norwich C.) 1958/9 *W*; 1959/60 *W*; 1960/1 *G* (Everton); 1963/4 *S, Sp, E.*

Hinton, E. (7) (Fulham) 1946/7 *S, W*; 1947/8 *S, E, W* (Millwall); 1950/1 *W, F.*

Hughes, W. (1) (Bolton Wanderers) 1950/1 *W.*

Humphries, W. (13) (Ards) 1961/2 *W* (Coventry City) *Holl*; 1962/3 *Pol, E, S, W, Sp*; 1963/4 *S, Sp, E*; 1964/5 *S, Holl, W.*

Hunter, A. (53) (Blackburn Rovers) 1969/70 *Rus*; 1970/1 *C* (2), *E, S, W*; 1971/2 (Ipswich Town) *Rus* (2), *Sp, S, E, W*; 1972/3 *Bulg, C, Port, C, E, S, W*; 1973/4 *Bulg, S, E, W*; 1974/5 *N, Swdn, Y, E, S, W*; 1975/6 *Swdn, N, Y, Isr, S, E, W*; 1976/7 *Holl, G, Bel, E, S, W, Ic*; 1977/8 *Ic, Holl, Bel*; 1978/9 *Eire, D, S, W, D*; 1979/80 *E, Eire.*

Irvine, R. (8) (Linfield) 1961/2 *Holl*; 1962/3 *Pol, E, S, Pol, W, Sp*; (Stoke City) 1964/5 *W.*

Irvine, W. (22) (Burnley) 1962/3 *W, Sp*; 1964/5 *Switz, S, Holl* (2), *W*; 1965/6 *S, E, A, W, Mex*; 1966/7 *E, S*; 1967/8 *E, W*; 1968/9 (Preston North End) *Isr, T, E*; (Brighton & Hove Albion) 1971/2 *S, E, W.*

Jackson, T. (35) (Everton) 1968/9 *Isr, E, S, W;* 1969/70 *Rus* (2); 1970/1 (Nottingham Forest) *Sp;* 1971/2 *S, E, W;* 1972/3 *C, E, S, W;* 1973/4 *Bulg, Port, S, E, W;* 1974/5 *N, Swdn, Y, E, S, W*; 1975/6 *Swdn, N, Y*; 1976/7 *Holl, G, Bel, E, S, W, Ic.*

Jamison, A. (1) (Glentoran) 1975/6 *N.*

Jennings, P. (105) (Watford) 1963/4 *W, U*; 1964/5 (Tottenham Hotspur) *E, Switz* (2), *S, Holl, A*; 1965/6 *S, E, A, W, G*; 1966/7 *E, S*; 1967/8 *S, E, W*; 1968/9 *Isr, T* (2), *E, S, W*; 1969/70 *Rus* (2), *S, E*; 1970/1 *C* (2), *E, S, W*; 1971/2 *Rus, Sp, S, E, W*; 1972/3 *Bulg, C, Port, E, S, W*; 1973/4 *Port, S, E, W*; 1974/5 *N, Swdn, Y, E, S, W*; 1975/6 *Swdn, N, Y, Isr, S, E, W*; 1976/7 *Holl, G, Bel, E, S, W, Ic*; (Arsenal) 1977/8 *Ic, Holl, Bel*; 1978/9 *Eire, D, Bulg, E, Bulg, E, S, W, D*; 1979/80 *E, Eire, Isr;* 1980/81 *S, Port, S, Swdn;* 1981/2 *S, Isr, E, W, Y, Hon, Sp, F*; 1982/3 *A, S, E, W;* 1983/4 Aust, T, G, S, W, Fin.

Johnston, W. (1) (Glentoran) 1961/2 *W.*

Johnston, W. (1) (Oldham Athletic) 1965/6 *Mex.*

Jones, J. (4) (Glenavon) 1955/6 *W*; 1956/7 *E, S, W.*

Keane, T. (1) (Swansea City) 1948/9 *S.*
Keith, R. (23) (Newcastle United) 1957/8 *E, W, Czecho, Arg, G, Czecho, F*; 1958/9 *It, E, S, W, Sp*; 1959/60 *S, E*; 1960/1 *E, G, S, W, It, Gr, G*; 1961/2 *W, Holl.*
Kelly, H. (4) (Fulham) 1949/50 *E, W* (Southampton); 1950/1 *E, S.*
Kelly, P. (1) (Barnsley) 1949/50 *S.*

Lawther, I. (4) (Sunderland) 1959/60 *W*; 1960/1 *It*; 1961/2 (Blackburn Rovers) *S, Holl.*
Lockhart, N. (8) (Linfield) 1946/7 *E*; 1949/50 (Coventry City) *W*; 1950/1 *W*; 1951/2 *W*; 1953/4 (Aston Villa) *S, E*; 1954/5 *W*; 1955/6 *W.*
Lutton, B. (5) (Wolverhampton Wanderers) 1969/70 *S, E*; 1972/3 (West Ham United) *S, W*; 1973/4 *Port.*

Magill, E. (25) (Arsenal) 1961/2 *S, Gr, E*; 1962/3 *Pol, E, S, Pol, W, Sp*; 1963/4 *S, Sp, E, W, U*; 1964/5 *E, Switz* (2), *S, Holl*; 1965/6 *S, E,* (Brighton & Hove Albion) *A, W, G, Mex.*
Martin, C. (6) (Glentoran) 1946/7 *S*; 1947/8 (Leeds United) *S, E, W*; 1948/9 (Aston Villa) *E*; 1949/50 *W.*
McAdams, W. (16) (Manchester City) 1953/4 *W*; 1954/5 *S*; 1956/7 *E, S*; 1957/8 *S, It*; 1960/1 (Bolton Wanderers) *E, G, S, W, It, Gr, G*; 1961/2 (Leeds United) *Gr, E, Holl.*
McAlinden, J. (2) (Portsmouth) 1946/7 *E*; 1948/9 (Southend United) *E.*
McCabe, J. (6) (Leeds United) 1948/9 *S, W*; 1949/50 *E*; 1950/1 *W*; 1952/3 *W*; 1953/4 *S.*
McCavana, T. (3) (Coleraine) 1954/5 *S*; 1955/6 *S. E.*
McCleary, J. W. (1) (Cliftonville) 1954/5 *W.*
McClelland, J. (6) (Arsenal) 1960/1 *G, W, It, Gr, G*; 1965/6 (Fulham) *Mex.*
McClelland, J. (30) (Mansfield Town) 1979/80 *S, Au, Au, Au;* 1980/81 *Swdn, S, S, Swdn;* 1981/2 (Rangers) *S, W, Y, Hon, Sp, Aust, F*; 1982/3 *Aust, G, A, T, A, S, E, W*; 1983/4 *Aust, T, G, S, E, W, Fin.*
McCourt, F. (6) (Manchester City) 1951/2 *E, W*; 1952/3 *E, S, F, W.*
McCreery, D. (46) (Manchester United) 1975/6 *S, E, W*; 1976/7 *Holl, G, Bel, E, S, W, Ic*; 1977/8 *Ic, Holl, Bel, S, E, W*; 1978/9 *Eire, D, Bulg, E, Bulg, W, D*; 1979/80 (Q.P.R.) *E, Eire, S, E, W, Au, Au;* 1980/81 *Swdn, Port, S, Port* (Tulsa Roughnecks), *Swdn;* 1981/2 *S, Isr, F, E, Y, Hon, Sp, Aust, F*; 1982/3 (Newcastle United) *Aust;* 1983/4 *T.*
McCrory, S. (1) (Southend United) 1957/8 *E.*
McCullough, W. (10) (Arsenal) 1960/1 *It*; 1962/3 *Sp*; 1963/4 *S, Sp, E, W, U*; 1964/5 *E, Switz*; 1966/7 (Millwall) *E.*
McCurdy, C. (1) (Linfield) 1979/80 *Au.*
McElhinney, G. (5) (Bolton W.) 1983/4 *G, S, E, W, Fin.*
McFaul, I. (6) (Linfield) 1966/7 *E*; 1969/70 (Newcastle United) *W*; 1970/1 *Sp*; 1971/2 *Rus*; 1972/3 *C*; 1973/4 *Bulg.*
McGarry, J. K. (3) (Cliftonville) 1950/1 *S, W, E.*
McGrath, R. (21) (Tottenham Hotspur) 1973/4 *S, E, W*; 1974/5 *N*; 1975/6 *Isr;* (Manchester United) 1976/7 *Holl, G, Bel, E, S, W, Ic*; 1977/8 *Ic, Holl, Bel, S, E, W*; 1978/9 *Bulg, E, E.*
McIlroy, J. (53) (Burnley) 1951/2 *S, E, W*; 1952/3 *E, S, W*; 1953/4 *S, E, W*; 1954/5 *E, S, W*; 1955/6 *S. E, W*; 1956/7 *E, S, W, It, Port*; 1957/8 *S, E, It, W, Czecho, Arg,*

Czecho, F, It; 1958/9 *E, S, W, Sp*; 1959/60 *S, W, E*; 1960/1 *E, G, W, Gr, G*; 1961/2 *S, Gr, E, Holl*; 1962/3 *Pol, E, S, Pol, W*; 1965/6 (Stoke City) *S, E, A*.

McIlroy, S. (75) (Manchester United) 1971/2 *Sp, S*; 1973/4 *S, E, W*; 1974/5 *N, Swdn, Y, E, S, W*; 1975/6 *Swdn, N, Y, S, E, W*; 1976/7 *Holl, Bel, E, S, W, Ic*; 1977/8 *Ic, Holl, Bel, S, E, W*; 1978/9 *Eire, D, Bulg, E, Bulg, E, S, W, D*; 1979/80 *E, Eire, Isr, S, E, W;* 1980/81 *Swdn, Port, S, Port, S, Swdn;* 1981/2 (Stoke C.) *F, E, S, W, Y, Hon, Sp, Aust, F*; 1982/3 *Aust, G, A, T, A, S, E, W;* 1983/4 *Aust, T, S, E, W, Fin.*

McKeag, W. (2) (Glentoran) 1967/8 *S, W*.

McKenna, J. (7) (Huddersfield Town) 1949/50 *S, E, W*; 1950/1 *E, S, F*; 1951/2 *E*.

McKenzie, R. (1) (Airdrieonians) 1966/7 *W*.

McKinney, W. (1) (Falkirk) 1965/6 *G*.

McLaughlin, J. (12) (Shrewsbury Town) 1961/2 *S, Gr, E, W*; 1962/3 *W*, (Swansea City); 1963/4 *W, U*; 1964/5 *E, Switz* (2); 1965/6 *W*.

McMichael, A. (39) (Newcastle United) 1949/50 *S, E*; 1950/1 *E, S, F*; 1951/2 *S, E, W*; 1952/3 *E, S, F, W*; 1953/4 *S, E, W*; 1954/5 *E, W*; 1955/6 *W*; 1956/7 *E, S, W, It, Port*; 1957/8 *E, S, It, W, Czecho, Arg, G, Czecho, F, It*; 1958/9 *S, W, Sp*; 1959/60 *S, E, W*.

McMillan, S. (2) (Manchester United) 1962/3 *E, S*.

McMordie, E. (21) (Middlesbrough) 1968/9 *Isr, T, T, E, S, W*; 1969/70 *Rus, S, E, W*; 1970/1 *C* (2) *E, S, W*; 1971/2 *Rus, Sp, S, E, W*; 1972/3 *Bulg.*

McMorran, E. (15) (Belfast Celtic) 1946/7 *E* (Barnsley); 1950/1 *E, S, W*; 1951/2 *E, S, W*; 1952/3 *E, S, F* (Doncaster Rovers), *W*; 1953/4 *E*; 1955/6 *W*; 1956/7 *It, Port.*

McParland, P. (34) (Aston Villa) 1953/4 *W*; 1954/5 *E, S*; 1955/6 *S, E*; 1956/7 *E, S, W, Port*; 1957/8 *S, E, It, W, Czecho, Arg, G, Czecho, F, It*; 1958/9 *E, S, W, Sp*; 1959/60 *S, F, W*; 1960/1 *E, G, S, W, It, Gr, G*; 1961/2 (Wolverhampton W.) *Holl.*

Montgomery, F.) (Coleraine) 1954/5 *E.*

Moore, C. (1) (Glentoran) 1948/9 *W*.

Moreland, A. (5) (Derby County) 1978/9 *Bulg, E, S*; 1979/80 *E, Eire.*

Morgan, S. (18) (Port Vale) 1971/2 *Sp*; 1972/3 *Bulg, Port, C, E, S, W*; 1973/4 (Aston Villa) *Bulg, Port, S, E*; 1974/5 *Swdn*; 1975/6 *Swdn, N, Y* (Brighton & Hove Albion), *S, W*; 1978/9 *D*.

Mullen, G. (3) (Glentoran) 1982/3 *S, E, W*.

Napier, R. (1) (Bolton Wanderers) 1965/6 *G*.

Neill, T. (58) (Arsenal) 1960/1 *It, Gr, G*; 1961/2 *S, Gr, E, W*; 1962/3 *E, Pol, W, Sp*; 1963/4 *S, Sp, E, W, U*; 1964/5 *E, Switz, S, Holl* (2), *W*; 1965/6 *S, E, A, W, G, Mex*; 1966/7 *S, W*; 1967/8 *S, E*; 1968/9 *Isr, T, T, E, S, W*; 1969/70 *Rus* (2), *S, E, W*; 1970/1 *Sp, C*; 1971/2 (Hull City) *Rus* (2), *Sp, S, E, W*; 1972/3 *Bulg, C, Port, C, E, S, W*.

Nelson, S. (51) (Arsenal), 1969/70 *E, W*; 1970/1 *Sp, C, E, S, W*; 1971/2 *Rus* (2), *Sp, S, E, W*; 1972/3 *Bulg, C, Port*; 1973/4 *S, E*; 1974/5 *Swdn, Y*; 1975/6 *Swdn, N, Isr, E*; 1976/7 *G, Bel, W, Ic*; 1977/8 *Ic, Holl, Bel*; 1978/9 *Eire, D, Bulg, E, Bulg, E, S, W, D*; 1979/80 *E, Eire, Isr;* 1980/81 *S, Port, S, Swdn;* 1981/2 (Brighton) *E, S, Sp, Aust.*

Nicholl, C. (52) (Aston Villa) 1974/5 *Swdn, Y, E, S, W*; 1975/6 *Swdn, N, Y, S, E, W*; 1976/7 *W*; 1977/8 *Bel, S, E, W* (Southampton); 1978/9 *Eire, Bulg, E, Bulg, E, W*; 1979/80 *E, Eire, Isr, S, E, W, Au, Au, Au* 1980/81 *Swdn, Port, S, Port, S, Swdn;* 1981/2 *S, Isr, F, E, W, Y, Hon, Sp, Aust, F*; 1982/3 *S, E, W;* (Grimsby T.) 1983/4 *Aust, T.*

Nicholl, J. (60) (Manchester United) 1975/6 *Isr, W*; 1976/7 *Holl, Bel, E, S, W, Ic*; 1977/8 *Ic, Holl, Bel, S, E, W*; 1978/9 *Eire, D, Bulg, E, Bulg, E, S, W, D*; 1979/80

Eire, Isr, S, E, W, Au, Au, Au; 1980/81 *Swdn, Port, S, Port, S, Swdn;* 1981/2 *S, Isr, F, E,* (Toronto Blizzards) *W, Y, Hon, Sp, Aust, F*; 1982/3 (Sunderland) *Aust, G, A, T,* (Toronto Blizzards) *A, S, E, W;* (Rangers) 1983/4 *T, G, S, E;* (Toronto Blizzards) *Fin.*
Nicholson, J. (40) (Manchester United) 1960/1 *S, W*; 1961/2 *Gr, E, W, Holl*; 1962/3 *Pol, E, S, Pol*; 1964/5 (Huddersfield Town) *Holl* (2), *W*; 1965/6 *S, E, A, W, Mex*; 1966/7 *S, W*; 1967/8 *S, E, W*; 1968/9 *T, T, E, S, W*; 1969/70 *Rus* (2), *S, E, W*; 1970/1 *C* (2), *E, S, W*; 1971/2 *Rus* (2).

O'Doherty, A. (3) (Coleraine) 1969/70 *S, E, W.*
O'Driscoll, J. (3) (Swansea City) 1948/9 *E, S, W.*
O'Kane, L. (20) (Nottingham Forest) 1969/70 *E, W, S*; 1970/1 *Sp, E, S, W*; 1971/2 *Rus* (2); 1972/3 *Port, C*; 1973/4 *Bulg, Port, S, E, W*; 1974/5 *N, Swdn, E, S.*
O'Neill, J. (1) (Sunderland) 1961/2 *W.*
O'Neill, J. (25) (Leicester City) 1979/80 *Isr, S, E, W, Au, Au, Au;* 1980/81 *Port, S, Port, S, Swdn;* 1981/2 *S, Isr, F, E, S, F*; 1982/3 *Aust, G, A, T, A, S;* 1983/4 *S.*
O'Neill, M. (62) (Distillery) 1971/2 *Rus,* (Nottingham Forest), *Sp, W*; 1972/3 *Port, C, E, S, W*; 1973/4 *Bulg, Port, E, W*; 1974/5 *Swdn, Y, E, S*; 1975/6 *Y*; 1976/7 *E, S*; 1977/8 *Ic, Holl, S, E, W*; 1978/9 *Eire, D, Bulg, E, Bulg, D*; 1979/80 *Eire, Isr, Au, Au, Au;* 1980/81 *Swdn, Port,* (Norwich C.) *Port, S, Swdn;* 1981/2 (Manchester C.) *S,* (Norwich C.) *F, E, S, Y, Hon, Sp, Aust, F*; 1982/3 *Aust, G, A, T, A, S, E;* (Notts Co.) 1983/4 *Aust, T, G, E, W, Fin.*

Parke, J. (13) (Hibernian) 1963/4 *S, Sp, E*; 1964/5 (Sunderland) *Switz, S, Holl* (2), *W*; 1965/6 *G*; 1966/7 *E, S*; 1967/8 *S, E.*
Peacock, R. (31) (Glasgow Celtic) 1951/2 *S*; 1952/3 *F*; 1953/4 *W*; 1954/5 *E, S*; 1955/6 *S, E*; 1956/7 *W, It, Port*; 1957/8 *S, E, It, W, Czecho, Arg, G, Czecho, It*; 1958/9 *E, S, W*; 1959/60 *S, E*; 1960/1 *E, G, S, It, Gr, G*; 1961/2 *S.*
Platt, J. (21) (Middlesbrough) 1975/6 *Isr*; 1977/8 *S, E, W*; 1979/80 *S, E, W, Au, Au, Au;* 1980/81 *Swdn, Port;* 1981/2 *F, S, Aust*; 1982/3 *Aust, G, A, T*; (Ballymena) 1983/4 *E, W.*

Rafferty, W. (1) (Wolverhampton Wanderers) 1979/80 *E.*
Ramsey, P. (3) (Leicester C.) 1983/4 *Aust, G, S.*
Rice, P. (49) (Arsenal) 1968/9 *Isr*; 1969/70 *Rus*; 1970/1 *E, S, W*; 1971/2 *Rus, Sp, S, E, W*; 1972/3 *Bulg, C, E, S, W*; 1973/4 *Bulg, Port, S, E, W*; 1974/5 *N, Y, E, S, W*; 1975/6 *Swdn, N, Y, Isr, S, E, W*; 1976/7 *Holl, G, Bel, E, S, Ic*; 1977/8 *Ic, Holl, Bel*; 1978/9 *Eire, D, E, E, S, W, D*; 1979/80 *E.*
Ross, E. (1) (Newcastle United) 1968/9 *Isr.*
Russell, A. (1) (Linfield) 1946/7 *E.*
Ryan, R. (1) (West Bromwich Albion) 1949/50 *W.*

Scott, J. (2) (Grimsby Town) 1957/8 *Czecho, F.*
Scott, P. (8) (Everton) 1974/5 *W*; 1975/6 (York City) *Y, Isr, S, W*; 1977/8 *S, E, W.*
Sharkey, P. (1) (Ipswich Town) 1975/6 *S.*
Shields, J. (1) (Southampton) 1956/7 *S.*
Simpson, W. (12) (Glasgow Rangers) 1950/1 *W, F*; 1953/4 *S, E*; 1954/5 *E*; 1956/7 *It, Port*; 1957/8 *S, E, It, W*; 1958/9 *S.*
Sloan, A. (1) (Manchester United) 1978/9 *S.*

Sloan, D. (2) (Oxford) 1968/9 *Isr*; 1970/1 *Sp*.
Sloan, W. (1) (Arsenal) 1946/7 *W*.
Smyth, S. (9) (Wolverhampton Wanderers) 1947/8 *S, E, W*; 1948/9 *S, W*; 1949/50 *S, E, W* (Stoke City); 1951/2 *E*.
Smyth, W. (4) (Distillery) 1948/9 *E, S*; 1953/4 *S, E*.
Spence, D. (27) (Bury) 1974/5 *Y, E, S, W*; 1975/6 *Swdn, Isr, E, W, S*; (Blackpool) 1976/7 *Holl, G, E, S, W, Ic*; 1978/9 *Eire, D, E, E, S, W, D*; 1979/80 *Eire, Isr, Au;* 1980/81 (Southend U.) *Swdn;* 1981/82 *F*.
Stevenson, A. (3) (Everton) 1946/7 *S, W*; 1947/8 *S*.
Stewart, A. (6) (Glentoran) 1966/7 *W*; 1967/8 *S, E*, (Derby) *W*; 1968/9 *Isr*. *T*.
Stewart, I. (16) (Q.P.R.) 1981/2 *F*; 1982/3 *Aust, G, A, T, A, S, E, W*; 1983/4 *Aust, T, G, S, E, W, Fin*.
Stewart, P. (1) (Linfield) 1960/1 *W*.
Stewart, D. (1) (Hull City) 1977/8 *Bel*.

Todd, S. (9) (Burnley) 1966/7 *E*; 1967/8 *W*; 1968/9 *E, S, W*; 1969/70 *Rus, S*; 1970/1 *Sp* (Sheffield Wednesday), *C* (2).
Trainor, D. (1) (Crusaders) 1966/7 *W*.
Tulley, C. (10) (Glasgow Celtic) 1948/9 *E*; 1949/50 *E*; 1951/2 *S*; 1952/3 *E, S, F, W*; 1953/4 *S*; 1955/6 *E*; 1958/9 *Sp*.

Uprichard, N. (18) (Swindon Town) 1951/2 *S, E, W*; 1952/3 *E, S*, (Portsmouth) *F, W*; 1954/5 *E, S, W*; 1955/6 *S, E, W*; 1957/8 *S, It, Czecho*; 1958/9 *S, Sp*.

Whiteside, N. (15) (Manchester U.) 1981/2 *Y, Hon, Sp, Aust, F*; 1982/3 *G, A, T*; 1983/4 *Aust, T, G, S, E, W, Fin*.
Worthington, N. (2) (Sheffield W.) 1983/4 *W, Fin*.

SCOTLAND

Aird, J. (4) (Burnley) 1953/4 *N* (2), *Aust, U*.
Aitken, G. (8) (East Fife) 1948/9 *E, F;* 1949/50 *I, W, Switz;* 1952/3 (Sunderland) *W, I;* 1953/4 *E*.
Aitken, R. (12) (Celtic) 1979/80 *Per, Bel, W, E, Pol*; 1982/3 *Bel, Can* (3); 1983/4 *Bel, I, W*.
Albiston, A. (6) (Manchester U.) 1981/2 *I*; 1983/4 *U, Bel, E/Germ, W, E*.
Allan, T. (2) (Dundee) 1973/4 *G, N*.
Anderson, J. (1) (Leicester City) 1953/4 *Fin*.
Archibald, S. (22) (Aberdeen) 1979/80 *Port, I, Pol, H;* 1980/81 (Tottenham H.) *Isr, I, Isr, I, E;* 1981/2 *I, Port, Holl, Sp, NZ, Braz, Rus*; 1982/3 *E/Germ, Switz, Bel*; 1983/4 *E/Germ, E, F*.
Auld, B. (3) (Celtic) 1958/9 *Holl, Port;* 1959/60 *W*.

Baird, H. (1) (Airdrieonians) 1955/6 *Aust*.
Baird, S. (7) (Rangers) 1956/7 *Y, Sp, Switz, G, Sp;* 1957/8 *I, F*.
Bannon, E. (6) (Heart of Midlothian) 1979/80 *Bel*; 1982/3 (Dundee U.) *I, W, E, Can*; 1983/4 *E/Germ*.
Bauld, W. (3) (Heart of Midlothian) 1949/50 *E, Switz, Port*.
Baxter, J. (34) (Rangers) 1960/1 *I, Eire* (2), *Czecho;* 1961/2 *Czecho, I, W, Czecho, E, U;* 1962/3 *W, I, E, Aust, N, Eire, Sp;* 1963/4 *N, W, E, G;* 1964/5 *W, Fin, I* (Sunderland); 1965/6 *I, It, W, E, Port, Braz;* 1966/7 *W, E, Rus;* 1967/8 *W*.

Bell, W. (2) (Leeds United) 1965/6 *Port, Braz.*
Bett, J. (6) (Rangers) 1981/2 *Holl*; 1982/3 *Bel*; 1983/4 *Bel, W, E, F.*
Black, I. (1) (Southampton) 1947/8 *E.*
Blacklaw, A. (3) (Burnley) 1962/3 *N, Sp;* 1965/6 *It.*
Blackley, J. (7) (Hibernian) 1973/4 *Czecho, E, Bel, Z;* 1975/6 *Switz;* 1976/7 *W, Swdn.*
Blair, J. (1) (Blackpool) 1946/7 *W.*
Blyth, J. (2) (Coventry City) 1977/8 *Bulg, W.*
Bone, J. (1) (Norwich City) 1972/3 *D.*
Brand, R. (8) (Rangers) 1960/1 *I, Eire* (2), *Czecho;* 1961/2 *I, W, Czecho, U.*
Brazil, A. (13) (Ipswich Town) 1979/80 *Pol, H;* 1981/2 *Holl, Sp, I, W, E, NZ, Rus*; 1982/3 *E/Germ, Switz,* (Tottenham Hotspur) *W, E.*
Bremner, D. (1) (Hibernian) 1975/6 *Switz.*
Bremner, W. (54) (Leeds United) 1964/5 *Sp;* 1965/6 *Pol, It* (2), *E, Port, Braz;* 1966/7 *W, I, E;* 1967/8 *W, E;* 1968/9 *D, C, Aust, G, W, I, E, C;* 1969/70 *Eire, G, Aust;* 1970/1 *W, E;* 1971/2 *Port, Bel, Holl, I, W, E, Y, Czecho, Braz;* 1972/3 *D* (2), *E, I, E, Switz, Braz;* 1973/4 *Czecho, G, I, W, E, Bel, N, Z, Braz, Y;* 1974/5 *Sp* (2); 1975/6 *D.*
Brennan, F. (7) (Newcastle United) 1946/7 *W, I;* 1952/3 *W, I, E;* 1963/4 *I, E.*
Brogan, J. (4) (Celtic) 1970/1 *Port, W, I, E.*
Brown, A. (14) (East Fife) 1949/50 *Switz, Port, F;* (Blackpool) 1951/2 *US, D, Swdn;* 1952/3 *W;* 1953/4 *W, E, N* (2), *Fin, Aust, U.*
Brown, H. (3) (Partick Thistle) 1946/7 *W, Bel, Lux.*
Brown, J. (1) (Sheffield United) 1974/5 *Rus.*
Brown, R. (3) (Rangers) 1946/7 *I;* 1948/9 *I;* 1951/2 *E.*
Brown, W. (28) (Dundee) 1957/8 *F;* 1958/9 *W, I, E;* 1959/60 (Tottenham Hotspur) *I, N, Pol, Aust, H, T;* 1961/2 *Czecho, I, W, E;* 1962/3 *W, I, E, Aust;* 1963/4 *I, N, W;* 1964/5 *E, Sp, Pol, Fin;* 1965/6 *I, Pol, It.*
Brownlie, J. (7) (Hibernian) 1970/1 *Rus;* 1971/2 *Per, I, E;* 1972/3 *D* (2); 1975/6 *Ru.*
Buchan, M. (34) (Aberdeen) 1971/2 *Bel* (Manchester United) *W, Y, Port, Czecho, Braz;* 1972/3 *D (2), E;* 1973/4 *G, I, W, N, Braz, Y;* 1974/5 *E/Germ, Sp, Port;* 1975/6 *D, Ru;* 1976/7 *Fin, Czecho, Ch, Arg, Braz;* 1977/8 *E/Germ, W, I;* 1978/9 *Per, Ir, Holl, Aust, N, Port.*
Buckley, P. (3) (Aberdeen) 1953/4 *N;* 1954/5 *W, I.*
Burley, G. (11) (Ipswich Town) 1978/9 *W, I, E, N, Arg;* 1979/80 *Port, I, E, Pol;* 1981/2 *W, E.*
Burns, F. (1) (Manchester United) 1969/70 *Aust.*
Burns, K. (20) (Birmingham City) 1973/4 *G;* 1974/5 *E/Germ, Sp* (2); 1976/7 *Czecho, W, Swdn, W;* (Nottingham Forest) 1977/8 *I, W, E;* 1978/9 *Per, Ir, N;* 1979/80 *Per, Aust, Bel;* 1980/81 *Isr, I, W.*
Burns, T. (5) (Celtic) 1980/81 *I;* 1981/2 *Holl, W*; 1982/3 *Bel, I.*

Caldow, E. (40) (Rangers) 1956/7 *E, Sp, Switz, G, Sp;* 1957/8 *I, Switz, W, H, Pol, Y, Per, F;* 1958/9 *W, I, E, G, Holl, Port;* 1959/60 *I, W, E, Aust, H, T;* 1960/1 *W, I, E, Eire* (2), *Czecho;* 1961/2 *Czecho, I, W, Czecho, E, U;* 1962/3 *W, I, E.*
Callaghan, T. (2) (Dunfermline) 1969/70 *Eire, W.*
Campbell, R. (3) (Chelsea) 1949/50 *Switz, Port, F.*
Campbell, W. (7) (Morton) 1946/7 *I, Bel, Lux;* 1947/8 *E, Bel, Switz, F.*
Carr, W. (6) (Coventry City) 1969/70 *I, W, E;* 1970/1 *D;* 1971/2 *Per;* 1972/3 *D.*

Chalmers, S. (5) (Celtic) 1964/5 *W, Fin;* 1965/6 *Port, Braz;* 1966/7 *I.*
Clark, J. (4) (Celtic) 1965/6 *Braz;* 1966/7 *W, I, Rus.*
Clark, R. (16) (Aberdeen), 1967/8 *W, Holl;* 1969/70 *I;* 1970/1 *Port, W, I, E, D, Rus;* 1971/2 *Bel, I, W, E, Czecho, Braz;* 1972/3 *D, E.*
Collins, R. (31) (Celtic) 1950/1 *W, I, Aust;* 1954/5 *Y, Aust, H;* 1955/6 *I, W;* 1956/7 *W, E, Sp, Switz, G, Sp;* 1957/8 *I, Switz, W, H, Pol, Y, Par, F;* 1958/9 (Everton) *W, I, E, G, Holl, Port;* 1964/5 (Leeds United) *E, Sp, Pol.*
Colquhoun, E. (9) (Sheffield United) 1971/2 *Port, Holl, Per, Y, Czecho, Braz;* 1972/3 *D (2), E.*
Combe, R. (3) (Hibernian) 1947/8 *E, Bel, Switz.*
Conn, A. (1) (Heart of Midlothian) 1955/6 *Aust.*
Conn, A. (2) (Tottenham Hotspur) 1974/5 *I, E.*
Connachan, E. (2) (Dunfermline Athletic) 1961/2 *Czecho, U.*
Connelly, G. (2) (Celtic) 1973/4 *Czecho, G.*
Connolly, J. (1) (Everton) 1972/3 *Switz.*
Cooke, C. (16) (Dundee) 1965/6 *W, It, Port, Braz* (Chelsea); 1967/8 *E, Holl;* 1968/9 *C, Aust, G, W, I, C;* 1969/70 *Aust;* 1970/1 *Bel;* 1974/5 *Sp, Port.*
Cooper, D. (4) (Rangers) 1979/80 *Per, Aust*; 1983/4 *W, E.*
Cormack, P. (9) (Hibernian) 1965/6 *Braz;* 1969/70 *Eire, G, Aust;* (Nottingham Forest) 1970/1 *D, Port, W, E;* 1971/2 *Holl.*
Cowan, J. (25) (Morton) 1947/8 *Bel, Switz, F;* 1948/9 *W, E, F;* 1949/50 *I, W, E, Switz, Port, F;* 1950/1 *W, I, Aust* (2), *E, D, F, Bel;* 1951/2 *I, W, US, D, Swdn.*
Cowie, D. (20) (Dundee) 1952/3 *E, Swdn;* 1953/4 *I, W, N, Fin, Aust, U;* 1954/5 *W, I, Aust, H;* 1955/6 *W, Aust;* 1956/7 *I, W;* 1957/8 *H, Pol, Y, Par.*
Cox, S. (25) (Rangers) 1947/8 *F;* 1948/9 *E, F;* 1949/50 *I, W, E, Switz, Port, F;* 1950/1 *E* (2), *F, Bel, Aust;* 1951/2 *I, W, US, D, Swdn;* 1952/3 *W, I, E;* 1953/4 *I, W, E.*
Craig, J. (1) (Celtic) 1967/8 *W.*
Craig, J. (1) (Celtic) 1976/7 *Swdn.*
Craig, T. (1) (Newcastle United) 1975/6 *Switz.*
Crerand, P. (16) (Celtic) 1960/1 *Eire* (2), *Czecho;* 1961/2 *Czecho, I, W, Czecho, E, W;* 1962/3 *W, I;* 1963/4 *I;* 1964/5 (Manchester United) *E, Pol, Fin;* 1965/6 *Pol.*
Cropley, A. (2) (Hibernian) 1971/2 *Port, Bel.*
Cruickshank, J. (6) (Heart of Midlothian) 1963/4 *G;* 1969/70 *W, E;* 1970/1 *D, Bel;* 1975/6 *Ru.*
Cullen, M. (1) (Luton Town) 1955/6 *Aust.*
Cumming, J. (9) (Heart of Midlothian) 1954/5 *H, E, Port, Y;* 1959/60 *E, Pol, Aust, H, T.*
Cunningham, W. (8) (Preston North End) 1953/4 *N (2), Fin, Aust, U;* 1954/5 *W, H, E.*
Curran, H. (5) (Wolverhampton Wanderers) 1969/70 *Aust;* 1970/1 *I, E, D, Rus.*

Dalglish, K. (92) (Celtic) 1971/2 *Bel, Holl;* 1972/3 *D* (2), *E, W, I, E, Switz, Braz;* 1973/4 *Czecho* (2), *G* (2), *I, W, E, Bel, N, Z, Braz, Y;* 1974/5 *E/Germ, Sp* (2), *Swdn, Port, W, I, E, Ru;* 1975/6 *D* (2), *Ru, Switz, I, E;* 1976/7 *Fin, Czecho, W, Swdn, W, I, E, Ch, Arg, Braz;* (Liverpool) 1977/8 *E/Germ, Czecho, W* (2), *Bulg, I, E;* 1978/9 *Per, Ir, Holl, Aust, N, Port, W, I, E, N, Arg;* 1979/80 *Per, Aust, Bel, Bel, Port, I, W, E, Pol, H;* 1980/81 *Swdn, Port, Isr;* 1981/2 *Swdn, I, Holl, Sp, I, W, E, NZ, Braz*; 1982/3 *Bel, Switz*; 1983/4 *U, Bel, E/Germ.*
Davidson, J. (8) (Partick Thistle) 1953/4 *N (2), Aust, U;* 1954/5 *W, I, H, E.*

Dawson, A. (5) (Rangers) 1979/80 *Pol, H*; 1982/3 *I, Can* (2).
Deans, D. (2) (Celtic) 1974/5 *E/Germ, Sp.*
Delaney, J. (4) (Manchester United) 1946/7 *E;* 1947/8 *I, W, E.*
Dick, J. (1) (West Ham United) 1958/9 *E.*
Dickson, A. (5) (Kilmarnock) 1969/70 *I, W, E;* 1970/1 *D, Rus.*
Docherty, T. (25) (Preston North End) 1951/2 *W;* 1952/3 *E, Swdn;* 1953/4 *N (2), Aust, U;* 1954/5 *W, H (2), F, Aust;* 1956/7 *E, Sp, Switz, G, Sp;* 1957/8 *I, Switz, W, E;* 1958/9 (Arsenal) *W, I, E.*
Dodds, D. (2) (Dundee U.) 1983/4 *U, I.*
Donachie, W. (35) (Manchester City) 1971/2 *Per, I, E, Y, Czecho, Braz;* 1972/3 *D, E, W, I;* 1973/4 *I;* 1975/6 *Ru, I, W, E;* 1976/7 *Fin, Czecho, W, Swdn, W, I, E, Ch, Arg, Braz;* 1977/8 *E/Germ, W* (2), *Bulg, E;* 1978/9 *Ir, Holl, Aust, N, Port.*
Dougall, C. (1) (Birmingham City) 1946/7 *W.*
Dougan, R. (1) (Heart of Midlothian) 1949/50 *Switz.*
Doyle, J. (1) (Ayr United) 1975/6 *Ru.*
Duncan, A. (6) (Hibernian) 1974/5 *Port, W, I, E, Ru;* 1975/6 *D.*
Duncan, D. (3) (East Fife) 1947/8 *Bel, Switz, F.*
Duncanson, J. (1) (Rangers) 1946/7 *I.*

Evans, A. (4) (Aston Villa) 1981/2 *Holl, I, E, NZ.*
Evans, R. (48) (Celtic) 1948/9 *W, I, E, F;* 1949/50 *I, W, Switz, Port;* 1950/1 *Aust, E;* 1951/2 *I;* 1952/3 *Swdn;* 1953/4 *I, W, E, N, Fin;* 1954/5 *I, Port, Y, Aust, H;* 1955/6 *I, W, E, Aust;* 1956/7 *G, Sp;* 1957/8 *I, Switz, W, E, H, Pol, Y, Par, F;* 1958/9 *E, G, Holl, Port;* 1959/60 *I, W, E,* (Chelsea) *Pol, Aust, H, T.*
Ewing, T. (2) (Partick Thistle) 1957/8 *W, E.*

Farm, G. (10) (Blackpool) 1952/3 *W, I, E, Swdn;* 1953/4 *I, W, E;* 1958/9 *G, Holl, Port.*
Ferguson, R. (7) (Kilmarnock) 1965/6 *W, E, Holl, Port, Braz;* 1966/7 *W, I.*
Fernie, W. (11) (Celtic) 1953/4 *Fin, Aust, U;* 1954/5 *W, I;* 1956/7 *Y, W, E;* 1957/8 *Switz, W, Per.*
Flavell, R. (2) (Airdrieonians) 1946/7 *Bel, Lux.*
Fleming, C. (1) (East Fife) 1953/4 *I.*
Forbes, A. (14) (Sheffield United) 1946/7 *E, Bel, Lux;* 1947/8 *I, W,* (Arsenal); 1949/50 *E, Port, F;* 1950/51 *W, I, Aust;* 1951/52 *W, D, Swdn.*
Ford, D. (3) (Heart of Midlothian) 1973/4 *Czecho, G, W.*
Forrest, J. (1) (Motherwell) 1957/8 *E.*
Forrest, J. (2) (Rangers) 1965/6 *W, It.*
Forrest, J. (3) (Aberdeen) 1970/1 *Bel, D, Rus.*
Forsyth, A. (18) (Partick Thistle) 1971/2 *Y, Czecho, Braz;* 1972/3 *D,* (Manchester United), *E;* 1974/5 *E/Germ, Sp, I, Ru;* 1975/6 *D;* 1977/8 *Czecho, W* (2), *I, E;* 1978/9 *Per, Ir, Holl.*
Forsyth, C. (3) (Kilmarnock) 1963/4 *E;* 1964/5 *W, Fin.*
Forsyth, T. (14) (Motherwell) 1970/1 *D* (Rangers); 1973/4 *Czecho;* 1975/6 *Switz, I, W, E;* 1976/7 *Fin, Swdn, W, I, E, Ch, Arg, Braz.*
Fraser, D. (2) (West Bromwich Albion) 1967/8 *Holl;* 1968/9 *C.*
Fraser, W. (2) (Sunderland) 1954/5 *D, I.*

Gabriel, J. (1) (Everton) 1960/1 *W.*

Gardiner, W. (1) (Motherwell) 1957/8 *W.*
Gemmell, T. (2) (St Mirren) 1954/5 *Port, Y.*
Gemmell, T. (18) (Celtic) 1965/6 *E;* 1966/7 *W, I, E, Rus;* 1967/8 *I, E;* 1968/9 *Aust, D, G, W, I, E, C;* 1969/70 *Eire, G, E;* 1970/1 *Bel.*
Gemmill, A. (43) (Derby County) 1970/1 *Bel;* 1971/2 *Port, Holl, Per, I, W, E;* 1975/6 *D, Ru, I, W, E,* 1976/7 *Fin, Czecho, W* (2), *I, E, Ch, Arg, Braz;* (Nottingham Forest) 1977/8 *E/Germ, Bulg, I, W, E;* 1978/9 *Per, Ir, Holl, Aust, N, Port, N;* (Birmingham City) 1979/80 *Aust, Port, I, W, E;* 1980/81 *Swdn, Port, Isr, I.*
Gibson, D. (7) (Leicester City) 1962/3 *Aust, N, Eire, Sp;* 1963/4 *I;* 1964/5 *W, Fin, H.*
Gilzean, A. (22) (Dundee) 1963/4 *N, W, E, G;* 1964/5 *I* (Tottenham Hotspur), *Sp;* 1965/6 *I, Pol, It, W;* 1967/8 *W;* 1968/9 *C, Aust, G, W, E, C;* 1969/70 *G, Aust, I, E;* 1970/1 *Port.*
Glavin, R. (1) (Celtic) 1976/7 *Swdn.*
Glen, A. (2) (Aberdeen) 1955/6 *I, E.*
Gough, R. (11) (Dundee United) 1982/3 *Switz, I, W, E, Can* (3); 1983/4 *U, Bel, E/Germ, I, W, E, F.*
Govan, J. (6) (Hibernian) 1947/8 *W, E, Bel, Switz, F;* 1948/9 *I.*
Graham, G. (11) (Arsenal) 1971/2 *Port, Holl, I, Y, Czecho, Braz;* 1972/3 *D* (2), (Manchester United) *E, W, I.*
Graham, A. (10) (Leeds United) 1977/8 *E/Germ;* 1978/9 *Aust, N, W, I, E, N, Arg;* 1979/80 *Aust;* 1980/81 *W.*
Gray, A. (19) (Aston Villa) 1975/6 *Ru, Switz;* 1976/7 *Fin, Czecho;* 1978/9 *Aust, N, Arg;* (Wolverhampton Wanderers) 1979/80 *Port, E;* 1980⅜81 *Swdn, Port, Isr, I;* 1981/2 *Swdn*; 1982/3 *I, W, E, Can* (2)
Gray, E. (12) (Leeds United) 1968/9 *E, C;* 1969/70 *G, Aust;* 1970/1 *W, I;* 1971/2 *Bel, Holl;* 1975/6 *W, E;* 1976/7 *Fin, W.*
Gray, F. (31) (Leeds United) 1975/6 *Switz;* 1978/9 *N, Port, W, I, E;* 1979/80 (Nottingham F.) *Bel;* 1980/81 *Swdn, Port, Isr, I, Isr* (Leeds U.) *W, I, E;* 1981/2 *Swdn, I, Port, Holl, Sp, W, NZ, Braz, Rus*; 1982/3 *E/Germ, Switz, Bel, Switz, W, E, Can.*
Grant, J. (2) (Hibernian) 1958/9 *W, I.*
Green, A. (16) (Blackpool) 1970/1 *Bel, Port, I, E;* (Newcastle United) 1971/2 *W, E.*
Greig, J. (44) (Rangers) 1963/4 *E, G;* 1964/5 *W, Fin, I, E, Sp, Pol, Fin;* 1965/6 *I, Pol, It, W, It, E, Holl, Port, Braz;* 1966/7 *W, I, E;* 1967/8 *I, W, E, Holl;* 1968/9 *D, C, Aust, G, W, I, E, C;* 1969/70 *Eire, G, Aust, W, E;* 1970/1 *D, Bel, W, I, E;* 1975/6 *D.*

Haddock, H. (6) (Clydebank) 1954/5 *H* (2), *E, Port, Y;* 1957/8 *E.*
Haffey, H. (2) (Celtic) 1959/60 *E;* 1960/1 *E.*
Hamilton, A. (24) (Dundee) 1961/2 *W, Czecho, E, U;* 1962/3 *W, I, E, Aust, N, I, Eire;* 1963/4 *I, N, W, E, G;* 1964/5 *W, Fin, I, E, Sp, Pol, Fin;* 1965/6 *I, Pol.*
Hamilton, G. (5) (Aberdeen) 1946/7 *I;* 1950/1 *Bel, Aust;* 1953/4 *N* (2).
Hamilton, W. (1) (Hibernian) 1964/5 *Fin.*
Hansen, A. (21) (Liverpool) 1978/9 *W, Arg;* 1979/80 *Bel, Port;* 1980/81 *Swdn, Port, Isr;* 1981/2 *Swdn, I, Port, Sp, I, W, E, NZ, Braz, Rus*; 1982/3 *E/Germ, Switz, Bel, Switz.*
Hansen, J. (1) (Partick Thistle) 1971/2 *Bel.*
Harper, J. (4) (Aberdeen) 1972/3 *D* (2); 1975/6 *D;* 1978/9 *Ir.*
Hartford, A. (49) (West Bromwich Albion) 1971/2 *Per, W, E, Y, Czecho, Braz;* 1975/6 (Manchester City) *D, Ru, I;* 1976/7 *Czecho, W, Swdn, W, I, E, Ch, Arg, Braz;*

1977/8 *E/Germ, Czecho, W* (2), *Bulg, E;* 1978/9 *Per, Ir, Holl, Aust, N, Port, W, I, E, N, Arg;* 1979/80 (Everton) *Per, Bel;* 1980/81 *Isr, W, I, E;* 1981/2 *Swdn,* (Manchester C.) *I, Port, Sp, I, W, E, Braz.*

Harvey, D. (16) (Leeds United) 1972/3 *D;* 1973/4 *Czecho, G, I, W, E, Bel, Z, Braz, Y;* 1974/5 *E/Germ, Sp* (2); 1975/6 *D* (2); 1976/7 *Fin.*

Haughney, M. (1) (Celtic) 1953/4 *E.*

Hay, D. (27) (Celtic) 1969/70 *I, W, E;* 1970/1 *D, Bel, Port, W;* 1971/2 *Port, Bel, Holl;* 1972/3 *W, I, E, Switz, Braz;* 1973/4 *Czecho* (2), *G, I, W, E, Bel, N, Z, Braz, Y.*

Hegarty, P. (7) (Dundee United) 1978/9 *W, I, E, Arg;* 1979/80 *W, E;* 1982/3 *I.*

Henderson, J. (7) (Portsmouth) 1952/3 *Swdn;* 1953/4 *I, E, N;* 1955/6 *W;* 1958/9 (Arsenal) *W, I.*

Henderson, W. (29) (Rangers) 1962/3 *W, I, E, Aust, N, Eire, Sp;* 1963/4 *I, N, W, E, G;* 1964/5 *E, Sp, Pol, Fin;* 1965/6 *I, Pol, It, W, Holl;* 1966/7 *W, I;* 1967/8 *Holl;* 1968/9 *I, E, C;* 1969/70 *Eire, Czecho.*

Herd, D. (5) (Arsenal) 1958/9 *W, I, E;* 1960/1 *Eire;* 1970/1 *Port.*

Herd, G. (5) (Clydebank) 1957/8 *E;* 1959/60 *H, T;* 1960/1 *W, I.*

Herriot, J. (8) (Birmingham City) 1968/9 *D, C, W, I, E, C;* 1969/70 *Eire, G.*

Hewie, J. (19) (Charlton Athletic) 1955/6 *E, Aust;* 1956/7 *Y, I, W, E, Sp, Switz, G, Sp;* 1957/8 *W, Pol, Y, F;* 1958/9 *Holl, Port;* 1959/60 *I, W, Pol.*

Holt, D. (4) (Heart of Midlothian) 1962/3 *Aust, N, Eire, Sp.*

Holton, J. (15) (Manchester United) 1972/3 *W, I, E, Switz, Braz;* 1973/4 *Czecho, G, I, W, E, N, Z, Braz, Y;* 1974/5 *E/Germ.*

Hope, R. (2) (West Bromwich Albion) 1967/8 *Hol;* 1968/9 *D.*

Houliston, W. (3) (Queen of the South) 1948/9 *I, E, F.*

Houston, S. (1) (Manchester United) 1975/6 *D.*

Howie, H. (1) (Hibernian) 1948/9 *W.*

Hughes, J. (8) (Celtic) 1964/5 *Sp, Pol;* 1965/6 *I, It* (2); 1967/8 *E;* 1968/9 *Aust;* 1969/70 *Eire.*

Hughes, W. (1) (Sunderland) 1974/5 *Swdn.*

Humphries, W. (1) (Motherwell) 1951/2 *Swdn.*

Hunter, A. (3) (Kilmarnock) 1971/2 *Per;* 1972/3 (Celtic) *E;* 1973/4 *Czecho.*

Hunter, N. (3) (Motherwell) 1959/60 *H, T;* 1960/1 *W.*

Husband, J. (1) (Partick Thistle) 1946/7 *W.*

Hutchison, T. (17) (Coventry City) 1973/4 *Czecho* (2), *G* (2), *I, W, Bel, N, Z, Y;* 1974/5 *E/Germ, Sp* (2), *Port, E, Ru;* 1975/6 *D.*

Imlach, S. (4) (Nottingham Forest) 1957/8 *H, Pol, Y, F.*

Jackson, C. (8) (Rangers) 1974/5 *Swdn, Port, W;* 1975/6 *D, Ru, I, W, E.*

Jardine, A. (37) (Rangers) 1970/1 *D;* 1971/2 *Port, Bel, Holl;* 1972/3 *E, Switz, Braz;* 1973/4 *Czecho* (2), *G* (2), *I, W, E, Bel, N, Z, Braz, Y;* 1974/5 *E/Germ, Sp* (2), *Swdn, Port, W, I, E;* 1976/7 *Swdn, Ch;* 1977/8 *Czecho, W, I;* 1978/9 *Ir;* 1979/80 *Per, Aust, Bel* (2).

Jarvie, A. (3) (Airdrieonians) 1970/1 *Port, I, E.*

Johnston, M. (3) (Watford) 1983/4 *W, E, F.*

Johnston, W. (21) (Rangers) 1965/6 *Pol, W, E, Holl;* 1967/8 *W, E;* 1968/9 *I;* 1969/70 *I;* 1970/1 *D;* (West Bromwich Albion) 1976/7 *Swdn, W, I, Ch, Arg, Braz;* 1977/8 *E/Germ, Czecho, W* (2), *E.*

Johnstone, D. (15) (Rangers) 1972/3 *W, I, E, Switz, Braz;* 1974/5 *E/Germ, Swdn;*

1975/6 *Switz, I, E;* 1977/8 *Bulg, I, W;* 1978/9 *Per;* 1979/80 *Bel.*
Johnstone, J. (23) (Celtic) 1964/5 *W, Fin;* 1965/6 *E;* 1966/7 *W, Rus;* 1967/8 *W;* 1968/9 *Aust, G;* 1969/70 *G, E;* 1970/1 *D, E;* 1971/2 *Port, Bel, Holl, I, E;* 1973/4 *W, E, Bel, N;* 1974/5 *E/Germ, Sp.*
Johnstone, L. (2) (Clydebank) 1947/8 *Bel, Switz.*
Johnstone, R. (17) (Hibernian) 1950/1 *E, D, F;* 1951/2 *I, E;* 1952/3 *E, Swdn;* 1953/4 *W, E, N, Fin;* 1954/5 *I, H,* (Manchester City), *E;* 1955/6 *I, W, E.*
Jordan, J. (52) (Leeds United) 1972/3 *E, Switz, Braz;* 1973/4 *Czecho* (2), *G, I, W, E, Bel, N, Z, Braz, Y;* 1974/5 *E/Germ, Sp* (2); 1975/6 *I, W, E;* 1976/7 *Czecho, W, I, E;* (Manchester United) 1977/8 *E/Germ, Czecho, W, Bulg, I, E;* 1978/9 *Per, Ir, Holl, Aust, Port, W, I, E, N;* 1979/80 *Bel, I, W, E, Pol;* 1980/81 *Isr, W, E;* 1981/2 (AC Milan) *Swdn, Holl, W, E, Rus.*

Kelly, H. (1) (Blackpool) 1951/2 *US.*
Kelly, J. (2) (Barnsley) 1948/9 *W, I.*
Kennedy, J. (6) (Celtic) 1963/4 *W, E, G;* 1964/5 *W, Fin, I.*
Kennedy, S. (12) (Rangers) 1974/5 *Swdn, Port, W, I, E;* 1977/8 *Bulg, W, E;* 1978/9 *Per, Holl, Aust, Port.*
Kerr, A. (2) (Partick Thistle) 1954/5 *Aust, H.*

Law, D. (55) (Huddersfield Town) 1958/9 *W, I, Holl, Port;* 1959/60 *I, W,* (Manchester City) *E, Pol, Aust;* 1960/1 *I, E;* 1961/2 (Torino) *Czecho* (2), *E;* 1962/3 (Manchester United) *W, I, E, Aust, N, Eire, Sp;* 1963/4 *N, W, E, G;* 1964/5 *W, Fin, I, E, Sp, Pol, Fin;* 1965/6 *I, Pol, E;* 1966/7 *W, E, Rus;* 1967/8 *I;* 1968/9 *Aust, G, I;* 1971/2 *Per, I, W, E, Y, Czecho, Braz;* 1973/4 (Manchester City) *Czecho* (2), *G* (2), *I, Z.*
Lawrence, T. (3) (Liverpool) 1962/3 *Eire;* 1968/9 *G, W.*
Leggat, G. (18) (Aberdeen) 1955/6 *E;* 1956/7 *W;* 1957/8 *I, H, Pol, Y, Par;* 1958/9 (Fulham) *W, I, E, G, Holl;* 1959/60 *I, W, E, Pol, Aust, H.*
Leighton, J. (14) (Aberdeen) 1982/3 *E/Germ, Switz, Bel, Switz, W, E, Can* (2); 1983/4 *U, Bel, I, W, E, F.*
Lennox, R. (10) (Celtic) 1966/7 *I, E, Rus;* 1967/8 *W, E;* 1968/9 *D, W, Aust, G, C.*
Leslie, L. (5) (Airdrieonians) 1960/1 *W, I, Eire* (2), *Czecho.*
Liddell, W. (28) (Liverpool) 1946/7 *W, I;* 1947/8 *I, W, E;* 1949/50 *W, E, Port, F;* 1950/1 *W, I, Aust, E;* 1951/2 *I, W, E, US, D, Swdn;* 1952/3 *W, I, E;* 1953/4 *W;* 1954/5 *Port, Y, Aust, H;* 1955/6 *I.*
Linwood, A. (1) (Clydebank) 1949/50 *W.*
Little, A. (1) (Rangers) 1952/3 *Swdn.*
Logie, J. (1) (Arsenal) 1952/3 *I.*
Long, H. (1) (Clyde) 1946/7 *I.*
Lorimer, P. (21) (Leeds United) 1969/70 *Aust;* 1970/1 *W, I;* 1971/2 *I, W, E;* 1972/3 *D* (2), *E* (2); 1973/4 *G, E, Bel, N, Z, Braz, Y;* 1974/5 *Sp;* 1975/6 *D* (2), *Ru.*

Macari, L. (24) (Celtic) 1971/2 *W, E, Y, Czecho, Braz;* 1972/3 *D,* (Manchester United) *F, W, I, E;* 1974/5 *Swdn, Port, W, E, Ru;* 1976/7 *I, E, Ch, Arg;* 1977/8 *E/Germ, W, Bulg;* 1978/9 *Per, Ir.*
Macaulay, A. (7) (Brentford) 1946/7 *E* (Arsenal); 1947/8 *I, W, E, Bel, Switz, F.*
Macdougall, E. (7) (Norwich City) 1974/5 *Swdn, Port, W, I, E;* 1975/6 *D, Ru.*
Mackay, D. (22) (Heart of Midlothian) 1956/7 *Sp;* 1957/8 *F;* 1958/9 *W, I,* (Tottenham Hotspur) *E, G;* 1959/60 *I, W, Pol, Aust, H, T;* 1960/1 *W, I, E;* 1962/3 *E,*

Aust, N; 1963/4 *I, N, W;* 1965/6 *I.*
Malpas, M. (1) (Dundee U.) 1983/4 *F.*
Martin, F. (7) (Aberdeen) 1953/4 *N* (2), *Aust, U;* 1954/5 *N, E, N.*
Martin, N. (3) (Hibernian) 1964/5 *Pol, Fin;* 1965/6 (Sunderland) *It.*
Martis, J. (1) (Motherwell) 1960/1 *W.*
Mason, J. (7) (Third Lanark) 1948/9 *W, I, E;* 1949/50 *I;* 1950/1 *I, Bel, Aust.*
Masson, D. (17) (Queens Park Rangers) 1975/6 *I, W, E;* 1976/7 *Fin, Czecho, W, I, E, Ch, Arg, Braz;* (Derby County) 1977/8 *E/Germ, Czecho, W, I, E;* 1978/9 *Per.*
Mathers, D. (1) (Partick Thistle) 1953/4 *Fin.*
McBride, J. (2) (Celtic) 1966/7 *W, I.*
McCalliog, J. (5) (Sheffield Wednesday) 1966/7 *E, Rus;* 1967/8 *I;* 1968/9 *D;* 1970/1 (Wolverhampton Wanderers) *Port.*
McCann, A. (5) (Motherwell) 1958/9 *G;* 1959/60 *I, W, E;* 1960/1 *E.*
McCloy, P. (4) (Rangers) 1972/3 *Switz, Braz, W, I.*
McColl, I. (14) (Rangers) 1949/50 *E, F;* 1950/1 *W, I, Bel;* 1956/7 *Y, I, W, E, Sp, Switz, G;* 1957/8 *I, E.*
McCreadie, E. (23) (Chelsea) 1964/5 *E, Sp, Pol, Fin;* 1965/6 *I, Pol, W, It, Port;* 1966/7 *E, Rus;* 1967/8 *I, W, E, Holl;* 1968/9 *D, C, Aust, G, W, I, E, C.*
MacDonald, A. (1) (Rangers) 1975/6 *Switz.*
MacDonald, J. (2) (Sunderland) 1955/6 *I, W.*
McFarlane, W. (1) (Heart of Midlothian) 1946/7 *Lux.*
McGarr, E. (2) (Aberdeen) 1969/70 *Eire, Aust.*
McGarvey, A. (1) (St Mirren) 1978/9 *Arg.*
McGarvey, F. (5) (Celtic) 1983/4 *U, Bel, E/Germ, I, W.*
McGhee, M. (4) (Aberdeen) 1982/3 *Can* (2); 1983/4 *I, E.*
McGrain, D. (62) (Celtic) 1972/3 *W, I, E, Switz, Braz;* 1973/4 *Czecho* (2); *G, W, E, Bel, N, Z, Braz, Y;* 1974/5 *Sp, Swdn, Port, W, I, E, Ru;* 1975/6 *D* (2), *Switz, I, W, E;* 1976/7 *Fin, Czecho, W, Swdn, W, I, E, Ch, Arg, Braz;* 1977/8 *E/Germ, Czecho;* 1979/80 *Bel, Port, I, W, E, Pol, H;* 1980/81 *Swdn, Port, Isr, I, Isr, W, I, E;* 1981/2 *Swdn, Holl, Sp, I, E, NZ, Rus.*
McGrory, J. (3) (Kilmarnock) 1964/5 *Fin, I;* 1965/6 *Port, Pol, H.*
McKay, D. (13) (Celtic) 1958/9 *E, G, Holl, Port;* 1959/60 *E, Pol, Aust, H, T;* 1960/1 *W, I;* 1961/2 *Czecho, I.*
McKean, R. (1) (Rangers) 1975/6 *Switz.*
McKenzie, J. (9) (Partick Thistle) 1953/4 *W, E, N, Fin, Aust, U;* 1954/5 *H, E;* 1955/6 *Aust.*
McKinnon, R. (28) (Rangers) 1965/6 *It, W, It, E, Holl, Braz;* 1966/7 *W, I, E;* 1967/8 *I, W, E, Holl;* 1968/9 *D, C, Aust, G;* 1969/70 *Eire, G, Aust, I, W, E;* 1970/1 *D, Bel, Port, D, Rus.*
McLaren, A. (4) (Preston North End) 1946/7 *E, Bel, Lux;* 1947/8 *W.*
McLean, G. (1) (Dundee) 1967/8 *Holl.*
McLean, T. (5) (Kilmarnock) 1968/9 *D, W;* 1969/70 *I, W;* 1970/1 (Rangers) *D.*
McLeish, A. (26) (Aberdeen) 1979/80 *Port, I, W, E, Pol, H;* 1980/81 *Swdn, Isr, I, Isr, I, E;* 1981/2 *Swdn, Sp, I, Braz*; 1982/3 *Bel, Switz, W, E, Can* (3); 1983/4 *U, Bel, E/Germ, I, W, E, F.*
McLeod, J. (4) (Hibernian) 1960/1 *E, Eire* (2), *Czecho.*
McLintock, F. (8) (Leicester City) 1962/3 *Eire, Sp;* 1964/5 (Arsenal) *I;* 1966/7 *Rus;* 1969/70 *I;* 1970/1 *W, I, E.*
McMillan, I. (6) (Airdrieonians and Rangers) 1951/2 *E, US, D;* 1954/5 *E;* 1955/6 *E;*

1960/1 *Czecho.*
McNaught, W. (5) (Raith Rovers) 1950/1 *W, I, Aust;* 1951/2 *E;* 1954/5 *I.*
McNeill, W. (28) (Celtic) 1960/1 *E, Eire* (2), *Czecho;* 1961/2 *Czecho, I, E, U;* 1962/3 *Eire, Sp;* 1963/4 *W, E, G;* 1964/5 *E, Sp, Pol, Fin;* 1965/6 *I, Pol;* 1966/7 *Rus;* 1967/8 *E;* 1968/9 *W, E, C;* 1969/70 *G;* 1971/2 *I, W, E.*
McPhail, J. (5) (Celtic) 1949/50 *W;* 1950/1 *W, I, Aust;* 1953/4 *I.*
McQueen, G. (30) (Leeds United) 1973/4 *Bel;* 1974/5 *Sp* (2), *Port, W, I, E, Ru;* 1975/6 *D;* 1976/7 *Czecho, W* (2), *I, E;* (Manchester U.) 1977/8 *E/Germ, Czecho, W* (2), *Bulg, I;* 1978/9 *Aust, N, Port, I, E, N;* 1979/80 *Per, Aust, Bel;* 1980/81 *W.*
McStay, P. (6) (Celtic) 1983/4 *U, Bel, E/Germ, I, W, E.*
Millar, W. (6) (Celtic) 1946/7 *W, E, Bel, Lux;* 1947/8 *I, W.*
Miller, J. (2) (Rangers) 1962/3 *Aust, Eire.*
Miller, W. (33) (Aberdeen) 1974/5 *Ru;* 1977/8 *Bulg;* 1979/80 *Bel, W, E, Pol, H;* 1980/81 *Swdn, Port, Isr, I, W, I, E;* 1981/2 *I, Port, Holl, Braz, Rus;* 1982/3 *E/Germ, Switz, Switz, W, E, Can* (3); 1983/4 *U, Bel, E/Germ, W, E, F.*
Mitchell, R. (2) (Newcastle United) 1950/1 *F, D.*
Mochan, H. (3) (Celtic) 1953/4 *N, Aust, U.*
Moir, W. (1) (Bolton Wanderers) 1949/50 *E.*
Moncur, R. (16) (Newcastle United) 1967/8 *Hol;* 1969/70 *Eire, I, W, E;* 1970/1 *D, Bel, Port, W, I, E, D;* 1971/2 *Per, I, W, E.*
Morgan, W. (21) (Burnley) 1967/8 *I;* (Manchester United) 1971/2 *Per, Y, Czecho, Braz;* 1972/3 *D* (2), *E, W, I, E, Switz, Braz;* 1973/4 *Czecho* (2), *G* (2), *I, Bel, Braz, Y.*
Morris, H. (1) (East Fife) 1949/50 *I.*
Mudie, J. (17) (Blackpool) 1956/7 *Y, I, W, E, Sp, Switz, G, Sp*; 1957/8 *I, Switz, W, E, H, Pol, Y, Par, F.*
Mulhall, G. (3) (Aberdeen) 1959/60 *I*; 1962/3 (Sunderland) *I*; 1963/4 *I.*
Munro, F. (9) (Wolverhampton Wanderers) 1970/1 *I, E, D, Rus*; 1974/5 *Swdn, W, I, E, Ru.*
Munro, J. (7) (St Mirren) 1978/9 *N, Arg*; 1979/80 *Per, Aust, Bel, W, E.*
Murdoch, R. (12) (Celtic) 1965/6 *It, W, It, E*; 1966/7 *I*; 1967/8 *I*; 1968/9 *C, G, W, I, E*; 1969/70 *Aust.*
Murray, J. (5) (Heart of Midlothian) 1957/8 *E, H, Pol, Y, F.*
Murray, S. (1) (Aberdeen) 1971/2 *Bel.*

Narey, D. (24) (Dundee United) 1976/7 *Swdn*; 1978/9 *Port, Arg*; 1979/80 *Port, I, Pol, H;* 1980/81 *W, E;* 1981/2 *Holl, W, E, NZ, Braz, Rus*; 1982/3 *E/Germ, Switz, Bel, I, W, E, Can* (3).
Nicholas, C. (8) (Celtic) 1982/3 *Switz, I, E, Can* (3); (Arsenal) 1983/4 *Bel, F.*

O'Hare, J. (13) (Derby County) 1969/70 *I, W, E*; 1970/1 *D, Bel, W, I*; 1971/2 *Port, Bel, Holl, Per, I, W.*
Ormond, W. (6) (Hibernian) 1953/4 *E, N, Fin, Aust, U*; 1958/9 *E.*
Orr, T. (2) (Morton) 1951/2 *I, W.*

Parker, A. (15) (Falkirk) 1954/5 *Port, Y, Aust*; 1955/6 *I, W, E, Aust*; 1956/7 *Y, I, W*; 1957/8 *I, Switz, W, E, Par.*
Parlane, D. (13) (Rangers) 1972/3 *W, Switz, Braz*; 1974/5 *Sp, Swdn, Port, W, I, E, Ru*; 1975/6 *D*; 1976/7 *W, Braz.*
Paton, A. (2) (Motherwell) 1951/2 *D, Swdn.*

Pearson, T. (2) (Newcastle United) 1946/7 *E, Bel.*
Penman, A. (1) (Dundee) 1965/6 *Holl.*
Pettigrew, W. (5) (Motherwell) 1975/6 *Switz, I, W*; 1976/7 *W, Swdn.*
Plenderleith, J. (1) (Manchester City) 1960/1 *I.*
Provan, D. (5) (Rangers) 1963/4 *I, N*; 1965/6 *It* (2), *Holl.*
Provan, D. (10) (Celtic) 1979/80 *Bel, Bel, Port, I;* 1980/81 *Isr, W, E;* 1981/2 *Swdn, Port, I.*

Quinn, P. (4) (Motherwell) 1960/1 *E, Eire* (2); 1961/2 *U.*

Redpath, W. (9) (Motherwell) 1948/9 *W, I*; 1950/1 *E, D, F, Bel, Aust*; 1951/2 *I, E.*
Reilly, L. (38) (Hibernian) 1948/9 *W, E, F*; 1949/50 *I, W, Switz, F*; 1950/1 *W, E, D, F, Bel, Aust*; 1951/2 *I, W, E, US, D, Swdn*; 1952/3 *W, I, E, Swdn*; 1953/4 *W*; 1954/5 *H* (2), *E, Port, Y, Aust*; 1955/6 *I, W, E, Aust*; 1956/7 *Y, I, W, E.*
Ring, T. (12) (Clydebank) 1952/3 *Swdn*; 1954/5 *W, I, H, E*; 1956/7 *E, Sp, Switz, G, Sp*; 1957/8 *I, Switz.*
Rioch, B. (24) (Derby County) 1974/5 *Port, W, I, E, Ru*; 1975/6 *D* (2), *Ru, I, W, E*; 1976/7 *Fin, Czecho, W,* (Everton) *W, I, E, Ch, Braz*; (Derby County) 1977/8 *Czecho, I, E*; 1978/9 *Per, Holl.*
Robb, D. (5) (Aberdeen) 1970/1 *Port, W, E, D, Rus.*
Robertson, A. (5) (Clydebank) 1954/5 *Port, Aust, H*; 1957/8 *Switz, Par.*
Robertson, H. (1) (Dundee) 1961/2 *Czecho.*
Robertson, J. (1) (Tottenham Hotspur) 1964/5 *W.*
Robertson, J. (26) (Nottingham Forest) 1977/8 *I*; 1978/9 *Ir, Port, N*; 1979/80 *Per, Aust, Bel, Bel, Port;* 1980/81 *Swdn, Port, Isr, I, Isr, I, E;* 1981/2 *Swdn, I, I, E, NZ, Braz, Rus*; 1982/3 *E/Germ, Switz;* (Derby Co.) 1983/4 *U, Bel.*
Robinson, B. (4) (Dundee) 1973/4 *G*;1974/5 *Swdn, I, Ru.*
Rough, A. (51) (Partick Thistle) 1975/6 *Switz, I, W, E*; 1976/7 *Fin, Czecho, W, Swdn, W, I, E, Ch, Arg, Braz*; 1977/8 *Czecho, W, I, E*; 1978/9 *Per, Ir, Holl, Aust, Port, W, N, Arg*; 1979/80 *Per, Aust, Bel, Bel, Port, W, E, Pol, H;* 1980/81 *Swdn, Port, Isr, I, Isr, W, E;* 1981/2 *Swdn, I, Holl, Sp, W, E, NZ, Braz, Rus.*
Rougvie, D. (1) (Aberdeen) 1983/4 *I.*
Rutherford, E. (1) (Rangers) 1947/8 *F.*

Schaedler, E. (1) (Hibernian) 1973/4 *G.*
Scott, A. (16) (Rangers) 1956/7 *Y, I, G*; 1957/8 *Switz, W*; 1958/9 *Port*; 1961/2 *Czecho, I, W, E, W* (Everton); 1963/4 *N, W*; 1964/5 *Fin*; 1965/6 *Port, Braz.*
Scott, A. (1) (Hibernian) 1965/6 *Holl.*
Scott, J. (2) (Dundee) 1970/1 *D, Rus.*
Scoular, J. (9) (Portsmouth) 1950/1 *D, I, Aust*; 1951/2 *E, US, D, Swdn*; 1952/3 *W, I.*
Shaw, D. (8) (Hibernian) 1946/7 *W, I*; 1947/8 *E, Bel, Switz, F*; 1948/9 *W, I.*
Shaw, J. (4) (Rangers) 1946/7 *E, Bel, Lux*; 1947/8 *I.*
Shearer, R. (4) (Rangers) 1960/1 *Eire* (2), *E, Czecho.*
Simpson, N. (2) (Aberdeen) 1982/3 *I*; 1983/4 *F.*
Simpson, R. (5) (Celtic) 1966/7 *E, Rus*; 1967/8 *I, E*; 1968/9 *Aust.*
Sinclair, J. (1) (Leicester City) 1965/6 *Port.*
Smith, D. (2) (Aberdeen) 1965/6 *Holl*; 1967/8 (Rangers) *Holl.*
Smith, E. (2) (Celtic) 1958/9 *Holl, Port.*
Smith, G. (19) (Hibernian) 1946/7 *I, E*; 1947/8 *W, Bel, Switz, F*; 1951/2 *E, US*;

1954/5 *Port, Y, Aust, H*; 1955/6 *I, E, W*; 1956/7 *E, Sp, Switz, Sp.*
Smith, J. (4) (Aberdeen) 1967/8 *Holl*; 1973/4 (Newcastle United) *G, I, W.*
Souness, G. (38) (Middlesbrough) 1974/5 *E/Germ, Sp, Swdn*; (Liverpool) 1977/8 *Bulg, W, E*; 1978/9 *Holl, Aust, N, W, I, E*; 1979/80 *Per, Aust, Bel, Port, I;* 1980/81 *Port, Isr, Isr;* 1981/2 *I, Port, Sp, W, E, NZ, Braz, Rus*; 1982/3 *E/Germ, Switz, Bel, Switz, W, E, Can* (3); 1983/4 *U, I, W.*
Stanton, P. (16) (Hibernian) 1965/6 *Holl*; 1968/9 *I*; 1969/70 *Eire, Aust*; 1970/1 *D, Bel, Port, D, Rus*; 1971/2 *Port, Bel, Holl, W*; 1972/3 *W, I*; 1973/4 *G.*
Steel, W. (30) (Morton) 1946/7 *E, Bel, Lux*; 1947/8 (Derby County) *I, W, E, F*; 1948/9 *W, I, E, F*; 1949/50 *I, W, E, Switz, Port, F* (Dundee); 1950/1 *W, I, Aust* (2), *E, D, F, Bel*; 1951/2 *W*; 1952/3 *W, I, E, Swdn.*
Stein, C. (20) (Rangers) 1968/9 *D, C, W, I, E, C*; 1969/70 *Eire, G, I, W, E*; 1970/1 *D, Bel, D, Rus*; 1971/2 *Czecho*; (Coventry City), *E, W, I, E.*
Stephen, J. (2) (Bradford City) 1946/7 *W*; 1947/8 *W.*
Stewart, D. (2) (Leeds United) 1977/8 *E/Germ*; 1978/9 *N.*
Stewart, J. (1) (Kilmarnock) 1976/7 *Ch.*
Stewart, R. (7) (West Ham U.) 1980/81 *W, I, E;* 1981/2 *I, Port, W*; 1983/4 *F.*
St John, I. (31) (Motherwell) 1958/9 *G*; 1959/60 *I, W, E, Pol, Aust*; 1960/1 *E*; 1961/2 (Liverpool) *Czecho, I, W, Czecho, E, W*; 1962/3 *W, I, E, N, Eire, Sp*; 1963/4 *I*; 1964/5 *E.*
Strachan, G. (28) (Aberdeen) 1979/80 *I, W, E, Pol, H;* 1980/81 *Swdn, Port;* 1981/2 *I, Port, Holl, Sp, NZ, Braz, Rus*; 1982/3 *E/Germ, Switz, Bel, Switz, I, W, E; Can* (3); 1983/4 *E/Germ, I, E, F.*
Sturrock, P. (14) (Dundee United) 1980/81 *W, I, E*; 1981/2 *Port, I, W, E*; 1982/3 *E/Germ, Switz, Bel*, Can (3); 1983/4 *W.*

Telfer, W. (1) (St Mirren) 1953/4 *W.*
Thomson, W. (8) (St Mirren) 1979/80 *I;* 1980/81 *I;* 1981/2 *Port*; 1982/3 *I*, Can (3); 1983/4 *E/Germ.*
Thornton, W. (7) (Rangers) 1946/7 *W*; 1947/8 *I, E*; 1948/9 *F*; 1951/2 *D, Swdn.*
Toner, W. (2) (Kilmarnock) 1958/9 *W, I.*
Turnbull, E. (8) (Hibernian) 1957/8 *Bel, Switz*; 1950/1 *Aust*; 1957/8 *H, Pol, Y, Par, F.*

Ure, I. (11) (Dundee) 1961/2 *W, Czecho*; 1962/3 *W, I, E, Aust, N, Sp,* (Arsenal); 1963/4 *I, N*; 1967/8 *I.*

Waddell, W. (17) (Rangers) 1946/7 *W*; 1948/9 *W, I, E, F*; 1949/50 *I, E*; 1950/1 *E, D, F, Bel, Aust*; 1951/2 *I, W*; 1953/4 *I*; 1954/5 *W, I.*
Wallace, I. (3) (Coventry City) 1977/8 *Bulg*; 1978/9 *Port, W.*
Wallace, W. (7) (Heart of Midlothian) 1964/5 *I*; 1965/6 *E, Holl*; 1966/7 (Celtic) *E, Rus*; 1967/8 *I*; 1968/9 *E.*
Wardhaugh, J. (2) (Heart of Midlothian) 1954/5 *H*; 1956/7 *I.*
Wark, J. (27) (Ipswich Town) 1978/9 *W, I, E, Arg*; 1979/80 *Per, Aust, Bel, Bel;* 1980/81 *Isr, I;* 1981/2 *Swdn, Holl, Sp, I, NZ, Braz, Rus*; 1982/3 *E/Germ, Switz, Switz, I, E*; 1983/4 *U, Bel, E/Germ,* (Liverpool) *E, F.*
Watson, J. (2) (Motherwell) 1947/8 *I*; 1953/4 *I.*
Watson, R. (1) (Motherwell) 1970/1 *Rus.*
Weir, A. (5) (Motherwell) 1959/60 *E, Pol, Aust, H, T.*

Weir, P. (6) (St Mirren) 1979/80 *I, W, Pol, H*; 1982/3 (Aberdeen) *Switz*; 1983/4 *I*.
White, J. (22) (Falkirk) 1958/9 *G, Holl, Port*; 1959/60 *I*, (Tottenham Hotspur) *W, Pol, Aust, T*; 1960/1 *W*; 1961/2 *Czecho, I, W, Czecho, E*; 1962/3 *W, I, E*; 1963/4 *I, N, W, E, G*.
Wilson, A. (1) (Portsmouth) 1953/4 *Fin*.
Wilson, D. (22) (Rangers) 1960/1 *W, I, E, Eire* (2), *Czecho;* 1961/2 *Czecho, I, W, E, U*; 1962/3 *W, E, Aust, N, Eire, Sp*; 1963/4 *E, G*; 1964/5 *I, E, Fin*.
Wilson, P. (1) (Celtic) 1974/5 *Sp*.
Wilson, R. (2) (Arsenal) 1971/2 *Port, Holl*.
Wood, G. (4) (Everton) 1978/9 *I, E, Arg;* 1981/2 (Arsenal) *I*.
Woodburn, W. (24) (Rangers) 1946/7 *E, Bel, Lux*; 1947/8 *I, W*; 1948/9 *Y, E, F*; 1949/50 *I, W, E, Port, F*; 1950/1 *W, I, Aust* (2), *E, D, F, Bel*; 1951/2 *I, W, E, US*.
Wright, T. (2) (Sunderland) 1952/3 *W, I, E*.

Yeats, R. (2) (Liverpool) 1964/5 *W*; 1965/6 *It*.
Yorston, H. (1) (Aberdeen) 1954/5 *W*.
Young, A. (9) (Heart of Midlothian) 1959/60 *F, Aust, H, E, T*; 1960/1 (Everton) *W, Eire*; 1965/6 *Port*.
Young, G. (53) (Rangers) 1946/7 *I, E, Bel, Lux*; 1947/8 *I, E, Bel, Switz, F*; 1948/9 *W, I, E, F*; 1949/50 *I, W, E, Switz, Port, F*; 1950/1 *W, I, Aust* (2), *E, D, F, Bel*; 1951/2 *I, W, E, US, D, Swdn*; 1952/3 *W, I, E, Swdn*; 1953/4 *I, W*; 1954/5 *W, I, Port, Y*; 1955/6 *I, W, E, Aust*; 1956/7 *Y, I, W, E, Sp, Switz*.
Younger, T. (24) (Hibernian) 1954/5 *Port, Y, Aust, H*; 1955/6 *I, W, E, Aust*; 1956/7 (Liverpool) *Y, I, N, E, Sp, Switz, G, Sp*; 1957/8 *I, Switz, W, E, H, Pol, W, Par*.

WALES

Allchurch, I. (68) (Swansea City) 1950/1 *E, I, Port, Switz*; 1951/2 *E, S, UK, I*; 1952/3 *S, E, I, F, Y*; 1953/4 *E, S, I, Aust*; 1954/5 *Y, S, E, I*; 1955/6 *E, S, Aust, I*; 1956/7 *S, E*; 1957/8 *Isr* (2), *I, H, Mex, Swdn, H, Braz*; 1958/9 (Newcastle United) *S, E, I*; 1959/60 *E, S*; 1960/1 *T, Sp* (2), *H*; 1961/2 *E, S, Braz* (2), *Mex*; 1962/3 (Cardiff City) *S, H, E, H, I*; 1963/4 *E*; 1964/5 *S, E, Gr, I, It, Rus*; 1965/6 (Swansea City) *E, Rus, S, D, Braz, Braz 'B', Ch*.
Allchurch, L. (11) (Swansea City) 1954/5 *I*; 1955/6 *Aust*; 1957/8 *E/Germ, S, Isr, I*; 1958/9 *S*; 1961/2 (Sheffield United) *S, I, Braz*; 1963/4 *E*.
Allen, B. (2) (Coventry City) 1950/1 *S, E*.

Baker, C. (7) (Cardiff City) 1957/8 *Mex*; 1959/60 *S, I*; 1960/1 *Eire, S, E*; 1961/2 *S*.
Baker, W. (1) (Cardiff City) 1947/8 *I*.
Barnes, W. (22) (Arsenal) 1947/8 *E, S, I*; 1948/9 *S, E, I*; 1949/50 *E, S, Bel, I*; 1950/1 *S, E, I, Port*; 1951/2 *E, S, UK, I*; 1953/4 *E, S*; 1954/5 *Y. S*.
Berry, G. (5) (Wolverhampton Wanderers) 1978/9 *G*; 1979/80 *Eire, G, T*; 1982/3 (Stoke City) *E*.
Bowen, D. (19) (Arsenal) 1954/5 *Y, S*; 1956/7 *I, Czecho, E/Germ*; 1957/8 *E/Germ, E, S, Isr* (2), *I, H, Mex, Swdn, H, Braz*; 1958/9 *S, E, I*.
Boyle, T. (2) (Crystal Palace) 1980/81 *Eire, S*.
Burgess, R. (32) (Tottenham Hotspur) 1946/7 *S, E, I*; 1947/8 *E, S*; 1948/9 *S, E, I, Port, Bel, Switz*; 1949/50 *E, S, Bel, I*; 1950/1 *S, I, Port, Switz*; 1951/2 *E, S, UK, I*; 1952/3 *S, E, I, F, Y*; 1953/4 *E, S, I, Aust*.

Burton, O. (9) (Norwich City) 1962/3 *H, I,* (Newcastle United); 1963/4 *E*; 1968/9 *It, E/Germ, S, E, I*; 1971/2 *Czecho.*

Cartwright, L. (6) (Coventry City) 1973/4 *E, S, I*; 1975/6 *S*; 1976/7 *G*; (Wrexham) 1978/9 *M.*

Charles, J. (38) (Leeds United) 1949/50 *I*; 1950/1 *Switz*; 1952/3 *I, F, Y*; 1953/4 *E, S, I, Aust*; 1954/5 *Y, S, E, I*; 1955/6 *E, S, Aust, I*; 1956/7 *S, E, I,* (Juventus Turin) *Czecho, E/Germ, Czecho*; 1957/8 *Isr* (2), *H, Mex, Swdn, H*; 1959/60 *S*; 1961/2 *E, Braz* (2), *Mex*; 1962/3 (Leeds United) *S,* (Cardiff City); 1963/4 *S*; 1964/5 *S, Rus.*

Charles, J. (14) (Swansea C.) 1980/81 *Czecho, T, S, Rus;* 1981/2 *Ic*; 1982/3 *N, Y, Bulg, S, I, Braz*; 1983/4 *Bulg, Y,* (Q.P.R.) *S.*

Charles, M. (31) (Swansea City) 1954/5 *I*; 1955/6 *E, S, Aust*; 1956/7 *E, I, Czecho, E/Germ, Czecho*; 1957/8 *E/Germ, E, S, Isr (2), H, Mex, Swdn, H, Braz*; 1958/9 *S, E,* (Arsenal) 1960/1 *I, Sp* (2), *H*; 1961/2 *E, S,* (Cardiff City) *I, Braz*; 1962/3 *S, H.*

Clarke, R. (22) (Manchester City) 1948/9 *E*; 1949/50 *S, Bel, I*; 1950/1 *S, E, I, Port, Switz*; 1951/2 *E, S, UK, I*; 1952/3 *S, E*; 1953/4 *E, S, I*; 1954/5 *Y, S, E*; 1955/6 *I.*

Crowe, V. (16) (Aston Villa) 1958/9 *E*; 1959/60 *E, I*; 1960/1 *Eire, S, E, I, Sp* (2), *H*; 1961/2 *E, S, Braz, Mex*; 1962/3 *H.*

Curtis, A. (30) (Swansea City) 1975/6 *E* (2), *S, I, Y* (2); 1976/7 *G, S, I*; 1977/8 *G, E, S*; 1978/9 *G, S, E, I, M*; 1979/80 *Eire, G, T;* 1981/2 *Czecho, Ic, Rus, Sp, E, S, I*; 1982/3 *N*; 1983/4 *Ru,* (Southampton) *S.*

Daniel, R. (21) (Arsenal) 1950/1 *E, I, Port*; 1951/2 *E, S, UK, I*; 1952/3 *S, E, I, F, Y*; 1953/4 (Sunderland) *E, S, I*; 1954/5 *E, I*; 1956/7 *S, E, I, Czecho.*

Davies, A. (4) (Manchester United) 1982/3 *I, Braz;* 1983/4 *E, I.*

Davies, D. (52) (Everton) 1974/5 *H, Lux, S, E, I*; 1975/6 *Y* (2), *E, I*; 1976/7 *G, S,* (2) *Czecho, E, I*; 1977/8 *K, S* (2), *Czecho, G, Ir, E, I*; (Wrexham) 1978/9 *M, T, G, S, E, I, M*; 1979/80 *Eire, G, T, E, S, I, Ic;* 1980/81 *T, Czecho, Eire, T, S, E, Rus;* 1981/2 *Czecho, Ic, Rus,* (Swansea C.) *Czecho, Ic, Rus, Sp, E, S, F*; 1982/3 *Y.*

Davies, G. (11) (Fulham) 1981/2 *Sp, F*; 1982/3 *E, Bulg, S, I, Braz*; 1983/4 *Ru, S, E, I.*

Davies, Reg (6) (Newcastle United) 1952/3 *S, E*; 1953/4 *E, S*; 1957/8 *E/Germ, E.*

Davies, Ron (29) (Norwich City) 1963/4 *I*; 1964/5 *E*; 1965/6 *Braz, Braz 'B', Ch*; 1966/7 (Southampton) *S, E, I*; 1967/8 *I, G*; 1968/9 *It, G, S, E, I*; 1969/70 *UK, E, S, I*; 1970/1 *Czecho, S, E, I*; 1971/2 *Ru, E, S, I*; 1973/4 (Portsmouth) *E.*

Davies, R. Wyn (34) (Bolton Wanderers) 1963/4 *E*; 1964/5 *S, D, E, Gr, I, Rus*; 1965/6 *E, Rus, S, D, I, Braz, Braz 'B', Ch*; 1966/7 *S* (Newcastle United) *E*; 1967/8 *S, I, G*; 1968/9 *It, S, E, I*; 1969/70 *E/Germ*; 1970/1 *Ru, Czecho*; 1971/2 (Manchester City) *E, S, I*; 1972/3 (Manchester United) *E, S, I*; 1973/4 *Pol.*

Davis, G. (4) (Wrexham) 1977/8 *I, E*; 1979/80 *T, Ic.*

Deacy, T. (11) (PSV Eindhoven) 1976/7 *Czecho, S, E, I*; 1977/8 *K, S* (2), *Czecho, G, I*; 1978/9 *T.*

Derrett, S. (4) (Cardiff City) 1968/9 *G, S*; 1969/70 *It*; 1970/1 *Fin.*

Durban, A. (26) (Derby County) 1966/7 *I*; 1967/8 *E, S, I, G*; 1968/9 *G, E/Germ, S, E, I*; 1969/70 *E/Germ, It, E, S, I*; 1970/1 *Ru, Czecho, S, E, I, Fin*; 1971/2 *Fin, Czecho, E, S, I.*

Dwyer, A. (8) (Wrexham) 1977/8 *E, S, I*; 1978/9 *T, S, E, I*; 1979/80 *G.*

Edwards, I. (4) (Chester) 1977/8 *K*; 1978/9 *M, G*; 1979/80 *T.*

Edwards, G. (12) (Birmingham City) 1946/7 *S, E, I*; 1947/8 *E, S, I*(Cardiff City);

1948/9 *I, Port, Bel, Switz*; 1949/50 *E, S.*
Edwards, T. (2) (Charlton Athletic) 1956/7 *I, E/Germ.*
Emanuel, J. (2) (Bristol City) 1972/3 *E, I.*
England, M. (44) (Blackburn Rovers) 1961/2 *I, Braz, Mex*; 1962/3 *H, I*; 1963/4 *E, S, I*; 1964/5 *D, E, Gr* (2), *I, It, Rus*; 1965/6 *E, Rus, S, D, I*; 1966/7 (Tottenham Hotspur) *S, E*; 1967/8 *E, I, G*; 1968/9 *E/Germ*; 1969/70 *UK, E/Germ, It, E, S, I*; 1970/1 *Ru*; 1971/2 *Fin, E, S, I*; 1972/3 *E* (2), *S, E*; 1973/4 *Pol*; 1974/5 *H, Lux.*
Evans, I. (13) (Crystal Palace) 1975/6 *Aust, E, Y* (2), *E, I*; 1976/7 *G, S* (2), *Czecho, E, I*; 1977/8 *K.*
Evans, R. (1) (Swansea City) 1963/4 *I.*

Felgate D. (1) (Lincoln C.) 1983/4 *Ru.*
Flynn, B. (65) (Burnley) 1974/5 *Lux* (2), *H, S, E, I*; 1975/6 *Aust, E* (2), *Y* (2), *I*; 1976/7 *G, S, Czecho, S, E, I*; 1977/8 *K* (2), *S* (2), *Czecho, G, E, I*; (Leeds United) 1978/9 *M, T, S, E, I, M*; 1979/80 *Eire, G, E, S, I, Ic;* 1980/81 *T, Czecho, Eire, T, S, E, Rus;* 1981/2 *Czecho, Rus, E, S, I, F*; 1982/3 *N,* (Burnley) *Y, E, Bulg, S, I, Braz*; 1983/4 *N, Ru, Bulg, Y, S, N, Isr.*
Ford, T. (38) (Swansea City) 1946/7 *S,* (Aston Villa) *I*; 1947/8 *S, I*; 1948/9 *S, E, I, Port, Bel, Switz;* 1949/50 *E, S, Bel, I*; 1950/1 *S,* (Sunderland), *E, I, Port, Switz*; 1951/2 *E, S, UK, I*; 1952/3 *S, E, I, F, Y* (Cardiff City); 1953/4 *Aust*; 1954/5 *Y, S, E, I*; 1955/6 *E, S, Aust, I, I*; 1956/7 *S.*
Foulkes, W. (11) (Newcastle United) 1951/2 *E, S, UK, I*; 1952/3 *S, E, F, Y*; 1953/4 *E, S, I.*

Giles, D. (12) (Wrexham) 1979/80 *E, S, I, Ic;* 1980/81 (Swansea City) *T, Czecho, T, E, Rus;* 1981/2 (Crystal Palace) *Sp*; 1982/3 *I, Braz.*
Godfrey, B. (3) (Preston North End) 1963/4 *I*; 1964/5 *D, It.*
Green, C. (15) (Birmingham City) 1964/5 *It, Rus*; 1965/6 *E, Rus, S, Braz, Braz 'B'*; 1966/7 *E*; 1967/8 *E, S, I, G*; 1968/9 *It, S, I.*
Griffiths, A. (17) (Wrexham) 1970/1 *Czecho*; 1974/5 *Aust, H* (2), *Lux* (2), *E, I*; 1975/6 *Aust, E* (2), *Y* (2), *S, I*; 1976/7 *G, S.*
Griffiths, H. (1) (Swansea City) 1952/3 *I.*
Griffiths, M. (11) (Leicester City) 1946/7 *I*; 1948/9 *Port, Bel*; 1949/50 *E, S, Bel*; 1950/1 *E, I, Port, Switz*; 1953/4 *Aust.*

Harrington, A. (11) (Cardiff City) 1955/6 *I*; 1956/7 *S, E*; 1957/8 *S, Isr* (2), *I*; 1960/1 *S, E*; 1961/2e, S.
Harris, C. (19) (Leeds United) 1975/6 *S, E*; 1977/8 *G, E, S, I*; 1978/9 *M, T, G, M*; 1979/80 *I;* 1980/81 *T, Czecho, Eire, T, S, E, Rus;* 1981/2 *Czecho, Ic.*
Harris, W. (6) (Middlesbrough) 1953/4 *Aust*; 1956/7 *E/Germ, Czecho*; 1957/8 *E/Germ, E, S.*
Hennessey, T. (39) (Birmingham City) 1961/2 *I, Braz* (2); 1962/3 *S, H, E, H*; 1963/4 *E, S*; 1964/5 *S, D, E, Gr, Rus*; 1965/6 *E, Rus,* (Nottingham Forest), *S, D, I, Braz, Braz 'B', Ch*; 1966/7 *S, E*; 1967/8 *E, S, I*; 1968/9 *G, E/Germ*; 1969/70 *UK, E/Germ* (Derby County), *E, S, I*; 1971/2 *Fin, Czecho, E, S*; 1972/3 *E.*
Hewitt, R. (5) (Cardiff City) 1957/8 *Isr, I, Swdn, H, Braz.*
Hill, M. (2) (Ipswich Town) 1971/2 *Czecho, Ru.*

Hockey, T. (9) (Sheffield United) 1971/2 *Fin, Ru*; 1972/3 *E* (1), (Norwich City), *Pol, S, E, I*; 1973/4 (Aston Villa) *Pol.*
Hodges, G. (2) (Wimbledon) 1983/4*N, Isr.*
Holden A. (1) (Chester C.) 1983/4 *Isr.*
Hole, B. (30) (Cardiff City) 1962/3 *I*; 1963/4 *I*; 1964/5 *S, D, E, Gr* (2), *I, It, Rus*; 1965/6 *E, Rus, S, D, I, Braz 'B', Ch*; 1966/7 (Blackburn Rovers) *S, E, I*; 1967/8 *E, S, I, G*; 1968/9 (Aston Villa) *It, G, E/Germ*; 1969/70 *It*; (Swansea City) 1970/1 *Ru.*
Hollins, D. (11) (Newcastle United) 1961/2 *Braz, Mex*; 1962/3 *H, I*; 1963/4 *E*; 1964/5 *Gr, I, It;* 1965/6 *S, D, Braz.*
Hopkins, J. (11) (Fulham) 1982/3 *I, Braz*; 1983/4 *N, Ru, Bulg, Y, S, E, I, N, Isr.*
Hopkins, M. (34) (Tottenham Hotspur) 1955/6 *I*; 1956/7 *S, E, I, Czecho, E/Germ, Czecho*; 1957/8 *E/Germ, E, S, Isr* (2), *I, H, Mex, Swdn, H, Braz*; 1958/9 *S, E, I*; 1959/60 *E, S*; 1960/1 *I, Sp* (2), *H*; 1961/2 *I, Braz* (2), *Mex*; 1962/3 *S, H, I.*
Howells, R. (2) (Cardiff City) 1953/4 *E, S.*
Hughes, I. (4) (Luton Town) 1950/1 *E, I, Port, Switz.*
Hughes, M. (2) (Manchester U.) 1983/4 *E, I.*
Hughes, W. (3) (Birmingham City) 1946/7 *S, E, I.*
Hughes, W. A. (5) (Blackburn Rovers) 1948/9 *E, I, Port, Bel, Switz.*
Humphreys, J. (1) (Everton) 1946/7 *I.*

Jackett, K. (12) (Watford) 1982/3 *N, Y, E, Bulg, S*; 1983/4 *N, Ru, Y, S, I, N, Isr.*
James, G. (9) (Blackpool) 1965/6 *Braz, Braz 'B', Ch*; 1966/7 *I*; 1967/8 *S*; 1970/1 *Czecho, S, E, I.*
James, L. (60) (Burnley) 1971/2 *Czecho, Rus, S*; 1972/3 *E* (2), *Pol, S, E, I*; 1973/4 *Pol, E, S, I*; 1974/5 *Aust, H* (2), *Lux* (2), *S, E, I*; 1975/6 *Aust, E, S, Y* (2), *I*; (Derby County) 1976/7 *G, S, Czecho, S, E, I*; 1977/8 *K* (2) *G* (Swansea City); 1978/9 *M, T, S, E, I, M*; 1979/80 *G, E, S, I, Ic;* 1980/81 *T, Eire, T, S, E;* 1981/2 *Czecho, Ic, Rus, E, S, I, F*; 1982/3 (Sunderland) *E.*
James, R. (20) (Swansea C.) 1981/2 *Czecho, Ic, Sp, E, S, I, F*; 1982/3 *N, Y, E, Bulg*; (Stoke C.) 1983/4 *N, Ru, Bulg, Y, S, E, I, N, Isr.*
Jarvis, A. (3) (Hull City) 1966/7 *S, E, I.*
Johnson, M. (1) (Swansea City) 1963/4 *I.*
Jones, Barrie (14) (Swansea City) 1962/3 *S, H, E, I*; 1963/4 *S, I*; 1964/5 (Plymouth Argyle) *D*; 1968/9 (Cardiff City) *G, E/Germ, S, E, I*; 1969/70 *UK.*
Jones, Bryn (4) (Arsenal) 1946/7 *S, I*; 1947/8 *E*; 1948/9 *S.*
Jones, C. (59) (Swansea City) 1953/4 *Aust*; 1955/6 *E, S, Aust, I*; 1956/7 *S, E, J, Czecho, E/Germ, Czecho*; 1957/8 *E/Germ, E, S, Isr* (2), (Tottenham Hotspur), *I, H, Mex, Swdn, H, Braz*; 1958/9 *I*; 1959/60 *E, S, I*; 1960/1 *Eire, S, E, I, Sp, H*; 1961/2 *E, S, I, Braz* (2), *Mex*; 1962/3 *S, H, I*; 1963/4 *E, S, I*; 1964/5 *S, D, E, Gr* (2), *I, It, Rus*; 1966/7 *S, E*; 1967/8 *E, S, G*; 1968/9 (Fulham) *It*; 1969/70 *UK.*
Jones, D. (11) (Norwich City) 1975/6 *E, S*; 1977/8 *S, Czecho, G, E*; 1979/80 *Eire, G, T, E, I, Ic.*
Jones, E. (4) (Swansea City) 1947/8 *S, E* (Tottenham Hotspur); 1948/9 *S, E.*
Jones, J. (55) (Liverpool) 1975/6 *Aust, E, S*; 1976/7 *G, S* (2), *Czecho, E, I*; 1977/8 *K* (2), *S* (2), *Czecho, G, E, I*; (Wrexham) 1978/9 *M, T, G, S, E, M*; 1979/80 *E, S;* 1980/81 *T, Eire, T, S, E, Rus;* 1981/2 *Czecho, Ic, Rus, Sp, E, S, I, F*; 1982/3 *N,* (Chelsea) *Y, E, Bulg, S, I, Braz*; 1983/4 *N, Ru, Bulg, Y, S, E, I, N, Isr.*

Jones, K. (1) (Aston Villa) 1949/50 *S.*
Jones, T. G. (13) (Everton) 1946/7 *S, E*; 1947/8 *E, S, I*; 1948/9 *E, I, Port, Bel, Switz*; 1949/50 *E, S, Bel.*
Jones, W. (1) (Bristol Rovers) 1970/1 *Fin.*

Kelsey, J. (41) (Arsenal) 1953/4 *I, Aust*; 1954/5 *Y, S, I*; 1955/6 *E, S, Aust, I*; 1956/7 *S, E, I, Czecho, E/Germ, Czecho*; 1957/8 *E, S, Isr* (2), *I, H, Mex, Swdn, H, Braz*; 1958/9 *S, E*; 1959/60 *E, S, I*; 1960/1 *S, E, I, Sp* (2), *H*; 1961/2 *E, S, I, Braz* (2).
King, J. (1) (Swansea City) 1954/5 *E.*
Kinsey, N. (7) (Norwich City) 1950/1 *I, Port, Switz*; 1951/2 *E*; 1953/4 (Birmingham City) *I*; 1955/6 *E, S.*
Krzywicki, R. (8) (West Bromwich Albion) 1969/70 *E/Germ, It,* (Huddersfield Town) *E, S, I*; 1970/1 *Ru, Fin*; 1971/2 *Czecho.*

Lambert, R. (5) (Liverpool) 1946/7 *S*; 1947/8 *E*; 1948/9 *Port, Bel, Switz.*
Lea, C. (2) (Ipswich Town) 1964/5 *I, It.*
Leek, L. (13) (Leicester City) 1960/1 *S, E, I, Sp* (2), *H*; 1961/2 (Newcastle United) *S,* (Birmingham City) *Braz, Mex*; 1962/3 *E*; 1964/5 *S, Gr* (2).
Lever, A. (1) (Leicester City) 1952/3 *S.*
Lewis, D. (1) (Swansea C.) 1982/3 *Braz.*
Lloyd, B. (3) (Wrexham) 1975/6 *Aust, S, E.*
Lovell, S. (1) (Crystal Palace) 1981/2 *Rus.*
Lowndes, S. (2) (Newport Co.) 1982/3 *S, Braz.*
Lowrie, G. (4) (Coventry City) 1947/8 *E, S, I*; 1948/9 (Newcastle United) *Port.*
Lucas, M. (4) (Leyton Orient) 1961/2 *I, Mex*; 1962/3 *S, E.*
Lucas, W. (7) (Swansea City) 1948/9 *S, I, Port, Bel, Switz*; 1949/50 *E*; 1950/1 *E.*

Mahoney, J. (50) (Stoke City) 1967/8 *E*; 1968/9 *E/Germ*; 1970/1 *Czecho*; 1972/3 *E* (2), *Pol, S, E, I*; 1973/4 *Pol, E, S, I*; 1974/5 *Aust, H* (2), *Lux* (2), *S, E, I*; 1975/6 *Aust, Y* (2), *E, I*; 1976/7 *G, Czecho, S, E, I*; 1977/8 *K* (2), *S*(2), *Czecho, E, I*; (Middlesbrough) 1978/9 *G, S, E, I, M*; 1979/80 *Eire, G, T;* 1981/2 (Swansea C.) *Ic Rus*; 1982/3 *Y, E.*
Marustik, C. (6) (Swansea C.) 1981/2 *Sp, E, S, I, F*; 1982/3 *N.*
Medwin, T. (30) (Swansea City) 1952/3 *I, F, Y*; 1956/7 (Tottenham Hotspur) *S, E, I, Czecho, E/Germ, Czecho*; 1957/8 *E, S, Isr* (2), *I, H, Mex, H, Braz*; 1958/9 *S, E, I*; 1959/60 *E, S, I*; 1960/1 *Eire, S, E, Sp*; 1962/3 *H, E.*
Mielczarek, R. (1) (Rotherham United) 1970/1 *Fin.*
Millington, A. (21) (West Bromwich Albion) 1962/3 *S, H, E*; 1964/5 (Crystal Palace) *E, Rus*; 1965/6 (Peterborough United) *Braz 'B', Ch*; 1966/7 *E, I*; 1967/8 *I, G*; 1968/9 *It, E/Germ*; 1969/70 (Swansea City) *E, S, I*; 1970/1 *Czecho, Fin*; 1971/2 *Fin, Czecho, Ru.*
Moore, G. (21) (Cardiff City) 1959/60 *E, S, I*; 1960/1 *Eire, Sp*; 1961/2 (Chelsea) *Braz*; 1962/3 *H, I*; (Manchester United) 1963/4 *S, I*; (Northampton Town) 1965/6 *I, Ch*; 1968/9 (Charlton Athletic) *S, E, I*; 1969/70 *UK, It, E, S, I*; 1970/1 *Ru.*
Morris, W. (5) (Burnley) 1946/7 *I*; 1948/9 *E*; 1951/2 *S, UK, I.*

Nardiello, D. (2) (Coventry City) 1977/8 *Czecho, G.*

Nicholas, P. (31) (Crystal Palace) 1978/9 *M*; 1979/80 *Eire, G, T, E, S, I, Ic;* 1980/81 *T, Czecho, Eire,* (Arsenal) *T, S, E, Rus;* 1981/2 *Czecho, Ic, Rus, Sp, E, S, I, F*; 1982/3 *Y, Bulg, S, I*; (Crystal Palace) 1983/4 *N, Bulg, N, Isr.*
Nurse, M. (12) (Swansea City) 1959/60 *E, I*; 1960/1 *Eire, S, E, I, Sp* (2), *H*; 1962/3 (Middlesbrough) *H, E*; 1963/4 *S.*

O'Sullivan, P. (3) (Brighton & Hove Albion) 1972/3 *S*; 1975/6 *S*; 1978/9 *M.*

Page, M. (27) (Birmingham City) 1970/1 *Fin*; 1971/2 *S, I*; 1972/3 *E* (2), *I*; 1973/4 *S, I*; 1974/5 *H, Lux, S, E, I*; 1975/6 *E* (2), *Y* (2), *I*; 1976/7 *G, S*; 1977/8 *K* (2), *G, E, S*; 1978/9 *M, G.*
Palmer, D. (3) (Swansea City) 1956/7 *Czecho*; 1957/8 *E/Germ, E.*
Parry, J. (1) (Swansea City) 1950/1 *S.*
Pascoe, C. (2) (Swansea C.) 1983/4 *N, Isr.*
Paul, R. (33) (Swansea City) 1948/9 *S, E, I, Port, Switz*; 1949/50 *E, S, Bel, I*; (Manchester City) 1950/1 *S, E, I, Port, Switz*; 1951/2 *E, S, UK, I*; 1952/3 *S, E, I, F, Y*; 1953/4 *E, S, I*; 1954/5 *Y, S, E*; 1955/6 *E, S, Aust, I.*
Phillips, D. (3) (Plymouth Arg.) 1983/4 *E, I, N.*
Phillips, J. (4) (Chelsea) 1972/3 *E*; 1973/4 *E*; 1974/5 *H*; 1977/8 *K.*
Phillips, L. (58) (Cardiff City) 1970/1 *Czecho, S, E, I*; 1971/2 *Czecho, Ru, S, I*; 1972/3 *E*; 1973/4 *Pol, I*; 1974/5 *Aust,* (Aston Villa) *H* (2), *Lux* (2), *S, E, I*; 1975/6 *Aust, E* (2), *Y* (2), *I*; 1976/7 *G, S, Czecho, S, E*; 1977/8 *K* (2), *S* (2), *Czecho, G, E*; 1978/9 *M, T, G,* (Swansea City) *S, E, I, M*; 1979/80 *Eire, G, T, S, I, Ic;* 1980/81 *T, Czecho, T, S, E, Rus;* 1981/2 (Charlton Ath.) *Czecho, Rus.*
Pontin, K. (2) (Cardiff City) 1979/80 *E, S.*
Powell, A. (8) (Leeds United) 1946/7 *S, E*; 1947/8 *E, S, I*; 1948/9 (Everton) *E*; 1949/50 *Bel*; 1950/1 (Birmingham City) *S.*
Powell, D. (11) (Wrexham) 1967/8 *G*; 1968/9 (Sheffield United) *It, G, S, E, I*; 1969/70 *E/Germ, E, S, I*; 1970/1 *Ru.*
Powell, J. (8) (Queen's Park Rangers) 1946/7 *E*; 1947/8 *E, S*; 1948/9 (Aston Villa) *Bel*; 1949/50 *S, Bel*; 1950/1 *S.*
Price, P. (25) (Luton Town) 1979/80 *E, S, I, Ic;* 1980/81 *T, Czecho, Eire, T, S, E, Rus;* 1981/2 (Tottenham H.) *Rus, Sp, F*; 1982/3 *N, Y, E, Bulg, S, I*; 1983/4 *N, Ru, Bulg, Y, S.*
Pring, K. (3) (Rotherham United) 1965/6 *D, Ch*; 1966/7 *I.*

Rankmore, F. (1) (Peterborough United) 1965/6 *Ch.*
Ratcliffe, K. (17) (Everton) 1980/81 *Czecho, Eire, T, S, E, Rus;* 1981/2 *Czecho, Ic, Rus, Sp, E*; 1982/3 *Y, E, Bulg, S, I, Braz*; 1983/4 *N, Ru, Bulg, Y, S, E, I, N, Isr.*
Reece, G. (29) (Sheffield United) 1965/6 *E, Rus, S, I*; 1966/7 *S*; 1969/70 *UK, It*; 1970/1 *S, E, I, Fin*; 1971/2 *Fin, Ru, E, S, I*; (Cardiff City) 1972/3 *E, I*; 1973/4 *Pol, E, S, I*; 1974/5 *Aust, H* (2), *Lux* (2), *S, I.*
Reed, W. (2) (Ipswich Town) 1954/5 *Y, S.*
Rees, A. (1) (Birmingham C.) 1983/4 *N.*
Rees, R. (37) (Coventry City) 1964/5 *S, D, E, Gr* (2), *I, It, Rus*; 1965/6 *E, Rus, S, D, I, Braz, Braz 'B', Ch*; 1966/7 *E, I*; 1967/8 *E, S, I* (West Bromwich Albion), *G*; 1968/9 *It,* (Nottingham Forest) *G, E/Germ, S*; 1969/70 *UK, E/Germ, It, E, S, I*; 1970/1 *Ru,*

Czecho, Fin; 1971/2 *Czecho, Ru.*
Rees, W. (4) (Cardiff City) 1948/9 *I, Bel, Switz,* (Tottenham Hotspur); 1949/50 *I.*
Richards, S. (1) (Cardiff City) 1946/7 *E.*
Roberts, D. (17) (Oxford United) 1972/3 *Pol, E, I*; 1973/4 *E, S*; 1974/5 *Aust,* (Hull City) *Lux, I*; 1975/6 *Y, S, I*; 1976/7 *E, I*; 1977/8 *K* (2), *S, I.*
Roberts, J. (21) (Arsenal) 1970/1 *S, E, I, Fin*; 1971/2 *Fin, E, I*; 1972/3 (Birmingham City) *E, Pol, S, E, I*; 1973/4 *Pol, E, S, I*; 1974/5 *Aust, H, S, E*; 1975/6 *S.*
Roberts, J. (1) (Bolton Wanderers) 1948/9 *Bel.*
Roberts, P. (4) (Portsmouth) 1973/4 *E*; 1974/5 *Aust, H, Lux.*
Rodrigues, P. (40) (Cardiff City) 1964/5 *Gr* (2), *I*; 1965/6 *E, Rus, S, D,* (Leicester City), *I, Braz, Braz 'B', Ch*; 1966/7 *S*; 1967/8 *E, S, I*; 1968/9 *E/Germ, E, I*; 1969/70 *UK, E/Germ, E, S, I*; (Sheffield Wednesday) 1970/1 *Ru, Czecho, S, E, I*; 1971/2 *Fin, Czecho, Ru, E, I*; 1972/3 *E* (2), *Pol, S, E, I*; 1973/4 *Pol.*
Rouse, V. (1) (Crystal Palace) 1958/9 *I.*
Rowley, T. (1) (Tranmere Rovers) 1958/9 *I.*
Rush, I. (19) (Liverpool) 1979/80 *S, I;* 1980/81 *E;* 1981/2 *Rus, E, S, I, F*; 1982/3 *N, Y, E, Bulg*; 1983/4 N, Ru, Bulg, Y, S, E, I.

Sayer, P. (7) (Cardiff City) 1976/7 *Czecho, S, E, I*; 1977/8 *K* (2), *S.*
Scrine, F. (2) (Swansea City) 1949/50 *E, I.*
Sear, C. (1) (Manchester City) 1962/3 *E.*
Sherwood, A. (41) (Cardiff City) 1946/7 *E*; 1947/8 *S, I*; 1948/9 *S, E, I, Port, Switz*; 1949/50 *E, S, Bel, I*; 1950/1 *S, E, I, Port, Switz*; 1951/2 *E, S, UK, I*; 1952/3 *S, E, I, F, Y*; 1953/4 *E, S, I, Aust*; 1954/5 *Y, S, E, I*; 1955/6 *S, E, Aust, I*; 1955/6 *S, E, Aust, I*; 1956/7 (Newport County) *S, E.*
Shortt, W. (12) (Plymouth Argyle) 1946/7 *I*; 1949/50 *Bel, I*; 1951/2 *E, S, UK, I*; 1952/3 *S, E, I, F, Y.*
Showers, D. (2) (Cardiff City) 1974/5 *E, I.*
Sidlow, C. (7) (Liverpool) 1946/7 *S, E*; 1947/8 *E, S, I*; 1948/9 *S*; 1949/50 *E.*
Slatter, N. (3) (Bristol Rovers) 1982/3 *S*; 1983/4 *N, Isr.*
Smallman, D. (7) (Wrexham) 1973/4 *E, S, I*; 1974/5 *H, E, I*; 1975/6 (Everton) *Aust.*
Southall, N. (16) (Everton) 1981/2 *I*; 1982/3 *N, E, Bulg, S, I, Braz*; 1983/4 *N, Ru, Bulg, Y, S, E, I, N, Isr.*
Sprake, G. (37) (Leeds United) 1963/4 *S, I*; 1964/5 *S, D, Gr*; 1965/6 *E, Rus, I*; 1966/7 *S*; 1967/8 *E, S*; 1968/9 *G, S, E, I*; 1969/70 *UK, E/Germ, It*; 1970/1 *Ru, S, E, I*; 1971/2 *Fin, E, S, I*; 1972/3 *E* (2), *Pol, S, I*; 1973/4 (Birmingham City) *Pol, S, I*; 1974/5 *Aust, H, Lux.*
Stansfield, G. (1) (Cardiff City) 1948/9 *S.*
Stevenson, B. (15) (Leeds United) 1977/8 *I*; 1978/9 *M, T, S, E, I, M*; 1979/80 *G, T, Ic;* 1981/2 *Czecho,* (Birmingham C.) *Sp, S, I, F.*
Stevenson, N. (4) (Swansea C.) 1981/2 *E, S, I*; 1982/3 *N.*
Stitfall, R. (2) (Cardiff City) 1952/3 *E*; 1956/7 *Czecho.*
Sullivan, D. (17) (Cardiff City) 1952/3 *I, F, Y*; 1953/4 *I*; 1954/5 *E, S*; 1956/7 *S, E*; 1957/8 *I, H, Swdn, H, Braz*; 1958/9 *S, I*; 1959/60 *E, I.*

Tapscott, D. (14) (Arsenal) 1953/4 *Aust*; 1954/5 *Y, S, E, I*; 1955/6 *E, S, Aust, I*; 1956/7 *I, Czecho, E/Germ*; 1958/9 (Cardiff City) *E, I.*
Thomas, D. (2) (Swansea City) 1956/7 *Czecho*; 1957/8 *E/Germ.*
Thomas, M. (39) (Wrexham) 1976/7 *G, S* (2), *I*; 1977/8 *K, S, Czecho, E*; 1978/9 *M,*

T, G; (Manchester United) 1979/80 *Eire, G, T, E, S, I;* 1980/81 *Czecho, S, E, Rus;* 1981/2 (Everton) *Czecho,* (Brighton) *Rus, Sp, E, S, I*; 1982/3 (Stoke City) *N, Y, E, Bulg, S, I, Braz*: 1983/4 *Ru, Bulg, Y,* (Chelsea) *S, E.*

Thomas, R. (50) (Swindon Town) 1966/7 *I*; 1967/8 *G*; 1968/9 *It, G, E, I*; 1969/70 *UK, E/Germ, It, E, S, I*; 1970/1 *Ru, Czecho, S, E, I*; 1971/2 *Fin, Czecho, Ru, E, S, I*; 1972/3 *E* (2), *Pol, S, E, I*; 1973/4 (Derby County) *Pol, E, S, I*; 1974/5 *H* (2), *Lux* (2), *S, E, I*; 1975/6 *Aust, Y, E*; 1976/7 *S, Czecho, E, I*; 1977/8 *K, S, Czecho.*

Thomas, S. (4) (Fulham) 1947/8 *E, S, I*; 1948/9 *S.*

Toshack, J. (39) (Cardiff City) 1968/9 *G, E/Germ, S, E, I*; 1969/70 *UK, E/Germ, It*; 1970/1 *S, E, I, Fin*; 1971/2 (Liverpool) *Fin, E*; 1972/3 *E* (2), *Pol, S, E*; 1974/5 *Aust, H* (2), *Lux* (2), *S, E*; 1975/6 *Y* (2), *E*; 1976/7 *S*; 1977/8 *K* (2), *S, Czecho*; (Swansea City) 1978/9 *S, E, I, M*; 1979/80 *G.*

Vaughan, N. (9) (Newport County) 1982/3 *Y, Braz*; 1983/4 *N Ru Bulg, Y,* (Cardiff C.) *I, N, Isr.*

Vearncombe, G. (2) (Cardiff City) 1957/8 *E/Germ*; 1960/1 *Eire.*

Vernon, R. (32) (Blackburn Rovers) 1956/7 *I, Czecho, E/Germ, Czecho;* 1957/8 *E/Germ, E, S, Swdn*; 1958/9 *S*; 1959/60 (Everton) *I*; 1960/1 *Eire, S, E*; 1961/2 *I, Braz* (2), *Mex*; 1962/3 *S, H, E*; 1963/4 *E, S*; 1964/5 (Stoke City) *Gr, I, It*; 1965/6 *E, Rus, S, D, I*; 1966/7 *I*; 1967/8 *E.*

Villars, A. (2) (Cardiff City) 1973/4 *E, S.*

Walley, T. (1) (Watford) 1970/1 *Czecho.*

Walsh, I. (18) (Crystal Palace) 1979/80 *Eire, T, E, S, Ic;* 1980/81 *T, Czecho, Eire, T, S, E, Rus;* 1981/2 *Czecho, Ic,* (Swansea C.) *Sp, S, I, F.*

Ward, D. (2) (Bristol Rovers) 1958/9 *E*; 1961/2 (Cardiff City) *E.*

Webster, C. (4) (Manchester United) 1956/7 *Czecho*; 1957/8 *H, Mex, Braz.*

Williams, G. (1) (Cardiff City) 1950/1 *Switz.*

Williams, G. E. (26) (West Bromwich Albion) 1959/60 *I*; 1960/1 *Eire, S, E*; 1962/3 *I*; 1963/4 *H, E, S, I*; 1964/5 *S, D, E, Gr* (2), *I, It, Rus*; 1965/6 *I, Braz, Braz 'B', Ch*; 1966/7 *S, E, I*; 1967/8 *I*; 1968/9 *It.*

Williams, G. G. (5) (Swansea City) 1960/1 *I, Sp* (2), *H*; 1961/2 *E.*

Williams, H. (4) (Newport County) 1948/9 *I, Switz* (Leeds United); 1949/50 *I*; 1950/1 *S.*

Williams, Herbert (3) (Swansea City) 1964/5 *Gr* (2); 1970/1 *Ru.*

Williams, S. (43) (West Bromwich Albion) 1953/4 *Aust*; 1954/5 *E, I*; 1955/6 *E, S, Aust*; 1957/8 *E, S, Isr* (2), *I, H, Mex, Swdn, H, Braz*; 1958/9 *S, E, I*; 1959/60 *E, S, I*; 1960/1 *Eire, I, Sp* (2), *H*; 1961/2 *E, S, I, Braz* (2), *Mex*; 1962/3 (Southampton) *S, H, E, H*; 1963/4 *E, S*; 1964/5 *S, D, E*; 1965/6 *D.*

Witcombe, D. (3) (West Bromwich Albion) 1946/7 *S, E,* Sheffield Wednesday) *I.*

Woosnam, P. (17) (Leyton Orient) 1958/9 *S,* (West Ham United), *E*; 1959/60 *E, S, I*; 1960/1 *Eire, S, E, I, Sp, H*; 1961/2 *E, S, I, Braz*; 1962/3 (Aston Villa) *H, I.*

Yorath, T. (58) (Leeds United) 1969/70 *It*; 1970/1 *S, E, I*; 1971/2 *Czecho, E, S, I*; 1972/3 *E, Pol, S*; 1973/4 *Pol, E, S, I*; 1974/5 *Aust, H* (2), *Lux* (2), *S*; 1975/6 *Aust, E* (2), *Y* (2), *S, I*; (Coventry City) 1976/7 *G, S, Czecho, S, E, I*; 1977/8 *K* (2), *S* (2), *Czecho, G, E, I*; 1978/9 *T, G, S, E, I*; (Tottenham Hotspur) 1979/80 *Eire, T, E, S, I, Ic;* 1980/81 *T, Czecho, Eire, T, Rus.*

THE WORLD CUP FINALS

URUGUAY 1930

Uruguay 4, Argentina 2 (1–2)
Uruguay: Ballesteros; Nasazzi (capt), Mascheroni, Andrade, Fernandez, Gestido, Dorado, Scarone, Castro, Cea, Iriarte.
Argentina: Botasso; Della Torre, Paternoster, Evaristo, J., Monti, Suarez, Peucelle, Varallo, Stabile, Ferreira (capt), Evaristo, M.
Scorers: Dorado, Cea, Iriarte, Castro for Uruguay; Peucelle, Stabile for Argentina.
Leading scorers: Stabile (Argentina) 8.

ITALY 1934

Italy 2, Czechoslovakia 1 (0–0) (1–1) after extra time. *Rome*
Italy: Combi (capt), Monzeglio, Allemandi, Ferraris IV, Monti, Bertolini, Guaita. Meazza, Schiavio, Ferrari, Orsi.
Czechoslovakia: Planicka (capt), Zenisek, Ctyroky, Kostalek, Cambal, Krcil, Junek, Svoboda, Sobotka, Nejedly, Puc.
Scorers: Orsi, Schiavio for Italy, Puc for Czechoslovakia.
Leading scorers: Schiavio (Italy), Nejedly (Czechoslovakia), Conen (Germany) each 4.

FRANCE 1938

Italy 4, Hungary 2 (3–1). *Paris*
Italy: Olivieri; Foni, Rava, Serantoni, Andreolo, Locatelli, Biavati, Meazza (capt), Piola, Ferrari, Colaussi.
Hungary: Szabo; Polgar, Biro, Szalay, Szucs, Luzar, Sas, Vincze, Sarosi, (capt), Szengeller, Titkos.
Scorers: Colaussi (2), Piola (2) for Italy, Titkos, Sarosi for Hungary.
Leading scorer: Leonidas (Brazil) 8.

BRAZIL 1950

Final pool replaced knock-out system.
Final pool
Uruguay 2, Spain 2
Brazil 7, Sweden 1
Uruguay 3, Sweden 2
Brazil 6, Spain 1
Sweden 3, Spain 1
Uruguay 2, Brazil 1

Final positions

	P	*W*	*D*	*L*	*F*	*A*	*Pts*
Uruguay	3	2	1	0	7	5	5
Brazil	3	2	0	1	14	4	4
Sweden	3	1	0	2	6	11	2
Spain	3	0	1	2	4	11	1

Leading scorers: Ademir (Brazil) 7, Schiaffino (Uruguay), Basora (Spain) 5.

SWITZERLAND 1954

West Germany 3, Hungary 2.
West Germany: Turek; Posipal, Kohlmeyer, Eckel, Liebrich, Mai, Rahn, Morlock, Walter, O., Walter, F. (capt), Schaefer.
Hungary: Grosics; Buzansky, Lantos, Boszik, Lorant, Zakarias, Czibor, Kocsis, Hidegkuti, Puskas (capt), Toth, J.
Scorers: Morlock, Rahn (2) for Germany, Puskas, Czibor for Hungary.
Leading scorer: Kocsis (Hungary) 11.

SWEDEN 1958

Brazil 5, Sweden 2 (2–1). *Stockholm.*
Brazil: Gilmar; Santos, D., Santos, N., Zito, Bellini, Orlando, Garrincha, Didi, Vava, Pele, Zagalo.
Sweden: Svensson; Bergmark, Axbom, Boerjesson, Gustavsson, Parling, Hamrin, Gren, Simonsson, Liedholm, Skoglund.
Scorers: Vava (2), Pele (2), Zagalo for Brazil, Liedholm, Simonsson for Sweden.
Leading scorer: Fontaine 13 (present record total).

CHILE 1962

Brazil 3, Czechoslovakia 1 (1–1). *Santiago.*
Brazil; Gilmar; Santos, D., Mauro, Zozimo, Santos, N., Zito, Didi, Garrincha, Vava, Amarildo, Zagalo.
Czechoslovakia: Schroiff; Tichy, Novak, Pluskal, Popluhar, Masopust, Pospichal, Scherer, Kvasniak, Kadraba, Jelinek.
Scorers: Amarildo, Zito, Vava for Brazil, Masopust for Czechoslovakia.
Leading scorers: Albert (Hungary), Ivanov (Russia), Sanchez, L. (Chile), Garrincha, Vava (Brazil), Jerkovic (Yugoslavia) each 4.

ENGLAND 1966

England 4, West Germany 2 (1–1) (2–2) after extra time. *Wembley.*
England: Banks; Cohen, Wilson, Stiles, Charlton, J., Moore, Ball, Hurst, Hunt, Charlton, R., Peters.
West Germany: Tilkowski; Hottges, Schulz, Weber, Schnellinger, Haller, Beckenbauer, Overath, Seller, Held, Emmerich.
Scorers: Hurst 3, Peters for England, Haller, Weber for Germany.
Leading scorer: Eusebio (Portugal) 9.

MEXICO 1970

Brazil 4, Italy 1. *Mexico City.*
Brazil: Felix; Carlos Alberto, Brito, Piazza, Everaldo, Gerson, Clodoaldo, Jairzinho, Pele, Tostao, Rivelino. No subs.
Italy: Albertosi, Burgnich, Cera, Rosato, Facchetti, Bertini, Riva, Domenghini, Mazzola, De Sisti, Boninsegna. Subs: Juliano for Bertini, Rivera for Boninsegna.
Scorers: Pele, Gerson, Jairzinho, Carlos Alberto for Brazil, Boninsegna for Italy.

WEST GERMANY 1974

West Germany 2, Netherlands 1 (2–1). *Munich.*
West Germany: Maier; Vogts, Schwarzenbeck, Beckenbauer, Breitner, Bonhof, Hoeness, Overath, Grabowski, Muller, Holzenbein.
Netherlands: Jongbloed; Suurbier, Rijsbergen (De Jong), Haan, Krol, Jansen, Van Hanegem, Neeskens, Rep, Cruyff, Rensenbrink (Van der Kerkhof, R.).
Scorers: Breitner (*pen*), Muller for West Germany, Neeskens (*pen*) for Netherlands.

ARGENTINA 1978

Argentina 3, Netherlands 1 (after extra time). *Buenos Aires.*
Argentina: Fillol; Olguin, Passarella, Galvan, Tarantini, Ardiles (Larossa), Gallego, Ortiz (Houseman), Bertoni, Luque, Kempes.
Netherlands: Jongbloed; Poortvliet, Brandts, Krol, Jansen (Suurbier), Neeskens, W. Van der Kerkhof, R. Van der Kerkhof, Haan, Rep (Nanninga), Rensenbrink.
Scorers: Kempes 2, Bertoni for Argentina, Nanninga for Netherlands.

SPAIN 1982

Italy 3, West Germany 1. *Madrid*
Italy: Zoff; Bergomi, Cabrini, Collovati, Scirea, Gentile, Oriali, Tardelli, Conti, Graziani (Altobelli) (Causio), Rossi.
West Germany: Schumacher; Kaltz, K-H. Forster, Stielike, B. Forster, Breitner, Dremmler (Hrubesch), Littbarski, Briegel, Fischer, Rummenigge (Muller).
Scorers: Rossi, Tardelli, Altobelli for Italy, Breitner for West Germany.

UEFA UNDER-21 TOURNAMENT 1982-84

Group 1 (Scotland, East Germany, Belgium, Switzerland)

Belgium 0, Switzerland 0	5 October 1982
Scotland 2, East Germany 0	12 October 1982
Switzerland 3, Scotland 4	16 November 1982
Belgium 1, Scotland 2	14 December 1982
Scotland 2, Switzerland 1	29 March 1983
East Germany 2, Belgium 1	29 March 1983
Belgium 4, East Germany 2	26 April 1983
Switzerland 5, East Germany 6	13 May 1983
East Germany 2, Switzerland 1	11October 1983
Scotland 0, Belgium 0	11 October 1983
Switzerland 0, Belgium 2	8 November 1983
East Germany 1, Scotland 1	15 November 1983

FINAL TABLE	*P*	*W*	*D*	*L*	*F*	*A*	*Pts*	*Diff*
Scotland	6	4	2	0	11	6	10	+5
East Germany	6	3	1	2	13	14	7	−1
Belgium	6	2	2	2	8	6	6	+2
Switzerland	6	0	1	5	10	16	1	−6

Group 2 (Portugal, Poland, USSR, Finland)

USSR 1, Poland 1	5 September 1982
Finland 0, Poland 0	8 September 1982
Finland 1, Portugal 1	21September 1982
Portugal 1, Poland 0	9 October 1982
USSR 2, Finland 2	12 October 1982
Poland 4, Finland 0	27 October 1982
USSR 1, Portugal 1	26 April 1983
Poland 2, USSR 1	21 May 1983
Finland 0, USSR 1	31 May 1983
Portugal 0, Finland 2	20 September 1983
Poland 2, Portugal 0	27 October 1983
Portugal 0, USSR 2	12 November 1983

FINAL TABLE	*P*	*W*	*D*	*L*	*F*	*A*	*Pts*	*Diff*
Poland	6	3	2	1	9	3	8	+6
USSR	6	2	3	1	8	6	7	+2
Finland	6	1	3	2	5	8	5	−5
Portugal	6	1	2	3	3	8	4	−5

Group 3 (England, Greece, Denmark, Hungary)

Denmark 1, England 4	21 September 1982
Greece 1, England 0	16 November 1982
England 2, Greece 1	29 March 1983
England 1, Hungary 0	26 April 1983
Denmark 1, Greece 1	26 April 1983

Hungary 1, Greece 1	14 May 1983
Denmark 2, Hungary 1	31 May 1983
England 4, Denmark 1	20 September 1983
Hungary 0, England 2	11 October 1983
Hungary 5, Denmark 1	25 October 1983
Greece 1, Denmark 0	15 November 1983
Greece 1, Hungary 0	2 December 1983

FINAL TABLE	*P*	*W*	*D*	*L*	*F*	*A*	*Pts*	*Diff*
England	6	5	0	1	13	4	10	+9
Greece	6	3	2	1	6	4	8	+2
Hungary	6	1	1	4	7	8	3	−1
Denmark	6	1	1	4	6	16	3	−10

Group 4 (Yugoslavia, Bulgaria, Norway, Wales)

Wales 0, Norway 0	21 September 1982
Norway 2, Yugoslavia 2	12 October 1982
Bulgaria 2, Norway 0	26 October 1982
Bulgaria 0, Yugoslavia 2	16 November 1982
Yugoslavia 2, Wales 0	14 December 1982
Wales 0, Bulgaria 1	26 April 1983
Norway 0, Bulgaria 2	6 September 1983
Norway 2, Wales 3	20 September 1983
Yugoslavia 6, Norway 2	11 October 1983
Bulgaria 1, Wales 1	15 November 1983
Wales 1, Yugoslavia 0	13 December 1983
Yugoslavia 0, Bulgaria 0	20 December 1983

FINAL TABLE	*P*	*W*	*D*	*L*	*F*	*A*	*Pts*	*Diff*
Yugoslavia	6	3	2	1	12	5	8	+7
Bulgaria	6	3	2	1	6	3	8	+3
Wales	6	2	2	2	5	6	6	−1
Norway	6	0	2	4	6	15	2	−9

Group 5 (Czechoslovakia, Italy, Rumania, Cyprus)

Cyprus 1, Rumania 2	1 May 1982
Italy 2, Rumania 0	27 October 1982
Czechoslovakia 2, Italy 1	11 November 1982
Cyprus 0, Italy 1	1 December 1982
Czechoslovakia 2, Cyprus 0	27 March 1983
Cyprus 1, Czechoslovakia 4	16 April 1983
Italy 2, Czechoslovakia 1	27 April 1983
Rumania 1, Czechoslovakia 4	14 May 1983
Rumania 0, Italy 1	12 October 1983
Rumania 3, Cyprus 2	12 November 1983
Czechoslovakia 2, Rumania 2	29 November 1983
Italy 2, Cyprus 0	21 December 1983

FINAL TABLE	P	W	D	L	F	A	Pts	Diff
Italy	6	5	0	1	9	3	10	+6
Czechoslovakia	6	4	1	1	15	7	9	+8
Rumania	6	2	1	3	8	12	5	−4
Cyprus	6	0	0	6	4	14	0	−10

Group 6 (Albania, West Germany, Austria, Turkey)

Austria 1, Albania 2	21 September 1982
Turkey 0, Albania 1	26 October 1982
Austria 1, Turkey 1	16 November 1982
Albania 1, West Germany 1	29 March 1983
Turkey 0, West Germany 1	22 April 1983
Austria 1, West Germany 1	26 April 1983
Albania 1, Turkey 0	10 May 1983
Albania 3, Austria 0	7 June 1983
West Germany 2, Austria 1	4 October 1983
West Germany 7, Turkey 0	25 October 1983
Turkey 5, Austria 0	15 November 198[illegible]
West Germany 1, Albania 1	19 November 19[illegible]

FINAL TABLE	P	W	D	L	F	A	Pts	Diff
Albania	6	4	2	0	9	3	10	+6
West Germany	6	3	3	0	13	4	9	+9
Turkey	6	1	1	4	6	11	3	−5
Austria	6	0	2	4	4	14	2	−10

Group 7 (Netherlands, Spain, Iceland)

Iceland 1, Netherlands 1	31 August 1982
Spain 1, Iceland 0	27 October 1982
Netherlands 5, Spain 0	16 February 1983
Iceland 0, Spain 0	28 May 1983
Netherlands 1, Iceland 1	6 September 1983
Spain 1, Netherlands 0	16 November 1983

FINAL TABLE	P	W	D	L	F	A	Pts	Diff
Spain	4	2	1	1	2	5	5	−3
Netherlands	4	1	2	1	7	3	4	+4
Iceland	4	0	3	1	2	3	3	−1

Group 8 (France, Sweden, Luxembourg)

Luxembourg 0, Sweden 4	27 October 1982
France 1, Sweden 0	11 November 1982
Luxembourg 0, France 5	23 March 1983
Sweden 4, Luxembourg 1	12 May 1983
Sweden 2, France 2	7 September 1983
France 2, Luxembourg 0	5 October 1983

FINAL TABLE	*P*	*W*	*D*	*L*	*F*	*A*	*Pts*	*Diff*
France	4	3	1	0	10	2	7	+8
Sweden	4	2	1	1	10	4	5	+6
Luxembourg	4	0	0	4	1	15	0	−14

QUARTER-FINALS, First Leg

England 6, France 1	Sheffield, 28 February 1984
Scotland 2, Yugoslavia 1	Aberdeen, 14 March 1984
Albania 0, Italy 1	Tirana, 14 March 1984
Poland 2, Spain 2	Opole, 21 March 1984

QUARTER-FINALS, Second Leg

France 0, England 1	Petit-Quevilly, 28 March 1984
Yugoslavia 3, Scotland 1, (aet)	Beograd, 4 April 1984
Italy 1, Albania 0	Brescia, 4 April 1984
Spain 4, Poland 1	Zaragoza, 11 April 1984

SEMI-FINALS, First Leg

England 3, Italy 1	Manchester, 18 April 1984
Yugoslavia 0, Spain 1	Beograd, 25 April 1984

SEMI-FINALS, Second Leg

Italy 1, England 0	Florence, 2 May 1984
Spain 2, Yugoslavia 0	Malaga, 2 May 1984

FINAL, First Leg

Spain 0, England 1 (Sterland)	Seville, 17 May 1984
	Attendance: 15,000

FINAL, Second Leg

England 2 (Hateley, Gayle), Spain 0	Sheffield, 24 May 1984
	Attendance: 11,478

THE FA CHARITY SHIELD

Year	*Winners*	*Runners-up*	*Score*
1908	Manchester United	QPR	4 – 0 after 1 – 1 draw
1909	Newcastle United	Northampton	2 – 0
1910	Brighton	Aston Villa	1 – 0
1911	Manchester United	Swindon Town	8 – 4
1912	Blackburn Rovers	QPR	2 – 1
1913	Professionals	Amateurs	7 – 2
1919	West Bromwich Albion	Tottenham Hotspur	2 – 0
1920	Tottenham Hotspur	Burnley	2 – 0
1921	Huddersfield	Liverpool	1 – 0
1922	No competition		
1923	Professionals	Amateurs	2 – 0
1924	Professionals	Amateurs	3 – 1
1925	Amateurs	Professionals	6 – 1
1926	Amateurs	Professionals	6 – 3
1927	Cardiff City	Corinthians	2 – 1
1928	Everton	Blackburn Rovers	2 – 1
1929	Professionals	Amateurs	3 – 0
1930	Arsenal	Sheffield Wednesday	2 – 1
1931	Arsenal	West Bromwich Albion	1 – 0
1932	Everton	Newcastle United	5 – 3
1933	Arsenal	Everton	3 – 0
1934	Arsenal	Manchester City	4 – 0
1935	Sheffield Wednesday	Arsenal	1 – 0
1936	Sunderland	Arsenal	2 – 1
1937	Manchester City	Sunderland	2 – 0
1938	Arsenal	Preston North End	2 – 1
1948	Arsenal	Manchester United	4 – 3
1949	Portsmouth	Wolverhampton W.	1 – 1*
1950	World Cup Team	Canadian Touring Team	4 – 2
1951	Tottenham Hotspur	Newcastle United	2 – 1
1952	Manchester United	Newcastle United	4 – 2
1953	Arsenal	Blackpool	3 – 1
1954	Wolverhampton W.	West Bromwich Albion	4 – 4*
1955	Chelsea	Newcastle United	3 – 0
1956	Manchester United	Manchester City	1 – 0
1957	Manchester United	Aston Villa	4 – 0
1958	Bolton Wanderers	Wolverhampton W.	4 – 1
1959	Wolverhampton W.	Nottingham Forest	3 – 1
1960	Burnley	Wolverhampton W.	2 – 2*
1961	Tottenham Hotspur	FA XI	3 – 2
1962	Tottenham Hotspur	Ipswich Town	5 – 1
1963	Everton	Manchester United	4 – 0
1964	Liverpool	West Ham United	2 – 2*
1965	Manchester United	Liverpool	2 – 2*
1966	Liverpool	Everton	1 – 0
1967	Manchester United	Tottenham Hotspur	3 – 3*
1968	Manchester City	West Bromwich Albion	6 – 1
1969	Leeds United	Manchester City	2 – 1
1970	Everton	Chelsea	2 – 1
1971	Leicester	Liverpool	1 – 0
1972	Manchester City	Aston Villa	1 – 0

1973	Burnley	Manchester City	1–0
1974	Liverpool†	Leeds United	1–1
1975	Derby County	West Ham United	2–0
1976	Liverpool	Southampton	1–0
1977	Liverpool	Manchester United	0–0*
1978	Nottingham Forest	Ipswich Town	5–0
1979	Liverpool	Arsenal	3–1
1980	Liverpool	West Ham United	1–0
1981	Aston Villa	Tottenham Hotspur	1–1*
1982	Liverpool	Tottenham Hotspur	1–0
1983	Manchester United	Liverpool	2–0

*Each club retained shield for six months. †Won on penalties

WORLD CLUB CHAMPIONSHIP

Played annually up to 1974 between the winners of the European Cup and the winners of the South American Champions Cup – known as the Copa Libertadores de America. Revived in February 1981, but played on a single match basis on a neutral ground.

Year	*Winners*	*Runners-up*	*Score*
1960	Real Madrid	Penarol	0–0, 5–1
1961	Penarol	Benfica	0–1, 5–0, 2–1
1962	Santos	Benfica	3–2, 5–2
1963	Santos	AC Milan	2–4, 4–2, 1–0
1964	Inter-Milan	Independiente	0–1, 2–0, 1–0
1965	Inter-Milan	Independiente	3–0, 0–0
1966	Penarol	Real Madrid	2–0, 2–0
1967	Racing Club	Celtic	0–1, 2–1, 1–0
1968	Estudiantes	Manchester United	1–0, 1–1
1969	AC Milan	Estudiantes	3–0, 1–2
1970	Feyenoord	Estudiantes	2–2, 1–0
1971	Nacianal	Panathinaikos	1–1, 2–1
1972	Ajax	Independiente	1–1, 3–0
1973	Independiente	Juventus	1–0
1974	Athletico Madrid	Independiente	0–1, 2–0
1981	Nacional (Uruguay)	Nottingham Forest	1–0 (in Tokyo)
1982	Penarol (Uruguay)	Aston Villa	2–0 (in Tokyo)
1983	Gremio Porto Alegre (Brazil)	SV Hamburg	2–1 (in Tokyo)

OTHER LEAGUE TABLES

Alliance Premier League

	P	W	D	L	F	A	Pts
Maidstone U.	42	23	13	6	71	34	70
Nuneaton Bor.	42	24	11	7	70	40	69
Altrincham	42	23	9	10	64	39	65
Wealdstone	42	21	14	7	75	36	62
Runcorn	42	20	13	9	61	45	62
Bath C.	42	17	12	13	60	48	53
Northwich Vic.	42	16	14	12	54	47	51
Worcester C.	42	15	13	14	64	55	49
Barnet	42	16	10	16	55	58	49
Kidderminster Har.	42	14	14	14	54	61	49
Telford U.	42	17	11	14	50	58	49
Frickley Ath.	42	17	10	15	68	56	48
Scarborough	42	14	16	12	52	55	48
Enfield	42	14	9	19	61	58	43
Weymouth	42	13	8	21	54	65	42
Gateshead	42	12	13	17	59	73	42
Boston U.	42	13	12	17	66	80	41
Dagenham	42	14	8	20	57	69	40
Kettering T.	42	12	9	21	53	67	37
Yeovil T.	42	12	8	22	55	77	35
Bangor C.	42	10	6	26	54	82	29
Trowbridge T.	42	5	7	30	33	87	19

Southern League – Premier Division

	P	W	D	L	F	A	Pts
Dartford	38	23	9	67	32	78	
Fisher Ath.	38	22	9	7	80	42	75
Chelmsford C.	38	19	9	10	67	45	66
Gravesend & N'fleet	38	18	9	11	50	38	63
Witney T.	38	18	6	14	75	50	60
King's Lynn	38	18	6	14	42	45	60
Folkestone	38	16	9	13	60	56	57
Cheltenham T.	38	16	7	15	63	56	55
Gloucester C.	38	13	15	10	55	50	54
Hastings U.	38	15	9	14	55	57	54
Bedworth U.	38	15	9	14	51	55	54
Welling U.	38	15	7	16	61	61	52
A. P. Leamington	38	14	9	15	73	83	51
Corby T.	38	12	14	12	55	54	50
Fareham T.	38	13	11	14	65	70	50
Alvechurch	38	12	12	14	56	63	48
Sutton Coldfield	38	6	15	17	31	64	33
Gosport Bor.	38	6	15	17	31	64	33
Dorchester T.	38	4	8	26	40	69	20
Stourbridge	38	4	7	27	30	82	19

Southern League– Midland Division

	P	W	D	L	F	A	Pts
Willenhall T.	38	27	4	7	100	44	85
Shepshed Charterhouse	38	25	5	8	88	37	80
Bromsgrove R.	38	20	8	10	73	43	68
Dudley T.	38	18	13	7	71	43	67
Aylesbury U.	38	17	15	6	62	35	66
Moor Green	38	18	12	8	63	44	66
Rushden T.	38	17	12	9	68	42	63
Merthyr Tydfil	38	18	8	12	63	44	62
Redditch U.	38	17	9	12	67	67	60
V.S. Rugby	38	15	12	11	68	51	57
Forest Green Rovers	38	15	12	11	67	51	57
Bridgnorth T.	38	16	9	13	64	52	57
Leicester U.	38	12	9	17	58	58	45
Oldbury U.	38	10	13	15	53	51	43
Coventry Sporting	38	11	7	20	40	67	40
Bridgwater T.	38	10	8	20	39	65	38
Wellingborough T.	38	7	9	22	43	80	30
Banbury U.	38	6	11	21	37	78	29
Milton Keynes C.	38	3	9	26	31	110	18
Tamworth	38	2	7	29	25	118	13

Southern League– Southern Division

	P	W	D	L	F	A	Pts
R.S. Southampton	38	26	6	6	83	35	84
Crawley T.	38	22	9	7	68	28	75
Basingstoke T.	38	20	9	9	54	36	69
Tonbridge A.F.C.	38	20	9	9	61	44	69
Addlestone & Weybridge	38	19	11	8	58	34	68
Poole T.	38	20	7	11	68	42	67
Hillingdon	38	18	11	9	43	20	65
Ashford T.	38	19	5	14	65	47	62
Salisbury	38	17	8	13	61	48	59
Cambridge C.	38	13	9	16	43	53	48
Canterbury C.	38	12	9	17	44	52	45
Waterlooville	38	12	9	17	56	69	45
Dover Ath.	38	12	9	17	51	74	45
Chatham T.	38	11	10	17	46	56	43
Andover	38	12	6	20	35	54	42
Erith & Belvedere	38	11	9	18	43	68	42
Dunstable	38	10	8	20	38	65	38
Thanet U.	38	9	8	21	40	65	35
Woodford T.	38	7	8	23	30	69	29
Hounslow	38	4	12	22	30	58	24

Northern Premier League

	P	W	D	L	F	A	Pts
Barrow	42	29	10	3	92	38	97
Matlock T.	42	23	8	11	72	48	77
S. Liverpool	42	22	11	9	55	44	77
Grantham	42	20	8	14	64	51	68
Burton A.	42	17	13	12	61	47	64
Macclesfield T.	42	18	10	14	65	55	64
Rhyl	42	19	6	17	64	55	63
Horwich	42	18	9	15	64	59	63
Gainsborough Tr.	42	17	11	14	82	66	62
Stafford R.	42	15	17	10	65	52	62
Hyde U.	42	17	8	17	61	63	59
Marine	42	16	10	16	63	68	58
Witton A.	42	14	14	14	64	57	56
Chorley	42	14	11	17	68	65	53
Workington	42	14	9	19	53	57	51
Southport	42	14	8	20	57	74	50
Worksop T.	42	13	8	21	57	74	47
Goole T.	42	12	10	20	59	80	46
Morecambe	42	11	12	19	59	75	45
Oswestry T.	42	11	8	23	66	97	41
Buxton	42	11	6	25	52	91	39
Mossley*	42	9	9	24	47	74	33

**3 points deducted for breach of rule.*

Isthmian League–Premier Division

	P	W	D	L	F	A	Pts
Harrow Bor.	42	25	13	4	73	42	88
Worthing	42	20	11	11	89	72	71
Slough T.	42	20	9	13	73	56	69
Sutton U.	42	18	12	12	67	45	66
Hayes	42	17	13	12	56	41	64
Hitchin T.	42	16	15	11	58	57	63
Wycombe W.	42	16	14	12	63	52	62
Wokingham T.	42	18	10	14	78	55	61
Hendon	42	17	10	15	62	51	61
Dulwich Hamlet	42	16	11	15	61	64	59
Bishop's Stortford	42	15	13	14	56	57	58
Harlow T.	42	15	11	16	64	70	56
Bognor Regis T.	42	14	13	15	62	69	55
Staines T.	42	15	9	18	63	72	54
Billericay T.	42	15	8	19	53	73	53
Barking	42	13	13	16	60	64	52
Croydon	42	14	10	18	52	58	52
Walthamstowe Ave.	42	13	10	19	53	67	49
Leytonstone-Ilford	42	13	9	20	54	67	48
Carshalton Ath.	42	11	10	21	59	72	43
Tooting & Mitcham	42	10	13	19	50	63	43
Bromley	42	7	11	24	33	72	32

The Football Combination

	P	W	D	L	F	A	Pts
Arsenal	42	29	8	5	96	30	66
Watford	42	28	6	8	94	50	62
Chelsea	42	25	5	12	84	38	55
Queens Park R.	42	23	9	10	80	37	55
West Ham U.	42	21	11	10	105	50	53
Southampton	42	20	12	10	75	51	52
Tottenham H.	42	21	8	13	110	64	50
Norwich C.	42	20	10	12	78	45	50
Luton T.	42	19	11	12	78	54	49
Ipswich T.	42	20	8	14	67	53	48
Leicester C.	42	18	9	15	96	63	45
Brighton & Hove A.	42	19	7	16	74	65	45
Fulham	42	17	6	19	71	73	40
Millwall	42	17	6	19	60	77	40
Birmingham C.	42	16	5	21	75	83	37
Swansea C.	42	15	5	22	70	95	35
Charlton Ath.	42	11	11	20	46	88	33
Oxford U.	42	11	10	21	56	87	32
Bristol R.	42	9	6	27	60	112	24
Crystal Palace	42	5	12	25	32	101	22
Swindon T.	42	6	8	28	42	11	20
Reading	42	3	5	34	31	153	11

Central League–Division One

	P	W	D	L	F	A	Pts
Liverpool	30	18	7	5	57	33	61
Manchester U.	30	17	6	7	64	34	57
Aston Villa	30	16	6	8	50	29	54
Nottingham F.	30	14	10	6	60	38	52
Everton	30	16	3	11	53	35	51
West Bromwich A.	30	14	7	9	46	35	49
Newcastle U.	30	14	7	9	44	37	49
Derby Co.	30	11	7	12	45	42	40
Stoke C.	30	11	6	13	52	59	39
Sheffield W.	30	11	5	14	52	61	38
Blackburn R.	30	10	6	14	38	46	36
Sheffield U.	30	10	6	14	38	59	36
Sunderland	30	9	3	18	36	54	30
Leeds U.	30	7	7	16	37	51	28
Bolton W.	30	8	3	19	35	68	27
Burnley	30	5	9	16	19	45	24

Northern Counties East– Premier Division

	P	W	D	L	F	A	Pts
Spalding U.	34	20	8	6	76	43	48
Arnold	34	22	3	9	82	37	47
Emley	34	20	7	7	59	32	47
Alfreton T.	34	18	6	10	56	32	42
Eastwood T.	34	17	7	10	75	49	41
Ilkeston T.	34	14	11	9	49	38	39
Guiseley	34	14	11	9	54	48	39
Guisborough T.	34	16	6	12	58	54	38
Thackley	34	14	6	14	61	54	34
Winterton R.	34	13	7	14	48	42	33
Belper T.	34	12	8	14	47	46	32
Boston	34	10	12	12	46	57	32
Sutton T.	34	10	7	17	36	63	27
Appleby Frodingham	34	8	9	17	51	75	25
Mexborough T.	34	6	12	16	34	68	24
Bridlington Tr.	34	7	9	18	40	60	23
Heanor T.	34	7	9	18	31	68	23
Bentley VW	34	6	6	22	45	82	18

Midland Football Combination– Premier Division

	P	W	D	L	F	A	Pts
Studley Sporting	38	22	8	8	83	49	52
Coleshill T.	38	22	7	9	77	43	51
West Midlands Pol.	38	20	10	8	82	52	50
Highgate U.	38	17	14	7	70	41	48
Racing Club Warwick	38	21	4	13	79	66	46
Paget R.	38	15	15	8	55	35	45
Hurley Daw Mill	38	16	11	11	68	55	43
Evesham U.	38	16	10	12	55	49	42
Stratford T.	38	16	6	16	58	71	38
Boldmere St. Michaels	38	14	9	15	46	37	37
Northfield T.	38	14	9	15	63	56	37
Mile Oak Rovers	38	15	7	16	58	53	37
Solihull Bor.	38	15	7	16	54	57	37
Chipping Norton T.	38	13	10	15	49	51	36
Kings Heath	38	11	14	13	50	59	36
Cinderford T.	38	12	9	17	51	63	33
Walsall Bor.	38	13	6	19	54	58	32
Smethwick Highfield	38	7	13	18	45	66	27
Southam U.	38	7	8	23	35	76	22
Knowle North Star	38	3	5	30	34	129	11

Northern League– Division One

	P	*W*	*D*	*L*	*F*	*A*	*Pts*
Blyth Spartans	34	23	9	2	74	22	78
North Shields	34	21	6	7	81	51	69
Whitby T.	34	20	7	7	79	33	67
Tow Law T.	34	19	8	7	72	44	65
Bishop Auckland	34	19	7	8	80	39	64
South Bank	34	18	7	9	62	35	61
Billingham Synth	34	14	8	12	56	54	50
Gretna —3	34	15	7	12	65	48	49
Whitley Bay	34	14	5	15	39	60	47
Horden C. W.	34	12	7	15	48	59	43
Spennymoor U.	34	10	9	15	41	57	39
Consett	34	10	8	16	43	58	38
Peterlee Newtown	34	11	5	18	50	78	38
Crook T.	34	9	10	15	38	50	37
Shildon	34	10	6	18	50	66	36
Ferryhill Ath.	34	9	6	19	47	61	33
Ashington —3	34	7	8	19	39	71	26
Evenwood	34	1	5	28	27	95	8

South-East Counties League– Senior League

	P	*W*	*D*	*L*	*F*	*A*	*Pts*
Chelsea	30	23	5	2	87	29	51
Norwich C.	30	19	6	5	66	44	44
Ipswich T.	30	19	4	7	78	40	42
Millwall	30	19	4	7	68	44	42
Arsenal	30	17	4	9	84	54	38
Watford	30	12	8	10	73	64	32
Queens Park R.	30	10	11	9	52	55	31
West Ham U.	30	12	6	12	65	52	30
Gillingham	30	9	10	11	50	63	28
Orient	30	8	9	13	40	54	25
Cambridge U.	30	7	8	15	48	65	22
Portsmouth	30	7	7	16	29	58	21
Charlton Ath.	30	7	6	17	38	68	20
Tottenham H.	30	5	9	16	43	82	19
Southend U.	30	6	6	18	45	62	18
Fulham	30	8	1	20	48	80	17

North West Counties League– Division One

	P	W	D	L	F	A	Pts
Stalybridge Celtic	38	26	8	4	81	30	60
Penrith	38	23	9	6	88	39	55
Radcliffe Bor.	38	26	3	9	79	41	55
Burscough	38	22	8	8	87	41	52
Curzon Ashton	38	21	5	12	74	51	47
Lancaster C.	38	21	3	14	76	56	43*
Accrington Stanley	38	17	8	13	67	60	42
St. Helens T.	38	17	7	14	69	55	41
Congleton T.	38	18	5	15	64	50	41
Prescot Cables	38	17	6	15	72	45	40
Leek T.	38	14	10	14	56	64	38
Winsford U.	38	12	12	14	49	54	36
Formby	38	14	7	17	48	61	35
Caernarfon T.	38	11	12	15	46	55	34
Glossop	38	11	11	16	38	61	33
Bootle	38	11	7	20	46	69	27*
Leyland Motors	38	9	9	20	44	79	27
Netherfield	38	5	11	22	27	73	21
Ashton U.	38	7	9	22	47	86	19**
Darwen	38	2	2	34	29	111	6

Eastern Counties League

	P	W	D	L	F	A	Pts
Braintree T.	42	29	9	4	125	45	67
Wisbech T.	42	29	9	4	91	37	67
Colchester U.R.	42	26	7	9	94	41	59
Lowestoft T.	42	24	7	11	77	46	55
Sudbury T.	42	21	11	10	87	56	53
Saffron Wald. T.	42	22	8	12	88	474	52
Gorleston	42	18	16	8	73	47	52
Tiptree U.	42	20	9	13	83	64	49
G. Yarmouth T.	42	19	10	13	75	51	48
Chatteris T.	42	17	10	15	57	58	44
Brantham A.	42	16	9	17	66	68	41
Newmarket T.	42	16	9	17	62	73	41
Bury T.	42	16	8	18	69	73	40
Felixstowe T.	42	13	13	16	53	57	39
March T. U.	42	13	11	18	57	63	37
Histon	42	12	11	19	53	60	35
Haverhill R.	42	16	3	23	68	91	35
Soham T. R.	42	11	7	24	49	90	29
Stowmarket T.	42	10	8	24	57	99	28
Ely C.	42	7	8	27	45	108	22
Clacton T.	42	6	4	32	47	120	16
Thetford T.	42	6	3	33	43	125	15

West Midlands (Regional) League–Premier Division

	P	W	D	L	F	A	Pts
Halesowen T.	38	32	3	3	112	36	67
Hednesford T.	38	23	10	5	70	34	56
Atherstone U.	38	17	11	10	63	44	45
Gresley R.	38	17	9	12	68	61	43
Lye T.	38	15	12	11	55	45	42
Wolverhampton U.	38	17	7	14	53	55	41
Oldswinford	38	15	11	12	61	64	41
Armitage	38	17	5	16	67	61	39
Shifnal T.	38	13	12	13	59	56	38
Wednesfield Soc.	38	15	8	15	52	58	38
Tividale	38	12	12	14	53	48	36
Malvern T.	38	14	7	17	64	61	35
Rushall Olympic	38	11	11	16	55	59	33
Hinckley Ath.	38	12	9	17	51	61	33
G K N Sankey	38	13	7	18	54	74	33
Brereton Soc.	38	10	12	16	46	62	32
Bilston T.	38	10	11	17	44	58	31
Blakenall	38	11	7	20	39	59	29
Chasetown	38	9	8	21	39	81	26
Cradley T.	38	9	4	25	44	72	22

Western League–Premier Division

	P	W	D	L	F	A	Pts
Exmouth T.	38	21	12	6	59	35	53
Saltash U.	38	22	7	9	72	39	51
Barnstaple T.	38	21	9	8	68	40	51
Frome T.	38	20	10	8	78	35	50
Liskeard Ath.	38	18	9	11	64	38	65
Bideford	38	16	10	12	71	49	42
Clevedon T.	38	16	8	14	55	56	40
Bristol Manor Farm	38	14	11	13	54	42	39
Plymouth Arg.	38	16	8	14	68	58	38
Minehead	38	15	7	16	55	68	37
Shepton Mallet T.	38	14	9	15	55	74	37
Taunton T.	38	10	15	13	46	52	35
Mangotsfield U.	38	12	10	16	47	48	34
Dawlish T.	38	13	8	17	38	43	34
Weston-Super-Mare	38	13	8	17	46	54	34
Chippenham T.	38	13	8	17	44	56	34
Clandown	38	12	10	16	34	51	34
Melksham T.	38	9	11	18	49	66	29
Devizes T.	38	7	11	20	41	74	25
Wellington	38	4	8	26	29	95	16

NORTHWICH VICTORIA WIN FA CHALLENGE TROPHY

First round	Second round	Third round	Fourth round	Semi-finals
Slough T. 3	Dulwich H. ..1 2 2†	Dulwich Hamet 0 0 0	Northwich Vic. 1	Northwich Vic. ...1 2
Dulwich Hamlet 4				
Chorley 2	Chorley 1 2 0			
Rhyl 1				
Barking 0	Aylesbury U. 0	Northwich Vic. ....0 0 1†		
Aylesbury U. 1				
Boston U. 11	Northwich Vic. 1			
Northwich Vic. 15				
Barnet 3	Barnet 4	Barnet 2	Barnet 0	
Dartford 0				
Durham C. 1	North Shields 1			
North Shields 3				
Merthyr Tydfil 2	Merthyr Tydfil 0	Kidderminster H. ...1		
Enfield 0				
Altrincham 0	Kidderminster H. ...1			
Kidderminster H. ...2				
Mossley 1	Telford U. 2	Telford U. 2	Telford U. 3 0	Marine 1 0
Telford U. 2				
Runcorn 1	Runcorn 1			
Matlock T. 0				
Bromsgrove R. 2	Bromsgrove R. 2	Bromsgrove R. 0		
South L'pool 1				
Wycombe W. 4	Wycombe W. 0			
Dorchester T. 0				
Windsor & Eton 2	Windsor & Eton .1 0	Fisher Ath. 0	Marine 3 2	
Bishops Stortford ...1				
Gloucester C. 3 1	Fisher Ath. 1 4			
Fisher Ath. 3 2				
Bishop Auckland .1 0	Grantham 0	Marine 1		
Grantham 1 1				
Marine 2	Marine 3			
Scarborough 1				

Final

NORTHWICH VICTORIA 2
at Wembley 1 – 1 after extra time

BANGOR CITY 1
at Stoke 2-1

Witton A. 3	AP Leamington 4	AP Leamington 4	AP Leamington 1	Bangor C. 1 2
AP Leamington 4				
Welling U. 2	Welling U. 1			
Hastings U. 1				
Sutton U. 0	Chelmsford C. 2	Chelmsford C. 0		
Chelmsford 3				
Weymouth 2	Hendon 1			
Hendon 3				
Carshalton Ath. 2 2	Carshalton Ath. 1	Gateshead 2 0	Bangor C. 6	
Harrow Bor. 2 0				
Gateshead 1 3	Gateshead 2			
Hordern CW 1 1*				
Bangor C. 3	Bangor C. 1	Bangor C. 2 2		
Spennymoor U. 1				
Croydon 0 0	Bath C. 0			
Bath C. 0 6				
Hampton 0	Maidstone U. 2 0	Nuneaton Bor. 2 0	Dagenham 2 3	Dagenham 0 2*
Maidstone U. 2				
Worcester C. 0 0	Nuneaton Bor. 2 1			
Nuneaton Bor. 0 2				
Dagenham 0 3	Dagenham 1 4	Dagenham 2 1		
Fareham T. 0 2				
Yeovil T. 4	Yeovil T. 1 1			
Wealdstone 3				
Ley'stone/Ilf. 0 2	Ley'stone/Ilf. 0	Whitby T. 2	Whitby T. 2 0	
Trowbridge T. 0 1				
Whitby T. 1 2	Whitby T. 1			
Blyth Spartansd 1 1				
Sutton T. 1	Frickley Ath. 5	Frickley Ath. 0		
Frickley Ath. 4				
Arnold 0	Barrow 2			
Barrow 1				

* *after extra time*
† *at Nuneaton Borough*

STANSTED WIN FA CHALLENGE VASE

Third round	Fourth round	Fifth round	Sixth round	Semi-finals	Final
Old Georgians 4	Old Georgians 3*	Old Georgians 1	Old Georgians ...1 0	Stansted 1 2	STANSTED 3
Devizes T. 1	Newport IOW 2	Baldock T. 0	Stansted 1 2	Whickham 1 0	at Wembley
Newport IOW 2	Baldock T. 1	Stansted 2	Leyton-Wingate 0		
Eastleigh 0	Grays Ath. 0	Bristol Manor F. 1	Whickham 1*		
Baldock T. 3	Heybridge Swifts ..1*	Leyton-Wingate 2			
Gt Yarmouth T. 0	Stansted 2	RS Southampton ...1			
Grays Ath. 4	Newbury T. 0	Whickham 2			
H. Hempstead 1	Bristol Manor F. 1	Hucknall CW 0			
Harefield U. 3	Leyton-Wingate 5				
Heybridge Swifts ...4	Crown & Manor 0				
Stansted 2	Abingdon T. 1*				
Wivenhoe T. 0	RS Southampton ...2				
Newbury T. 3	Whickham 3*				
Yate T. 1	Denaby U. 2				
Bicester T. 0	Hucknall CW 2				
Bristol Manor F. 1	VS Rugby 0				
Leyton-Wingate 3					
Arundel 1					
Holbeach U. 2 0					
Crown & Manor .2 1					
Wantage T. 2					
Abingdon T. 5					
RS Southampton ...3					
Exmouth T. 0					
Whickham 1					
Fleetwood T. 0					
Denaby U. 2					
Halesowen T. 1					
Hucknall CW 4					
Cheadle T. 0					
VS Rugby 2					
Atherstone U. 1					

* after extra time

STAMFORD 2

Round 1		Round 2		Round 3		Round 4		Semi-final	
Uxbridge	2	Uxbridge	0	I'borough Dmds	1	I'borough Dmds	5	I'borough Dmds	1 0
S. Walden T.	1	I'borough Dmds	2	Buckingham T.	0	Brandon U.	0	Stamford	2 2
I'borough D'mds	2	Buckingham T.	3	Guiseley	0	Stamford	3		
Ampthill T.	1	Crockenhill	1	Brandon U.	1	Staveley Works	0		
Tunbridge Wells	2*	Warrington T.	0	Corinthian Cas.	2				
Buckingham T.	4	Guiseley	3	Stamford	4*				
Crockenhill	4	Brandon U.	2	Staveley Works	4				
Swanley T.	0	Farsley Celtic	1	Rainworth MW	2				
Warrington T.	4	Corinthian Cas.	1						
Appleby F'ham	0	Whitehawk	0						
Guiseley	2*	Stamford	3						
Harrowgate T.	0	Shifnal T.	1						
Chester-Le-St.	3	Staveley Works	2						
Brandon U.	5	Hatfield Main	1						
Blue Star	1 0	Rothwell T.	3 2						
Farsley Celtic	1 1	Rainworth MW	3 3						
Bracknell T.	0								
Corinthian Cas.	4								
Tiptree U.	1								
Whitehawk	4								
Stamford	2								
Potton U.	1								
Shifnal T.	1 2								
Bridgnorth T.	1 1								
Staveley Works	3								
Paget Rangers	1								
Lincoln U.	0								
Hatfield Main	1								
Rothwell T.	4*								
Dorking	3								
Rylands	†4* 0								
Rainworth MW	1 1								

* after extra time

† match ordered to be replayed

EVERTON WIN FA YOUTH CHALLENGE CUP

Third round		Fourth round		Fifth round		Semi-finals		Final	
Ipswich T.	1 0	Millwall	2	Everton	2	Everton	1 1	**Everton**	**2 2**
Millwall	1 1								
Everton	2	Everton	3						
Blackpool	0								
Newcastle U.	1	Newcastle U.	3	Newcastle U.	1				
Leeds U.	0								
Southampton	5	Southampton	2						
AP Leamington	0								
Barnsley	3	Barnsley	2 1	Barnsley	2	Barnsley	0 1*		
Manchester C.	1								
Derby Co.	0	Manchester U.	2 0						
Manchester U.	9								
Sunderland	1	Sunderland	2	Sunderland	1				
Mansfield T.	0								
York C.	0	Liverpool	0						
Liverpool	2								
Chelsea	1	Chelsea	5	Chelsea	1	Stoke C.	3 3	**Stoke C.**	**2 0**
Portsmouth	0								
Q.P.R.	0	Brentford	0						
Brentford	3								
Stoke C.	3	Stoke C.	3	Stoke C.	2				
Walsall	0								
Plymouth Arg.	1	Luton T.	2						
Luton T.	2								
Bristol R.	4 1	Arsenal	2	Arsenal	2	Arsenal	2 0		
Arsenal	4 3								
Norwich C.	2 1	Cambridge U.	0						
Cambridge U.	2 4								
Chesterfield	0	Aston Villa	2	Aston Villa	1				
Aston Villa	2								
Fulham	4 0	West Ham U.	0						
West Ham U.	4 3								

** after extra time*

LEE CHAPEL NORTH WIN FA SUNDAY CUP

Third round	Fourth round	Fifth round	Semi-finals	Final
Shirley Crusaders 2*	Shirley Crusaders 0			
Inter-Volante 1		Beaufort 0		
Ranelagh Sports 1	Beaufort 1			
Beaufort 6			Troy Ath. 0	
Quebec Rovers	Lion Rangers 1		(played at	
Lion Rangers ....◇		Troy Ath. 2	Gravesend	
Rainham WMC 0	Troy Ath. 2		& Northfleet)	
Troy Ath. 4				**Lee Chapel Nth.** 4
Lee Chapel Nth. 6	Lee Chapel Nth. 2			at Dagenham
Ollis T'sport Comb'd ..0		Lee Chapel Nth. 2		
Leight Billet 7	Leigh Billet 0			
IBM Portsmouth 1			Lee Chapel Nth. 1	
Leggatts Ath. 2	Leggatts Ath. 4			
Two-Seven-Nine 1		Leggatts Ath. 4		
N Breakspear OB 2	N. Breakspear OB 2			
Halesowen H. 1				
Sunderland HPF 1	Winlaton WE 3			
Winlaton WE 3		Winlaton WE 0		
Whetley Lane 2	Hartlepool LH 2*			
Hartlepool LH 4			Eagle 2	
Phoenix 1	Eagle 2		(played at	
Eagle 3		Eagle 2	Marine)	
Hoval Farrar 2	Newbiggin D. 1			
Newbiggin D. 5				**Eagle** 3
Garrington S'day 2	Garrington S'day 0			
Brereton T. 1		Avenue 0		
Avenue 1	Avenue 3			
Dudley & W'slade 0			Lodge Cottrell 1	
Acorn 1	Marston Sports 0			
Marston Sports 4		Lodge Cottrell 3		
Lodge Cottrell 2	Lodge Cottrell 3			
Olympic Star 1				

* *after extra time*

◇ *As QUEBEC ROVERS failed to arrive for the match, LION RANGERS received a walkover to the fourth round*

ALLIANCE PREMIER LEAGUE —

	Altrincham	Bangor C.	Barnet	Bath C.	Boston U.	Dagenham	Enfield	Frickley Ath.
Altrincham	—	2–1	3–2	2–0	3–0	4–0	1–3	1–0
Bangor C.	1–3	—	0–1	1–0	0–0	2–4	2–1	4–1
Barnet	1–2	3–1	—	1–2	1–2	3–1	2–1	3–2
Bath C.	0–0	5–1	0–1	—	4–2	0–1	3–2	1–0
Boston U.	2–2	3–2	0–0	0–0	—	3–0	3–2	2–2
Dagenham	0–2	3–1	3–1	3–1	2–0	—	1–4	1–1
Enfield	0–1	3–1	0–1	2–0	1–0	3–0	—	3–3
Frickley Ath.	3–1	2–0	3–1	1–2	7–1	4–0	1–1	—
Gateshead	0–1	2–1	2–3	3–1	5–5	1–1	1–1	2–0
Kettering T.	1–1	1–3	0–1	0–0	2–1	2–2	1–0	0–1
Kidderminster H.	0–2	2–1	4–4	1–1	1–1	4–2	1–1	1–1
Maidstone U.	1–0	2–0	1–1	1–1	2–2	2–0	1–1	3–1
Northwich Vic.	1–1	2–1	0–0	3–2	3–1	3–1	3–1	1–1
Nuneaton Bor.	0–1	3–0	2–2	5–2	4–0	1–1	4–0	1–0
Runcorn	0–0	0–2	2–0	2–1	3–1	1–0	0–0	2–1
Scarborough	3–1	3–0	1–0	0–0	2–0	0–0	0–4	3–1
Telford U.	2–1	2–1	0–0	3–2	3–2	3–1	0–3	0–1
Trowbridge T.	0–0	1–2	0–4	1–2	0–2	1–4	0–0	0–1
Wealdstone	3–1	5–0	3–0	0–3	1–1	1–0	2–1	0–0
Weymouth	0–1	5–0	2–2	0–1	0–2	3–1	1–3	0–2
Worcester C.	0–1	0–0	2–0	2–4	2–2	2–2	1–3	0–0
Yeovil T.	1–2	1–1	2–4	0–2	4–2	0–2	3–2	3–0

1983-84 RESULTS

	Gateshead	Kettering T.	Kidderminster H.	Maidstone U.	Northwich Vic.	Nuneaton Bor.	Runcorn	Scarborough	Telford U.	Trowbridge T.	Wealdstone	Weymouth	Worcester C.	Yeovil T
	5–0	1–1	0–1	1–0	1–1	0–1	1–3	2–0	1–1	4–0	1–0	2–1	3–4	2–1
	3–3	3–1	1–2	0–2	0–1	1–2	2–3	1–1	4–0	4–0	0–0	1–3	2–4	3–0
	0–1	0–3	0–2	0–4	2–1	1–2	2–0	0–1	0–0	2–1	1–1	1–1	2–0	2–0
	1–1	1–1	3–0	1–2	2–0	0–1	1–1	4–1	1–1	2–1	0–0	1–0	0–0	3–1
	0–4	3–1	2–3	1–0	3–1	3–0	1–2	1–1	2–3	2–0	2–2	4–3	0–1	3–2
	1–2	2–0	0–0	0–1	3–1	4–2	0–2	1–1	1–2	6–2	1–0	1–2	0–1	1–0
	0–3	2–2	0–1	0–3	1–2	0–1	0–1	2–1	3–1	2–1	0–2	0–1	2–2	3–0
	4–1	1–1	0–2	2–0	4–1	1–3	2–1	2–1	1–1	2–0	2–5	1–2	3–1	3–0
	—	1–2	1–0	0–2	1–3	1–1	1–1	1–1	2–1	2–2	1–1	3–0	1–1	4–2
	3–0	—	4–2	0–2	1–0	3–4	1–0	2–3	4–1	3–2	1–2	0–2	0–1	2–3
	1–0	3–1	—	0–0	2–2	3–3	0–2	1–3	1–0	1–1	3–1	0–1	2–1	1–2
	1–0	1–0	3–1	—	0–1	1–0	1–1	1–1	6–0	4–1	2–1	2–2	1–1	4–0
	3–1	4–0	4–2	1–1	—	1–1	0–1	3–1	0–0	0–2	1–1	1–0	1–0	0–0
	3–2	1–0	2–1	2–2	1–0	—	2–2	3–0	1–1	2–1	1–1	3–0	1–0	2–1
	4–2	4–1	1–1	0–0	0–0	0–1	—	2–0	0–0	2–0	4–2	1–1	2–1	4–4
	1–1	0–0	2–0	1–1	1–1	1–0	2–1	—	3–0	0–0	1–1	1–1	4–4	3–0
	4–0	1–0	3–0	3–1	0–2	1–0	1–1	1–0	—	1–0	0–1	0–1	2–0	2–2
	0–2	1–2	1–2	1–2	1–1	0–2	0–1	1–0	2–2	—	1–2	1–2	2–1	1–0
	4–0	4–2	2–0	1–2	1–0	0–0	4–2	1–1	4–0	6–0	—	2–0	3–1	1–0
	2–0	1–1	0–0	1–3	1–1	0–1	3–1	6–1	2–3	0–1	0–4	—	0–2	1–3
	3–1	0–3	1–1	3–0	2-0	1–1	3–0	3–0	0–1	5–2	1–1	1–0	—	4–0
	0–0	2–0	1–1	1–3	2–0	1–0	0–1	1–2	1–0	3–1	0–0	6–3	2–2	—

NORTHERN PREMIER LEAGUE –

	Barrow	Burton A.	Buxton	Chorley	Gainsboro' T.	Goole T.	Grantham	Howich R.M.I.
Barrow	—	5–0	2–0	2–2	3–0	4–3	1–0	2–0
Burton A.	0–0	—	4–1	2–4	0–2	0–0	0–2	1–2
Buxton	1–2	0–1	—	1–0	1–4	1–2	1–0	0–2
Chorley	0–2	0–2	4–0	—	3–4	4–1	1–3	2–2
Gainsboro' T.	1–2	1–1	3–2	1–1	—	0–1	3–1	0–2
Goole T.	2–3	0–0	2–2	0–0	6–3	—	3–1	2–0
Grantham	1–1	1–2	4–2	1–1	2–1	2–0	—	2–1
Howich R.M.I.	0–0	0–0	3–0	3–4	2–1	4–0	1–2	—
Hyde U.	0–0	0–0	3–1	4–1	1–2	2–1	2–1	2–0
Macclesfield T.	1–3	2–0	1–2	3–1	0–2	1–2	2–2	2–2
Marine	2–3	1–3	2–2	0–3	3–1	4–1	2–0	0–1
Matlock T.	1–2	1–1	2–1	0–1	3–1	5–2	0–0	1–0
Morecambe	2–1	1–1	4–0	1–2	1–2	1–4	1–0	1–1
Mossley	1–1	1–1	2–4	1–4	0–2	2–0	1–1	1–2
Oswestry T.	3–0	2–3	3–3	2–1	2–1	2–1	0–2	0–6
Rhyl	0–1	2–4	1–2	1–0	0–0	1–0	2–3	3–0
S. Liverpool	3–0	0–0	2–0	0–2	2–1	1–1	1–1	1–0
Southport	1–3	2–0	0–1	0–4	2–1	1–2	0–1	2–2
Stafford R.	1–1	1–1	1–2	0–0	3–1	4–0	4–0	3–1
Witton A.	1–3	2–1	4–1	2–1	3–1	0–2	1–2	7–1
Workington	1–3	0–1	6–1	2–1	0–1	0–0	4–1	3–1
Worksop T.	0–4	1–5	4–1	3–1	3–3	3–0	0–1	1–3

1983-84 RESULTS

Hyde U.	Macclesfield T.	Marine	Matlock T.	Morecambe	Mossley	Oswestry T.	Rhyl	S. Liverpool	Southport	Stafford R.	Witton A.	Workington	Worksop T.
2–2	2–0	4–0	3–0	4–1	3–1	4–0	1–0	2–1	5–1	1–1	2–2	3–1	2–1
1–2	0–2	1–2	3–0	1–0	1–1	4–0	2–1	0–1	3–1	2–2	2–0	3–0	4–1
0–1	1–3	2–2	0–1	3–3	2–3	1–0	1–2	0–1	3–2	2–2	1–0	3–1	0–2
1–1	4–2	0–2	4–4	2–1	1–0	3–2	0–1	1–1	1–2	1–1	0–0	1–3	1–2
4–1	2–2	2–2	1–1	1–1	4–1	5–1	1–1	5–0	1–1	3–1	1–1	3–1	6–2
2–4	0–2	1–1	2–3	2–2	0–0	3–3	1–4	1–2	3–1	2–0	2–5	0–2	2–0
1–3	2–1	4–0	0–1	1–0	2–1	0–1	4–0	1–1	3–0	0–1	4–1	0–0	5–3
2–1	1–1	1–0	0–1	3–1	2–0	4–2	0–3	1–1	2–1	2–1	1–1	1–0	2–3
—	2–0	0–2	0–2	3–1	1–3	2–0	2–4	0–2	0–3	0–1	2–2	1–2	2–0
1–3	—	4–1	2–2	1–0	2–0	2–1	3–1	2–1	2–0	2–2	2–0	2–1	1–0
5–2	2–1	—	1–1	1–1	2–1	0–1	1–1	1–1	5–2	2–2	1–3	1–0	1–2
2–2	2–1	0–1	—	2–0	3–0	4–1	3–1	2–3	1–0	3–0	0–1	2–0	1–0
2–0	1–1	4–1	2–0	—	1–0	2–1	0–1	1–3	1–2	0–0	2–2	2–2	5–1
0–1	1–1	3–0	0–5	5–1	—	1–0	0–2	0–0	2–2	2–3	2–0	1–2	0–3
2–2	2–0	0–4	1–1	4–4	0–2	—	5–2	0–1	2–3	1–4	3–3	3–0	1–4
2–0	1–2	0–2	2–1	6–1	1–2	3–1	—	3–0	0–0	1–2	2–1	3–1	1–0
1–1	1–0	2–1	1–2	2–1	1–0	1–0	2–1	—	4–2	4–3	1–0	1–0	0–0
2–1	2–0	3–0	1–2	0–2	4–2	3–3	3–0	1–0	—	1–1	2–1	1–1	1–1
0–2	1–3	1–2	2–1	4–0	3–2	1–4	2–1	1–1	4–0	—	1–0	0–0	0–0
2–0	1–1	3–1	2–3	1–1	1–1	2–1	0–0	0–1	2–1	0–0	—	2–1	2–0
1–2	0–3	1–1	2–0	2–0	1–0	3–4	0–2	4–2	2–0	0–0	1–1	—	0–0
2–1	1–1	0–1	1–3	2–3	4–1	2–2	1–1	2–1	0–1	0–1	2–1	0–2	—

SOUTHERN LEAGUE PREMIER DIVISION –

	A.P. Leamington	Alvechurch	Bedworth U.	Chelmsford C.	Cheltenham T.	Corby T.	Dartford	Dorchester T.
A.P. Leamington	—	3–1	0–0	2–2	4–2	3–1	3–4	2–2
Alvechurch	3–1	—	2–3	2–4	0–2	4–3	0–4	2–2
Bedworth U.	2–3	2–0	—	0–0	3–0	2–1	0–1	1–0
Chelmsford C.	2–3	2–2	2–0	—	2–1	2–1	1–0	5–0
Cheltenham T.	5–1	2–2	2–2	0–2	—	0–3	3–0	2–1
Corby T.	3–1	2–0	5–2	0–0	1–0	—	1–2	2–0
Dartford	2–0	1–1	0–0	3–0	1–0	2–2	—	2–0
Dorchester T.	4–1	2–2	0–2	2–4	2–0	1–2	0–0	—
Fareham T.	3–4	4–2	2–1	4–1	3–2	3–2	1–2	1–0
Fisher Ath.	5–0	0–0	2–3	2–1	2–0	2–2	1–1	2–0
Folkstone	2–1	1–1	2–1	1–3	1–3	1–0	1–0	3–2
Gloucester C.	2–1	1–2	5–2	2–0	0–0	1–1	1–1	3–3
Gosport Bor.	1–1	0–1	3–1	0–4	0–3	0–0	2–2	1–0
Gravesend & Northfl't.	1–0	2–0	2–0	1–1	2–0	1–1	1–1	1–0
Hastings U.	2–1	1–3	0–0	2–0	1–2	2–1	2–1	3–2
King's Lynn	1–1	1–1	2–0	1–0	3–2	0–1	0–0	2–0
Stourbridge	1–3	1–1	0–3	1–3	3–5	1–2	1–3	1–0
Sutton Coldfield T.	4–4	0–1	0–2	3–1	1–0	4–1	0–2	1–1
Welling U.	4–3	3–2	1–1	0–1	2–3	5–5	0–4	1–0
Witney T.	5–1	3–0	8–0	1–1	3–0	1–1	0–1	3–2

1983-84 RESULTS

Fareham T.	Fisher Ath.	Folkestone	Gloucester C.	Gosport Bor.	Gravesend and Northfl't	Hastings U.	King's Lynn	Stourbridge	Sutton Coldfield	Welling U.	Witney T.
4–2	0–5	1–1	4–1	2–3	3–1	3–1	1–0	2–1	1–1	1–1	4–2
3–3	0–4	2–1	0–0	5–0	0–1	1–3	2–0	2–0	3–1	2–0	2–1
1–2	1–1	3–1	0–0	2–2	1–0	4–1	2–0	2–1	0–1	1–3	1–0
1–1	1–1	4–2	2–1	1–1	1–2	3–1	0–1	6–1	2–0	2–0	1–0
0–0	1–4	1–1	4–1	4–1	1–1	2–0	2–0	2–0	2–2	3–0	2–1
0–0	2–7	1–1	0–0	0–0	0–0	0–0	0–1	2–0	2–0	2–1	2–4
2–1	3–1	4–1	0–2	2–1	4–1	2–1	0–1	3–0	1–0	2–1	4–1
4–0	0–1	2–3	1–3	1–0	1–2	1–2	0–3	1–2	0–0	1–3	2–2
—	0–1	4–2	2–0	1–2	2–2	1–2	2–2	0–1	0–3	1–0	2–1
6–3	—	1–3	2–0	3–2	3–2	1–0	2–3	0–0	3–2	1–2	1–0
1–1	1–1	—	1–3	3–0	1–0	0–0	2–1	1–0	3–0	0–2	1–2
3–3	2–1	0–0	—	3–0	1–0	2–2	1–2	4–0	1–1	1–1	0–4
0–0	0–2	0–2	1–1	—	0–2	1–1	1–1	0–1	1–1	0–3	0–2
1–0	1–2	2–0	3–1	0–0	—	2–1	0–1	1–1	1–1	2–0	5–1
3–3	3–2	0–3	1–1	3–0	2–0	—	2–0	3–1	2–3	1–1	0–3
1–0	0–3	3–2	1–2	3–2	0–1	1–2	—	1–0	1–1	2–1	0–3
4–6	1–1	1–4	1–2	0–1	0–2	1–1	0–1	—	0–1	0–4	0–0
1–2	0–1	4–4	1–1	1–1	1–2	2–1	2–0	1–1	—	0–1	3–1
2–3	1–1	1–0	1–3	2–2	4–1	1–3	1–2	4–0	2–1	—	1–0
3–1	1–2	1–3	1–0	1–1	2–1	2–0	3–0	4–3	1–1	4–1	—

SOUTHERN LEAGUE MIDLAND DIVISION –

	Aylesbury U.	Banbury U.	Bridgnorth T.	Bridgwater T.	Bromsgrove R.	Coventry Sporting	Dudley T.	Forest Green R.
Aylesbury U.	—	0–0	4–0	2–0	1–1	2–1	1–1	0–2
Banbury U.	1–1	—	0–3	1–1	1–2	0–1	1–1	1–1
Bridgnorth T.	0–2	4–1	—	5–0	1–0	2–3	1–0	2–2
Bridgwater T.	0–3	2–0	0–1	—	0–1	1–0	1–3	5–0
Bromsgrove R.	0–0	4–1	1–2	6–0	—	1–0	2–2	2–1
Coventry Sporting	0–1	1–2	2–0	1–2	1–0	—	1–1	0–2
Dudley T.	1–3	4–1	1–0	2–0	1–2	5–1	—	1–0
Forest Green R.	2–2	1–1	5–1	2–1	3–2	4–0	1–1	—
Leicester U.	2–2	2–1	2–1	4–0	0–0	1–2	1–0	0–1
Merthyr Tydfil	0–1	3–0	0–0	3–1	1–2	4–0	0–3	3–1
Milton Keynes C.	0–5	2–0	0–4	1–4	0–3	1–2	0–2	2–2
Moor Green	1–2	1–1	1–0	1–1	2–5	1–1	2–2	3–2
Oldbury U.	1–1	2–0	0–0	3–0	1–2	4–0	1–1	0–0
Redditch U.	2–0	2–1	0–0	5–3	1–1	1–1	4–0	2–1
Rushden T.	4–3	0–1	1–0	1–0	2–0	1–1	1–1	1–0
Shepshed Charterh'se	3–2	8–0	3–0	1–0	4–1	3–1	4–1	1–0
Tamworth	0–0	2–2	0–3	1–0	0–6	2–4	0–4	0–3
V.S. Rugby	0–0	2–0	1–1	0–1	2–3	2–0	3–3	1–2
Wellingborough T.	2–3	1–3	2–2	0–1	0–2	1–1	0–5	2–1
Willenhall T.	0–2	4–1	1–2	2–0	1–3	4–1	4–2	3–3

1983-84 RESULTS

Leicester U.	Merthyr Tydfil	Milton Keynes C.	Moor Green	Oldbury U.	Redditch U.	Rushden T.	Shepshed Chaterh'se	Tamworth	V.S. Rugby	Wellingborough T.	Willenhall T.
1–0	0–0	0–0	2–1	2–2	3–4	1–1	1–0	6–0	1–2	2–1	0–1
0–0	1–2	4–1	0–1	0–2	1–4	1–3	1–1	2–1	3–3	2–1	1–4
2–1	2–2	7–1	2–1	2–2	4–1	1–1	2–3	4–1	3–2	0–3	0–2
1–4	1–1	1–1	1–3	3–0	2–4	1–1	0–0	1–0	2–2	0–0	1–0
1–2	3–2	6–0	0–2	1–0	2–2	1–1	1–1	5–0	0–2	1–0	0–3
2–1	1–0	1–3	0–1	2–2	1–0	1–0	1–2	2–2	0–2	0–1	3–5
0–0	1–0	1–1	2–1	1–0	3–0	1–1	2–2	5–1	1–0	1–0	5–2
1–1	2–0	4–3	1–1	1–0	2–2	1–1	1–2	3–1	4–0	4–1	1–2
—	0–2	0–1	2–5	2–1	2–2	0–1	0–2	7–0	0–1	2–1	0–2
1–1	—	2–0	1–1	4–1	0–2	3–0	0–2	3–0	3–2	6–0	1–1
3–4	1–2	—	0–2	0–2	0–2	1–4	0–5	1–5	1–2	0–0	0–5
2–2	2–2	2–2	—	1–0	2–0	1–0	2–1	1–0	2–1	5–0	0–2
4–1	0–1	5–0	0–0	—	2–0	2–4	0–3	4–0	0–0	2–5	1–2
2–1	0–2	3–0	1–2	2–1	—	2–4	3–2	4–2	1–1	2–1	4–3
2–1	5–0	3–3	2–2	1–1	2–1	—	0–1	8–0	0–1	3–0	0–3
4–2	3–2	5–0	3–1	2–3	3–0	0–2	—	5–0	2–0	2–0	0–1
1–3	0–2	1–1	0–3	0–0	1–1	0–3	0–3	—	0–3	2–2	1–3
3–2	1–2	4–0	1–1	2–2	4–0	1–1	3–1	3–0	—	7–1	0–4
1–3	1–3	1–1	1–3	1–1	1–3	2–1	1–1	3–0	2–2	—	4–1
2–2	2–0	5–0	1–0	4–1	6–0	3–2	3–0	5–1	2–2	2–0	—

SOUTHERN LEAGUE SOUTHERN DIVISION –

	Addlestone & Weybridge	Andover	Ashford T.	Basingstoke T.	Cambridge C.	Canterbury C.	Chatham T.
Addlestone & Weybridge	—	1–1	2–1	1–1	0–0	2–0	4–0
Andover	1–2	—	1–0	0–2	1–1	0–1	2–1
Ashford T.	1–2	2–1	—	1–0	3–1	3–1	2–2
Basingstoke T.	1–0	6–0	0–2	—	1–0	2–0	3–1
Cambridge C.	0–1	1–0	3–4	0–1	—	2–1	3–0
Canterbury C.	3–1	0–0	0–1	0–2	4–1	—	0–1
Chatham T.	1–3	0–0	0–2	1–0	0–2	1–1	—
Crawley T.	1–0	5–0	2–2	0–1	2–1	1–1	2–0
Dover Ath.	3–1	2–1	1–0	2–2	0–0	1–0	1–1
Dunstable	0–2	0–4	0–0	1–0	1–0	0–3	0–3
Erith & Belvedere	1–1	2–1	1–1	1–1	0–2	1–0	3–1
Hillingdon.	2–0	2–0	1–0	0–1	2–0	0–2	2–0
Hounslow	1–2	0–1	3–2	0–1	1–1	2–2	0–2
Poole T.	1–2	1–2	1–0	3–0	0–1	4–1	2–1
R.S. Southampton	2–1	4–2	4–2	4–1	1–1	4–1	2–1
Salisbury	2–0	0–0	4–2	0–1	3–1	2–1	1–1
Thanet U.	1–2	1–0	1–2	1–1	0–2	1–2	1–2
Tonbridge	2–1	1–0	2–1	2–2	3–0	3–0	1–2
Waterlooville	3–3	0–1	2–4	0–2	1–2	1–1	1–3
Woodford T.	0–0	0–2	0–2	1–1	2–3	1–2	2–0

1983-84 RESULTS

Crawley T.	Dover Ath.	Dunstable	Erith & Belvedere	Hillingdon	Hounslow	Poole T.	R.S. Southampton	Salisbury	Thanet U.	Tonbridge	Waterlooville	Woodford T.
1–1	6–0	1–0	1–0	0–0	2–0	0–0	1–0	2–0	1–1	0–0	3–2	6–1
0–1	1–2	1–4	2–0	0–0	1–0	1–4	0–2	0–2	1–0	2–3	3–1	2–0
0–2	3–0	4–1	3–0	1–2	2–0	3–1	1–2	2–1	2–0	2–2	0–1	2–0
0–0	3–2	5–1	1–0	1–0	0–0	2–0	0–3	2–1	3–3	1–4	0–1	3–0
0–3	4–3	2–2	1–2	0–2	1–4	1–0	2–1	0–0	1–0	2–2	1–1	0–1
0–1	1–2	0–0	1–2	1–2	2–1	1–1	1–1	3–2	3–1	2–1	1–1	1–0
0–2	5–2	1–1	3–0	0–2	0–0	2–3	1–2	3–0	2–2	0–0	2–0	2–2
—	2–0	1–1	2–2	1–1	2–1	1–3	0–1	2–0	0–1	2–0	4–1	5–0
0–0	—	3–0	2–2	2–0	0–1	3–2	1–3	0–3	2–0	1–1	6–0	0–1
0–2	2–0	—	4–2	0–0	0–2	1–0	2–1	2–4	1–0	0–0	3–1	2–3
0–3	1–0	0–2	—	0–1	3–1	1–3	0–0	1–1	3–4	0–1	1–4	3–1
1–0	4–1	2–0	5–0	—	0–0	0–1	1–2	1–1	0–0	0–0	0–0	2–0
1–3	2–2	0–0	0–1	0–0	—	1–2	0–2	1–1	1–2	3–4	1–1	1–1
2–1	7–1	4–0	1–1	0–0	1–0	—	2–1	2–1	4–1	0–1	2–3	3–1
2–0	3–0	2–1	6–1	1–2	4–0	3–3	—	1–0	1–1	2–1	5–0	2–1
2–2	3–2	3–2	4–1	3–1	2–0	0–1	1–0	—	1–0	4–1	3–4	0–0
0–6	1–1	2–1	0–2	1–0	3–2	2–1	2–3	1–0	—	1–2	1–2	0–1
2–3	1–1	3–2	1–0	1–0	1–0	1–2	0–3	3–1	4–1	—	2–0	2–0
2–1	6–0	2–0	1–3	0–2	4–0	0–0	1–1	1–2	1–1	3–2	—	2–3
0–1	1–2	2–1	2–2	0–3	0–0	1–1	0–2	1–3	1–3	0–1	0–2	—

FOOTBALL LEAGUE DIVISION ONE FIXTURES

Subject to alteration; copyright of the Football League Limited, and may not be reproduced in whole or

	Arsenal	Aston Villa	Chelsea	Coventry C.	Everton	Ipswich T.	Leicester C.	Liverpool	Luton T.
Arsenal	—	10-11	25-8	2-2	6-10	12-1	16-3	8-9	1-12
Aston Villa	16-2	—	8-9	25-8	16-3	2-2	2-3	15-12	6-5
Chelsea	19-1	9-2	—	3-11	1-9	27-10	29-9	1-12	13-4
Coventry C.	29-9	19-1	23-2	—	9-2	10-11	1-9	6-5	6-4
Everton	23-3	13-10	22-12	8-9	—	4-9	3-11	9-3	1-1
Ipswich T.	15-9	29-9	2-3	16-2	29-12	—	9-2	27-4	27-8
Leicester C.	13-10	27-10	2-2	22-12	23-2	8-9	—	6-4	15-12
Liverpool	9-2	11-5	4-5	8-12	20-10	24-11	26-12	—	29-12
Luton T.	4-5	8-12	22-9	26-12	9-4	30-3	11-5	4-9	—
Manchester U.	3-11	23-3	5-9	12-1	2-3	22-12	16-2	22-9	17-11
Newcastle U.	29-12	1-9	10-11	16-3	15-9	6-10	19-1	17-11	23-2
Norwich C.	26-12	9-3	6-10	30-3	24-11	8-4	20-4	25-8	10-11
Nottingham F.	27-8	29-12	9-4	20-4	11-5	26-12	24-11	27-10	15-9
Q.P.R.	20-4	24-11	26-12	20-10	8-12	16-3	4-5	22-12	6-10
Sheffield W	24-11	26-12	8-12	2-3	4-5	22-9	20-10	2-2	16-3
Southampton	8-12	20-4	20-10	11-5	30-3	4-5	9-4	16-2	9-2
Stoke C.	30-3	27-8	11-5	8-4	20-4	8-12	15-9	3-11	19-1
Sunderland	9-3	4-5	30-3	22-9	26-12	11-5	8-12	12-1	27-10
Tottenham H.	8-4	30-3	24-11	4-5	19-1	20-4	27-8	13-10	29-9
Watford	1-9	15-9	16-3	6-10	29-9	23-2	29-12	1-1	9-3
W.B.A.	11-5	8-4	20-4	24-11	27-8	9-3	30-3	23-3	1-9
West Ham U.	27-10	23-2	12-1	4-9	10-11	25-8	6-10	13-4	27-4

1984-85

in part without their consent.

Manchester U.	Newcastle U.	Norwich C.	Nottingham F.	Q.P.R.	Sheffield W.	Southampton	Stoke C.	Sunderland	Tottenham H.	Watford	W.B.A.	West Ham U.
23-2	4-9	6-4	13-4	17-11	27-4	6-5	22-9	20-10	1-1	22-12	15-12	2-3
6-10	22-12	20-10	5-9	27-4	6-4	17-11	13-4	1-12	22-9	12-1	1-1	3-11
29-12	16-2	23-3	1-1	6-4	6-5	9-3	15-12	27-8	27-4	13-10	17-11	15-9
15-9	13-10	27-8	17-11	9-3	27-10	15-12	1-1	13-4	1-12	23-3	27-4	29-12
27-10	12-1	27-4	15-12	6-5	1-12	22-9	17-11	6-4	25-8	2-2	13-4	16-12
1-9	23-3	1-1	6-4	13-10	13-4	1-12	6-5	15-12	17-11	3-11	20-10	19-1
10-11	25-8	17-11	27-4	1-12	9-3	1-1	12-1	6-5	13-4	5-9	22-9	23-3
30-3	20-4	19-1	2-3	1-9	29-9	10-11	23-2	15-9	16-3	9-4	6-10	27-8
20-4	3-11	16-2	12-1	23-3	13-10	8-9	25-8	2-3	2-2	20-10	22-12	24-11
—	8-9	1-12	6-5	15-12	1-1	13-4	6-4	27-4	20-10	25-8	2-2	13-10
9-2	—	15-12	20-10	13-4	27-8	27-4	1-12	1-1	6-5	2-3	6-4	29-9
4-5	11-5	—	2-2	27-10	23-2	12-1	8-9	16-3	22-12	22-9	5-9	8-12
8-12	9-3	29-9	—	9-2	19-1	23-2	6-10	1-9	10-11	4-5	16-3	30-3
11-5	22-9	2-3	8-9	—	10-11	2-2	4-9	23-2	12-1	30-3	25-8	8-4
9-4	30-3	3-11	25-8	16-2	—	4-9	22-12	6-10	8-9	20-4	12-1	11-5
27-8	24-11	15-9	3-11	29-9	29-12	—	16-3	19-1	6-10	26-12	2-3	1-9
26-12	4-5	9-2	23-3	29-12	1-9	13-10	—	29-9	2-3	24-11	16-2	20-10
24-11	8-4	13-10	22-12	3-11	23-3	25-8	2-2	—	4-9	16-2	8-9	20-4
9-3	8-12	1-9	16-2	15-9	9-2	23-3	27-10	29-12	—	11-5	3-11	26-12
19-1	27-10	13-4	1-12	27-8	17-11	6-4	27-4	10-11	15-12	—	6-5	9-2
29-9	26-12	29-12	13-10	19-1	15-9	27-10	10-11	9-2	23-2	8-12	—	4-5
16-3	2-2	6-5	22-9	1-1	15-12	22-12	9-3	17-11	6-4	8-9	1-12	—

FOOTBALL LEAGUE DIVISION TWO FIXTURES

Subject to alteration; copyright of the Football League Limited, and may not be reproduced in whole or

	Barnsley	Birmingham C.	Blackburn R.	Brighton & H.A.	Cardiff C.	Carlisle U.	Charlton Ath.	Crystal Palace	Fulham
Barnsley	—	27-4	1-1	9-3	15-9	27-8	27-10	23-3	1-12
Birmingham C.	24-11	—	13-10	23-3	4-5	15-9	20-4	9-2	29-12
Blackburn R.	8-4	16-3	—	10-11	18-9	1-9	24-11	19-1	9-2
Brighton & H. A.	20-10	6-10	16-2	—	9-2	19-1	8-4	15-9	29-9
Cardiff C.	12-1	1-12	13-4	8-9	—	17-11	25-8	6-5	9-3
Carlisle U.	30-3	12-1	22-12	25-8	20-4	—	4-5	13-10	3-11
Charlton Ath.	2-3	17-11	27-4	1-1	19-1	1-12	—	6-4	13-10
Crystal Palace	6-10	8-9	25-8	12-1	8-12	16-3	26-12	—	27-10
Fulham	4-5	4-9	8-9	2-2	20-10	23-2	16-3	2-3	—
Grimsby T.	25-8	6-4	12-1	6-5	2-3	20-10	4-9	15-12	17-11
Huddersfield T.	22-9	2-2	4-9	22-12	24-11	2-3	30-3	16-2	23-3
Leeds U.	16-3	15-12	6-4	17-11	29-12	10-11	23-2	13-4	27-8
Manchester C.	26-12	10-11	27-10	23-2	30-3	9-2	11-5	29-9	1-9
Middlesbrough	10-11	6-5	17-11	27-4	29-9	6-4	6-10	1-12	13-4
Notts Co.	4-9	20-10	22-9	13-4	13-10	27-4	22-12	1-1	15-12
Oldham Ath.	22-12	25-8	9-3	22-9	16-2	15-12	12-1	27-4	6-5
Oxford U.	11-5	2-3	3-11	13-10	26-12	29-9	8-12	29-12	15-9
Portsmouth	8-9	13-4	1-12	6-4	23-3	6-5	2-2	17-11	1-1
Sheffield U.	23-2	1-1	6-5	15-12	1-9	13-4	10-11	18-9	6-4
Shrewsbury T.	20-4	23-2	23-3	27-10	9-4	29-12	9-3	1-9	19-1
Wimbledon	8-12	22-12	2-2	4-9	11-5	6-10	22-9	3-11	16-2
Wolverhampton W.	2-2	22-9	15-12	1-12	3-11	1-1	8-9	20-10	27-4

1984-85

in part without their consent.

Grimsby T.	Huddersfield T.	Leeds U.	Manchester C.	Middlesbrough	Notts Co.	Oldham Ath.	Oxford U.	Portsmouth	Sheffield U.	Shrewsbury T.	Wimbledon	Wolverhampton W.
19-1	13-4	13-10	6-4	16-2	29-12	1-9	15-12	9-2	3-11	17-11	6-5	29-9
26-12	29-9	11-5	16-2	8-12	9-3	19-1	27-10	18-9	8-4	3-11	1-9	30-3
15-9	29-12	26-12	2-3	20-4	30-3	20-10	23-2	4-5	8-12	6-10	29-9	11-5
8-12	1-9	20-4	3-11	24-11	27-8	30-3	16-3	26-12	11-5	2-3	29-12	4-5
27-10	27-4	4-9	22-9	2-2	16-3	10-11	6-4	6-10	22-12	1-1	15-12	23-2
9-3	27-10	16-2	8-9	26-12	24-11	11-5	2-2	8-12	22-9	4-9	23-3	8-4
29-12	27-8	3-11	15-12	23-3	1-9	15-9	6-5	29-9	16-2	20-10	13-4	9-2
11-5	10-11	22-9	2-2	4-5	9-4	24-11	4-9	20-4	30-3	22-12	23-2	9-3
20-4	6-10	30-3	22-12	22-9	11-5	8-12	12-1	8-4	26-12	25-8	10-11	24-11
—	1-1	8-9	13-4	22-12	23-2	6-10	22-9	16-3	2-2	1-12	27-4	10-11
9-4	—	20-10	12-1	3-11	20-4	26-12	25-8	11-5	4-5	8-9	13-10	8-12
9-2	9-3	—	1-1	27-10	19-1	29-9	27-4	15-9	6-10	6-5	1-12	1-9
27-8	15-9	8-4	—	9-3	8-12	4-5	6-10	24-11	20-4	16-3	19-1	29-12
1-9	23-2	2-3	20-10	—	9-2	29-12	1-1	19-1	16-3	15-12	18-9	15-9
3-11	17-11	25-8	6-5	8-9	—	2-3	1-12	16-2	12-1	2-2	6-4	23-3
23-3	6-4	2-2	1-12	4-9	27-10	—	17-11	3-11	8-9	13-4	1-1	13-10
30-3	19-1	24-11	23-3	8-4	4-5	20-4	—	1-9	20-10	16-2	9-2	19-9
13-10	15-12	12-1	27-4	25-18	10-11	23-2	22-12	—	4-9	22-9	9-3	27-10
29-9	1-12	23-3	17-11	13-10	15-9	9-2	9-3	29-12	—	27-4	27-10	19-1
4-5	9-2	8-12	13-10	11-5	29-9	18-9	10-11	30-3	24-11	—	15-9	26-12
24-11	16-3	4-5	25-8	30-3	26-12	8-4	8-9	20-10	2-3	12-1	—	20-4
16-2	6-5	22-12	4-9	12-1	6-10	16-3	13-4	2-3	25-8	6-4	17-11	—

FOOTBALL LEAGUE DIVISION THREE FIXTURES

	Bolton W.	Bournemouth	Bradford C.	Brentford	Brisol C.	Bristol R.	Burnley	Cambridge U.	Derby Co.	Doncaster R.
Bolton W.	—	13-10	6-5	27-4	5-3	25-8	2-3	22-12	12-1	2-2
Bournemouth	16-3	—	27-4	24-11	15-12	2-2	6-10	6-4	25-8	22-9
Bradford C.	29-12	1-12	—	23-3	20-10	13-2	20-4	25-8	10-11	26-12
Brentford	1-12	20-4	6-10	—	23-2	26-12	5-3	2-2	30-3	2-10
Bristol C.	23-10	4-5	9-3	3-11	—	10-11	29-12	26-1	12-2	30-3
Bristol R.	15-1	29-9	18-9	6-4	13-4	—	19-1	1-1	6-10	20-10
Burnley	27-10	23-3	24-11	23-10	6-5	8-9	—	13-4	26-1	12-1
Cambridge U.	11-5	26-12	5-1	29-9	15-9	8-4	10-11	—	1-12	5-3
Derby Co.	1-9	5-1	13-4	7-11	19-9	23-3	15-9	27-4	—	3-11
Doncaster R.	29-9	9-2	6-4	16-2	6-11	9-3	1-9	23-10	23-2	—
Gillingham	20-4	9-4	27-10	9-3	16-3	29-12	30-3	8-9	26-12	11-5
Hull C.	19-1	1-9	16-2	22-12	1-1	2-3	9-2	6-11	9-3	13-10
Lincoln C.	23-2	20-10	22-12	13-4	27-4	22-9	16-3	3-10	2-2	26-1
Millwall	4-5	29-12	23-2	13-10	27-10	20-4	1-12	12-1	2-10	12-2
Newport Co.	10-11	18-9	9-2	15-9	1-9	4-5	12-2	3-11	11-5	1-12
Orient	9-4	11-5	29-9	5-1	9-2	1-12	18-9	13-10	4-5	29-12
Plymouth Arg.	9-2	15-9	6-11	1-1	6-4	3-11	5-1	15-12	16-3	2-3
Preston N. E.	9-3	2-3	23-10	15-12	24-11	12-1	3-11	16-2	8-9	25-8
Reading	6-10	3-11	15-12	22-12	6-5	26-1	20-10	24-11	22-9	8-9
Rotherham U.	15-9	19-1	1-1	18-9	16-2	13-10	29-9	6-5	27-10	23-3
Swansea C.	18-9	12-2	15-9	9-2	19-1	11-5	4-5	2-3	29-12	20-4
Walsall	12-2	10-11	19-1	1-9	29-9	30-3	11-5	23-3	23-10	8-4
Wigan Ath.	26-12	30-3	1-9	19-1	5-1	23-10	9-4	9-3	20-4	4-5
York C.	30-3	5-3	16-3	2-3	6-10	2-10	26-12	22-9	8-4	10-11

1984-85

in part without their consent.

Gillingham	Hull C.	Lincoln C.	Millwall	Newport Co.	Orient	Plymouth Arg.	Preston N. E.	Reading	Rotherham U.	Swansea C.	Walsall	Wigan Ath.	York C.
24-11	8-9	3-11	15-12	13-4	1-1	22-9	20-10	23-3	26-1	16-2	2-10	6-4	6-11
1-1	12-1	9-3	6-5	16-2	22-12	26-1	27-10	23-2	8-9	2-10	13-4	6-11	23-10
2-3	3-10	11-5	3-11	22-9	2-2	30-3	6-3	4-5	8-4	26-1	8-9	12-1	13-10
20-10	11-5	10-11	16-3	26-1	25-8	8-4	4-5	29-12	12-2	22-9	12-1	8-9	27-10
13-10	8-4	1-12	2-3	12-1	22-9	26-12	20-4	11-5	2-10	8-9	2-2	25-8	23-3
6-5	27-10	9-2	24-11	15-12	27-4	23-2	1-9	15-9	16-3	22-12	6-11	5-3	16-2
6-11	22-9	13-10	27-4	2-10	16-2	25-8	23-2	9-3	2-2	15-12	22-12	1-1	6-4
19-1	30-3	12-2	1-9	23-2	16-3	4-5	18-9	20-4	29-12	27-10	6-10	20-10	9-2
6-4	20-10	29-9	16-2	22-12	15-12	13-10	19-1	9-2	2-3	6-5	6-3	24-11	1-1
22-12	16-3	15-9	18-9	27-4	6-5	27-10	5-1	19-1	16-10	24-11	1-1	15-12	13-4
—	12-2	4-5	6-10	25-8	12-1	2-10	1-12	23-10	10-11	2-2	22-9	26-1	23-2
18-9	—	5-1	6-4	24-11	13-4	23-3	15-9	29-9	3-11	23-10	15-12	27-4	6-5
15-12	25-8	—	6-3	7-11	6-4	8-9	6-10	27-10	12-1	1-1	6-5	16-2	24-11
23-3	26-12	23-10	—	2-2	8-9	11-5	10-11	9-4	30-3	25-8	26-1	22-9	9-3
5-1	20-4	30-3	29-9	—	20-10	29-12	8-4	26-12	5-3	13-10	2-3	23-3	19-1
1-9	10-11	26-12	19-1	9-3	—	23-10	12-2	30-3	20-4	23-3	3-11	2-3	15-9
16-2	6-10	19-1	22-12	6-5	5-3	—	29-9	1-9	20-10	27-4	24-11	13-4	18-9
27-4	26-1	23-3	13-4	1-1	2-10	2-2	—	13-10	22-9	6-11	6-4	6-5	22-12
6-3	2-2	2-3	1-1	6-4	7-11	12-1	16-3	—	25-8	13-4	16-2	3-10	27-4
13-4	23-2	1-9	6-11	23-10	24-11	9-3	9-2	5-1	—	6-4	27-4	22-12	15-12
29-9	5-3	9-4	5-1	16-3	6-10	1-12	30-3	10-11	26-12	—	20-10	3-11	1-9
9-2	4-5	29-12	15-9	27-10	23-2	20-4	26-12	18-9	1-12	9-3	—	13-10	5-1
15-9	1-12	18-9	9-2	6-10	27-10	10-11	29-12	12-2	11-5	23-2	16-3	—	29-9
3-11	29-12	20-4	20-10	8-9	26-1	12-2	11-5	1-12	4-5	12-1	25-8	2-2	—

FOOTBALL LEAGUE DIVISION FOUR FIXTURES

Subject to alteration; copyright of the Football League Limited, and may not be reproduced in whole or

	Aldershot	Blackpool	Bury	Chester C.	Chesterfield	Colchester U.	Crewe Alex.	Darlington	Exeter C.	Halifax T.
Aldershot	—	23-3	13-10	1-9	5-1	9-2	26-12	29-9	15-9	19-1
Blackpool	6-10	—	20-10	29-9	9-2	19-1	8-4	15-9	1-9	5-1
Bury	16-3	9-3	—	19-1	29-9	15-9	10-11	5-1	9-2	1-9
Chester C.	12-1	2-2	8-9	—	27-10	20-10	6-3	23-2	16-3	6-10
Chesterfield	25-8	22-9	2-2	2-3	—	3-11	4-5	6-10	20-10	16-3
Colchester U.	22-9	8-9	26-1	9-3	23-2	—	11-5	16-3	6-10	27-10
Crew Alex.	6-4	1-1	13-4	23-10	15-12	22-12	—	6-5	27-4	24-11
Darlington	2-2	26-1	25-8	3-11	23-3	13-10	29-12	—	2-3	9-3
Exeter C.	26-1	12-1	22-9	13-10	9-3	23-3	1-12	27-10	—	23-2
Halifax T.	8-9	25-8	12-1	23-3	13-10	2-3	20-4	20-10	3-11	—
Hartlepool U.	27-4	6-5	1-1	22-12	19-9	13-4	29-9	16-2	7-11	6-4
Hereford U	22-12	24-11	6-3	19-9	16-2	6-4	19-1	7-11	6-5	15-12
Mansfield T.	6-3	27-4	24-11	7-11	6-4	19-9	15-9	1-1	16-2	13-4
Northampton T.	20-10	2-3	3-11	9-2	1-9	29-9	30-3	19-1	5-1	15-9
Peterborough U	16-2	7-11	22-12	1-1	6-5	27-4	3-11	24-11	15-12	24-10
Port Vale	13-4	16-2	6-4	24-11	22-10	6-5	6-10	15-12	1-1	27-4
Rochdale	2-10	6-4	6-11	27-4	22-12	24-11	2-3	5-3	13-4	1-1
Scunthorpe U.	3-11	13-10	2-3	5-1	15-9	1-9	18-9	9-2	19-1	29-9
Southend U.	2-3	3-11	23-3	15-9	19-1	5-1	11-2	1-9	29-9	9-2
Stockport Co.	5-11	13-4	1-10	15-12	27-4	4-3	20-10	22-12	24-11	6-5
Swindon T.	24-11	2-10	16-2	6-5	1-1	15-12	16-3	27-4	5-3	22-12
Torquay U.	1-1	15-12	27-4	13-4	24-11	16-2	5-1	18-9	6-4	6-11
Tranmere R.	15-12	22-10	6-5	16-2	13-4	5-11	1-9	6-4	22-12	17-9
Wrexham	6-5	22-12	15-12	6-4	6-11	1-1	9-2	13-4	18-9	16-2

1984-85

in part without their consent.

Hartlepool U.	Hereford U.	Mansfield T.	Northampton T.	Peterborough U.	Port Vale	Rochdale	Scunthorpe U.	Southend U.	Stockport Co.	Swindon T.	Torquay U.	Tranmere R.	Wrexham
1-12	11-5	23-10	9-3	18-9	10-11	12-2	23-2	27-10	30-3	20-4	9-4	4-5	29-12
29-12	20-4	1-12	27-10	30-3	18-9	26-12	16-3	23-2	10-11	12-2	4-5	5-3	11-5
8-4	23-10	20-4	23-2	11-5	26-12	30-3	27-10	6-10	12-2	18-9	1-12	29-12	4-5
11-5	13-2	30-3	22-9	5-4	20-4	1-12	25-8	26-1	4-5	29-12	10-11	3-10	26-12
12-2	2-10	26-12	12-1	29-12	5-3	11-5	26-1	8-9	1-12	9-4	20-4	10-11	30-3
10-11	26-12	12-2	2-2	1-12	29-12	20-4	12-1	25-8	23-10	4-5	2-10	30-3	5-4
2-2	8-9	26-1	6-11	23-2	23-3	27-10	16-2	2-10	9-3	13-10	25-8	12-1	22-9
2-10	30-3	9-4	8-9	20-4	4-5	23-10	22-9	12-1	11-5	1-12	12-2	26-12	10-11
30-3	29-12	3-10	25-8	4-5	8-4	10-11	8-9	2-2	20-4	24-10	26-12	11-5	13-2
26-12	4-5	10-11	26-1	5-3	1-12	8-4	2-2	22-9	29-12	11-5	30-3	12-2	2-10
—	13-10	27-10	15-12	9-2	19-1	15-9	24-11	24-10	5-1	1-9	9-3	23-3	23-2
16-3	—	6-10	27-4	1-9	29-9	5-1	13-4	1-1	15-9	9-2	23-2	20-10	27-10
2-3	23-3	—	22-12	19-1	5-1	1-9	15-12	6-5	9-2	29-9	13-10	3-11	20-10
4-5	1-12	11-5	—	26-12	12-2	18-9	6-10	16-3	9-4	10-11	29-12	20-4	5-3
22-9	12-1	8-9	6-4	—	2-3	9-3	3-10	13-4	13-10	23-3	2-2	25-8	26-1
8-9	2-2	25-8	1-10	27-10	—	16-3	22-12	5-11	23-2	9-3	26-1	22-9	12-1
26-1	25-8	12-1	16-2	20-10	13-10	—	6-5	15-12	23-3	3-11	22-9	2-2	8-9
20-4	10-11	4-5	23-3	12-2	11-5	29-12	—	9-3	26-12	30-3	23-10	9-4	17-12
4-3	8-4	29-12	13-10	10-11	30-3	4-5	20-10	—	17-9	26-12	11-5	1-12	20-4
25-8	26-1	22-9	1-1	16-3	3-11	6-10	6-4	16-2	—	2-3	12-1	8-9	2-2
12-1	22-9	2-2	13-4	6-10	20-10	23-2	6-11	6-4	27-10	—	8-9	26-1	25-8
20-10	3-11	16-3	6-5	29-9	15-9	9-2	5-3	22-12	1-9	19-1	—	2-3	6-10
6-10	9-3	23-2	24-11	5-1	9-2	29-9	1-1	27-4	19-1	15-9	27-10	—	16-3
3-11	2-3	9-3	23-10	15-9	1-9	19-1	27-4	24-11	29-9	5-1	23-3	13-10	—

THE GOLA (ALLIANCE PREMIER) LEAGUE FIXTURES 1984-85

Sat 18 August 1984
Altrincham v Kettering Town
Barrow v Weymouth
Barnet v Telford United
Dagenham v Frickley Athletic
Dartford v Scarborough
Gateshead v Worcester City
Kidderminster Harriers v Enfield
Maidstone United v Runcorn
Northwich Victoria v Wealdstone
Nuneaton Borough v Bath City
Yeovil Town v Boston United

Mon 20 August 1984
Worcester City v Altrincham

Tues 21 August 1984
Bath City v Maidstone United
Enfield v Nuneaton Borough
Runcorn v Barrow
Telford United v Yeovil Town
Wealdstone v Dartford

Wed 22 August 1984
Boston United v Barnet
Kettering Town v Dagenham
Scarborough v Northwich Victoria
Weymouth v Kidderminster Harriers

Sat 25 August 1984
Bath City v Barrow
Boston United v Maidstone United
Enfield v Altrincham
Frickley Athletic v Dartford
Kettering Town v Northwich Victoria
Runcorn v Nuneaton Borough
Scarborough v Yeovil Town
Telford United v Dagenham
Wealdstone v Kidderminster Harriers
Weymouth v Gateshead
Worcester City v Barnet

Mon 27 August 1984
Maidstone United v Scarborough
Altrincham v Frickley Athletic
Barrow v Runcorn
Barnet v Enfield
Dagenham v Wealdstone
Dartford v Kettering Town
Gateshead v Boston United
Kidderminster Harriers v Weymouth
Northwich Victoria v Bath City
Nuneaton Borough v Telford United
Yeovil Town v Worcester City

Sat 1 September 1984
Altrincham v Nuneaton Borough
Dagenham v Worcester City
Dartford v Telford United
Enfield v Frickley Athletic
Kettering Town v Bath City
Kidderminster Harriers v Boston United
Maidstone United v Northwich Victoria
Scarborough v Barnet
Wealdstone v Gateshead
Weymouth v Runcorn
Yeovil Town v Barrow

Mon 3 September 1984
Dagenham v Weymouth
Gateshead v Scarborough

Tues 4 September 1984
Dartford v Yeovil Town
Frickley Athletic v Barrow
Telford United v Enfield
Barnet v Nuneaton Borough
Bath City v Kidderminster Harriers
Runcorn v Altrincham

Wed 5 September 1984
Boston United v Kettering Town

Sat 8 September 1984
Barnet v Altrincham
Barrow v Dartford
Bath City v Dagenham

Boston United v Wealdstone
Frickley Athletic v Kidderminster Harriers
Gateshead v Enfield
Northwich Victoria v Weymouth
Nuneaton Borough v Yeovil Town
Runcorn v Kettering Town
Telford United v Maidstone United
Worcester City v Scarborough

Mon 10 September 1984
Altrincham v Runcorn
Kidderminster Harriers v Bath City
Northwich Victoria v Worcester City

Tue 11 September 1984
Wealdstone v Nuneaton Borough
Barrow v Frickley Athletic
Enfield v Telford United

Wed 12 September 1984
Maidstone United v Barnet
Kettering Town v Boston United
Scarborough v Gateshead
Weymouth v Dagenham
Yeovil Town v Dartford

Sat 15 September 1984
Altrincham v Yeovil Town
Dagenham v Northwich Victoria
Dartford v Worcester City
Maidstone United v Kettering Town
Scarborough v Enfield
Telford United v Boston United
Weymouth v Barnet

Mon 17 September 1984
Dagenham v Maidstone United
Gateshead v Runcorn
Northwich Victoria v Scarborough
Worcester City v Weymouth

Tues 18 September 1984
Dartford v Enfield
Telford United v Frickley Athletic

Wed 19 September 1984
Boston United v Nuneaton Borough
Yeovil Town v Wealdstone

Sat 22 September 1984
Barnet v Northwich Victoria
Bath City v Altrincham
Boston United v Weymouth
Enfield v Barrow
Gateshead v Telford United
Kettering Town v Scarborough
Kidderminster Harriers v Dagenham
Nuneaton Borough v Frickley Athletic
Runcorn v Enfield
Worcester City v Wealdstone
Yeovil Town v Maidstone United

Mon 24 September 1984
Altrincham v Worcester City
Northwich Victoria v Nuneaton Borough

Tues 25 September 1984
Enfield v Barnet
Frickley Athletic v Gateshead
Wealdstone v Boston United

Wed 26 September 1984
Kettering Town v Nuneaton Borough
Scarborough v Barrow
Weymouth v Bath City

Sat 29 September 1984
Barnet v Kettering Town
Barrow v Frickley Athletic
Bath City v Wealdstone
Dartford v Yeovil Town
Dagenham v Altrincham
Maidstone United v Boston United
Nuneaton Borough v Kidderminster Harriers
Runcorn v Gateshead
Telford United v Northwich Victoria
Weymouth v Scarborough
Worcester City v Enfield

Mon 1 October 1984
Altrincham v Gateshead

Tues 2 October 1984
Dartford v Wealdstone

Wed 3 October 1984
Kettering Town v Telford United

Sat 6 October 1984
Altrincham v Maidstone United
Bath City v Gateshead

Boston United v Barrow
Enfield v Runcorn
Kettering Town v Worcester City
Kidderminster Harriers v Barnet
Northwich Victoria v Dartford
Nuneaton Borough v Weymouth
Scarborough v Dagenham
Yeovil v Frickley Athletic

Sat 13 October 1984
Barnet v Yeovil Town
Dagenham v Boston United
Gateshead v Frickley Athletic
Maidstone United v Enfield
Northwich Victoria v Altrincham
Runcorn v Bath City
Scarborough v Dartford
Telford United v Nuneaton Borough
Wealdstone v Barrow
Weymouth v Kettering Town
Worcester City v Kidderminster Harriers

Tues 16 October 1984
Dartford v Kidderminster Harriers

Sat 20 October 1984
Altrincham v Weymouth
Barrow v Telford United
Bath City v Scarborough
Boston United v Dartford
Enfield v Northwich Victoria
Frickley Athletic v Barnet
Kettering Town v Gateshead
Kidderminster Harriers v Runcorn
Nuneaton Borough v Maidstone United
Wealdstone v Worcester City
Yeovil Town v Dagenham

Sat 27 October 1984
Bath City v Nuneaton Borough
Gateshead v Barrow
Runcorn v Wealdstone
Telford United v Altrincham

Sat 3 November 1984
Altrincham v Kidderminster Harriers
Barnet v Runcorn
Barrow v Enfield
Boston United v Northwich Victoria
Dagenham v Bath City
Dartford v Weymouth
Frickley Athletic v Kettering Town
Maidstone United v Gateshead
Nuneaton Borough v Worcester City
Wealdstone v Telford United
Yeovil Town v Scarborough

Sat 10 November 1984
Bath City v Barnet
Dartford v Nuneaton Borough
Enfield v Wealdstone
Kettering Town v Boston United
Kidderminster Harriers v Altrincham
Northwich Victoria v Yeovil Town
Runcorn v Dagenham
Scarborough v Frickley Athletic
Telford United v Gateshead
Weymouth v Maidstone United
Worcester City v Barrow

Sat 17 November 1984
Frickley Athletic v Barrow
Runcorn v Weymouth

Sat 24 November 1984
Altrincham v Scarborough
Barnet v Dartford
Barrow v Kidderminster Harriers
Boston United v Worcester City
Dagenham v Weymouth
Frickley Athletic v Telford United
Kettering Town v Enfield
Maidstone United v Yeovil Town
Northwich Victoria v Gateshead
Nuneaton Borough v Runcorn
Wealdstone v Bath City

Sat 1 December 1984
Bath City v Kettering Town
Dartford v Boston United
Enfield v Maidstone United
Gateshead v Dagenham
Kidderminster Harriers v Northwich Victoria
Runcorn v Barnet
Scarborough v Nuneaton Borough
Telford United v Barrow
Weymouth v Wealdstone
Worcester City v Frickley Athletic
Yeovil Town v Altrincham

Sat 8 December 1984
Altrincham v Telford United
Barnet v Kidderminster Harriers
Barrow v Kettering Town
Boston United v Gateshead

Dagenham v Dartford
Frickley Athletic v Bath City
Maidstone United v Weymouth
Nuneaton Borough v Northwich Victoria
Scarborough v Runcorn
Wealdstone v Enfield
Worcester City v Yeovil Town

Sat 15 December 1984
Barrow v Nuneaton Borough
Bath City v Telford United
Dartford v Barnet
Enfield v Worcester City
Frickley Athletic v Wealdstone
Gateshead v Altrincham
Kidderminster Harriers v Maidstone United
Nuneaton Borough v Dagenham
Runcorn v Scarborough

Sat 22 December 1984
Barnet v Frickley Athletic
Dagenham v Kidderminster Harriers
Kettering Town v Barrow
Maidstone United v Bath City
Runcorn v Gateshead
Scarborough v Boston United
Telford United v Runcorn
Wealdstone v Altrincham
Weymouth v Enfield
Worcester City v Northwich Victoria
Yeovil Town v Dartford

Wed 26 December 1984
Altrincham v Barrow
Barnet v Wealdstone
Bath City v Worcester City
Boston United v Frickley Athletic
Dagenham v Enfield
Dartford v Maidstone United
Kidderminster Harriers v Telford United
Northwich Victoria v Runcorn
Nuneaton Borough v Kettering Town
Scarborough v Gateshead
Yeovil Town v Weymouth

Sat 29 December 1984
Altrincham v Dagenham
Barrow v Northwich Victoria
Bath City v Dartford
Enfield v Boston United
Frickley Athletic v Nuneaton Borough
Gateshead v Kettering Town
Kidderminster Harriers v Scarborough
Runcorn v Yeovil Town
Telford United v Barnet
Wealdstone v Maidstone United
Weymouth v Worcester City

Tues 1 January 1985
Barrow v Altrincham
Enfield v Dagenham
Frickley Athletic v Boston United
Gateshead v Scarborough
Kettering Town v Nuneaton Borough
Maidstone United v Dartford
Runcorn v Northwich Victoria
Telford United v Kidderminster Harriers
Wealdstone v Barnet
Weymouth v Yeovil Town
Worcester City v Bath City

Sat 5 January 1985
Altrincham v Bath City
Barnet v Weymouth
Boston United v Telford United
Dagenham v Runcorn
Dartford v Frickley Athletic
Kidderminster Harriers v Gateshead
Northwich Victoria v Barrow
Nuneaton Borough v Enfield
Scarborough v Wealdstone
Worcester City v Maidstone United
Yeovil Town v Kettering Town

Sat 19 January 1985
Barrow v Worcester City
Bath City v Yeovil Town
Dagenham v Gateshead
Frickley Athletic v Scarborough
Kettering Town v Altrincham
Kidderminster Harriers v Dartford
Maidstone United v Nuneaton Borough
Northwich Victoria v Barnet
Runcorn v Boston United
Telford United v Enfield
Wealdstone v Weymouth

Sat 26 January 1985
Barnet v Barrow
Boston United v Kidderminster Harriers
Dartford v Bath City
Enfield v Kettering Town
Frickley Athletic v Maidstone United
Gateshead v Wealdstone
Nuneaton Borough v Dagenham
Scarborough v Telford United
Weymouth v Altrincham

Worcester City v Runcorn
Yeovil Town v Northwich Victoria

Sat 2 February 1985
Runcorn v Weymouth

Sat 9 February 1985
Altrincham v Northwich Victoria
Barrow v Boston United
Dagenham v Barnet
Enfield v Gateshead
Kettering Town v Kidderminster Harriers
Maidstone United v Worcester City
Runcorn v Frickley Athletic
Telford United v Dartford
Wealdstone v Scarborough
Weymouth v Nuneaton Borough
Yeovil Town v Bath City

Sat 16 February 1985
Barnet v Worcester City
Bath City v Enfield
Boston United v Kettering Town
Dartford v Dagenham
Frickley Athletic v Weymouth
Gateshead v Maidstone United
Kidderminster Harriers v Wealdstone
Northwich Victoria v Telford United
Nuneaton Borough v Barrow
Scarborough v Altrincham
Yeovil Town v Runcorn

Tues 19 February 1985
Wealdstone v Frickley Athletic

Wed 20 February 1985
Weymouth v Dartford

Sat 23 February 1985
Barnet v Scarborough
Boston United v Bath City
Dagenham v Nuneaton Borough
Dartford v Yeovil Town
Frickley Athletic v Northwich Victoria
Kettering Town v Maidstone United
Kidderminster Harriers v Barrow
Telford United v Weymouth
Worcester City v Gateshead

Sat 2 March 1985
Barrow v Wealdstone
Bath City v Boston United
Altrincham v Dagenham
Gateshead v Yeovil Town
Kettering Town v Barnet
Maidstone United v Frickley Athletic
Northwich Victoria v Enfield
Nuneaton Borough v Dartford
Runcorn v Kidderminster Harriers
Scarborough v Worcester City
Weymouth v Telford United

Sat 9 March 1985
Altrincham v Wealdstone
Barrow v Bath City
Boston United v Dagenham
Enfield v Weymouth
Gateshead v Dartford
Kidderminster Harriers v Frickley Athletic
Runcorn v Maidstone United
Telford United v Scarborough
Worcester City v Kettering Town

Mon 11 March 1985
Gateshead v Northwich Victoria

Wed 13 March 1985
Kettering Town v Weymouth

Sat 16 March 1985
Barnet v Boston United
Bath City v Runcorn
Dartford v Barrow
Frickley Athletic v Enfield
Maidstone United v Altrincham
Northwich Victoria v Kidderminster Harriers
Nuneaton Borough v Scarborough
Wealdstone v Kettering Town
Weymouth v Dagenham
Worcester City v Telford United
Yeovil Town v Gateshead

Tues 19 March 1985
Wealdstone v Yeovil Town

Wed 20 March 1985
Boston United v Runcorn

Sat 23 March 1985
Altrincham v Enfield
Barrow v Barnet
Dagenham v Kettering Town
Dartford v Northwich Victoria
Frickley Athletic v Yeovil Town
Gateshead v Bath City
Nuneaton Borough v Boston United
Runcorn v Worcester City
Scarborough v Maidstone United
Telford United v Wealdstone

Tues 26 March 1985
Enfield v Yeovil Town
Frickley Athletic v Dagenham

Wed 27 March 1985
Maidstone United v Telford United
Scarborough v Kidderminster Harriers

Sat 30 March 1985
Barnet v Gateshead
Bath City v Frickley Athletic
Boston United v Altrincham
Enfield v Scarborough
Kettering Town v Dartford
Kidderminster Harriers v Nuneaton Borough
Northwich Victoria v Maidstone United
Wealdstone v Runcorn
Weymouth v Barrow
Worcester City v Dagenham
Yeovil Town v Telford United

Mon 1 April 1985
Nuneaton Borough v Boston United

Tues 2 April 1985
Barrow v Scarborough

Sat 6 April 1985
Altrincham v Barnet
Dagenham v Barrow
Dartford v Runcorn
Frickley Athletic v Worcester City
Gateshead v Nuneaton Borough
Maidstone United v Kidderminster Harriers
Scarborough v Kettering Town
Telford United v Bath City
Wealdstone v Northwich Victoria
Weymouth v Boston United
Yeovil Town v Enfield

Mon 8 April 1985
Barnet v Dagenham
Barrow v Gateshead
Bath City v Weymouth
Boston United v Scarborough
Enfield v Dartford
Kettering Town v Yeovil Town
Kidderminster Harriers v Worcester City
Maidstone United v Wealdstone
Northwich Victoria v Frickley Athletic
Nuneaton Borough v Altrincham
Runcorn v Telford United

Sat 13 April 1985
Barrow v Maidstone United
Boston United v Yeovil Town
Dagenham v Scarborough
Enfield v Bath City
Frickley Athletic v Altrincham
Gateshead v Kidderminster Harriers
Nuneaton Borough v Barnet
Telford United v Kettering Town
Weymouth v Northwich Victoria
Worcester City v Dartford

Mon 15 April 1985
Northwich Victoria v Kettering Town

Sat 20 April 1985
Barnet v Maidstone United
Barrow v Dagenham
Gateshead v Weymouth
Kettering Town v Frickley Athletic
Nuneaton Borough v Wealdstone
Runcorn v Enfield
Scarborough v Bath City
Worcester City v Boston United
Yeovil Town v Kidderminster Harriers

Mon 15 April 1985
Nuneaton Borough v Kettering Town

Sat 27 April 1985
Altrincham v Dartford
Bath City v Northwich Victoria
Boston United v Enfield
Frickley Athletic v Runcorn
Gateshead v Barnet
Kidderminster Harriers v Kettering Town
Maidstone United v Barrow
Scarborough v Weymouth
Telford United v Worcester City
Wealdstone v Dagenham
Yeovil Town v Nuneaton Borough

Sat 4 May
Altrincham v Boston United
Barnet v Bath City
Barrow v Yeovil Town
Dagenham v Telford United
Dartford v Gateshead
Enfield v Kidderminster Harriers
Kettering Town v Wealdstone
Maidstone United v Scarborough
Weymouth v Frickley Athletic
Worcester City v Nuneaton Borough

Saturday 11 May 1985
F.A. TROPHY FINAL

INTERNATIONAL, REPRESENTATIVE

All fixtures subject to alteration.

August 1984

Sat 11	Official opening of season
Sat 18	FA Charity Shield
Sat 25	League Season starts
Wed 29	Milk Cup, first round, first leg

September 1984

Sat 1	FA Cup, preliminary round
Wed 5	Milk Cup, first round, second leg
Sat 8	FA Trophy, preliminary round
	FA Vase, extra preliminary round
	FA Youth Cup, preliminary round★
Wed 12	Iceland v Wales (WC)
	Northern Ireland v Rumania (WC)
	England v East Germany (F)
	Scotland v Yugoslavia (F)
Sat 15	FA Cup, first qualifying round
Wed 19	European Cups, first round, first leg
Wed 26	Milk Cup, second round, first leg
Sat 29	FA Cup, second qualifying round
	FA Youth Cup, first qualifying round★

October 1984

Wed 3	European Cups, first round, second leg
Sat 6	FA Vase, preliminary round
Sun 7	FA Sunday Cup, first round
Wed 10	Milk Cup, second round, second leg
Sat 13	FA Cup, third qualifying round
Tue 16	England v Finland (Under-21)
Wed 17	England v Finland (WC)
	Scotland v Iceland (WC)
	Spain v Wales (WC)
Sat 20	FA Trophy, first qualifying round
	FA Youth Cup, second qualifying round★
Wed 24	European Cups, second round, first leg
Sat 27	FA Cup, fourth qualifying round
	FA County Youth Cup, first round★
Wed 31	Milk Cup, third round

November 1984

Sat 3	FA Vase, first round
Sun 4	FA Sunday Cup, second round
Wed 7	European Cups, second round, second leg
Tue 13	England v New Zealand (B)
	Turkey v England (Under-21)
Wed 14	Turkey v England (WC)
	Northern Ireland v Finland (WC)
	Scotland v Spain (WC)
	Wales v Iceland (WC)
Sat 17	FA Cup, first round
	FA Youth Cup, first round★
Wed 21	Milk Cup, fourth round
Sat 24	FA Trophy, second qualifying round
Wed 28	UEFA Cup, third round, first leg

December 1984

Sat 1	FA Vase, second round
Sun 2	FA Sunday Cup, third round
Wed 5	England v Australia (B)
Sat 8	FA Cup, second round
	FA County Youth Cup, second round★
Wed 12	UEFA Cup, third round, second leg
Sat 15	FA Trophy, third qualifying round
	FA Youth Cup, second round
Sat 22	FA Vase, third round

AND CUP FIXTURES 1984-85

January 1985

Sat 5	FA Cup, third round
Sun 6	FA Sunday Cup, fourth round
Sat 12	FA Trophy, first round
	FA Youth Cup, third round*
Wed 16	Milk Cup, fifth round
Sat 19	FA Vase, fourth round
Sat 26	FA Cup, fourth round
	FA County Youth Cup, third round*

February 1985

Sat 2	FA Trophy, second round
Sun 3	FA Sunday Cup, fifth round
Wed 6	Milk Cup, semi-final, first leg
Sat 9	FA Vase, fifth round
	FA Youth Cup, fourth round*
Wed 13	Milk Cup, semi-final, second leg
Sat 16	FA Cup, fifth round
Sat 23	FA Trophy, third round
Wed 27	Northern Ireland v England (WC)
	Spain v Scotland (WC)

March 1985

Sat 2	FA Vase, sixth round
Wed 6	European Cups, third and fourth rounds, first leg
Sat 9	FA Cup, sixth round
	FA Youth Cup, fifth round*
	FA County Youth Cup, fourth round*
Sat 16	FA Trophy, fourth round
Sun 17	FA Sunday Cup, semi-final
Wed 20	European Cups, third and fourth rounds, second leg
Sat 23	FA Vase, semi-final, first leg
Sun 24	Milk Cup Final
Wed 27	Scotland v Wales (WC)
Sat 30	FA Vase, semi-final, second leg

April 1985

Sat 6	FA Trophy, semi-final, first leg
	FA Youth Cup, semi-final*
Wed 10	European Cups, semi-final, first leg
Sat 13	FA Cup, semi-final
	FA Trophy, semi-final, second leg
	FA County Youth Cup, semi-final*
Wed 24	European Cups, semi-final, second leg
Sat 27	FA Vase Final (Wembley)
Sun 28	FA Sunday Cup Final
Tue 30	Wales v Spain (WC)
	Rumania v England (Under-21)

May 1985

Wed 1	Rumania v England (WC)
	Northern Ireland v Turkey (WC)
Sat 4	FA Youth Cup Final*
	FA County Youth Cup Final
Wed 8	UEFA Cup Final, first leg
Sat 11	FA Trophy Final (Wembley)
Wed 15	European Cup-Winners' Cup Final
Sat 18	FA Cup Final (Wembley)
Tue 21	Finland v England (Under-21)
Wed 22	UEFA Cup Final, second leg
	Finland v England (WC)
Tue 28	Iceland v Scotland (WC)
Wed 29	European Cup Final

Key
*=Closing date for round
F=Friendly International
WC=World Cup
B='B' International

FIFA WORLD CUP 1986

Fixtures for the Preliminary Competition

Introduction

There are six confederations of Football Associations in FIFA. At the time of going to press, fixture dates were known only for the European confederation (UEFA). Details of the groupings in the other confederations are listed below, together with notes explaining the system for qualification.

EUROPE (UEFA)

Italy qualify automatically as World Champions. Groups 2, 3, 4 and 6 will be decided on a League basis, with teams playing each other home and away. The top two teams in each group will qualify for the final tournament. Groups 1, 5 and 7 will also be decided on a League basis, but only the top team will qualify. The runners-up in these three groups will play an additional round on a League basis, and the top team will qualify. The runner-up in this additional round will play a two-match play-off against the winner of the Oceania group for a place in the finals. The team coming third in the additional round will be eliminated.

Group 1 (Albania, Belgium, Greece, Poland)

Belgium v Albania 17 October 1984; Poland v Greece 17 October 1984; Poland v Albania 31 October 1984; Greece v Belgium 19 December 1984; Albania v Belgium 22 December 1984; Greece v Albania 27 February 1985; Belgium v Greece 27 March 1985; Albania v Greece 17 April 1985; Belgium v Poland 1 May 1985; Greece v Poland 19 May 1985; Albania v Poland 30 May 1985; Poland v Belgium 11 September 1985.

Group 2 (Czechoslovakia, Malta, Portugal, Sweden, West Germany)

Sweden 4, Malta 0 23 May 1984; Sweden v Portugal 12 September 1984; Portugal v Czechoslovakia 14 October 1984; West Germany v Sweden 17 October 1984; Czechoslovakia v Malta 31 October 1984; Portugal v Sweden 14 November 1984; Malta v West Germany 16 December 1984; Malta v Portugal 10 February 1985; Portugal v West Germany 24 February 1985; West Germany v Malta 27 March 1985; Malta v Czechoslovakia 20/21 April 1985; Czechoslovakia v West Germany 1 May 1985; Sweden v Czechoslovakia 5 June 1985; Sweden v West Germany 25 September 1985; Czechoslovakia v Portugal 25 September 1985; Portugal v Malta 12 October 1985; Czechoslovakia v Sweden 16 October 1985; West Germany v Portugal 16 October 1985; West Germany v Czechoslovakia 16/17 November 1985; Malta v Sweden 17 November 1985.

Group 3 (England, Finland, Northern Ireland, Rumania, Turkey)

Finland (0) 1 (*Valvee*)
Northern Ireland (0) 0 27 May 1984

Finland: Huttonen; Tekonen, Kymalainen, Ikalainen (Europaeus), Petaja, Turunen, Houtsonen, Ukkonen, Rantaen (Kousa), Rautianinen, Valvee.

Northern Ireland: Jennings, Nicholl J., McClelland, McElhinney, Donaghy, O'Neill M., McIlroy (Worthington), Armstrong (Cochrane), Hamilton, Whiteside, Stewart.

Attendance: 8115.

Northern Ireland v Rumania 12 September 1984

England v Finland 17 October 1984; Turkey v Finland 31 October 1984; Northern Ireland v Finland 14 November 1984; Turkey v England 14 November 1984; Northern Ireland v England 27 February 1985; Rumania v Turkey 3 April 1985; Northern Ireland v Turkey 1 May 1985; Rumania v England 1 May 1985; Finland v England 22 May 1985; Finland v Rumania 6 June 1985; Rumania v Finland 28 August 1985; Turkey v Northern Ireland 11 September 1985; England v Rumania 11 September 1985; Finland v Turkey 25 September 1985; Rumania v Northern Ireland 16 October 1985; England v Turkey 16 October 1985; England v Northern Ireland 13 November 1985; Turkey v Rumania 14 November 1985;

Group 4 (Bulgaria, East Germany, France, Luxembourg, Yugoslavia)

Yugoslavia v Bulgaria 29 September 1984; Luxembourg v France 13 October 1984; East Germany v Yugoslavia 20 October 1984; Luxembourg v East Germany 17

November 1984; France v Bulgaria 21 November 1984; Bulgaria v Luxembourg 5 December 1984; France v East Germany 8 December 1984; Yugoslavia v Luxembourg 27 March 1985; Yugoslavia v France 3 April 1985; Bulgaria v East Germany 6 April 1985; Luxembourg v Yugoslavia 1 May 1985; Bulgaria v France 2 May 1985; East Germany v Luxembourg 18 May 1985; Bulgaria v Yugoslavia 1 June 1985; East Germany v France 11 September 1985; Luxembourg v Bulgaria 25 September 1985; Yugoslavia v East Germany 28 September 1985; France v Luxembourg 30 October 1985; France v Yugoslavia 16 November 1985; East Germany v Bulgaria 16 November 1985.

Group 5 (Austria, Cyprus, Hungary, Netherlands)
Cyprus 1 Austria 2 2 May 1984; Hungary v Austria 26 September 1984; Netherlands v Hungary 17 October 1984; Austria v Netherlands 14 November 1984; Cyprus v Hungary 17 November 1984; Cyprus v Netherlands 23 December 1984; Netherlands v Cyprus 27 February 1985; Hungary v Cyprus 3 April 1985; Austria v Hungary 17 April 1985; Netherlands v Austria 1 May 1985; Austria v Cyprus 14 May 1985; Hungary v Netherlands 14 May 1985.

Group 6 (Denmark, Eire, Norway, Switzerland, USSR); Eire v USSR 12 September 1984; Norway v Switzerland 12 September 1984; Denmark v Norway 26 September 1984; Norway v USSR 10 October 1984; Switzerland v Denmark 17 October 1984; Norway v Eire 17 October 1984; Denmark v Eire 14 November 1984; Switzerland v USSR 17 April 1985; Eire v Norway 1 May 1985; USSR v Switzerland 2 May 1985; Eire v Switzerland 2 June 1985; Denmark v USSR 5 June 1985; Switzerland v Eire 11 September 1985; USSR v Denmark 25 September 1985; Denmark v Switzerland 9 October 1985; Norway v Denmark 16 October 1985; USSR v Eire 16 October 1985; USSR v Norway 30 October 1985; Switzerland v Norway 13 November 1985; Eire v Denmark 13 November 1985.

Group 7 (Iceland, Scotland, Spain, Wales)
Iceland v Wales 12 September 1984; Spain v Wales 17 October 1984; Scotland v Iceland 17 October 1984; Scotland v Spain 14 November 1984; Wales v Iceland 14 November 1984; Spain v Scotland 27 February 1985; Scotland v Wales 27 March 1985; Wales v Spain 30 April 1985; Iceland v Scotland 28 May 1985; Iceland v Spain 12 June 1985; Wales v Scotland 10 September 1985; Spain v Iceland 25 September 1985.

SOUTH AMERICA

Group 1: Argentina, Colombia, Peru, Venezuela.
Group 2: Chile, Ecuador, Uruguay.
Group 3: Bolivia, Brazil, Paraguay.

The winners in each group qualify. The runners-up, together with the third-placed team in Group 1, play off for the fourth qualifying place.

OCEANIA

Australia, Israel, New Zealand, Taiwan.

The winner of this group enters a two-match play-off against the runner-up of the European supplementary group for a place in the finals.

ASIA

Group 1: Sub-group 1: Oman, Saudi Arabia, United Arab Emirates.
Sub-group 2: Iraq, Jordan, Lebanon, Qatar.
Group 2: Sub-group 1: Kuwait, North Yeman, Syria.
Sub-group 2: Bahrain, Iran, South Yeman.
Group 3: Sub-group 1: Malaysia, Nepal, South Korea.
Sub-group 2: Bangladesh, India, Indonesia, Thailand.
Group 4: Sub-group1: Brunei, China, Hong Kong, Macao.
Sub-group 2: Japan, North Korea, Singapore.

Two teams qualify for the finals.

NORTH AND CENTRAL AMERICA AND CARIBBEAN (CONCACAF)

Group 1: Canada v Jamaica, Dutch Antilles v USA, El Salvador v Puerto Rico *(home and away ties)*.

Group 2: Barbados v Costa Rica, Guatemala bye, Panama v Honduras *(home and away ties)*.

Group 3: Antigua v Haiti, Surinam v Guyana, Trinidad & Tobago v Grenada *(home and away ties).*
The three group winners play off to decide which team will join Mexico (who qualify automatically as host nation) as Concacaf's two representatives in the finals.

AFRICA

Group 1: Egypt v Zimbabwe, Kenya v Ethiopia, Mauritius v Malawi, Madagascar v Lesotho, Tanzania v Sudan, Zambia v Uganda.

Group 2: Benin v Tunisia, Libya v Niger, Sierra Leone v Morocco.

Group 3: Angola v Senegal, Ivory Coast v Gambia, Nigeria v Liberia, Togo v Guinea.

Algeria, Cameroon and Ghana receive byes into the second round of the qualifying tournament. Two teams will qualify for the finals.

FOOTBALL AWARDS 1983-84

Footballer of the Year

The Football Writers' Association this year voted Ian Rush (Liverpool) Footballer of the Year. Ian therefore became the seventh Liverpool player in the last eleven seasons to win this coveted award.

Past winners

1947-48	Stanley Matthews (Blackpool)
1948-49	Johnnie Carey (Manchester United)
1949-50	Joe Mercer (Arsenal)
1950-51	Harry Johnston (Blackpool)
1951-52	Billy Wright (Wolverhampton Wanderers)
1952-53	Nat Lofthouse (Bolton Wanderers)
1953-54	Tom Finney (Preston North End)
1954-55	Don Revie (Manchester City)
1955-56	Bert Trautmann (Manchester City)
1956-57	Tom Finney (Preston North End)
1957-58	Danny Blanchflower (Tottenham Hotspur)
1958-59	Sid Owen (Luton Town)
1959-60	Bill Slater (Wolverhampton Wanderers)
1960-61	Danny Blanchflower (Tottenham Hotspur)
1961-62	Jimmy Adamson (Burnley)
1962-63	Stanley Matthews (Stoke City)
1963-64	Bobby Moore (West Ham United)
1964-65	Bobby Collins (Leeds United)
1965-66	Bobby Charlton (Manchester United)
1966-67	Jackie Charlton (Leeds United)
1967-68	George Best (Manchester United)
1968-69	Dave Mackay (Derby County)
	Tony Book (Manchester City)
1969-70	Billy Bremner (Leeds United)
1970-71	Frank McLintock (Arsenal)
1971-72	Gordon Banks (Stoke City)
1972-73	Pat Jennings (Tottenham Hotspur)
1973-74	Ian Callaghan (Liverpool)
1974-75	Alan Mullery (Fulham)
1975-76	Kevin Keegan (Liverpool)
1976-77	Emlyn Hughes (Liverpool)
1977-78	Kenny Burns (Nottingham Forest)
1978-79	Kenny Dalglish (Liverpool)
1979-80	Terry McDermott (Liverpool)

1980-81 Frans Thijssen (Ipswich Town)
1981-82 Steve Perryman (Tottenham Hotspur)
1982-83 Kenny Dalglish (Liverpool)

PFA Player of the Year
The Professional Footballers' Association this year chose Ian Rush (Liverpool) as their Player of the Year.

Past winners: 1974 – Norman Hunter (Leeds U.), 1975 – Colin Todd (Derby Co.), 1976 – Pat Jennings (Tottenham H.), 1977 – Andy Gray (Aston Vila),1978–Peter Shilton (Nottingham F.), 1979 – Liam Brady (Arsenal), 1980 – Terry McDermott (Liverpool), 1981 – John Wark (Ipswich T.), 1982 – Keven Keegan O.B.E. (Southampton), 1983 – Kenny Dalglish (Liverpool).

PFA Young Player of the Year 1983-84: Paul Walsh (Luton Town)

Scottish PFA Player of the Year 1983-84: Willie Miller (Aberdeen)

Scottish PFA Young Player of the Year 1983-84: John Robertson (Hearts)

Manager of the Year
Joe Fagan (Liverpool)
Joe Fagan set a record by receiving this award from the Bell's Whisky Panel in his first-ever season as a team manager, but of course he had been a vital member of the Anfield set-up for many years, and was at the helm during a season when Liverpool continued their domination of English football by taking the Milk Cup, the League Championship for a record fifteenth time (and the third time in succession) and reaching the European Cup final.

European Footballer of the Year 1983
Michel Platini (Juventus)

Previous winners
1956 Stanley Matthews (Blackpool)
1957 Alfredo Di Stefano (Real Madrid)
1958 Raymond Kopa (Real Madrid)
1959 Alfredo Di Stefano (Real Madrid)
1960 Luis Suarez (Barcelona)
1961 Omar Sivori (Juventus)
1963 Josef Masopust (Dukla Prague)
Lev Yashin (Moscow Dynamo)
1964 Denis Law (Manchester United)
1965 Eusebio (Benfica)
1966 Bobby Charlton (Manchester United)
1967 Florian Albert (Ferencvaros)
1968 George Best (Manchester United)
1969 Gianni Rivera (AC Milan)
1970 Gerd Muller (Bayern Munich)
1971 Johan Cruyff (Ajax)
1972 Franz Beckenbauer (Bayern Munich)
1973 Johan Cruyff (Barcelona)
1974 Johan Cruyff (Barcelona)
1975 Oleg Blokhin (Dynamo Kiev)
1976 Franz Beckenbauer (Bayern Munich)
1977 Alan Simonsen (Borussia Moench)
1978 Kevin Keegan (SV Hamburg)
1979 Kevin Keegan (SV Hamburg)
1980 Karl-Heinz Rummenigge (Bayern Munich)
1981 Karl-Heinz Rummenigge (Bayern Munich)
1982 Paolo Rossi (Juventus)

IMPORTANT ADDRESSES

Football Association: E. A. Croker, 16 Lancaster Gate, London W2 3LW.

Scottish FA: E. Walker, 6 Park Gardens, Glasgow G3 7YE.

Irish FA: D. Bowen, 20 Windsor Avenue, Belfast BT9 6EG.

Welsh FA: A.E. Evans B.Sc., 3 Fairy Road, Wrexham LL13 7PS.

FA of Ireland (Eire): P. J. O'Driscoll, 80 Merrion Square, South Dublin 2.

League of Ireland: E. J. Dowling, 80 Merrion Square, Dublin 2.

Federation Internationale de Football Association (FIFA): J. Blatter, FIFA House, 11 Hitzigweg, 8032 Zurich, Switzerland.

Union des Associations Europeenes de Football (UEFA): H. Bangerter, Jupiterstrasse 33, PO Box 16, CH-3000 Berne 15, Switzerland.

Football League: R. H. G. Kelly, FCIS, Lytham St Annes, Lancashire FY8 1JG.

Scottish League: J. Farry, 188 West Regent Street, Glasgow G2 4RY.

Irish League: J. H. Long, 16 Donegall Square South, Belfast.

Welsh League: J. T. Burrows, 16 Meyer Street, Thomastown, Tonyrefail, Glamorgan.

Alliance Premier League: P. D. Hunter, 24 Barnehurst Road, Bexley Heath, Kent DA7 6EZ.

Southern League: D. J. Strudwick, 42 Cotswold Court, Burford Road, Horsham, West Sussex

Northern Premier League: R. D. Bayley, 22 Woburn Drive, Hale, Altrincham, Cheshire WA15 8LZ.

The Association of Football League Referees and Linesmen: R. G. Warnke, 7 Ferndale Road, Binley Woods, Nr Coventry CV3 2BG.

Football League Managers and Secretaries Association: K. Friar, c/o Arsenal FC, Arsenal Stadium, Highbury, London N5.

Women's Football Association: P. Gregory, 7 Mayfield Road, London N8.

Universities Athletic Union: B. Byrne, 28 Woburn Square, London WC1.

English Schools FA: G. Evans, 4a Eastgate Street, Stafford ST16 2NN.

Professional Footballers' Association: G. Taylor, 124 Corn Exchange Buildings, Hanging Ditch, Manchester M4 3BN.

England Supporters' Association: R. Coates, Hill End House, Butlers Cross, Aylesbury, Buckinghamshire.